The Illustrated Directory of

TANKS
OF THE WORLD

David Miller

MBI Publishing Company

...blished in 2000 by
...Company,
...Avenue, PO Box 1, Osceola,
...0001 USA

Salamander Books Limited 2000

The information in this book is true and
complete to the best of our knowledge.
All recommendations are made without
any guarantee on the part of the author
or publisher, who also disclaim any
liability incurred in connection with the
use of this data or specific details.

We recognize that some words, model
names and designations, for example,
mentioned herein are the property of the
trademark holder. We use them for
identification purposes only. This is not
an official publication.

MBI Publishing Company books are also
available at discounts in bulk quantity for
industrial or sales-promotional use. For
details write to Special Sales Manager at
Motorbooks International Wholesalers &
Distributors, 729 Prospect Avenue, PO
Box 1, Osceola, WI 54020-0001 USA.

Library of Congress Cataloging-in-
Publication Data Available

ISBN 0-7603-0892-6

Printed in Slovenia

Credits

Project Manager: Ray Bonds
Designed by: Interprep Ltd
Color reproduction by:
Studio Technology

The Author

David Miller is a former officer in the British Army and subsequently was a staff journalist with the Jane's Information Group, serving with *International Defense Review* and as Editor of Jane's *Major Surface Warships.* He has written for many international defence publications, and is author of more than 30 books on weapons and warfare.

The publishers wish to point out that many of the entries in this book were originally written by Christopher F. Foss and published in *The Illustrated Encyclopedia of the World's Tanks and Armoured Fighting Vehicles.*

Other Contributors

The publishers wish to thank the various armed services, companies and private individuals (including Christopher F. Foss) for providing photographs for use in this book, and make special mention of Ssg. Ralph Brewer for permission to use photographs of the Russian Chiormy Oriol (Black Eagle) tank from his website, ssgbrewer@hotmail.com.

Contents

Introduction

The tank brought a unique combination of firepower, mobility and protection to the 20th Century battlefield, with the number and quality of their tanks being the yardstick by which armies were measured. Tracked, armoured vehicles were first used in 1916 by the British, who shipped them to France labelled, for security reasons, as "water tanks", giving them the name by which they have been known ever since. Naturally, such a novel weapon created fresh problems, including new methods of command and control, co-operation with infantry and artillery, and logistic support, none of which was ever really resolved during World War I.

It is inescapable that tank designers must achieve a balance between firepower (more destructive guns), protection (more resistant armour) and mobility (greater battlefield agility). This has resulted in a development cycle in which weight increases to the point where the tank is either too big or too heavy (or both) forcing designers to revert to smaller, lighter tanks, thus starting the cycle over again. During World War II weight increased inexorably,

culminating in such giants as the German Tiger II (70 tons) and the British Tortoise (79 tons), which led to determined efforts throughout the 1950s and 1960s to keep weight down to about 40-50 tons, but today's tanks weigh 60 tons or more.

Between 1919 and 1939 the major European armies put much effort into tank design and tactics, but it was the Germans who evolved the highly mobile and effective "Blitzkrieg" which enabled them to overrun Western and most of Eastern Europe between 1939 and 1942. Thereafter, American, British and Russian tanks increased in quality and, more importantly, in numbers, so that by 1945 Germany's armoured forces, good as they were, had been defeated.

Following World War II, tank design continued at a high pace, one continuing priority being to reduce their weight, but despite major

Below: German forces were taken by surprise when they encountered tanks on the battlefield for the first time. Here they try to manoeuvre captured British Mk IVs.

efforts the weight of main battle tanks (MBT), as they were now called, crept back up to 60 tons again. Indeed, the importance of the tank had never been greater, playing a vital role in actual combat in Korea, the Arab-Israeli wars, the Iran/Iraq wars, and, most recently, in Operation *Desert Storm* in the Gulf and in Russia's war against Chechnya. Tanks had also been a major feature of the Cold War confrontation in Central Europe and it was for this theatre that the most advanced designs were built.

The last two decades have seen some remarkable advances in composite and explosive reactive armours (ERA); more powerful guns, growing through 120mm to 140mm and even 152mm; autoloaders enabling the crew to be reduced; and far more powerful engines. In addition, sophisticated fire control systems (FCS) enable the crew today to use their weapon with greater accuracy and effectiveness, while new detectors enable them to spot the enemy and to know when the enemy is trying to find them.

Tank designers have also had to counter ever more sophisticated anti-tank weapons, of which the most important has long been the main gun of an opposing tank. Next came wheeled anti-tank guns, but these have now almost completely disappeared, although tracked anti-tank guns (tank destroyers) appear from time to time.

Ground- and air-launched missiles are also important enemies of the tank although, since they are all capped by a high-explosive anti-tank (HEAT) warhead, these missiles suffer from the limitations of the warhead rather than of the system itself. Artillery is currently achieving something of a comeback since it can deliver bomblets which attack the top of the tank, traditionally an area which needs less protection than the sides.

This book shows every tank of any importance developed between 1916 and 2000. It is arranged by country so that the story of each nation's development becomes clear. The book concentrates on battle tanks, including MBTs, heavy, medium and light tanks; it does not include other tracked fighting vehicles such as tank destroyers, self-propelled artillery, and armoured personnel carriers.

As the continuing development shows, although the future of the tank has been brought into question from time to time as new weapons have challenged its supremacy on the battlefield, it is clear that, at the start of the 21st Century, its place on the battlefield is secure.

Below: Late in the Cold War period, a US Army M60 demonstrates its impressive firepower while on exercise in Germany.

TAM Medium Tank

Countries of origin: Germany (design), Argentina (production).
Crew: 4.
Armament: One 105mm gun; one 7.62mm machine-gun co-axial with main armament; one 7.62mm anti-aircraft machine-gun; eight smoke dischargers.
Armour: Classified.
Dimensions: Length (with gun forwards) 27ft (8.23m); length (hull) 22ft 3in (6.78m); width 10ft 8in (3.25m); height 7ft 11in (2.42m).
Weight: Combat 67,252lb (30,500kg).
Ground pressure: 11.23lb/in² (0.79kg/cm²).
Engine: MTU six-cylinder diesel developing 710hp at 2,200rpm.
Performance: Road speed 46mph (75km/h); road range 342 miles (550km); vertical obstacle 3ft 3in (1m); trench 8ft 2in (2.5m); gradient 60 per cent.
History: Production complete. In service with Argentinian Army (350).

The Argentinian Army has in the past obtained most of its equipment from the United States but recent American policy has led to a drastic curtailment in the supply of arms to many countries, especially those in South America. So in 1974 the Argentinian Army placed a contract with the West German company of Thyssen Henschel for the design and development of the Tanque Argentino Mediano (TAM) medium tank, and a contract was placed at the same time for the design and development of an infantry fighting vehicle to operate with the TAM, called the Véhiculo Combate Infanteria (VCI). Under the terms of the contract three prototypes of both the TAM and the VCI were to be supplied and a factory was to be established in Argentina to undertake production of both vehicles, which would initially be assembled from components supplied from West Germany but in time would be mostly manufactured in Argentina, not only providing some employment but also saving the country valuable foreign exchange costs.

Both the TAM and the VCI are based to a large extent on the chassis of the Marder Mechanised Infantry Combat Vehicle which entered service with the West German Army in 1971. The hull of the TAM is of all-welded steel construction with the driver seated at the front of the well-sloped hull on the left with the engine to his right. The all-welded turret is mounted at the rear of the hull with the commander and gunner on the right and the loader on the left. The suspension system is of the torsion bar type and consists of six dual rubber-tyred road wheels with the drive sprocket at the front, idler at

Above: The TAM medium tank has an operational range of 342 miles (550km) which can be increased to 559 miles (900km) by fitting two long-range auxiliary fuel tanks to the rear of the hull. The TAM is essentially a Marder Mechanised Infantry Combat Vehicle hull with a new turret and a 105mm gun at the rear of the hull.

Above: The TAM medium tank was originally developed by the German company Thyssen Henschel to meet the requirements of the Argentinian Army. 350 were acquired for service.

the rear and three track return rollers. The first, second, fifth and sixth road wheel stations are provided with a hydraulic shock absorber. The basic model has a range on internal fuel tanks of some 342 miles (550km) but to increase the range to 559 miles (900km) two long range fuel tanks can be mounted at the rear of the hull. The basic vehicle can ford to a depth of 4ft 7in (1.4m) without any preparation but with a snorkel fitted it can ford to a depth of 13ft 2in (4m).

Main armament consists of a 105mm gun which can fire fixed APFSDS, HEAT, HE-T, HESH and WP-T rounds, with a total of 50 rounds being carried, and loaded into the TAM via a door in the rear of the hull or via a small circular door in the left side of the turret. A 7.62mm machine-gun is mounted co-axial with the main armament and a similar weapon is mounted on the turret roof for anti-aircraft fire; four electrically-operated smoke dischargers are fitted either side of the turret. The fire control system consists of a panoramic sight for the commander which has a magnification of from x6 to x20, a coincidence rangefinder which is also operated by the commander, while the gunner is provided with a sight with a magnification of x8.

Below: The TAM medium tank sports a well-sloped glacis plate, leading up and back to a turret which extends almost to the rear of the hull. Visible in this view is the external mantlet which houses the tank's 105mm main gun.

11

Panzerjäger K 4KH7FA SK105 Light Tank/Tank Destroyer

Country of origin: Austria.
Crew: 3.
Armament: One 105mm gun; one 7.62mm machine-gun co-axial with main armament; three smoke dischargers each side of turret.
Armour: 0.4in-1.6in (10mm-40mm).
Dimensions: Length (with gun forwards) 25ft 6in (7.76m); length (hull) 18ft 3in (5.58m); width 8ft 2in (2.5m); height 8ft 2in (2.51m).
Weight: Combat 38,587lb (17,500kg).
Ground pressure: 9.67lb/in² (0.68kg/cm²).
Engine: Steyr 7FA turbo-charged 6-cylinder diesel developing 320hp at 2,300rpm.
Performance: Road speed 40.4mph (65km/h); range 323 miles (520km); vertical obstacle 2ft 8in (0.8m); trench 7ft 11in (2.41m); gradient 75 per cent.
History: Entered service with Austrian Army in 1973. Now in service with following armies: Argentina (150), Austria (250), Bolivia (34), Botswana (30), Morocco (109), Tunisia (54).

In 1965 Saurer-Werke commenced the development of this well-armed and highly mobile tank destroyer to meet the requirements of the Austrian Army. The chassis uses many components of an earlier range of APCs but its layout is quite different with the driver's compartment at the front, turret in the centre and the engine and transmission at the rear. The hull is of all-welded construction and provides the crew with protection from small arms fire and shell splinters. The suspension is of the torsion bar type and consists of five dual rubber-tyred road wheels with the drive sprocket at the rear, idler at the front and three track return rollers. The first and last road wheel stations have an hydraulic shock absorber.

The FL-12 turret is made under licence in Austria from the French company Fives-Lille-Cail and is identical to that fitted to the AMX-13 light tank and the Brazilian EE-17 (6x6) tank destroyer. This turret is of the oscillating type with the 105mm gun fixed in the upper half which in turn pivots on the lower part. The gun can be elevated from –6° to +13° and the turret traversed through a full 360° in 12 to 15 seconds. The 105mm gun is fed from two revolver-type magazines in the turret bustle, each of which holds six rounds of ammunition. Empty cartridge cases are ejected outside of the turret through a small trap door in the turret rear. The two magazines have enabled the crew to be reduced to three men –

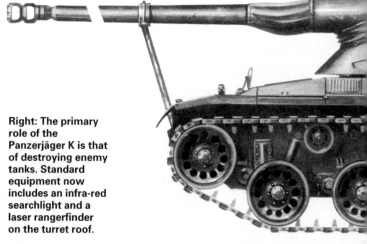

Right: The primary role of the Panzerjäger K is that of destroying enemy tanks. Standard equipment now includes an infra-red searchlight and a laser rangefinder on the turret roof.

Above: A Panzerjäger is firing its 105mm gun. Empty cartridge cases are ejected through a door in the rear of the turret.

commander, gunner and driver – and also allow a high rate of fire to be achieved for a short period; on the other hand, once the 12 rounds have been fired at least one of the crew has to leave the vehicle to carry out manual reloading of the two magazines. A total of 44 rounds of 105mm ammunition are carried, which can be a mixture of the following types: HE with the complete round weighing 41lb (18.4kg); HEAT with the complete round weighing 39lb (17.7kg) which will penetrate 14in (360mm) of armour at an incidence of 0° or 6in (150mm) of armour at an incidence of 65°; smoke with the complete round weighing 42lb (19.1kg). Mounted co-axial to the right of the main armament is a 7.62mm MG42/49 machine-gun and mounted on each side of the turret are three electrically operated smoke dischargers; a total of 2,000 rounds of 7.62mm ammunition are carried. Recently most vehicles have been fitted with a laser rangefinder mounted externally on the turret roof and above this has been mounted an infrared/white-light searchlight. The Kürassier K, as the vehicle is often called, has no NBC system and no deep fording capability.

X1A2 Medium Tank

Country of origin: Brazil.
Crew: 3
Armament: One 90mm gun; one 7.62mm machine-gun co-axial with main armament; one 12.7mm anti-aircraft machine-gun; six smoke dischargers
Armour: Classified.
Dimensions: Length 9 with armament) 23ft 3in (7.1m); length (hull) 21ft 4in (6.5m); width 8ft 6in (2.6m); height (to turret top) 8ft 2.45m).
Weight: Combat 41,895lb (19,000kg).
Ground pressure: 8.96lb/in^2 (0.63kg/cm^2).
Engine: Scania DS-11 6-cylinder diesel developing 300hp at 2,200rpm.
Performance: Road speed 34mph (55km/h); range 466 miles (750km); vertical obstacle 2ft 3in (0.7m); trench 6ft 10in (2.1in); gradient 70 per cent.
History: Delivered to Brazilian Army in 1980s; some remain in service.

The X1A2 is an entirely new tank produced for the Brazilian Army by Bernardini of Sâo Paulo. It does incorporate features of the earlier X1A and X1A1 tanks, but these essentially rebuilds of the American M3A1 Stuart light tank, some 200 of which were supplied by the US over 40 years ago.

The hull is of all-welded construction and is divided up into three compartments, driver's at the front, fighting in the centre and the engine at the rear. The driver is seated on the left side with ammunition stowed to his right. The two other crew members are seated in the all-welded steel turret, the commander on the left and the gunner on the right, both with a single piece hatch cover that opens to the rear and vision devices. The engine is made under licence in Brazil and is coupled to a

manual transmission with two forward and one reverse gear. The suspension is of the vertical volute type, each side having three bogies each with two road wheels and the drive sprocket at the front, idler at the rear and three tank return rollers that support the inside of the track only.

Main armament consists of a 90mm gun which has a double baffle muzzle brake; this fires a HEAT projectile weighing 8.04lb (3.65kg) with a muzzle velocity of 831 yards/s (760m/s), which will penetrate 12in (320mm) of armour at an incidence of 0°, and an HE projectile weighing 12.56lb (5.7kg) with a muzzle velocity of 711 yards/s (650m/s). Mounted co-axial with the main armament is a 7.62mm machine-gun and mounted on the turret roof is a 12.7mm anti-aircraft machine-gun. A total of 66 rounds of 90mm, 2,500 rounds of 7.62mm and 750 rounds of 12.7mm ammunition are carried. Three electrically operated smoke dischargers are mounted either side of the turret. Optional equipment includes the replacement of the 90mm gun with a 105mm gun, the installation of a laser rangefinder, infra-red night vision equipment and an air-conditioning system. The X1A2 has no inherent amphibious capability although it can ford to a depth of 4ft 3in (1.3m).

Approximately 50 of these tanks entered service with the Brazilian Army. A small number remain in service, but are being replaced by the more modern and much more capable Leopard 1s acquired from Belgium.

Below: Incorporating lessons learnt on the X1A and X1A1 medium Tanks, the X1A2 was built specifically for the Brazilian Army, with a final total of 50 being acquired.

Engesa Osório Main Battle Tank

EE-T1 and EE-T2.
Country of origin: Brazil.
Crew: 4.
Armament: GIAT 120mm smoothbore main gun (see text); one 7.62mm machine-gun coaxial with main gun; one 7.62mm/12.7mm machine-gun on turret roof; three single-barrelled smoke grenade dischargers on each side of turret.
Armour: Not known.
Dimensions: Length 33ft 1in (10.1m); width 10ft 8in (3.26m); height 9ft 6in (2.89m)
Weight: Combat 90,388lb (41,000kg).
Ground pressure: 11.4lb/in² (0.8kg/cm²).
Engine: Deutz MWM TBD-234-V12 12-cylinder turbocharged diesel; 765bhp at 2,300rpm.
Performance: Road speed 43mph (70km/h); range 342 miles (550km); vertical obstacle 3ft 8in (1.15m); trench 9ft 10in (3.0m); gradient 65 per cent.
History: Prototype (105mm gun) 1985; prototype (120mm) gun 1986; Saudi Arabian order placed 1990; Saudi Arabian order cancelled 1992.
(*Specifications are for EE-T2 armed with 120mm gun.*)

The Osório main battle tank was developed in the 1980s by the Brazilian company Engesa as a company project, using the company's own money. Engesa was one of the world's largest manufacturers of wheeled AFVs,

was also the major producer of ordnance and ammunition in South America, and was well-placed at the time. The Osório was designed principally for the Brazilian Army, although the export market was also borne strongly in mind in the design.

Major efforts were made to keep the weight within reasonable bounds and the heaviest versions had a combat weight of no more than 44 tons (which was considerably less than most other MBT designs of its era) and appeared in two versions: EE-T1 armed with a British L7A1 rifled 105mm gun, for which 45 rounds were carried; and EE-T2 armed with the GIAT 120mm smoothbore (38 rounds). There was a 7.62mm coaxial machine-gun and either a 7.62mm or 12.7mm machine-gun could be mounted on the turret roof. A computerized fire-control system was installed. This turret was designed, built and equipped by the British company, Vickers, under contract to Engesa.

The Osório was powered by a Deutz 12-cylinder turbocharged diesel engine, coupled to a *Zahnradfabrik* (ZF) LSG-3000 transmission; with a power output of 765bhp, this gave a respectable power/weight ratio of 18.6hp per tonne. The suspension was designed and manufactured by Dunlop and was hydropneumatic, a system which featured in a number of late 1970s/early 1980s designs, with six roadwheels on each side.

Below: The Brazilian Osório tank was developed in the 1980s. A sound, advanced design, it would have been produced in large numbers, but the company encountered severe financial problems.

Several countries showed a lot of interest in the Osório. The most important of these was Saudi Arabia, and in a series of desert trials against the US M1 and various European tanks, the Osório did particularly well. Indeed, serious consideration was given to a plan to build the Osório in Saudi Arabia, where it would have been named *Al Fahd*. In addition, the Brazilian Army took a strong interest in a tank which had been designed in its own country. In the end, however, circumstances combined to bring the project to naught. First, the Cold War ended, which meant that a large number of much cheaper tanks became available as the larger armies

down-sized and the Brazilian Army was able to acquire ex-US Army M60s and ex-Belgian Army Leopard 1s at virtually give-away prices. Then various other deals in which Engesa was involved went wrong, including a number with Iraq and Libya, and the company went bankrupt and ceased trading. It was a sad end to a very promising design.

Below: The EE-2 Osório weighed 40 tons, was armed with French 120mm gun in a British-designed turret, and was powered by a German Deutz 12-cylinder diesel engine.

Ram I and II Cruiser Tanks

Country of origin: Canada.
Crew: 5.
Armament: One 2pounder gun; one .3in machine-gun co-axial with main armament; one .3in machine-gun in cupola on hull top; one .3in machine-gun for anti-aircraft use.
Armour: 90mm (3.56in) maximum.
Dimensions: Length 19ft (5.971m); width 9ft 5in (2.87m); height 8ft 9in (2.667m).
Weight: Combat 64,000lb (29,030kg).
Ground pressure: 13.3lb/in^2 (0.94kg/cm^2).
Engine: Continental R975-EC2 nine-cylinder radial developing 400bhp at 2,400rpm.
Performance: Road speed 25mph (40.2km/h); road range 144 miles (232km); vertical obstacle 2ft (0.609m); trench 7ft 5in (2.26m); gradient 60 per cent.
History: Used only for training.

In 1940 the Canadian armoured forces consisted of two Vickers tanks, 12 Carden-Loyd carriers and 14 new Mk VI light tanks. Further tanks were not available as Britain did not have enough tanks to meet even her own requirements. The Canadians were able to purchase 219 American M1917 two-man tanks and a few Mk VIII tanks from the United States as scrap. These fulfilled a valuable training role until further and more modern tanks were available. Canada's first venture into tank construction was to build the British Valentine tank, 1,420 being built between 1941 and 1943. Of these 30 were kept in Canada for training and the remaining 1,390 were supplied to the

Below: The RAM I tank was designed and built by the Montreal Locomotive works in 1941 and was based on M3 Grant chassis.

Russians. Manufacture of the Valentine was undertaken at the Canadian Pacific Railway workshops at Angus, Montreal, and was a result of a British rather than a Canadian order.

In 1940 the Canadians started looking for a cruiser tank to meet the requirements of the Canadian armoured Corps, and finally decided to take the chassis of the American M3 Grant tank and redesign the hull to accept a turret with a traverse of 360°, rather than have a gun mounted in the side of the hull with limited traverse. The first prototype was completed by the Montreal Locomotive Works in June 1941, production starting late in 1941. The first vehicles were known as the Ram I, but only 50 of these were built before production switched to the Ram II, which had a 6pounder gun. Some 1,899 Ram IIs had been built by the time production was completed in July 1943.

The Ram I had a hull of all-cast construction. The driver was seated at the front of the hull on the right with the small machine-gun turret to his left. This latter was armed with a .3in machine-gun and had a traverse of 120° left and 50° right. The other three crew members were in the turret in the centre of the hull, the turret being a casting with the front part bolted into position. The main armament consisted of a 2pounder gun with an elevation of +20° and a depression of −10° and a .3in M1919A4 machine-gun was mounted co-axially with the main armament. A similar weapon could be mounted on the commander's cupola for use in the anti-aircraft role. Some 171 round so 2pounder and 4,275 rounds of .3in machine-gun ammunition were carried.

The Ram II was armed with a 6pounder gun, and the small turret on the hull was replaced by a more conventional ball-type mounting. A total of 92 rounds of 6pounder and 4,000 rounds of .3in machine-gun ammunition was carried. Other modifications of the Ram II over the earlier vehicle included the elimination of the side doors in the hull, a modified suspension, a modified clutch, new air cleaners and so on. Most Rams were shipped to Britain where

they were used by the 4th and 5th Canadian Armoured Divisions, although these formations were re-equipped with Shermans before the invasion of Europe in June 1944, so the Ram did not see combat.

There were a number of variants of the Ram tank, and some of these did see combat. The Ram Command and Observation Post Vehicle had a crew of six, and in appearance was almost identical to the normal tank, although it had only a dummy gun and the turret could be traversed through a mere 90° by hand wheel. Internally, additional communication equipment was provided. Eighty-four Ram COPVs were built. A Ram Armoured Vehicle Royal Engineers was developed, but this did not enter service. The Ram was also used as an ammunition carrier and as a towing vehicle for the 17pounder anti-tank gun. Perhaps the most famous version of the vehicle was the Ram Kangaroo. In 1944 the Canadian II Corps had to carry out an assault in Falaise in Normandy, and as there were not sufficient half-tracks available, they used as APCs

Above: The Ram II was armed with a 6pounder in place of the 2pounder of the Ram I. Neither version was ever used in combat.

some American M7 105mm Priest SPGs with their guns removed. Later it was decided to do the same with the Rams, as there were plenty of these in England. By the end of 1944 special battalions, equipped with Kangaroos, had been formed by both the British and Canadians. The conversion of the Ram was simple, and carried out at REME workshops. Basically, the turret was removed and benches were provided for 10 to 12 troops. The Kangaroo remained in service with the British the Canadian Armies for some years after the war. There was also a Ram Armoured Recovery Vehicle. Finally there was the Ram flamethrower, known as the Badger, which was used operationally in Holland early in 1945. The flame-gun was mounted in place of the bow machine-gun.

Type 59 Main Battle Tank

Country of origin: China.
Crew: 4.
Armament: One Type 59 (D-10T copy) 100mm rifled gun; one Type 59T 7.62mm co-axial machine-gun; one Type 59T AA 7.652mm machine-gun.
Armour: 1.5in-8in (39mm-203mm).
Dimensions: Length (including armament) 29ft 6in (9.00m); length (hull) 19ft 10in (6.04m); width 10ft 8in (3.27m); height 8ft 6in (2.59m).
Weight: Combat 79,300lb (36,000kg).
Ground pressure: 11.38lb/in² (0.80kg/cm²).
Engine: Model 12150L V-12 liquid-cooled diesel developing 520hp at 2,000rpm.
Performance: Road speed 31mph (50km/h); range 273 miles (440km); vertical obstacle 2ft 7in (0.79m); trench 8ft 10in (2.7m), gradient 60 per cent.
History: First production Type 59 completed in 1957; production complete. In service with: Albania (700), Bangladesh (80), Cambodia (150), China (c6,000), Congo (15), Iran (c220), Iraq (c200), North Korea (175), Pakistan (c1,100), Sudan (10), Tanzania (10), Vietnam (c300), Zaire (20), Zambia (20), Zimbabwe (35).

When the People's Liberation Army (PLA) defeated Chiang Kai-Shek's Kuomintang in 1949 they inherited a mixture of old Japanese and American tanks to supplement their own small numbers of elderly Soviet MBTs. There was an obvious need to establish their own MBT production facilities as soon as possible and to this end a small number of T-54s were procured from the then friendly Soviet Union. This model was copied exactly and put into production at a new factory at Baotou, near Peking. Designated the Type 59 by the West, the first production versions reached the PLA in about 1957 and production rose steadily to a rate of some 500-700 per year by the 1970s, peaking at about 1,000 per year in the early 1980s. Although not officially confirmed, it would appear that production has now ended.

The original Type 59 was identical to the Soviet Type 54, but the tank has

been progressively developed during its long production run in China. Two versions exist with a 105mm gun. One has been developed in China and is designated the Type 59-II by the PLA and the Type 59M1984 by the US Army. This is fitted with a 105mm gun with a thermal sleeve and fume extractor, which from visual inspection looks very similar to the British L7. The other version has been produced in the United Kingdom by Royal Ordnance and mounts a standard L7A3 105mm gun, and also sports additional armour. This MBT was tested in Pakistan in 1987, but no order was forthcoming.

The producers of the tank, the Chinese North Industries Corporation, offer no fewer than eight separate packages to enable current users of the Type 59 or T-54/-55 to upgrade their fleet. These enhancements include everything from appliqué armour, through new optical and electronic devices to either a new-model 100mm gun or a new Chinese-developed 105mm gun.

Above: T-59 MBTs of the PLA move into action during a live-fire exercise. Based on the Soviet T-54 MBT, the Type 59 has provided the backbone of the PLA's tank force for many years, as well as winning a healthy number of export orders.

Left: : A Chinese Type 59 MBT fitted experimentally with a 120mm smoothbore gun. Note the thermal jacket and bore evacuator, but there is no muzzle reference system.

Type 63 Light Tank

Country of origin: China.
Crew: 4.
Armament: One 85mm gun; one 7.62mm machine-gun co-axial with main armament; one 12.7mm anti-aircraft machine-gun.
Armour: 0.4-0.5in (10-14mm).
Dimensions: Length (with armament) 26ft 10in (8.2m); length (hull) 22ft 8in (6.91m); width 10ft 2in (3.1m); height (turret roof) 7ft 2in (2.19m).
Weight: (combat) 35,280-39,690lb (16,000-18,000kg).
Engine: 6-cylinder diesel developing 240hp.
Performance: Road speed 25mph (40kmh); range 149 miles (240km); vertical obstacle 3ft 3in (1m); trench 9ft 2in (2.8m); gradient 60 per cent.
History: Entered service with PLA in 1963. In service with: China (1,200), North Korea (c100), Myanmar (Burma) (c100), Vietnam (c1500).

The Chinese Type 63 was developed from the Soviet-supplied PT-76 light amphibious tank (*qv*), from which it differed mainly in having a new cast (as opposed to welded) turret, a heavier main gun (85mm as opposed to 76mm), and a more powerful engine. The hull of the Type 63 is of all-welded steel construction and is divided into three, with the driver's compartment at the front, the fighting compartment in the centre, and the engine/transmission bay at the rear. The driver is seated on the left side of the hull and has a single-piece hatch cover that opens to the left, and periscopes for observation when the hatch is in the closed position. To his right is ammunition stowage. The other three crew members are seated in the turret, with the commander and gunner on the left and the loader on the right. On the turret roof, the commander's hatch opens forward and the loader's hatch to the rear. The engine and transmission are at the rear and the suspension is of the torsion-bar type, consisting of six rubber-tyred road wheels, with the idler at the front and the drive sprocket at the rear; there are no track return rollers. The Type 63 is fully amphibious and is

Below: Communist Chinese People's Liberation Army regular and militia practise anti-tank tactics against T-59s, which are Chinese versions of the Soviet T-54 MBT. Such tactics, involving the use of satchel charges, would probably be suicidal in fairly open country such as this, but might be more successful in close country and heavily built-up areas.

propelled in the water by two water-jets mounted at the rear of the hull, enabling it to travel at about 7mph (12km/hr) in still water. Like the Russian PT-76, the main disadvantage of the Type 63 is its relatively large size, necessitated by the volume needed to make it amphibious.

The Type 63 is armed with an 85mm main gun similar to that in the Type 62 light tank. This weapon was based on the Chinese 85mm Type 56 field gun (which was itself a development of the Soviet 85mm D-44), but the barrel of the tank gun is considerably shorter and is fitted with a fume extractor rather than a muzzle brake. The tank gun fires fixed ammunition, with APDS, HEAT and HE rounds being available. Range in the direct fire role is 5,700yd (5,200m), but HE rounds can also be fired in the indirect role to a range of 14,000yd (12,900m). One 7.62mm machine-gun is mounted to the right of the main gun, while anti-aircraft defence is provided by a Chinese Type 54 12.7mm heavy machine gun mounted on the turret roof above the loader's station.

The Type 63 is no longer in production. Some 1,200 were supplied to the PLA in the 1960s and some of these have subsequently been passed to the rapidly expanding marine corps, which is part of the PLA-Navy. The tank has seen combat in the Vietnam War, the 1971 Indo-Pakistani War and during the Chinese invasion of Vietnam in 1979.

Below: The Type 63 light tank has been developed by the Chinese from the Soviet PT-76 amphibious light tank and has a new turret mounting an 85mm and 7.62mm co-axial machine-gun.

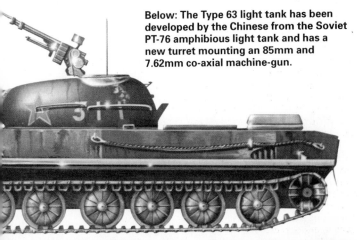

Type 69 Main Battle Tank

Type 69-I and Type 69-II
Country of origin: China.
Crew: 4.
Armament: (Type 69-I) One 100mm smoothbore gun; one Type 54 12.7mm co-axial machine-gun; one Type 59T 7.62mm anti-aircraft machine-gun. **(Type 69II)**. One 100mm rifled gun; one Type 54 12.7mm co-axial machine-gun; one Type 59T 7.62mm anti-aircraft machine-gun.
Armour: 1.5in-8in (39mm-203mm).
Dimensions: Length (including main armament) 28ft 5in (8.66m); length (hull) 20ft 6in (6.24m); width 10ft 10in (3.29m); height 9ft 3in (2.81m).
Weight: Combat 81,500lb (37,000kg)
Ground pressure: 11.80lb/in² (0.83g/cm²).
Engine: Model 12150L-7BW V-12 liquid-cooled diesel developing 580hp at 2,000rpm.
Performance: Road speed 31mph (50km/h); range 273 miles (440km); vertical obstacle 2ft 7in (0.79m); trench 8ft 10in (2.7m); gradient 60 per cent.
History: First production Type 69 completed in early 1980s. Production continuing. In service with: China (6,000), Iran (several hundred), Iraq (c1,000), Thailand (c50). Production has also recently started in Pakistan.

The Type 69 is a development of the Chinese Type 59, from which it differs mainly in armament, fire control and night vision devices. As in the Type 59, the driver sits in the front on the left, while the remaining three crewmen are housed in the turret.

The main difference between the Type 69-I and the Type 69-II is in the armament. In the first production batch two different types of gun were installed: some had a 100mm rifled tube and the others a 100mm smoothbore. The tanks with the smoothbore weapon were designated Type 69-I; this had a slightly longer tube, with a bore evacuator near the muzzle. After extensive testing, however, it was concluded that the rifled gun was superior and production of the Type 69-I terminated with the 150th tank.

The Type 69-II has the same rifled 100mm gun as the Type 59 tank, and fires a range of Chinese-designed and produced ammunition, including three types of APFSDS, HEAT, HE and APHE. The gun is fully stabilized, there is a Tank Laser Rangefinder-1 laser mounted above the mantlet and the Tank Simplified Fire Control System (TSFCS) is fitted. Most Type 69-IIs have an externally-mounted laser rangefinder, but the TSFCS-L system incorporates a laser integrated with the gun sight and mounted inside the turret.

The Type 69 has been exported in respectable quantities, Iraq having received several hundred in the early 1980s, while Iran has taken delivery of over 1,000 examples. The Royal Thai Army ordered some 500 Type 69-IIs under the local designation Type 30, but it is believed that only about 50 were delivered.

Below: First seen in 1982, the Chinese Type 69 main battle tank is a development of the Type 59 MBT. Mounted above and to the right of the 100mm gun is a large infra-red searchlight.

Type 80 Main Battle Tank

Type 80 and Type 80-II.
Country of origin: People's Republic of China.
Crew: 4.
Armament: One 105mm rifled main gun; one 7.62mm machine-gun coaxial with the main armament; one 12.7mm anti-aircraft machine-gun on loader's cupola; one four-barrelled smoke discharger on each side of turret.
Armour: All-welded steel.
Dimensions: Length (including main armament) 30ft 7in (9.33m); length (hull) 20ft 9in (6.33m); width 11ft 0in (3.35m); height (to turret roof) 7ft 6in (2.29m).
Weight: Combat 83,774lb (38,000kg).
Ground pressure: 11.5lb/in^2 (0.81 kg/cm^2).
Engine: Model VR36 diesel developing 700hp at 2,000rpm.
Performance: Speed 37 mph (60km/h); range 270 miles (430km); vertical obstacle 2ft 7in (0.8m); trench 8ft 10in (2.7m); gradient 60 per cent.
History: Entered service with the People's Liberation Army in the late 1980s. Still in service with China (approx 400) and Myanmar (approx 20).

The Type 69 (*qv*), armed with a 100mm gun, was produced in very large numbers and sold well abroad. The next Chinese MBT was the Type 79, which was essentially a Type 69 hull and turret but with a 105mm gun, the first PLA MBT to be armed with such a weapon, and other minor improve-

ments. About 800 are believed to have been produced for the PLA and none was exported.

The next major design was the Type 80, which took the Chinese tank progression, which began with the Type 59 and continued through the Types 69 and 79, a step further. The Type 80 has an all-steel, welded hull, which is marginally longer and wider than that of the Type 69 and which runs on a new torsion-bar suspension system, with six road wheels, compared to five on the Types 59/69/79. Another major change is that it is armed with the Chinese 105mm rifled gun, which is fitted with a fume extractor at the mid-point of the barrel and a thermal sleeve. The weapon bears at least a passing resemblance to the British-designed L7 105mm gun. Ammunition is Chinese-designed and manufactured, with three types of anti-tank round, APFSDS-T, HEAT-T and HESH, and an HE round for use against personnel and ground fortifications. Secondary armament comprises a 7.62mm machine-gun mounted co-axially with the main armament, and a 12.7mm heavy machine-gun on a pintle-mounting above the loader s hatch.

Like all Chinese MBTs the Type 80 can carry two long-range fuel tanks externally on the rear of the hull, as well as a large, wooden unditching beam. A further development was the Type 80-II which was approximately 1,100lb (0.5kg) heavier, marginally longer (30ft 7in/9.34m) and had a semi-automatic transmission system.

Left: The Chinese Type 80-II was armed with a Chinese-developed, rifled 105mm gun, fitted with a thermal sleeve and a bore evacuator, firing APFSDS, HEAT and HESH rounds.

Type 85 Main Battle Tank

Types 85-II, 85-IIA, 85-IIM, 85-IIAP, and 85-III.
Country of origin: People's Republic of China.
Crew: 3.
Armament: One 125mm smoothbore gun; one 7.62mm machine-gun coaxial with the main armament; one 12.7mm heavy anti-aircraft machine-gun on loader s cupola; one six-barrelled smoke discharger on each side of turret.
Armour: Not known.
Dimensions: Length (including main armament) 34ft 2in (10.43m); width 11ft 2in (3.40m); height (to turret roof) 6ft 7in (2.20m).
Weight: Combat 91,930lb (41,700kg).
Ground pressure: Not known.
Engine: Diesel, 1,000bhp (estimated).
Performance (estimated): Road speed 41mph (65km/h); range 370miles (600km); vertical obstacle 3ft 0in (0.9m); trench 9ft 2in (2.8m); gradient 60 per cent.
History: Type 85-II/-IIA: entered service with PLA in 1990/1991; now in service with China (500) and Pakistan (300). Type 85-III: ready for production, but no known orders to date.
(*Specifications for Type 85-III.*)

The Type 85, which was publicly announced in 1989, started as a progressive development of the Type 80 MBT (*qv*) and is in essence a Type 80 chassis with a totally new turret and main gun. It has now appeared in five models: Type 85-II; Type 85-IIA; Type 85-IIM; Type 85-IIAP; and Type 85-III.

First to appear were the Type 85-II and Type 85-IIA, which were developed

Below: A Chinese tank factory full of Type 85-IIM tanks armed with a 125mm gun. Note the drive sprocket and the tracks with their rubber pads lying on the floor.

Above: The Type 85-IIA was essentially a Type 80 hull with the same 105mm rifled gun, but mounted in a completely new welded steel turret. Some 500 are in service with the PLA.

in parallel with each other and are both armed with the same rifled 105mm gun as the Type 80. They also share a common hull and a completely new type of welded steel turret, which replaced the cast turret fitted to all previous Chinese tanks. Both have a four-man crew and are fitted with a collective NBC protection system, compared to the individual systems in earlier tanks. There are, however, a number differences, some of which have not been publicly announced. It is known that the Type 85-IIA is marginally heavier and shorter than the Type 85-II and carries 44 rounds of 105mm ammunition compared to the Type 85-II's 46 rounds.

It was announced in 1992 that a new version had been developed – the Type 85-IIM – which is generally similar to earlier models but is armed with a 125mm rifled gun and auto loader, enabling the crew to be reduced to three men. It is of interest that only two *rifled* large bore tank guns ever entered service, the British 120mm and this Chinese 125mm; all others have been smoothbores. The Type 85-IIAP is the Type 85-IIM manufactured under licence in Pakistan.

Yet another version was announced in 1995: the Type 85-III. This is a Type 85-II but with a considerable number of improved features, of which the most important is the main armament, which is a 125mm smoothbore gun with an automatic loader, similar to that fitted to contemporary Russian tanks such as the T-80. It fires three types of ammunition: APFSDS (muzzle velocity of 5,674ft/sec [1,730m/s]), HEAT and HE-FRAG. A total of 42 rounds are carried, with rounds and propellants carried separately and loaded sequentially. Firing rate is eight rounds per minute. Both commander and gunner have roof-mounted, stabilised image-intensifier sights and a new computerised fire-control system allows stationary or moving targets to be engaged with a high first round hit probability when the vehicle is moving. Secondary armament comprises a 7.62mm co-axially mounted machine-gun, and a pintle-mounted 12.7mm heavy machine-gun on the turret roof.

The Type 85-III is powered by a new integrated power-pack, based on a transversely-mounted diesel engine, with a rated output of 1,000bhp, giving a power/weight ratio of 24hp/tonne and a road speed of 41mph (65km/h). The transmission has also been upgraded. Both hull and turret have improved armoured protection. Road range is approximately 370 miles (600km) but, as is usual on Chinese MBTs, this can be extended by drum-type, jettissonable fuel tanks mounted on brackets on the rear of the vehicle.

Type 90-II Main Battle Tank

Types 90 and 90-II.
Country of origin: People's Republic of China.
Crew: 3.
Armament: One 125mm smoothbore main gun; one 7.62mm machine-gun co-axial with the main armament; one 12.7mm heavy anti-aircraft machine-gun on turret roof; one six-barrelled smoke discharger on each side of turret.
Armour: All-welded steel with additional ERA.
Dimensions: Length (including main armament) 33ft 0in (10.07m); width 11ft 6in (3.50m); height (to turret roof) 7ft 9in (2.37m).
Weight: Combat 105,820lb (48,000kg).
Ground pressure: 12.3lb/in^2 (0.86kg/cm^2).
Engine: Perkins CV12-1200 TA 12-cylinder, water-cooled, electronic-controlled diesel, 1,200hp at 2,300rpm
Performance: Road speed 39mph (62.3km/h); range 280 miles (450km); vertical obstacle 2ft 10in (0.85m); trench 8ft 10in (2.7m); gradient 60 per cent.
History: First prototype completed in 1991; trials started in 1992 and, as far as is known, continue. No production orders, as of early 2000.

The latest Chinese main battle tank design to be revealed, the Type 90 first appeared in 1991, but by the end of the decade production had still not started and it is thought that this design might be intended for export rather than for deployment with the People's Liberation Army. A development of the basic Type 90 design – the Type 90-II – was revealed in 1997. It is generally similar but is fitted with explosive reactive armour (ERA).

A significant change from previous Chinese practice is that the Type 90-II incorporates Western automotive and transmission systems. The fully-integrated power pack is based on the British Perkins CV12-1200 diesel engine, is very similar to that fitted in the British Challenger 1 and 2 tanks, and has a power output of 1,200hp at 2,300rpm. The transmission, however, is French: the ESM 500, which is the same as that fitted in the French Army's Leclerc tank. Thus, although the Type 90-II is heavier than the Type 85-IIM, the new engine/transmission system gives it a better power/weight ratio: 25hp/tonne compared to 24hp/tonne.

Below: The first Chinese tank to incorporate a Western power-train, Type 90-II has a British Perkins CV12-1200 diesel engine, and French ESM 500 transmission. Power/weight ratio is 25hp/t.

Above: Rear view of the Chinese NORINCO Type 90, showing the neat hull design, heavy track skirts, very low turret, 120mm smoothbore main gun and roof-mounted 12.7mm machinegun.

The gun is a 125mm smoothbore with a fume extractor and thermal sleeve, but is not fitted with a muzzle reference system. The autoloader loads the projectiles and charges separately, and after firing returns the barrel to an angle of 4 degrees for reloading, before automatically resuming the correct angle for the next shot. There are 22 projectiles and charges in the autoloader and another 17 of each stowed elsewhere in the tank. Normal rate of fire is six rounds per minute, but this can be increased to eight if the tactical situation so demands.

Below: The Type 90-II was designed for export and is armed with a 125mm main gun fitted with an auto-loader, which is capable of firing up to eight rounds per minute.

LT-35 (LTM-35) S-IIa Light Tank

Country of origin: Czechoslovakia.
Crew: 4.
Armament: One 37.2mm gun; one 7.92mm Type 37 machine-gun co-axial with main armament; one 7.92mm Type 32 machine-gun in hull front.
Armour: 35mm (1.38in) maximum; 12mm (0.47in) minimum.
Dimensions: Length 16ft 1in (4.9m); width 7ft 1in (2.159m); height 7ft 3in (2.209m).
Weight: Combat 23.148lb (10,500kg).
Ground pressure: 7.6lb/in² (0.6kg/cm²).
Engine: Skoda six-cylinder water-cooled inline petrol engine developing 120hp at 1,800rpm.
Performance: Road speed 25mph (40km/h); range 120 miles (193km); vertical obstacle 2ft 7in (0.787m); trench 6ft 6in (1.981m); gradient 60 per cent
History: Used by Czech Army from 1937-39, German Army from 1940-45, Hungarian Army (see text) and Romanian Army.

The LT-35 was developed by Skoda in the 1930s and was officially designated the Skoda 10.5ton tank Model T-11 or LT-35 (LTM-35) S-IIa. After trials it went into production in 1936 and entered service with the Czech Army the following year. When the Germans invaded Czechoslovakia they took all remaining LT-35s and also continued production for the German Army. The Germans called the tank the *PzKpfw* 35(t) and issued the type to the 6th *Panzer* Division in time for the invasion of France in 1940. The tank remained in front-line service until at least 1942, when most were withdrawn and converted to tow mortars and

artillery. Some were also used in the recovery role.

Main armament of the LT-35 was a Skoda Type A3 37.2mm gun, with an elevation of +25° and a depression of –10°, and a co-axial 7.92mm CZ Type 37 machine-gun. There was a similar machine-gun in the hull front, on the left. Some 90 rounds of 37mm (AP and HE) and 2,550 rounds of 7.92mm ammunition were carried. The hull and turret of the tank were of riveted and bolted armour plate with a maximum thickness of 35mm (1.38in) and a minimum thickness of 12mm (0.47in). The driver and bow machine-gunner were in the front of the hull, and the commander and loader/radio-operator in the turret.

The tank was rather complex, however, and was very prone to mechanical breakdowns. After their experiences in Russia with the tank, the Germans carried out some redesign work on the tank's engine and steering system. Further development resulted in the Skoda S-IIb medium tank, one of which was tested in 1938 but not placed in production. Another Skoda medium was the S-11r/T-21. Once again this was tested by the Czech Army but not placed in production. The Hungarians obtained a licence to build the latter tank in 1940, and they carried out a major redesign of the vehicle. This included a new three-man turret and a more powerful 260hp engine. This entered service as the 40M *Turan I* and was armed with a 40mm gun and two 8mm machine-guns, combat weight being 15.75 tons (16,000kg). The *Turan II* had a 75mm gun but did not enter service, and there was also a 105mm self-propelled gun on a *Turan* chassis.

Left: An LT-35 – the *PzKpfw* 35(t) in German service – operates with a *Panzer* division in Russia. Many LT-35s were taken over by the German Army after the occupation of Czechoslovakia.

LT-38 (TNHP) Light Tank

Country of origin: Czechoslovakia.
Crew: 4.
Armament: One 37.2mm gun; one 7.92mm Type 37 machine-gun co-axial with main armament; one 7.92mm Type 37 machine-gun in hull.
Armour: 30mm (1.18in) maximum; 8mm (0.3in) minimum.
Dimensions: Length 14ft 11in (4.546m); width 7ft (2.133m); height 7ft 7in (2.311m).
Weight: Combat 21,385lb (9,700kg).
Engine: Six-cylinder water-cooled inline petrol engine developing 150hp at 2,600rpm
Performance: Road speed 26mph (42km/h); road range 125 miles (201km); vertical obstacle 2ft 7in (0.787m); trench 6ft 2in (1.879m); gradient 60 per cent.
History: Entered service with Czech Army in 1938 and later used by German Army until 1942. Variants remained in service with German Army until 1945. (*Note: Data relate to late production LT-38.*)

There were two main tank manufacturers in Czechoslovakia before World War II, Skoda of Pilsen and CKD (*Ceskomoravska Kolben Danek),* the latter being an amalgamation of four companies. In addition, the Tatra company did some development work, mainly on wheel-cum-track vehicles. The two major companies built a variety of AFVs for the Czech Army and for export before World War II started. The CKD LTLH (or TNHB) was developed in the early 1930s and aimed at the export market, where it was known as the LT-34. Further development of this resulted in the LTL-P (TNHS). This was entered in trials organised by the Czech Army in 1937 to find a new light tank for the army. The TNHS was found to meet the army requirement and a modified version was placed in production the following year as the TNHP (or LT-38). Other countries which purchased CKD vehicles in the 1930s included Afghanistan, Latvia, Peru, Sweden (which also built the vehicle as the Strv.m/41),

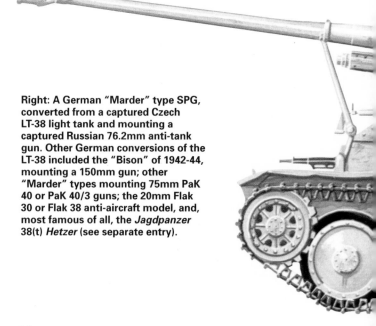

Right: A German "Marder" type SPG, converted from a captured Czech LT-38 light tank and mounting a captured Russian 76.2mm anti-tank gun. Other German conversions of the LT-38 included the "Bison" of 1942-44, mounting a 150mm gun; other "Marder" types mounting 75mm PaK 40 or PaK 40/3 guns; the 20mm Flak 30 or Flak 38 anti-aircraft model; and, most famous of all, the *Jagdpanzer* 38(t) *Hetzer* (see separate entry).

Switzerland, and Yugoslavia. One even went to Great Britain for trials.

The LT-38 served with the Czech Army until the German invasion. The Germans then took over these tanks and also continued production for themselves. The Germans designated the tank the PzKpfw 38(t), which continued in production in Czechoslovakia until 1942. The tank was used in action by the 7th and 8th *Panzer* Divisions during the invasion of France in 1940.

The main armament consisted of a Skoda A7 37.2mm gun which fired AP and HE rounds. The gun had an elevation of +12° and a depression of –6°. A 7.92mm 7165 CZ Type 37 machine-gun was mounted co-axial with the main armament, and there was a similar weapon in the front of the hull. Ninety rounds of 37mm and 2,550 rounds of 7.92mm machine-gun ammunition were carried. The hull was mainly of riveted construction, although the top of the superstructure was bolted in place. The suspension was of the semi-elliptic leaf-spring type, with one spring controlling a pair of road wheels. There were four road wheels, with the idler at the rear and the drive sprocket at the front. Two return rollers were fitted, although these supported the inside of the track only.

The LT-38 was renowned for its reliability and ease of maintenance. The hull was also adopted for a wide range of other roles, including a smokelayer, reconnaissance vehicle, ammunition carrier and artillery prime mover. Its chassis was most widely used to mount artillery, anti-tank and anti-aircraft weapons. The Bison was in production from 1942 to 1944, and was armed with a 15cm gun. The *Marder III*, or SkKfz 139, was armed with a captured Russian 76.2mm anti-tank gun with a limited traverse of 21° left and 21° right, 28 rounds of HE and APC ammunition being carried. There were two other *Marder III* types, one armed with a 7.5cm Pak 40 and the other with a Pak 40/3. The anti-aircraft model was known as the 2cm Flak 30 or Flak 38, this being armed with a 20mm gun with an elevation of 90° and full traverse through 360°, 1,040 rounds of 20mm ammunition being carried.

T-72CZ Main Battle Tank

T-72M3CZ and T-72M4CZ.
Country of origin: Czech Republic.
Crew: 3.
Armament: One 2A46M 125mm smoothbore gun; one 7.62mm PKT machine-gun coaxial with main gun; one NSVT 12.7mm machine-gun on turret roof; four single-barrelled smoke grenade dischargers on each side of turret.
Armour: Advanced composite armour with ERA package.
Dimensions: Length (including main armament) 31ft 5in (9.56m); length (hull) 22ft 10in (6.95m); width 12ft 4in (3.76m); height (to turret roof) 7ft 2in (2.19m).
Weight: Combat 101,411lb (46,000kg).
Ground pressure: 12.8lb/in^2 (0.9kg/cm^2).
Engine: V-46 TC diesel, 858hp at 2,000rpm.
Performance: Road speed 37mph (60km/h); range 300 miles (480km); vertical obstacle 2ft 10in (0.85m); trench 9ft 2in (2.8m); gradient 60 per cent.
History: T-72s entered service with Czech Army in 1980. Current holding is 541 of which at least 250 will be upgraded.
(*Specifications for T-72M3 CZ.*)

As described in the Russian T-72 entry (*qv*), large numbers of these tanks were manufactured and have been sold to a variety of armies around the world. Many of these are now being upgraded and the Czech Republic's T-72CZ has been selected as typical of many programmes. Czechoslovakian State Arsenals undertook the licence manufacture of the Russian-designed T-54/-55 and T-62, so it was a natural progression for them to undertake

Below: The Czech Army is taking delivery of T-72s upgraded to T-72M3 CZ standard (refurbished powerpack) and may soon approve the full modernisation to T-72M4 CZ standard.

Above : An interesting design which did not get beyond the prototype stage, the Slovakian T-72M1 Moderna combined a 125mm main gun with two Oerlikon Contraves 20mm cannon.

production of the T-72 as well. Production of the standard T-72 for the Czechoslovak Army started in 1979, with hulls being produced by ZTS Martin and turrets by ZTS Dubnica, but when Czechoslovakia split into two separate states both these factories were in the newly created Slovakian Republic, leaving the Czech Republic with no production facilities.

The Czech Army operates a fleet of some 514 T-72s and when it decided to upgrade these the responsibility was placed on a vehicle repair workshop, which ran a competition open to both indigenous and foreign suppliers for the supply of the various components, which it would then incorporate. This resulted in two models – T-72M3CZ and T-72M4CZ – which differ, principally, in their power-packs, both of which are supplied by the Israeli company, NIMDA. In the T-72M3CZ the power-pack is a refurbished and upgraded version of the original V-46 TC unit, with added turbo-blowers for the supercharger and an upgraded version of the original transmission. In the T-72M4CZ, the power-pack is based on the British Perkins CV-12 1000 diesel, which has a much higher power output (1,000bhp at 2,300rpm), coupled to an Allison transmission. The result is a tank which weighs some 1.9 tons (2,000kg) more than the T-72M3CZ, but which has a much improved 21hp/tonne power/weight ratio.

The two versions are identical in all other respects. The original fire-control system is replaced by a new digital Officine Galileo TURMS, which provides an overall improvement in fighting efficiency, and improves the probability of a first-round hit, particularly at longer ranges. A new muzzle reference system is also installed.

Other upgrades include new communications systems for both internal and external communications; a laser warning system; a combined inertial/global positioning system (GPS) navigation system; passive night vision sight for the driver, and one of the increasingly widely used Kidde fire detection and suppression systems. The tanks are also fitted with an explosive reactive armour (ERA) package.

The Czech Army has already authorized the upgrading of T-72s to T-72M3CZ standard (ie, with the refurbished power-pack). A decision has not yet been made to go ahead with the T-72M4CZ upgrade (ie, with the new power-pack and transmission).

Schneider Assault Tank

Country of origin: France.
Crew: 6
Armament: One 75mm howitzer in nose; one 8mm machine-gun in each side of the hull.
Armour: 0.45in (11.5mm) maximum.
Dimensions: Length 20ft 9in (6.32m); width 6ft 9in (2.05m); height 7ft 7in (2.3m).
Weight: Combat 32,187lb (14,600kg).
Ground pressure: 11.3lb/in^2 (0.72kg/cm^2).
Engine: Schneider four-cylinder water-cooled petrol engine developing 55hp.
Performance: Road speed 4.6mph (7.5km/h); range 30 miles (48km); vertical obstacle 2ft 9in (0.787m); trench 5ft 9in (1.752m); gradient 57 per cent.
History: Entered service with French Army in 1916 and phased out of service after end of World War I.

In 1915, the French company of Schneider was acting as agent for the American Holt tractor, which had already been adopted by the British Army for towing heavy artillery. In May 1915 Schneider purchased two Holt crawler tractors, one of 45hp and the other of 75hp, for trials. As a result of these trials the French Army placed an order for 15 of the 45hp model, or Baby Holt as the type became known, for delivery in 1916. Late in 1915 the Baby Holt was fitted with mock-up armour to the engine and the driver's position and demonstrated to General Pétain. For some time a French officer named Colonel Estienne had been pressing for a tank-like vehicle to cross trenches and barbed wire, and in December 1916, he and Brillé (of the Schneider company) designed a vehicle whose chassis owed a lot to the American Holt tractor.

The hull was of armour plate on 0.45in (11.5mm) thick the front was shaped like a boat and a barbed-wire cutter was mounted at the front of the hull. The rear of the hull was square cut and two doors were provided in the rear of the hull for entry and exit. The engine was at the front of the hull, offset to the left. The driver was located to the right of the engine. On later production models an additional layer of armour 0.31in (8mm) thick was added to give protection

Above: The Schneider tank negotiates a steep gradient on trials. One of the most successful French tanks of World War I, the Schneider saw extensive service on the Western Front.

against the armour-piercing bullet which the Germans introduced. This was known as the "K" bullet and had a tungsten-carbide core. Armament consisted of a 75mm Schneider gun (it was to have been a 37mm gun in the original design) mounted in the front of the hull on the right, and a single Hotchkiss Model 1914 machine-gun mounted in each side of the hull. Some 90 rounds of 75mm and 4,000 rounds of machine-gun ammunition were carried.

The first production Schneiders were delivered for training purposes late in 1916 and they were first used in action on 16 April 1917, at Chemin des Dames. Of the 132 Schneider tanks used in this battle some 57 were destroyed, with many more damaged beyond repair. Most of the losses were attributable to the petrol tanks catching fire and the tank blowing up. These fuel tanks were right next to the hull machine-gun positions. Just over 400 Schneider tanks were built, the last being delivered in August 1918. Some were disarmed and used as supply carriers during the later stages of the war. Schneider also built the prototype of a vehicle (*CA3*) which had a turret-mounted 47mm gun, but unfortunately this was not placed in production. The *CA3* had numerous improvements over the original Schneider tank but this never even reached the prototype stage.

Left: Side view of a Schneider tank. The 75mm howitzer and 8mm machine-gun mountings can be clearly seen.

43

Renault FT-17 Light Tank

Country of origin: France.
Crew: 2.
Armament: One Hotchkiss 8mm machine-gun (see text).
Armour: 22mm (0.87in) maximum; 6mm (0.24in) minimum.
Dimensions: Length (with tail) 16ft 5in (5m); width 5ft 9in (1.74m); height 6ft 7in (2.14m).
Weight: Combat 15,432lb (7,000kg).
Ground pressure: 8.5lb/in² (0.59kg/cm²).
Engine: Renault four-cylinder water-cooled petrol engine developing 35bhp at 1,500rpm.
Performance: Road speed 4.7mph (7.7km/h); road range 22 miles (35km); vertical obstacle 2ft (0.6m); trench crossing (with tail) 5ft 11in (1.8m); (without tail) 4ft 6in (1.35m); gradient 50 per cent.
History: Entered service with the French Army in 1918 and continued in service until 1940. Remaining vehicles taken over by the Germans in 1940. Also used by the United States (also built in the US as the 6 Ton Tank M1917), Belgium, Brazil, Canada (from the United States in 1940), China, Czechoslovakia, Finland, Greece, Great Britain (used in France in 1918 for command role), Holland, Italy (also further developed to become FIAT 3000 light tank), Japan (used as the Type 79 until 1940), Manchuria, Poland, Romania, Soviet Union (also built in Russia as the KS and with modifications as the MS-1 and MS-2), Spain and Yugoslavia.

Colonel J. E. Estienne first approached Louis Renault in 1915 to build his *Char d'Assaut,* but at that time Renault had no experience of building tracked vehicles and was heavily committed to other projects. By the following year, however, Renault had received contracts from the French Army to design tracked vehicles, mainly for the artillery. Some sources have stated that the FT-17 (*Faible Tonnage*) was designed by Estienne, others that it was designed by Renault, and some that it was a joint development! By late 1916 a mock-up had been completed with the first prototype following in February and March 1917. In the early days of the project there was a considerable amount

Right: Side view of a Renault FT-17 – a standard production model of 1918 with the round turret mounting a 37mm gun. This tank was built in very large numbers and served with numerous armies throughout the 1930s. Many modifications were made to the FT-17 by the countries which it served, including the US-built 6-ton Tank M1917.

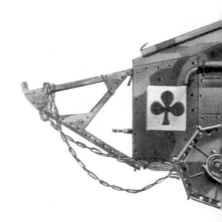

Above: Renault FT-17 light tanks of the US 326th Bn, 311th Tank Center, move up the line near 35th Division HQ, near Boureuilles, Meuse, on 26 September 1918. In the foreground, the machine-gun version; behind, the 37mm-gunned version.

of conflict within the various sections of the army not only on the value of the vehicle, but also on what its armament should be. The first production contract was awarded to Renault, but as subsequent orders went up in leaps and bounds to 3,500 tanks, it was apparent that Renault alone could not hope to build these tanks by the end of 1918. Therefore other companies were brought into the programme, including Berliet, Delaunay Belleville and SOMUA (*Societé d'Outillage Mécanique et d'Usinage d'Artillerie*). In addition there were many other component manufacturers, including some in Great Britain who supplied a proportion of the armour plate. Renault completed its

first production tanks in September 1917, but the whole programme was delayed by acute shortages of components. By the end of 1917, just 83 FT-17s had been built and most of these had no armament. Other manufacturers did not start delivering vehicles until mid-1918, and as a result of the shortage of turrets each manufacturer designed its own to start with.

The FT-17 was essentially a narrow armoured box with the driver at the front, turret with a traverse of 360° in the centre, and the engine and transmission at the rear. The driver entered the tank via twin doors over his compartment, whilst the commander/gunner entered via doors in the turret rear. Maximum armour thickness was 16mm (0.63in) and the hull was of riveted construction. The Renault FT-17 was the first tank with a turret that could be traversed through 360° to enter service. The suspension consisted of coil and leaf springs and pivoted bogies. There were nine small road wheels on four bogies, with the drive sprocket at the rear and the large idler at the front. The latter was of laminated wood with a steel rim. There were six return rollers. Most FT-17s were fitted with a tail at the rear of the hull to increase the trench-crossing capabilities of the tank, but this could be removed for transport.

From a very early stage it was decided that there would be four basic models of the FT-17. The first model to enter service was the *Char Mitrailleur* 8mm, which was armed with an 8mm machine-gun with an elevation of +35° and a depression of −20° 4,800 rounds of machine gun ammunition were carried. This was followed by the 37mm model, armed with a 37mm Puteaux gun with an elevation of +35° and a depression of −20°; 237 rounds of ammunition were carried − 200 HE, 25 AP and 12 shrapnel. The signals vehicle had no turret but was fitted with a superstructure, carrying a single radio, and had a crew of three (radio-operator, observer and driver). The self-propelled gun was called the *Char Canon* 75S and was armed with a 75mm gun in an open mount. This did not enter service, however. Subsequently many other variants were developed, including an amphibious version, bridgelayer, bulldozer, cargo carrier with redesigned hull, fascine carrier for crossing trenches (*Char Fascine*), mineclearing tank (*Char Demineur*),

Below: Late production models of the Renault FT light tank. The special unditching tail, fitted at the rear, can be clearly seen.

Above: Obsolete Renault FT light tanks captured by the Germans in 1940 in use by the internal security forces of the occupying power. Many French AFV s were used by the *Wehrmacht* from 1940 on.

searchlight carrier (this had a searchlight on a high tower and was used for internal security operations by the French police after the war) and a smoke-laying tank. Most of these were for trials purposes, although some were used in the war.

The Renault FT-17 was first used in action on 31 May 1918, when 21 tanks supported infantry in the battle of the Forest of Retz. Later that day the Germans counter-attacked and most of the ground was lost again. At the end of the day only three FT-17s were still operational. Losses were heavy in many of the early engagements, but as the crews gained experience and tactics were improved, losses dropped considerably. By the end of the war just over 3,000 tanks had been completed and production continued for a short time afterwards. After the war the tank was used in action in most of the French colonies including Morocco, Syria and Tunisia.

One of the advantages of the Renault was that its small size enabled it to be transported by lorry from one part of the front to another, whereas the heavier tanks had to be brought up by rail and then proceed to the front line under their own power. After the end of the war many FT-17s were exported, and in many cases these were the first armoured vehicles of some armies. Such was the demand that eventually exports were stopped as the French Army would have ended up with no Renaults at all. In the 1920s many attempts were made to modernise the FT-17, and some were fitted with Citroën-Kégresse rubber band tracks, although these were for trials only. Further development by Renault resulted in the NC1 (or NC27) light tank which had an up-armoured hull and new suspension. This was tested by the French Army but was not adopted, though some examples were sold to Japan and Yugoslavia. This was followed by the NC2 (or NC31) which had a more powerful engine and weighed 9.5tons (9.653kg). Armament consisted of turret-mounted twin 7.5mm machine-guns, and some of this model were purchased by Greece. In the 1930s those FT-17s remaining in service were rearmed with new 0.75mm Hotchkiss machine-guns and then became known as the FT-31. These carried 3,600 rounds of standard ammunition plus a further 450 rounds of armour-piercing ammunition. There were still some 1,600 FT-17s in service when the Germans invaded France in 1940, and many of these were captured by the Germans. The Germans called them the *PzKpfw* 18R 730(f) and used them mainly for the internal security role and for guarding airfields and other strategic targets. Some of the tanks had their turrets removed, the turrets being installed in coastal defences. Some remain to this day in the Channel Islands.

Saint Chamond Assault Tank

Country of origin: France.
Crew: 8.
Armament: One 75mm gun; four 8mm machine-guns.
Armour: 0.67in (17mm) maximum.
Dimensions: Length 28ft 6in (8.687m); width 8ft 9in (2.667m); height 7ft 9in (2.362m).
Weight: Combat 48.50lb (22,000kg).
Ground pressure: 11.3lb/in² (0.79kg/cm²).
Engine: Panhard four-cylinder petrol engine developing 90hp.
Performance: Road speed 5mph (8km/h); range 37 miles (59.5km); vertical obstacle 1ft 3in (0.381m); trench 9ft (2.438m); gradient 57 per cent.
History: Entered service with the French Army in 1916 and phased out of service shortly after the end of the war. Also used by Russia, Italy and the

United States (in France), although it was not used operationally by the latter two countries.

The Schneider was the first tank to be designed and built in France but it was nothing to do with the STA (*Service Technique Automobile*) whose job it was

Below: French Saint Chamond tanks on their way to the front. Better-armoured than the Schneider (France's first tank), the 23-ton Saint Chamond mounted a 75mm gun and four 8mm machine-guns. But faulty design revealed itself when the first of 500 Saint Chamonds built went into action in May 1917. The hull overhung the tracks so much that when crossing trenches the tank's nose became embedded in the far side of the obstacle.

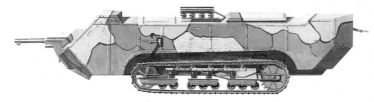

to supply such vehicles for the French Army. The STA therefore quickly started work on an "official" tank without even consulting Colonel Estienne who had designed the Schneider tank. The first prototype was completed in February 1916 at the Saint Chamond works of the *Compagnie des Forges et Aciéries de la Marine et Homécourt*, and two months later it was decided to build 400 of the tank, which became known as the Saint Chamond.

Like the Schneider, the Saint Chamond was also based on a Holt Tractor type chassis, although in this case the chassis was longer. The hull was of riveted construction with a maximum thickness of 0.67in (17mm), this being a great improvement over that of the Schneider tank. The front of the hull was boat-shaped, with the driver and commander seated at the front of the hull, one on each side, each being provided with a circular cupola in the roof. On the prototypes the suspension was covered by armoured plates, but these were left off the production tanks, for when these were fitted, the tracks soon became blocked up with mud. The suspension consisted of three bogies. The front bogie had the idler and two small road wheels, the centre bogie had three small road wheels whilst the last bogie had three small road wheels and the drive sprocket; there were five small return rollers. One of the more unusual features of the Saint Chamond was that each track was powered by an electric motor, power for these being provided by a dynamo driven by the Panhard petrol engine mounted in the centre of the hull. The transmission was a Crochat-Collardeau.

First production vehicles were armed with a 75mm Saint Chamond gun but these were later replaced by the standard 75mm Model 1897 gun. Four 8mm Hotchkiss machine-guns were fitted, one in the front of the hull on the right, one in each side of the hull and one in the rear. Some 106 rounds of 75mm and 7,600 rounds of machine-gun ammunition were carried.

The Saint Chamond was first used in action at Laffaulx Mill on 5 May 1917. During this action all but one of the 16 Saint Chamonds used became stuck in the first line of German trenches. The main disadvantage of this tank was that the front and rear of the hull hung over the tracks, and when crossing trenches or ditches the nose just dug into the ground and the tank was immobilised. The French did modify some tanks to overcome this problem but none of the various schemes tried was satisfactory. The inability of the French tanks to cross the German trenches stemmed from the fact that both the Schneider and the Saint Chamond were based to a large extent on a commercial crawler tractor. The British also had Holt tractors, but soon realised that something more was required to cross the German trenches. The lozenge shape of the British tanks enabled them to cross wide trenches. The Mark I, for example, could cross a trench 11ft 6in wide (3,505m) when fitted with its tail, and climb a vertical obstacle of 4ft 6in (1.372m). Several modifications were carried out on production tanks, including revised commander's and driver's cupola and the roof was angled so that grenades would roll off the roof before they exploded.

In all, 400 Saint Chamonds were built, the last of these being completed in March 1918. Some Saint Chamond tanks had their 75mm guns removed for use in the supply role. Production of the Schneider and Saint Chamond was finally stopped as it had been decided to concentrate on building larger numbers of the smaller Renault FT 17 two-man tanks.

Char 2C Heavy Tank

Char 1A, Char 1B and Char 2C
Country of origin: France.
Crew: 12-13.
Armament: One 75mm gun; four 8mm machine-guns.
Dimensions: Length 33ft 8in (10.27m); width 9ft 8in (2.95m); height 13ft 2in (4.01m).
Weight: Combat 154,320lb (70,000kg).
Engine: See text.
Performance: Road speed 8mph (12km/h); range 100 miles (160km); vertical obstacle 4ft (1.219m); trench 13ft 6in (4.114m); gradient 50 per cent.
History: Entered service with French Army shortly after end of World War I and destroyed in 1940.

The first French tanks were the Schneider and the Saint Chamond, but these both had one major short-coming, their inability to cross German trenches. In 1916 the FCM (*Forges et Chantiers de la Méditerranée*) at La Seyne, near Toulon, started the design of a new "breakthrough tank", the first of two prototypes being completed late in 1917. One of the prototypes had an electrical transmission and the other a mechanical transmission. These tanks

**Above: Front view of the massive Char 2C.
Apart from it's main 75mm gun, it had four
8mm machine-guns, two of which can be seen
protruding from the hillsides.**

were known as the *Char* FCM 1A, weighed 39.37 tons (40,000kg) and had a crew of seven men. They were powered by Renault 12-cylinder petrol engines, giving them a top speed of just 4mph (6.4km/h). Armament consisted of a 75mm gun and machine-guns. The 1B was similar, but the 75mm gun was replaced by a 105mm weapon.

The FCM 1A was not placed in production but was followed by the *Char* 2C. Ten of these were built by 1918, but they did not enter service with the French Army until after the war. If the war had not ended, it was anticipated that 300 *Char* 2Cs would have been built for the 1919 campaigns. These 10 tanks were modified in the 1930s and were still operational with the 51st Battalion when war broke out in 1939. They took no part in the Battle of France as most of them were destroyed on their special railway wagons by the *Luftwaffe*.

Main armament of the *Char* 2C consisted of a turret-mounted 75mm gun. The four 8mm machine-guns were mounted as follows: one in the hull front, one in each side of the hull in the forward part of the tank, and the last turret-mounted on the hull top towards the rear of the tank. When built the tanks were powered by German six-cylinder Mercedes engines developing 180hp each, but these were later replaced by more powerful Maybach engines developing 250hp each. The *Char* 2C had the distinction of being the first tank to have two turrets. It was very heavy and if it had been used operationally would have been more of a liability than an asset. One *Char* 2C was rebuilt as the only *Char 2C-bis*, which had additional armour, Sautter-Harlé engines and a 155mm howitzer.

Above and Below: The French *Char 2C* was one of the largest AFVs built. It was developed near the end of WWI and served until 1940, supplementing the Maginot Line defences. Only 10 were built.

Renault AMC 35 Light Tank

AMC 35 (ACG1), plus Belgian and German variants.
Countries of origin: France.
Crew: 3.
Armament: One 47mm gun; one 7.5mm machine-gun co-axial with main armament.
Armour: 25mm (1in) maximum.
Dimensions: Length 15ft (4.572m); width 7ft 4in (2.235m); height 7ft 8in (2.336m).
Weight: 31,967lb (14,500kg).
Engine: Renault four-cylinder petrol engine developing 180hp.
Performance: Maximum road speed 25mph (40km/h); range 100 miles (161km); vertical obstacle 2ft (0.609m); trench 6ft (1.828m); gradient 60 per cent.
History: In service with the French Army from 1935 to 1940. Also used by the Belgian and German Armies (see text).

As well as building a light tank to met the AMR requirement (the Renault AMR 33 VM), Renault also built a tank to meet the AMC (*Auto-Mitrailleuse de Reconnaissance*) requirement. The first prototype, which was completed in 1933, had a turret from the Renault light tank, featuring a 37mm gun. Trials with this prototype were not satisfactory so a further prototype was built, under the designation AMC Renault 34 YR.

This was the first French light tank to have a two-man turret, at last enabling the tank commander to carry out his proper role, that is to command the tank, and not operate the armament. AMC 34 YR armament consisted of a 25mm gun and a co-axial 7.5mm machine-gun. It was powered by a Renault four-cylinder petrol engine which developed 120hp, giving the tank a maximum road speed of 25mph (40km/h). Combat weight was 10.63 tons (10,800kg).

This tank was followed by the Renault AMC 35 or ACG1, of which early models were built by Renault, but then the majority by AMX. The tank had a crew of three, with the driver at the front of the hull and the other two crew members in the turret. Armament consisted of a 47mm gun and a co-axial 7.5mm machine-gun, although some tanks had the 47mm gun replaced by a long barrelled 25mm anti-tank gun. The suspension was of the scissors type with horizontal springing. There were five road wheels on each side, with the drive sprocket at the front and the idler at the rear, and five track-return rollers.

Production of the AMC 35 amounted to about 100 tanks, of which 12 were purchased by the Belgians in 1937. The tanks were re-designated *Auto-Mitrailleuses de Corps de Cavalerie*, and had a turret of Belgian design and construction armed with a 47mm anti-tank gun and a co-axial 13.2mm machine-gun. After the fall of France some AMC 35s were taken over by the Germans, who called them the *PzKpfw* AMC 738 (f).

Above right: The three-crew AMC 35 was a significant departure from previous French designed tanks in that it had a two-man-turret.

Centre right: AMC 35 with its original short-barrelled 47mm gun replaced by a long-barrelled 25mm Hotchkiss anti-tank gun, but retaining co-axial machine gun.

Right: The AMC 35 was designed by Renault but later production was undertaken by AMX. This is the 47mm-gunned version which had a cast turret.

Hotchkiss H-35 and H-39 Light Tank

H-35, H-39 and German variants.
Country of origin: France.
Crew: 2.
Armament: One 37mm SA 38 gun; one 7.5mm Model 1931 machine-gun co-axial with main armament.
Armour: 40mm (1.57in) maximum; 12mm (0.47in) minimum.
Dimensions: Length 13ft 10in (4.22m); width 6ft 1in (1.85m) height 6ft 7in (2.14m).
Weight: Combat 26,456lb (12,000kg).
Ground pressure: 12.8lb/in^2 (0.90kg/cm^2).
Engine: Hotchkiss six-cylinder water-cooled petrol engine developing 120bhp at 2,800rpm.
Performance: Road speed 22.5mph (36km/h); range 93 miles (150km); vertical obstacle 1ft 8in (0.5m); trench 5ft 11in (1.8m); gradient 60 per cent.
History (H-35): Entered service with the French Army in 1936 and used until fall of France. Also used by Free French, Germany and Israel (after World War II). (*Note: data relate to the H-39.*)

When the first *DML (Division Légère Mécanique)* was formed in 1934, the French Army wanted a light tank to operate with the *SOMUA* S-35 medium tank. In 1933 the French infantry ordered a light tank, the prototype of which

Below: Side view of Hotchkiss H-39 light tank with a near horizontal rear engine deck as compared to the downward-sloping deck of the earlier Hotchkiss H-35. By the beginning of the war 821 H-35/H-39 tanks were in service with the French Army.

Above: Hotchkiss H-35 light tank armed with the short barrelled SA 18 37mm gun which had a muzzle velocity of 1,273fps (388m/s) compared to the more common SA 38 (33 calibre) long barrel weapon with a muzzle velocity of 2,300fps (701m/s). Some 100 rounds of 37mm and 2,400 rounds of 7.5mm machine gun ammunition were carried, with the empty cartridge cases for the latter being deposited outside via a chute.

was completed by Hotchkiss in 1934. This was rejected by the infantry in favour of the similar Renault 35 tank. The cavalry, however, accepted the tank for service as the *Char Léger* Hotchkiss *modèle* 35H, and in the end the infantry also accepted the tank for its *DCs (Divisions Cuirassées)* formed shortly before war broke out.

The H-35 weighed 11.22 tons (11,400kg) and was powered by a six-cylinder petrol engine which developed 75bhp at 2,700rpm and gave the tank a top road speed of 17mph (28km/h). The H-35's maximum armour thickness was 34mm (1.34in). The H-35 was followed by the H-38 and the H-39, which had a number of modifications, including thicker armour and more powerful engines which increased their speed. Production of the H-35/H-39 family amounted to about 1,000 tanks, of which some 821 were in front-line service when World War II broke out.

The hull of the H-39 was of cast sections bolted together. The driver was seated at the front of the hull, slightly offset to the right, and was provided with a two-piece hatch cover, one part of which opened upwards and the other part forwards A hull escape hatch was provided in the floor of the tank. The turret was also of cast construction and this was built by APX and was identical to that fitted to the Renault R-35 and R-40 tanks. The turret was provided with a cupola, which could be traversed, and the commander entered via a hatch in the turret rear, which also folded down horizontally to form a seat, this being used when the tank was not in action. The engine was at the rear of the hull on the left, with the fuel tank on the right, these being separated from the fighting compartment by a fireproof bulkhead. Compared with the earlier H-35, the deck of the H-39 was almost horizontal, the earlier model's deck having been more sloped. An external fuel tank could be fitted if required, as could a detachable skid tail, the latter being designed to increase the tank's cross-country performance. Power was transmitted to the gearbox and transmission at the front of the hull by a shaft. The suspension on each side comprised three bogies, each with two wheels. These were mounted on bellcranks with double springs between the upper arms. The drive sprocket was at the front and the idler at the rear; there were two track-return rollers.

Main armament consisted of a 37mm gun with a 7.5mm machine-gun mounted co-axially to the right. Two different models of 37mm gun were fitted: the SA38 with a long (33 calibre) barrel, giving a muzzle velocity of 2,300fps (701m/s), or the shorter SA 18 gun (21 calibre) with a muzzle velocity of 1,273fps (388m/s). The former was the more common weapon for the H-39.

Above: Front and top views of H-39 light tank which, together with the H-35, was used in the cavalry role, or in a direct support role with the infantry.

Right: The H-35 tank, like many other French tanks, had the drawback of having a one-man turret.

Some 100 rounds of 37mm and 2,400 rounds of 7.5mm machine-gun ammunition were carried. The empty cartridge cases for the latter went into a chute which deposited them outside of the tank. Like most French tanks of this period, the Hotchkiss H-35/H-39 had one major drawback, and this was that the commander also had to aim and load the gun.

When France fell the Germans took over many H-35 and H-39 tanks, some being used on the Russian Front without modification apart from the installation of a German radio and a new cupola. This had a flat roof and was provided with a two-piece hatch cover which opened to the left and right. Some were also provided with a searchlight over the main armament. The Germans also developed two self-propelled guns based on the Hotchkiss H-35 and H-39 chassis. The anti-tank model was known as the 7.5cm *Pak* 40 L/48 *auf Gw* 39H (f), and had its turret removed and replaced by an open-topped armoured superstructure mounted at the rear of the hull. In the front of this superstructure was mounted a 7.5cm anti-tank gun. Twenty-four such conversions were produced from 1942. This version weighed 12.3 tons (12,500kg) and had a crew of five. The second model was the 10.5cm *Panzer-feldhaubitze* 18 *auf Sfh 39H (f)* or *10.5cm le* FH 18 *GW* 39H (f), 48 of these being built from 1942. This model was armed with a 10.5cm howitzer and was provided with a similar superstructure to the anti-tank model.

When the state of Israel was formed after the end of World War II, it could not obtain any modern tanks at all and had to rely on what equipment was left in the area after the war. These included some French H-39 tanks and a number of these were rearmed with British 6pounder anti-tank guns.

Char B1 Heavy Tank

Char B1, B1-*bis*, B1-*ter* and German variants.
Country of origin: France.
Crew: 4.
Armament: One 75mm gun in hull; one 7.5mm machine-gun in hull; one 47mm turret-mounted gun; one 7.5mm machine-gun co-axial with 47mm gun (see text).
Armour: 60mm (2.36in) maximum.
Dimensions: Length 21ft 5in (6.52m); width 8ft 2in (2.5m); height 9ft 2in (2.79m).
Weight: Combat 70,548lb (32,000kg).
Ground pressure: 19.7lb/in² (1.39kg/cm²).
Engine: Six-cylinder inline water-cooled petrol engine developing 307bhp at 1,900rpm.
Performance: Road speed 17mph (28km/h); range 93 miles (150km); vertical obstacle 3ft 1in (0.93m); trench 9ft (2.75m); gradient 50 per cent.
History: Entered service with the French Army in 1936 and used until fall of France in 1940. Also used by the German Army (see text).

In 1921 the *Section Technique des Chars de Combat*, under the leadership of the famous French exponent of armour, General Estienne, requested five companies to draw up a design for a tank weighing 14.75 tons (15,000kg), to be armed with a hull-mounted 47mm or 75mm gun. In 1924 four different mock-ups were presented at Rueil and three years later orders were given for the construction of three tanks, one each from FAMH (*Forges et Aciéries de la Marine et d'Homécourt*), FCM (*Forges et Chantiers de la Méditerranée)* and Renault/Schneider. These were completed between 1929 and 1931 and were known as the *Char* B. these weighed 24.6 tons (25,000kg) and were armed with a hull-mounted 75mm gun, two fixed machine-guns in the front of the hull, and two turret-mounted machine-guns. They had a crew of four. With modifications the type entered production as the *Char* B1, but only 35 of these had been built before it was decided to place in production an improved model with heavier armour and a more powerful engine, to be known as the *Char*
B1-*bis*. Some 365 were built by the fall of France in 1940. Of these there were 66 *Char* B1-*bis* tanks in the 1st, 2nd, 3rd and 4th DCRs *(Division Cuirassées de Réserve),* and a further 57 in independent companies.

Right and below: Front and top views of the *Char* B1-*bis*. The main 75mm gun, to the right and below the driver, was operated by the driver. It was fixed and the driver had to aim it by pointing the entire tank at the target. Elevation was +25° and depression −15°. Ammunition for the weapons was stored on the walls and under the floor of the fighting compartment of the tank.

The *Char* B1-*bis* had excellent armour which could withstand attack from any German anti-tank gun except the famous 88mm. The hull of the tank was of cast sections bolted together. The driver was seated at the front of the hull on the left and steered the tank with a conventional steering wheel which was connected in turn to a hydrostatic system. Mounted to the driver's right was the 75mm SA 35 gun, which had a very short barrel (17.1 calibres), elevation being +25° and depression −15°. The gun was fixed in traverse and was aimed by the driver, who swung the tank until the gun was lined up with the target. An unusual feature of this gun was that an air compressor was provided to blow fumes out of the barrel. A 7.5mm Chatellerault machine-gun was fixed in the front of the hull on the right, lower than the 75mm gun. This machine-gun could be aimed by the driver or commander. The APX turret was identical to that installed on the *SOMUA* S-35 tank and was armed with a 37mm gun with an elevation of +18° and a depression of −18°. A 7.5mm

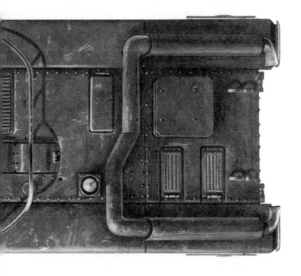

machine-gun was also mounted in the turret, and this had an independent traverse of 10° left and 10° right. Some 74 rounds of 75mm (HE), 50 rounds of 47mm (AP and HE) and 5,100 rounds of machine-gun ammunition were carried.

The tank had a crew of four, the driver/gunner, wireless operator, loader and commander. The last had to aim, load and fire the turret guns as well as command the tank. The loader was just as busy, as he had to pass ammunition to the commander as well as load the hull-mounted 75mm gun. The wireless operator was seated near the turret. Normal means of entry and exit was via a large door in the right of the hull. The driver had a hatch over his position, and there was also a hatch in the turret rear on the right. There were two emergency exits, one in the floor of the tank and another hatch in the roof of the engine compartment. The engine, transmission and fuel tanks were at the rear of the hull, and a compressed air starting system was fitted in addition to the normal electric starting system. Another interesting feature of

Above: The German Army removed the hull-mounted 75mm gun from a small number of *Char* B1 tanks and fitted a flame-thrower. These became known as *PzKpfw* B1 (f) *Fahrschulewagen*.

Right: A *Char* B1 knocked out in the summer of 1940. At that time the *Char* B1 was one of the most formidable tanks in service.

the tank was the installation of a gyroscopic direction indicator, also driven by the compressor. The suspension on each side consisted of 16 double steel bogie wheels. Of these, three assemblies had four wheels each and these were controlled by vertically mounted coil springs and semi-elliptical leaf springs. There were also three independent bogie wheels forward and one to the rear, with quarter-elliptic leaf springs. The drive sprocket was at the rear and the idler at the front, the latter being coil sprung to act as the tensioner.

Further development of the *Char* B1-*bis* resulted in the *Char* B1-*ter*. This had additional armour, a fifth crew member (a mechanic) and the 75mm hull gun had a traverse of 5° left and 5° right. Only five of these were built and none was used in action. The tank was also used by the German Army for a variety of roles. The driver training model had the turret and hull-mounted gun removed, the latter being replaced by a machine-gun. The type was then known as the *PzKpfw* B1 (f) *Fahrschulewagen*. The Germans also modified 24 tanks in 1942-43 for use in the flamethrower role. These had flameguns fitted in place of the hull guns and the type was known as the *PzKpfw* B1-*bis* (*Flamm*). The gun turret was retained to give the vehicle some anti-tank capability. Finally there was a self-propelled gun model. This had the hull gun and turret removed, and on top of the tank was mounted a standard German 105mm howitzer. The conversion work was carried out by Rheinmetall-Borsig. Very few such conversions were effected and most of these served in France.

A few *Char* B1 -*bis* tanks were used by the French when they liberated the port of Royan in 1944. The *Char* B1-*bis* would have probably been followed in production by the ARL 40 but this was still at the design stage when France fell. The type was eventually placed in production as the ARL 44 in 1946. The main other French infantry tanks (medium/heavy) were the *Char* D1 and *Char* D2. The *Char* D1 was developed in the early 1930s and 160 were built for the infantry between 1932 and 1935. These weighed 12.8 tons (13,000kg) and were armed with a turret-mounted 47mm gun and a fixed machine-gun in the front of the hull, fired by the driver. Later production models had thicker armour, a more powerful engine and a machine-gun mounted co-axially with the main armament. Before production of the D1 was even completed, work started on a more powerful and heavier armoured tank called the *Char* D2. This weighed 15.75 tons (16,000kg) and was powered by a six-cylinder petrol engine developing 150hp. By 1940 about 100 had been built.

Renault AMR 33 VM Light Tank

AMR 33 VM, 32 ZT and German variants.
Country of origin: France.
Crew: 2.
Armament: One 7.5mm machine-gun.
Armour: 13mm (0.51).
Dimensions: Length 11ft 6in (3.504m); width 5ft 3in (1.6m); height 5ft 8in (1.727m).
Weight: 11.023lb (5000kg).
Engine: Reinastella eight-cylinder liquid-cooled petrol engine developing 84bhp.
Performance: Maximum road speed 37mph (60km/h); vertical obstacle 2ft (0.609m); trench 5ft (1.524m); gradient 60 per cent.
History: Entered service with the French Army in 1934–35 and used until fall of France in 1940.
(*Note: data relate to AMR 33 VM.*)

During World War I the French cavalry used armoured cars for the reconnaissance role in small numbers. These lacked mobility for cross-country operations, however, and in 1922–23 specifications were issued for a new vehicle to be called the AMC, or *Auto-Mitrailleuse de Cavalerie*. Various projects were started over the next few years but little progress was made. In 1931 requirements for three different types of vehicle for the cavalry were drawn up: firstly, the AMD (*Auto-Mitrailleuse de Découverte*), a requirement eventually filled by the Panhard AMD 178 armoured car; secondly, the AMR (*Auto-Mitrailleuse de Reconnaissance*), a light tracked vehicle with a crew of two, to be armed with a single 7.5mm machine gun; and thirdly, the AMC (*Auto-Mitrailleuse de Combat*), to support the lighter AMR with heavier armour and more powerful armament. Renault built a small tracked vehicle to meet the AMR requirement, and after trials an order for 123 production vehicles was placed in 1933. These vehicles entered service with the French Army under the designation AMR Renault 33 VM.

The hull was of riveted construction, with the driver at the front, the commander/gunner in the turret, which was offset to the left of the hull, and the engine on the right side. The suspension was unusual and consisted of four

Above: One of the most widely-used French light reconnaissance tanks was the AMR 33 Renault VM, mounting a 7.5mm machine-gun. The tank served with French mechanised cavalry units until the German occupation.

road wheels: a twin-wheeled bogie in the centre, pivoted at the lower end of a vertical coil, and single wheels, front and rear, on bell cranks. The drive sprocket was at the front and the idler at the rear, and there were four track-return rollers.

Further development resulted in the Renault AMR 35 ZT, of which 200 were built. This weighed 6.4 tons (6,500kg) and was powered by a Renault four-cylinder water-cooled petrol engine which developed 85hp and gave the vehicle a top road speed of 34mph (55km/h). Armament consisted of a 7.5mm machine-gun, or a 13.2mm Hotchkiss machine-gun or a 25mm Hotchkiss anti-tank gun.

Quantities of both the AMR 33 VM and the AMR 35 ZT were captured by the Germans, the former being given the designation *PzSpWg* VM 701 (*f*) and the latter *PzSpWg* ZTI 702 (*f*). Some of these had their turrets removed and replaced by a new superstructure mounting an 80mm mortar. The (*f*) stood for French, captured British tanks having the suffix (*e*), American (*a*), Czecho-slovakian (*t*) and so on.

Left: Pilot model of the AMC 34. In the inter-war years the French did much light tank development.

Renault R-35 Light Tank

R-35 and German variants.
Country of origin: France.
Crew: 2.
Armament: One 37mm gun; one 7.5mm machine-gun co-axial with main armament.
Armour: 1.77in (45mm) maximum.
Dimensions: Length 13ft 10in (4.2m); width 6ft 1in (1.85m); height 7ft 9in (2.37m).
Weight: 22,046lb (10,000kg).
Ground pressure: 9.52lb/in² (0.67kg/cm²).
Engine: Renault four-cylinder petrol engine developing 82bhp at 2,200rpm.
Performance: Road speed 12.42mph (20km/h); range 87 miles (140km); vertical obstacle 1ft 10in (0.5m); trench 5ft 3in (1.6m) or 6ft 7in (2m) with tail; gradient 60 per cent.
History: Entered service with the French Army in 1936 and used until fall of France. Also used by Germany, Italy (tanks received from Germany), Poland, Romania, Turkey and Yugoslavia.

In 1934 the French infantry issued a requirement for a new light tank to replace the large number of World War I Renault FT-17 two-man tanks which were still in service (these in fact remained in service with French Army until 1940, and with the German Army for some years later still). This new light tank was to weigh 7.87 tons (8,000kg), have a crew of two, a maximum road speed of 12.42mph (20km/h), to be armed with twin 7.5mm machine-guns or a single 37mm gun, and have a maximum armour thickness of 1.57in (40mm). Four companies submitted designs: *Compagnie Général de Construction des Locomotives*, Delaunay-Belleville, FCM and Renault.

Below: Side view of Renault R-35 light tank clearly showing the scissor-type suspension, common to many French tanks of this period, trailing idler wheel and the special tail that was fitted to enable the tank to cross wide trenches. It was one of the better French light tanks of the period.

The Renault model, called the Renault ZM (or R-35) was selected for production and the first 300 were order in May 1935. The prototype was armed with twin turret-mounted 7.5mm machine-guns and differed in many details to the production models. The suspension was based on that used in the Renault *Auto-Mitrailleuse de Reconnaissance* 1935 Type ZT (AMR) which had already been accepted for service. Production of the Renault R-35 amounted to between 1,600 and 1,900 tanks, and when war was declared this was the most numerous of all of the French

Above: Repairs had often to be accomplished in the field to allow the damaged AFVs to be returned to front line service as quickly as possible. Here, in a temporary field workshop, the front armour of a Renault R-35 light tank has been lifted off to allow repair work to be carried out on the differential and final drive assemblies. The R-35 was the most numerous of all French infantry tanks, but had a one-man turret and was very slow.

tanks, and many were also exported. In May 1940 there were some 945 R-35/R-40 tanks in front line use, and of these 810 were organic to armies and another 135 were with the 4th *DCR* (*Division Cuirassée de Réserve*). Their role was the support of the infantry and their slow road speed gave them little strategic mobility.

The FCM entry in the original competition was also adopted for service as the *Char Léger Modèle* 1936 FCM, but only 100 were built by 1940 and these were sufficient to equip a mere two battalions. The FCM tank was faster than the R-35 and had a much larger radius of action. It was powered by a 90hp diesel and its suspension was similar to that used on the *Char* B1. Its hull was of welded construction and in this respect was quite advanced. Combat weight was about 10.33 tons (10,500kg). Some of these FCMs were converted to self-propelled guns after the German invasion.

Like most French tanks, the hull of the R-35 was of cast sections which were then bolted together. The driver was seated at the front of the hull, slightly offset to the left, and was provided with two hatch covers, one of which opened forwards and the other upwards, the operation of the latter being assisted by a hydraulic ram. The APX turret was in the centre of the hull and was identical to that installed on the Hotchkiss H-35 and H-39 tanks. This was provided with a cupola but the commander entered the turret via a hatch in the rear of the turret, and this hatch also acted as a seat for the commander when the tank was not in action. Main armament consisted of a 37mm SA 18 gun with a 7.5mm machine-gun mounted co-axially. Some 100 rounds of 37mm and 2,400 rounds of 7.5mm ammunition were carried. The empty cartridge cases from the machine-gun were deposited into a chute which carried them out through a hold in the floor of the tank. Late production tanks were armed with the long-barrelled SA 38 37mm gun. The engine was at the rear of the hull on the right, with the fuel tank (this being of the self-sealing type) on the left. A fireproof bulkhead separated the engine and fighting compartments. The suspension on each side consisted of five rubber-tired wheels, the first being mounted independently and the others on two bogies. These were mounted on bellcranks with springs. The drive sprocket was at the front and the idler at the rear, and there were three track-return rollers. Most tanks had a tail fitted to increase their trench-crossing capabilities. When first developed the tank was not provided with a radio, although these were fitted to late production tanks. This addition meant even more work for the commander, who already had to command the tank as well as aim, load and fire the armament.

Another development of the R-35 was the AMX-40. This had a new suspension designed by AMX, consisting of 12 small road wheels, with the drive sprocket at the front and the idler at the rear, and there were four track-return rollers. This suspension was an improvement over the Renault suspension. Two battalions were equipped with the AMX-40, or R-40 as the type was sometimes called. The R-35 was also used as a fascine carrier. This model had a frame running from the front of the hull over the turret to the rear, on top of which was carried a fascine for dropping into trenches. Some tanks were also provided with FCM turrets of cast or

Left: The Germans fitted about 100 Renault R-35 tanks with a Czech 47mm anti-tank gun in place of the turret. These were known as the 4.7cm *Pak(t)* auf *GW* R35 (*f*), but were already obsolete by the time they entered service. Others were used as carriers for ammunition and a few were even fitted with a 105mm howitzer and designated *leFH* 18 auf *GW* 35R (*f*).

Above and left: Front and rear views of an R-35 tank. Playing card insignia were often painted on the turret for identification of sub-units. When open, the door in the turret rear provided a seat for the tank commander who also had to aim, load and fire the 37mm SA 18 gun and the co-axial machine-gun. Turret was the same as that fitted to the H-35/H-39 tanks.

welded construction, although these were not adopted for service. Other trials version included a mine-detection tank and remote controlled tank.

The Germans used the R-35 for various roles. The basic tank was used for the reconnaissance role on the Eastern Front from 1941 onwards under the designation *PzKpfw* R-35 (4.7cm). Many had their turrets removed and were used for towing artillery (*Traktor*) or for carrying ammunition, the latter version being known as the *Munitionpanzer* 35R (*f*). The anti-tank variant was known as the 4.7cm *Pak (t) auf GW* R35 (*f*), this consisting of an R-35 with its turret removed and replaced by a new open topped superstructure in the front of which was mounted a Czech 47mm anti-tank gun. About 100 of these were converted, but they were already obsolete by the time conversion work was completed. Alfred Becker fitted some with a 105mm howitzer and these were known as the 10.5cm *leFH* 18 *auf GW* 35R (*f*). Some examples, known as the *Mörserträger* 35r (*f*), were also fitted with an 80mm mortar.

Char SOMUA S-35
Medium Tank

S-35 and S-40.
Country of origin: France.
Crew: 3.
Armament: One 47mm gun; one 7.5mm Model 31 machine-gun co-axial with main armament.
Armour: 56mm (2.2in) maximum.
Dimensions: Length 17ft 11in (5.46m); width 6ft 11in (2.108m); height 8ft 10in (2.692m).
Weight: Combat 44,2000lb (20,048kg).
Ground pressure: 13.08lb/in^2 (0.92kg/cm^2).
Engine: *SOMUA* eight-cylinder water-cooled petrol engine developing 190hp at 2,000rpm.
Performance: Maximum road speed 23mph (37km/h); road range 160 miles (257km); vertical obstacle 1ft 8in (0.508m); trench 7ft 8in (2.336m); gradient 65 per cent.
History: Entered service with the French Army in 1936 and used until fall of France in 1940. Also used by Germany and Italy (see text).

In the early 1930s the French cavalry issued a requirement for a tank to be called the AMC, or *Automitrailleuse de Combat*. A vehicle to this specification

**Below: Side view of SOMUA S-35
showing access doors in left side of hull.
A hull escape hatch was also provided.
The hull consisted of cast sections
bolted together.**

Above: The *Char* SOMUA S-35 medium tank was more than a match for any German tanks during the Battle of France in 1940, by which time some 500 had been built. The S-35 was well armed, had good mobility and firepower but, as in most other French tanks of this period, the commander had to load, aim and fire the guns as well as command the tank. The turret of the S-35 was identical to that fitted to the *Char* B1-bis and D2 tanks and mounted a 47mm SA 35 gun and a 7.5mm Model 31 MG coaxial.

Above: After the fall of France in the summer of 1940, the occupying German forces took over all available French tanks and other weapons. This photograph shows a SOMUA S-35 medium tank leading Hotchkiss light tanks though Paris with their German crews. The Germans called the S-35 the *PzKpfw* 35C 739(*f*) and these were used on the Russian front. Some of these tanks were also supplied to the Italians.

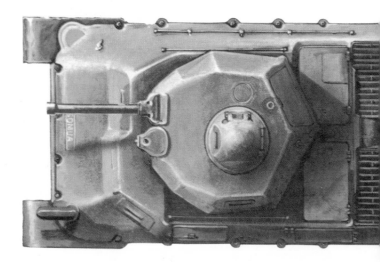

was built by *SOMUA* (*Société d'Outillage Mécanique et d'Usinage d'Artillerie*) at Saint Ouen. After trials this was accepted for service with the cavalry under the designation AMC *SOMUA* AC-3. Soon afterwards it was decided that the type would be adopted as the standard medium tank of the French Army, and it was redesignated the *Char* S-35, the "S" standing for *SOMUA* and the "35" for the year of introduction, 1935. About 500 had been built by the fall of France. Tank for tank, the S-35 was more than a match for any of the German tanks of that time, but bad tactics gave them little chance to prove their worth apart from a few isolated actions.

The S-35 had good armour, mobility and firepower, but it also had the usual French weakness in that the commander was also the gunner and loader. The hull was of three cast sections bolted together. These sections were the hull

Right and below: Front, top and rear views of the SOMUA S-35 medium tank. The hull was cast in three sections and then bolted together just above the tops of the tracks. This proved one of the weak points as a hit on one of these joints generally split the tank wide open. The driver and radio operator, seated at the front, entered the tank through the door in the left side of the hull. The tank was well laid out, with ample vision devices provided. Note in particular the wide area of engine air-intake grilles at the rear, the shrouded turret machine gun, and the twin exhaust pipes running down the centre of the rear deck.

floor, front superstructure and rear superstructure, which were joined by bolts just above the tops of the tracks, with the vertical join between the front and rear parts near the rear of the turret. These joints were one of the weak points of the tank as a hit on one of these was likely to split the tank wide open. The hull had a maximum thickness of 1.6in (41mm). The driver was seated at the front of the hull on the left, and was provided with a hatch to his front. This hatch was normally left open as the tank moved up to the front. The radio operator was located to the right of the driver. Normal means of entry and exit for the driver and radio operator were through a door in the left side of the hull; a floor escape hatch was also provided for use in an emergency. The turret was also of cast construction and had a maximum thickness of 2.2in (56mm). It was identical to that of the *Char* B1-*bis* and D2.

Main armament consisted of a 47mm SA 35 gun with an elevation of +18° and a depression of −18°, the turret being traversible through 360° by an electric motor. The 47mm gun could fire both HE and AP rounds with a maximum muzzle-velocity of 2,200fps (670m/s). A 7.5mm Model 31 machine-gun was mounted co-axially to the right of the main armament. This machine-gun was unusual in that it had a limited traverse of 10° left and 10° right of the main armament. Some 118 rounds of 47mm and 1,250 rounds of machine-gun ammunition were normally carried. Provision was also made for mounting another 7.5mm machine-gun on the commander's cupola for use in the anti-aircraft role. This last does not appear to have been fitted in action as no doubt the commander already had enough to do without having to cope with this weapon as well!

The engine and transmission were at the rear of the hull, with the engine on the left and the self-sealing petrol tank on the right. The engine compartment was separated from the fighting compartment by a fireproof bulkhead. The suspension on each side consisted of two assemblies, each of which had four bogie wheels mounted in pairs on articulated arms, these being controlled by semi-elliptic springs. The ninth bogie wheel at the rear was provided with its own spring. The idler was at the front and the drive sprocket at the rear, and there were two small track-return rollers. The lower part of the suspension was provided with an armoured cover which could be hinged up to allow access to the bogie assemblies.

In 1940 production of an improved model, the S-40, started. This had a more powerful 220hp engine and modified suspension, but few of these had been completed by the fall of France. Another interesting vehicle was the SAu 40 self-propelled gun, although this existed only in prototype form. This had a

Above: The final version of the SOMUA medium tank, considered by many to be the best French tank built, was the S-40. This had a more powerful 220hp engine and modified suspension, but few were built by the fall of France in 1940. This S-40 was captured by the Resistance towards the end of the war.

Right: A new S-40 on a low loader awaits delivery to the French Army. At one time it was thought that production for the French Army would be undertaken in the USA.

Above: A captured S-35 medium tank is used to patrol an airfield in occupied France. This photograph shows the use of the standard German wireless aerial base to turret rear.

hull-mounted 75mm gun to the right of the driver, and a different turret.

The S-35 was also used by the Germans for a variety of roles including crew training and internal security; some were even used on the Russian front. The Germans called the type the *PzKpfw* 35C 739 (*f*). Some were also fitted as command vehicles, and a few were handed over to the Italians.

ARL-44 Heavy Tank

Country of origin: France.
Crew: 5.
Armament: One 90mm gun; one 7.5mm machine-gun co-axial with main armament; one 7.5mm anti-aircraft machine-gun.
Armour: Not known.
Dimensions: Length 34ft 6in (10.52m); width 11ft 2in (3.4m); height 10ft 6in (3.2m).
Weight: About 105,820lb (48,000kg).
Engine: Maybach petrol engine developing 700hp.
Performance: Road speed 23mph (37.3km/h); range 93 miles (150km); vertical obstacle 3ft (0.93m); trench 9ft (2.75m); gradient 50 per cent.
History: In service with the French Army from 1947 to 1953.

One of the drawbacks of the *Char* B1 was that the 75mm gun mounted in the front of the hull had very limited traverse. So in 1938 the *ARL* (*Atelier de Construction de Rueil*) started a project to mount a 75mm gun in a new turret on a *Char* B1 chassis. By the fall of France in 1940 this project, known as the ARL-40, was still on the drawing board. During the occupation of France design work continued in secret at Rueil, and once Paris was liberated in 1944 the new design was placed in immediate production. The first production tank was completed in 1946. This was a considerable achievement for the French at that time. The tank became known as the ARL-44 or *Char de Transition*, and at one time it was intended to build 300 of them. In the end, however, only 60 were built. These were issued to the 503rd Regiment and made only one public appearance, on 14 July 1951. Production was undertaken by Renault and the FAMH (*Forges et Aciéries de la Marine et d'Homecourt*), with the turrets being supplied by Schneider. Whilst the tracks and suspension were similar to those of the earlier *Char* B1, the hull was new, as was the turret and engine. The driver and co-driver were seated at the front of the hull with the other three crew members in the turret. The engine was at the rear of the hull. The ARL-44 was to have been followed by the AMX-50, but although various prototypes of this later tank were built and tested, the type was not placed in production as large quantities of M47 tanks were available from the United States.

Above: ARL-44s of the French 503rd Regiment made their only public appearance in Paris on 14 July 1951. Only 60 ARL-44s were completed, although it was originally intended to build 300. It was to have been replaced by the AMX-50, but this plan was abandoned when large numbers of US M47 tanks became available under the Military Aid Program. These were in service until replaced by the AMX-30 in the 1960s. Main armament of the ARL-44 was a 90mm gun with a 7.5mm co-axial machine-gun, with a similar machine-gun for anti-aircraft duty.

Below: The ARL-44 heavy tank was the first French-designed AFV to enter service with the French Army after World War II. Its design dated back to the ARL-40 of 1940; the ARL-44 was designed by the *Atelier de Construction de Rueil* (ARL) during the German occupation. The first production model of the ARL-44 was completed in 1946 – a remarkable achievement when the condition of the French engineering industry after five years of German occupation is taken into account.

AMX-13 Light Tank

Country of origin: France.
Crew: 3.
Armament: One 90mm gun; one 7.5mm or 7.62mm machine-gun co-axial with main armament; two smoke discharges on each side of turret.
Armour: 0.4in-1.6in (10mm-40mm).
Dimensions: Length (gun forward) 20ft 10in (6.36m); length (hull) 15ft (4.88m); width 8ft 2in (2.50m); height 7ft 7in (2.30m).
Weight: Combat 33,069lb (15,000kg).
Ground pressure: 10.81lb/in² (0.76kg/cm²).
Engine: SOFAM Model 8 GXb eight-cylinder water-cooled petrol engine developing 250hp at 3,200rpm.
Performance: Road speed 37mph (60km/h); range 218 miles (350km); vertical obstacle 2ft 2in (0.65m); trench 5ft 3in (1.6m); gradient 60 per cent.
History: Entered service with French Army in 1953. Currently in service with following armies; Argentina (58), Dominican Republic (2), Ecuador

Below: This AMX-13 Light Tank sports a 105mm gun which can fire a HEAT projectile that can penetrate 14in (360mm) of armour at an incidence of 0° and a range of 3,280ft (1,000m).

Above: This Armoured Recovery Vehicle derivative of the AMX-13 Light Tank is used to recover disabled tanks via three winches.

(108), Indonesia (100+), Ivory Coast (5), Lebanon (35), Peru (110), Singapore (350), and Venezuela (36). Production complete.

The AMX-13 was designed by the *Atelier de Construction d'Issy-les-Moulineaux (AMX)* near Paris and the first prototype was completed in 1948. The type entered production at the *Atelier de Construction Roanne* in 1952 and production continued at that plant until the early 1960s when it was transferred to the civilian Creusot-Loire plant at Chalons-sur-Saône. The AMX-13 remained in production until the late 1980s by which time no fewer than 7,700 light tanks, self-propelled guns and armoured personnel carriers (APCs) in this family of armoured fighting vehicles (AFVs) had been constructed. The AMX-13 was designed for use as a tank destroyer and reconnaissance vehicle, and was the standard light tank of the French Army for many years.

The hull is of all-welded steel construction, with a maximum thickness of 1.58in (40mm). The driver sits at the front of the hull on the left, with the engine to his right. The turret is at the rear of the hull, with the commander on the left and the gunner to his right. To keep the hull as low as possible the tank was designed for crew members no taller than 5ft 8in (1.73m). The turret is of an unusual "oscillating" design and consists of two parts, the lower one being mounted on the turret ring and has two trunnions. The gun is mounted rigidly in the upper part, which elevates as a complete unit. This design enabled the French to fit an automatic loader and thus reduce the crew from the standard four to three.

The gun is fed from two revolving, 6-round magazines and once 12 rounds have been expended a crew member must physically leave the tank to reload. The empty cartridge cases are ejected through a hatch in the rear of the turret. The first AMX-13s were armed with a 75mm gun firing HE or HEAT rounds. Later models are armed with either a 105mm or a 90mm gun. Many AMX-13s have been fitted with anti-tank missiles, usually the French SS-11. There is a co-axial machine-gun of either 7.5mm or 7.62mm calibre and there is a mounting on the turret

Overleaf: An AMX-13 VCG Engineer Combat Vehicle puts its large, hydraulically-powered dozer blade to good use on rough terrain.

roof for an optional 7.5mm or 7.62mm anti-aircraft machine-gun.

The AMX-13 chassis has been used as the basis for a large number of variants. These include the AMX VCI APC and two self-propelled howitzers: the Mk 61 105mm and Mk F3 155mm. There is also a bridgelayer, the *Char Poseur du Pont*, carrying a Class 25 scissors bridge, and an armoured recovery vehicle, the *Char de Depannage*.

The AMX-13 is no longer in use with its two former, largest users, the

Below and right: AMX-13 Model 51 armed with 75mm gun in FL-10 oscillating turret; a total of 37 rounds are carried for main armament.

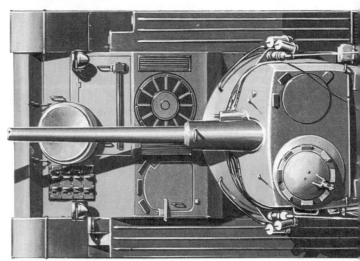

French and Dutch armies. The Singapore Army is now the largest single operator and Singapore Automotive Engineering converted these to the new AMX-13 SM1 standard which includes a completely new automative package, with a diesel engine and a fully automatic transmission. An alternative retrofit kit is available from Creusot-Loire, which includes a GIAT 105mm main gun mounted in a Fives Cail Babcock FL-15 turret.

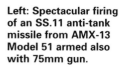

Left: Spectacular firing of an SS.11 anti-tank missile from AMX-13 Model 51 armed also with 75mm gun.

AMX-30B2 Main Battle Tank

AMX-30, AMX-30B2, AMX-305, AMX-30 ER1, AMX-30 ER2.
Country of origin: France.
Crew: 4.
Armament: One 105mm gun; one 20mm cannon or one 12.7mm machine-gun co-axial with the main armament (see text); on 7.62mm machine-gun on commander's cupola; two smoke discharges.
Armour: 3.1in (79mm) maximum.
Dimensions: Length (including main armament) 31ft 1in (9.48m); length (hull) 21ft 8in (6.59m); width 10ft 2in (3.1m); height (including searchlight) 9ft 4in (2.85m).
Weight: Combat 79,366lb (36,000kg).
Ground pressure: 12.08lb/in² (0.85kg/cm²).
Engine: Hispano-Suiza HS-110 12-cylinder water-cooled multi-fuel engine developing 720hp at 2,600rpm.
Performance: Speed 40mph (65km/h); range 373 miles (600km); vertical obstacle 3ft 1in (0.93m); trench 9ft 6in (2.9in); gradient 60 per cent.
History: Entered service with the French Army in 1967. Now in service with Chile (19 AMX-30); Croatia (42 AMX-30); Cyprus (102 AMX-30B2); France (387 AMX-30; 659 AMX-30B2); Greece (154 AMX-30 [in reserve]); Qatar 24 AMX-30S); Saudi Arabia (290 AMX-30S); Spain (210); UAE (64 AMX-30); Venezuela (81 AMX-30).

After the end of World War II France quickly developed three vehicles, the AMX-13 light tank, the Panhard EBR 8x8 heavy armoured car and the AMX-50 heavy tank. The last was a very interesting vehicle with a hull and suspension very similar to the German *PzKpfw* V Panther tank used in some numbers by the French Army

in the immediate post-war period. The AMX-50 had on oscillating turret, a feature that was adopted for the AMX-13 tank. The first AMX-50s had a 90mm gun, this being followed by a 100mm and finally a 120mm weapon. At one time it was intended to place the AMX-50 in production, but as large numbers of American M47s were available under the US Military Aid Program (MAP) the whole programme was cancelled.

In 1956 France, Germany and Italy drew up their requirements for a new MBT for the 1960s. The basic idea was good: the French and Germans were each to design a tank to the same general specifications; these would then be evaluated together; and the best tank would then enter production in both countries, for use in all three. But like many international tank programmes which were to follow, this came to nothing: France placed her AMX-30 in production and Germany placed her Leopard 1 in production.

The AMX-30 is built at the *Atelier de Construction* at Roanne, which is a government establishment and the only major tank plant in France. The first production AMX-30s were completed in 1966 and entered service with the French Army the following year, where it replaced the American M47. The hull of the AMX-30 is of cast and welded construction, whilst the turret is cast in one piece. The driver is seated at the front of the hull on the left, with the other three crew members in the turret. The commander and gunner are on the right of the

Below: The AMX-30 is the standard MBT of the French Army and is manufactured at the *Atelier de Construction Roanne* where the AMX-10P MICV and AMX-10RC recce vehicles were also built.

The AMX-30S was developed specifically for desert operations and has been ordered by Saudi Arabia (290) and Qatar (24). Modifications include the additions of a laser rangefinder, sand shields and a modified engine, as well as a modified transmission which reduced the tank's speed to 37.3mph (60km/h).

turret with the loader on the left. The engine and transmission are at the rear of the hull, and can be removed as a complete unit in under an hour. Suspension is of the torsion-bar type and consists of five road wheels, with the drive sprocket at the rear and the idler at the front, and there are five track-return rollers. These support the inner part of the track. The main armament of the AMX-30 is the CN-105-F1 (L56) 105mm gun of French design and manufacture, with an elevation of +20° and a depression of –8°, and a traverse of 360°, both elevation and traverse being powered. A 12.7mm machine-gun or a 20mm cannon is mounted to the left of the main armament. This installation is unusual in that it can be elevated independently of the main armament to a maximum of 40°, enabling it to be used against slow-flying aircraft and helicopters. There is a 7.62mm machine-gun mounted on the commander's cupola and this can be aimed and fired from within the turret. Two smoke dischargers are mounted each side of the turret. 47 rounds of 105mm, 500 rounds of 20mm and 2,050 rounds of 7.62mm ammunition are carried. There are five types of ammunition available for the 105mm gun: APFSDS, HEAT, HE, Smoke, Illuminating and Practice. The HEAT round weighs 48.5lb (22kg) complete, has a muzzle velocity of 3,281ft/s (1,000m/s) and will penetrate 14.17in (360mm) of armour at an angle of 0°. Other HEAT projectiles spin rapidly in flight as they are fired from a rifled tank gun, but the French HEAT round has its shaped charge mounted in ball bearings, so as the outer body of the projectile spins rapidly, the charge itself rotates much more slowly. In 1980 an APFSDS projectile entered production, this being able to penetrate 1.96in (50mm) of armour at an incidence of 60° and a range of 5,470 yards (5,000m).

The AMX-30 can ford streams to a maximum depth of 6ft 7in (2m) without preparation. A schnorkel can be fitted over the loader's hatch, and this enables the AMX-30 to ford to a depth of 13ft 2in (4m). Infra-red driving equipment is fitted, as is an infra-red searchlight on the commander's cupola and another such searchlight to the left of the main armament. An NBC system is fitted as standard equipment.

A special model, designated AMX-30S, was developed for use in desert

Above: To the left of the AMX-30's main armament is a Sopelem PH-8-B searchlight with a range of 2,623ft (800m) in infra-red mode.

conditions. The modifications included reducing engine power output to 620hp at 2,400rpm and changing the gearbox ratios, both of which were intended to limit the maximum speed to 37.5mph (60km/h) to improve desert performance. Sandshields were also fitted over the air intakes. The opportunity was also taken to upgrade the fire control system, with the installation of a laser rangefinder, infra-red nightsights and new optical sights. The AMX-30S was purchased by the armies of Saudi Arabia (299) and Qatar (24).

Above: An example of the versatility of the AMX-30 MBT is this much-modified example used as a transporter/launcher for the Pluton tactical nuclear missile system.

In 1979 is was decided to upgrade the French Army's version with a much-improved and fully integrated fire-control system, a new gearbox and other more minor improvements. The French Army received 166 new-build AMX-30B2 in the early 1980s and a further 493 AMX-30s were brought up to the -B2 standard, although plans to upgrade a further 90 were cancelled due to the ending of the Cold War. An ERA package was developed for the AMX-30B2; the tanks of two tank battalions in the rapid reaction force have been fitted with the ERA, while a further two battalions have had their tanks "fitted-for-but-not-with" ERA. Further development of the French MBT fleet is now concentrated solely on the Leclerc (*qv*).

The Spanish Army received 299 AMX-30s, of which the first 19 were supplied direct by GIAT and the remaining 280 were built under licence by Santa Barbara between 1974 and 1984. The fleet has received two upgrades. The first concentrated on the power train and driver, and was carried out in army workshops. The work involved replacing the transmission, modifying the cooling system and the engine compartment, and upgrading the equipment in the driver's compartment. This involved the entire fleet and the modified tanks were designated AMX-30 ER1. Next came the AMX-30 ER2 upgrade which involved replacing the power-pack with a new MTU MB-833 Ka-501 diesel and a new transmission, and installing a new fire-control system and a 12.7mm machine-gun on the turret roof. Other enhancements include a muzzle reference system, fire suppression system and improved suspension. Plans to install a Spanish ERA package appear to have been shelved as the numbers of Leopard 2 in Spanish service increases.

The AMX-30 sold reasonably well abroad but never as well as had been anticipated. Later French tanks aimed specifically at the export market were the AMX32 (see next entry) and the AMX-40 with a 120mm gun, but neither went into production.

89

AMX-32 Main Battle Tank

Country of origin: France.
Crew: 4.
Armament: One 105mm gun; one 20mm cannon co-axial with main armament; one 7.62mm anti-aircraft machine-gun; six smoke dischargers.
Armour: Classified.
Dimensions: Length (with armament) 31ft 1in (9.48m); length (hull) 21ft 7in (6.59m); width 10ft 7in (3.24m); height 9ft 8in (2.96m).
Weight: (combat) 83,790lb (38,000kg).
Ground pressure: 0.85kg/cm².
Engine: Hispano-Suiza HS 110 12-cyclinder multi-fuel developing 720hp at 2000rpm.
Performance: Road speed 40mph (65k/mh); road range 329 miles (530km); vertical obstacle 3ft (0.93m); trench 9ft 6in (2.9m); gradient 60 per cent.
History: Prototype completed in 1979. No production orders..

Most second generation MBTs such as the American M1 (XM1), West German Leopard 2 and British Shir 2 were characterised by a size and weight which made them unsuitable for employment in many parts of the world, even if their manufacturers were allowed to sell them on the world market. A classic example was the German Leopard 1, which was only sold to NATO countries, apart from Australia, and prospective buyers in the Middle East and elsewhere were forced to look elsewhere and have usually ended up buying French or Soviet equipment as a result. France exported large numbers of AMX-30 MBTs to countries that include Greece, Iraq, Libya, Peru, Saudi Arabia, Spain and Venezuela.

Rather than develop a new tank for the early 1980s the French Army elected to carry out a mid-life modernisation programme to its existing AMX-30 tank fleet (in a similar manner to the British Army's policy in updating their Chieftains so that they would remain effective through the 1980s until the arrival of Challenger). The modernised AMX-30 was known as the AMX-30 B2 and is basically an AMX-30 with the automatic COTAC integrated fire-control system, LLLTV system, new transmission and a new collective pressurisation system.

Above: The AMX-32 MBT was derived from the AMX-30 and was developed by France specifically for the export market, but no firm orders were received.

For the export market the AMX-32 was developed; this was announced in 1977 and the first prototype was unveiled in June 1979. The AMX-32 was a further development of the AMX-30 B2 but has increased armour protection which improved the tank's chances of survival when encountering ATGWs and other infantry anti-tank weapons fitted with HEAT warheads.

The hull of the AMX-32 like that of the AMX-30 was of rolled steel plates welded together with the driver's compartment at the front,

Below: The AMX-32 had the same armament and fire control system as the AMX-30 B2, but had a new all-welded turret which offered additional armour protection and more room for the crew.

Above: The AMX-32 had a 105mm gun which traversed with the turret through 360° and had an elevation of –8° to +20°.

fighting compartment in the centre and the engine at the rear. The nose and glacis plate were of cast and welded construction rather than cast construction as in the case of the AMX-30. The driver was seated on the left side and had a single piece hatch cover that opened to the left, in front of which were three periscopes for forward observation when driving with the hatch closed. The driver steered the tank with a steering wheel rather than two sticks as in the case of most other tanks.

The turret of the AMX-32 was all of welded construction and offered both increased protection and more room for the crew than the AMX-30 turret. The commander is seated on the right of the turret with the gunner forward and below his position. The commander's cupola had periscopes for all round observation and mounted in its roof was a stabilised sight which enables him to lay and fire the main armament or designate the target for the gunner and then resume his primary role of commanding the tank. This sight had a magnification of x2 or x8 in the day mode and x1 in the night mode. The gunner had an optical sight with a magnification of x10 and a laser range-finder. Mounted to the right of the mantlet was a LLLTV camera which moved in elevation with the main armament and provided a picture to both the commander's and gunner's TV monitor screens. The integrated COTAC fire control system gave the tank a high hit probability under both day and night conditions. The loader was seated on the left of the turret and had a single piece hatch cover that opened to the rear and periscopes for observation. In the left side of the turret was an ammunition resupply hatch.

The engine was identical to that installed in the AMX-30 and AMX-30 B2 tanks and the transmission was the same as that installed in the latter. The transmission was composed of a hydraulic torque converter, electrohydraulically controlled gearbox with five forward gears and a reverser, and a hydrostatic steering system. This enabled the driver to change gear under torque, carry out pivot turns, change gears while turning and it also reduced driver fatigue and training.

The suspension was similar to that of the AMX-30 but the torsion bars, shock absorbers, and bump stops were strengthened to take account of the increased weight and mobility of the tank. The upper parts of the tracks were covered by armoured skirts which hinged upwards for maintenance gave protection against HEAT attack.

Main armament was identical to that of the AMX-30 but provision was made to replace this with a new French 120mm smooth bore gun firing

the same ammunition as the German Leopard 2. In addition to the rounds described in the entry for the AMX-30 the AMX-32 could also fire the recent French APFSDS projectile, which when complete weighs 12.78lb (5.8kg) with the penetrator weighing 7.93lb (3.6kg), and has a muzzle velocity of 143 yards a second (130 metres a second) and will penetrate 6in (150mm) of a armour at an incidence of 60°. Mounted co-axially to the left of the main armament was a 20mm M693 F2 cannon which could be linked to the main armament or elevated independently to +40° to enable it to be used against low flying helicopters. A 7.62mm machine-gun was mounted on the commander's cupola and this could be aimed and fired from within the tank. Three electrically operated smoke dischargers were mounted each side of the turret. A total of 47 rounds of 105mm, 500 rounds of 20mm and 2050 rounds of 7.62mm machine-gun ammunition were carried.

Despite intense marketing and some overseas interest no orders were ever placed.

Below: View from rear clearly shows ammunition resupply case to left of turret. Loader had access to it from inside turret.

Leclerc Main Battle Tank

Country of origin: France.
Crew: 3.
Armament: One GIAT 120-26 120mm smoothbore gun; one 12.7mm co-axial machine-gun; one 7.62mm anti-aircraft machine-gun; two nine-barreled smoke grenade discharges.
Armour: Spaced, multi-layer.
Dimensions: Length (including main armament) 32ft 5in (9.87m); length (hull) 22ft 7in (6.88m); width 12ft 2in (3.71m); height 8ft 4in (2.53m).
Weight: Combat 1120,172lb (54,500kg).
Ground pressure: 12.80lb/in^2 (0.90kg/cm^2).
Engine: Uni-Diesel V8X-1500 Hyperbar 8-cylinder liquid-cooled diesel engine developing 1,500hp at 2,500rpm; SACM Turbomeca gas turbine auxiliary power unit.
Performance: Road speed 44mph (71km/h); range 341 miles (550km); vertical obstacle 4ft 1in (1.25m); trench 9ft 10in (3m), gradient 60 per cent.
History: Entered production in 1990. At least 420 on order for French Army; 388 on order for UAE (Abn Dhabi).

In the late 1970s the French and West German armies undertook a second collaborative project to develop a replacement for the AMX-30 and Leopard 1 MBTs, which were themselves the separate outcomes of a previous attempt at a joint design. But, like all previous collaborative tank ventures, this one also collapsed (in December 1982) and the French Army set about the design of a new tank for the 1990s designated *Engin Principal de Combat* (*EPC*). Project definition was completed in 1986 and the first prototype was up and running by the end of 1989. By this time the tank had been named the Leclerc after one of the most successful of French World War II commanders.

The Leclerc is generally similar in size and armament to other contemporary Western MBTs, except that, unlike the Leopard 2 (Germany), Challenger 2 (UK) and M1 (USA), it has a crew of only three men. This is achieved through the replacement of the fourth crewman by an automatic loader, a feature the Leclerc shares with the Japanese Type 90 and the Soviet T-64/-72/-80.

The hull and turret shells are constructed of welded steel to which is added modular segments of composite armour. The current armour is claimed to have high resistance to kinetic energy and chemical rounds, but being modular can be

Below : French Leclerc tank travelling at speed. The outcome of a very lengthy development process, the Leclerc is now in service with the French Army and is on order for the army of the UAE.

Above: A prototype Leclerc MBT being put through its paces. Of particular note is the early turret – quite different in shape to that sported by the Leclerc on the previous page.

replaced by new or improved armour later in the tank's life, if required. The original turret fitted to the prototypes was very angular in shape, but the production tanks sport a very long and low turret of excellent ballistic shape, which offers armour protection for the laser, machine-gun and even the grenade launchers.

The driver sits well to the rear of the glacis plate and just to the left of the centreline of the tank, with a drum of 18 rounds of 120mm ammunition to his right. The commander is in the turret to the left of the main gun, with the gunner on the right, the reverse of the arrangement in most other MBTs where the commander is on the right. The crew is supplied with a sophisticated, computerised battle management system, which controls and monitors all activities within the vehicle, and which will even give status reports to a higher headquarters either at given intervals or on request.

The gun is a 120mm smoothbore, designed and built by GIAT. Its chamber is the same size as that on the German and US 120mm guns, thus ensuring commonality of ammunition, but the tube is somewhat longer (52 as opposed to 44 calibres), which imparts a higher muzzle velocity to the projectiles, particularly APFSDS. The gun has a thermal sleeve, but rather than a fume extractor fitted to the barrel it uses a compressed-air system to expel fumes automatically after firing. A muzzle reference system is fitted.

The automatic loader is made by Creusot-Loire and contains 22 rounds of ready-use ammunition. The system can distinguish between five different natures of ammunition and will load the appropriate round as selected by the commander or gunner. To reload, the gun automatically returns to the –1.8° position and then resumes the elevation directed by the commander or gunner. The system is claimed to be capable of a firing rate of 15 rounds per minute, although the normal maximum would be about 12. The automatic loader is mounted in the long turret bustle and is separated from the fighting compartment by a bulkhead, and there are blow-out panels in the roof to divert any explosion away from the crew.

There are currently two principal rounds. The APFSDS round has a tungsten penetrator with a muzzle velocity (mv) of 5,742ft/sec (1,750m/sec), while the HEAT round has an mv of 3,610ft/sec (1,100m/s).

The French mounted a 20mm co-axial cannon in the AMX-30/-32 and AMX-40 series of MBTs, which could elevate independently of the main armament. In the Leclerc they have dropped the idea of independent elevation, but the co-axial weapon is a 12.7mm machine-gun, which is again unusual, since virtually all other MBTs use 7.62mm calibre machine-guns for this application. A 7.62mm machine-gun is located on the turret roof, which has an armoured casing and is fully-controlled from within the tank.

The power unit is a 1,500hp SACM diesel engine, which gives the very high power:weight ratio of 28.3hp/tonne. There is also a Turbomeca TM-7038 gas turbine, which is used to provide power when the tank is stationary, so that the main engine can be closed down.

LK II Cavalry Tank

***Leichte Kampfwagen** II.*
Country of origin: Germany.
Crew: 3.
Armament: One 5.7cm gun or two 7.92mm Maxim machine-guns.
Armour: 0.24in (6mm) minimum; 0.43in (11mm) maximum.
Dimensions: Length 16ft 7in (5.06m); width 6ft 4in (1.95m); height 8ft 2in (2.5m).
Weight: 18,739lb (8,500kg).
Engine: Daimler four-cylinder water-cooled inline petrol engine developing 55bhp.
Performance: Road speed 10mph (16km/h); range 40 miles (65km); trench 6ft 6in (2.04m); gradient 45 degrees, for short climbs only.
History: Prototypes only built.

The Germans awoke late to the possibility of the tank and by 1918, realising that they were behind, were prepared to copy anything that the British used. When the Whippet (*qv*) appeared it was duly captured and copied, but some of the faults of that unhappy vehicle were corrected. The same general layout was copied, but this may have been for another reason. In their haste to get the design going, the Germans took an armoured car and replaced the wheels with tracks. This immediately gave them the front engine layout, the central driver, rear turret and rear final drive. A rotating turret was too difficult to make in quantity and an alternative fixed box with a front-mounted gun was fitted. It was intended to use the rotating turret for the machine-gun version.

By more careful designing and perhaps good fortune, the *LK* II came out considerably lighter than the Whippet, yet had roughly the same protection. It was thus able to make better use of its power and was both faster and more agile. From the driver's point of view, it was far easier to control than the British tank and the commander could give more time to controlling the tank, since he did not have the responsibility for firing a gun as did the Whippet's commander.

Unfortunately this vehicle never came into service and it seems that no more than two were actually completed. When the war ended the design was sold to Sweden, which took it into service as the m/21. Krupp, who had designed the *LK* II, lent their experience to the Swedes and the m/21 incorporated what would have been built into the *LK* III. One change was to fit a small rotating turret on top of the fixed one and mount a 3.7cm gun in it. Another was to increase the crew to four and fit a small radio to a proportion of the fleet. Later, in 1926, another *LK* II appeared, though this one was far more advanced than the previous model and was really an amalgam of the *LK* and the Vickers Medium. It had a sprung track, using coupled bogies, a lower silhouette, a fully rotating turret carrying the 3.7cm gun, and reasonably sloped armour. The weight increased by 0.98 ton (1,000kg) but the speed and agility improved markedly.

Above and below: The German *LK* II cavalry tank, mounting a 57mm gun. Designed by Krupp, it incorporated features of captured British Whippet tanks on a modified armoured car chassis. Only prototypes had been built by the end of WWI.

A7V Battle Tank

A7V *Sturmpanzerwagen.*
Country of origin: Germany.
Crew: 18.
Armament: One 5.7cm gun; six or seven 7.92mm Maxim machine-guns.
Armour: 0.59in (15mm) minimum; 1.18in (30mm) maximum.
Dimensions: Length 24ft 1in (7.34m); width 10ft 0½in (3.07m); height 10ft 10in (3.3m).
Weight: 65.918lb (29,900kg).
Engines: Two Daimler four-cylinder water-cooled inline engines each developing 100bhp at 1.600rpm.
Performance: Road speed 5mph (8km/h); range 25 miles (40km); trench 7ft (2.13m).
History: Used in limited numbers by the German Army during 1918.

Badly shaken by the British success with their first tanks, the German general staff cast around for a quick answer, and late in 1916 decided to build their own, and better, type of tank. Design contracts were hurriedly let in November of that year and finalised on 22 December. Having no background of tracked vehicles to call upon, the resident representative of Holt tractors, a Mr. Steiner, was brought in to produce the chassis. Throughout the summer of 1917 the prototypes underwent their trials, revealing many weaknesses, particularly in the engine cooling and tracks. On 1 December 1917 the general staff could wait no longer, and 100 tanks were ordered to be ready in time for the great spring offensives. Since nobody could think of a suitable name, it was decided to call the machine the A7V, from the initial letters of the committee that first called for it – the *Allgemeine Kriegsdepartment 7 Abteilung Vehkerwesen.*

The design was uninspired and showed every sign of weakness. All that had been done was in effect to take a large Holt tractor chassis and suspension, put on it a large rectangular steel box and then to fit in as many weapons as possible; a 5.7cm gun with 250 or 500 rounds and six or seven machine-guns with 36,000 rounds. The result was thoroughly unwieldy and

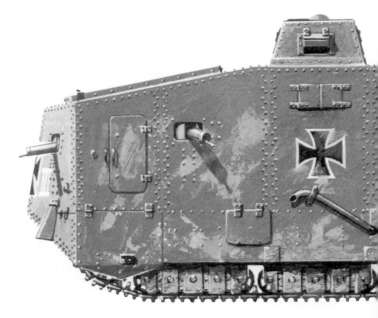

Above: A7V moving forward with crew riding outside of the vehicle for comfort, when in action all of the 18-man crew were inside of the hull and conditions in side of the tank were unbearable: they were often overcome by heat and fumes.

sharply lacking in any ability to move on any surface other than a flat and hard road. The thinking behind the design had been to produce a mobile fortress for the support of the infantry, and the concentration had been on the fortress aspect to the virtual exclusion of anything which gave suitable mobility on the battlefields of the Western Front. The very limited ground clearance of 15.75in (40cm) ensured that rough and muddy ground caused the tank to belly down and stick. The absence of any "lift" at the front idler meant that there was barely any ability to climb a step, or to pull out from a hole or trench, since all that happened was that the nose dug in. The one advantage to the track arrangement was that it was protected by armour, and perhaps the Germans had seen enough Mark IVs with shattered tracks to feel that there system was worthwhile.

Left: Side view of the A7V *"Elfriede"*: identified at the time of her loss as belonging to *Abteilung* III, Imperial German Army Tank Force. An *Abteilung* comprised a total of five tanks, with six officers and 170 other ranks. By 1918, Germany had eight tank units, most of which used captured tanks.

The interior of the hull was in the form of one large compartment with the engines sited below the cupola housing driver and commander. These were linked to a common transmission shaft which drove through a gearbox to the final drive at the rear of the body. From there the drive went by shafts to the sprockets, passing through steering brakes on the way. It was an easier arrangement than on the British tanks. The tracks ran on 24 sprung bogies and allowed a top speed of 8mph (13km/h) under ideal conditions. However, the tank's weight was far too much for the engine and transmission, despite gearing down, and engines reliability suffered. The driver's task was easier than on the Mark IV, and two engineers were carried for running repairs, and played no part in the actual driving. The commander sat in the square cupola above the fighting compartment, but he could only give his instructions by shouting, and in the infernal din of the engines and tracks this must have been difficult. The driver and engineers came from the engineer corps, but the two men who manned the 5.7cm gun were artillerymen. Their gun was a low velocity version, from captured Belgian stock. The machine-gunners worked in pairs to each gun, and were infantrymen. The crew was thus drawn from three different military disciplines, and this led to a lack of cohesion in their performance – a fact which several German commentators touch upon. Vision for the crew was poor, as with all World War I tanks, and comfort was negligible. The thickness of armour was good, but this was nullified by the fact that most of it had to be supplied in an unhardened state. However, on the one occasion when a British Mark IV male met an A7V in action, there is good reason to think that the three hits scored with British 6pounder guns did not penetrate the German armour.

Actual battle use of the A7V was very limited. The 100 ordered in 1917 were never delivered, and perhaps no more than 35 were completed. These were grouped into battalions of five vehicles, and were invariably used unimaginatively, to their detriment. Their first operation seems to have been on 29 March 1918 and the last was on 8 October. Despite the poor showing of their first tank, the German general staff were not discouraged, and quietly set about learning where they had gone wrong, with results clear to everyone when the *Blitzkrieg* was launched some 20 years later.

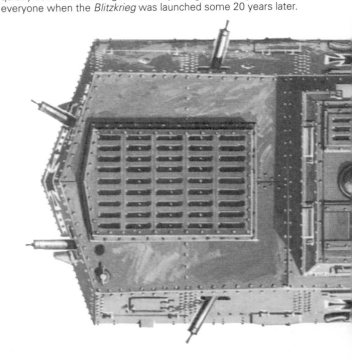

Right and below: Top, front and rear views of the A7V tank *"Elfriede"*, the first enemy tank to be engaged and captured by British tank units in WWI. She was hit by four 6-pounder shells fired by a male Mk IV tank of A Coy, 1st Bttn, Tank Corps, and immobilized. After her capture she was taken for detailed examination by Allied intelligence. Known names of other A7Vs include *"Woten"*, *"Hagen"* and *"Schnuck"*.

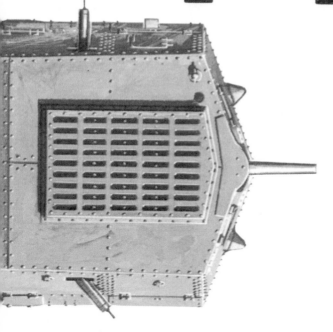

PzKpfw V Experimental Medium Tank

Country of origin: Germany.
Crew: 7.
Armament: One 7.5cm *KwK* L/24 gun; 3.7cm gun co-axial with main armament; four 7.92mm MG 13 machine-guns in pairs in two sub-turrets.
Armour: 0.57in (14.5mm).
Dimensions: Length about 21ft 4in (6m); width 9ft 6in (2.9m); height 8ft 6in (2.65m).
Weight: 47,950lb (21,750kg).
Engine: Maybach V-12 water-cooled inline petrol engine developing 360bhp.
Performance: Road speed 19mph (30km/h); trench 7ft 2in (2.2m); gradient 30 degrees.
History: In service with the German Army from 1936 to 1940.

The Versailles Treaty forbade Germany to possess any tanks, and various devices were resorted to in order that the restrictions might be overcome. One was to produce tanks and call them by innocuous names. Heavy tanks were known as Heavy Tractors, and light tanks as Light Tractors. In January 1934 there was a conference to decide on the specifications for medium tanks (or tractors) which would equip the medium tank companies in the new *Werhmacht*. These tanks would carry a large-calibre gun to give effective HE fire to support the smaller high-velocity guns of the more numerous battle tanks. The 7.5cm gun was chosen for the main armament. This was a Krupp gun, whose performance was well known and approved. In addition there was a requirement for the new tank to carry machine-guns.

Three firms undertook the design study: Krupp, Rheinmetall-Borsig and MAN. Rheinmetall's solution used the existing suspension from their commercial tractor, and the tank was designed round this as it stood, merely one more set of bogies being added on each side. The resulting vehicle was an amalgam of existing French, British and Russian designs, though it showed some features of its own which were laudable.

In broad outline the *PzKpfw V* was one of the multi-turreted tanks of the early 1930s, of which there were many examples, but it had its special points. The turret was a better design than most of the uninspired box shapes of the day, there was a reasonable cupola for the commander, and the suspension bogies had a good range of travel. About six were built, and there is reason to believe that none may have actually carried armour plate. They were made in steel, as were most prototypes at that time. The hull shape was derived directly from the *Grosstraktor* (large tractor) of 1929, and may well have been almost unchanged. The suspension was greatly improved by using the commercial bogies, and at the top the track returned over four rollers. The driver and the front gunner sat in the bows; behind was the fighting compartment; and the engine was in the rear, driving a rear sprocket. The turret was mounted on a small pedestal and to its right front was a small machine-gun turret. There was another such turret behind and to the left of the main turret, a layout which both Vickers and the Japanese had tried.

In the event the *PzKpfw V* was no more than a test bed for the gun and mounting. It never saw

Above: Factory assembly of an *NbFz* tank, along with a number of other German AFVs including several experimental vehicles. The small machine-gun turret on the right-hand side of the *PzKpfw* V was the same as that fitted to the *PzKpfw* I light tank and mounted two 7.92mm machine-guns. The tank never went into full-scale production; only about six were built.

service as a production tank, but there is a well known propaganda photograph of two of them driving through Oslo in 1940, which shows that the German Army was prepared to make intelligent use of its surplus experimental vehicles.

Below: When Germany re-armed in the 1930s many experimental tanks were built. The multi-turreted *PzKpfw* V (*NbFz*) was one of the most famous.

PzKpfw I Light Tank

SdKfz 101.
Country of origin: Germany.
Crew: 2.
Armament: Two 7.92mm MG 34 machine-guns.
Armour: 0.28in (7mm) minimum; 0.51in (13mm) maximum.
Dimensions: Length 13ft 3in (4.03m); width 6ft 9in (2.05m); height 5ft 8in (1.72m).
Weight: 11,905lb (5,400kg).
Ground pressure: 5.71lb/in^2 (0.4kg/cm^2).
Engine: Krupp M305 four-cylinder horizontally-opposed air-cooled petrol engine developing 60hp at 2,500rpm.
Performance: Road speed 23mph (37km/h); range 125 miles (200km); vertical obstacle 1ft 2in (0.355m); trench 4ft 7in (1.4m); gradient 58 per cent.
History: Served with German Army from 1934 to 1941 as a tank, and to 1945 in other roles. Also used by Spain. (*Note: Data relate to PzKpfw 1 A.*)

In 1933, when Germany began openly to rearm, it was realised that the development of a full family of armoured vehicles would take several years. In the meantime it was decided to build light vehicles which the new armoured formations could use for training and experience. Contracts were therefore laid for a series of armoured vehicles between 3.9 and 6.9 tons (4,000 and 7,000kg) overall weight, and Krupp's design was the one chosen.

The *PzKpfw* 1 A was a small two-man tank which was inadequate in most respects even by the modest standards of the day. The hull was lightly armoured and had many openings, cervices and joints, all of which generally weakened it and made it vulnerable to attack. The engine was low powered and as a result performance was poor. The gearbox was a standard commercial crash type, with five forward speeds and one reverse. Fittings were minimal, and there was little evidence of designing for crew comfort. The suspension showed evidence of plagiarisation of some of the features of the Carden-Loyd light tanks of the 1920s, in that an external beam carried the

Below: The *PzKpfw* Model B differed from the Model A in having a more powerful engine. This necessitated a longer hull. To compensate for the extra length an additional road wheel was fitted, the idler was raised off the ground and an extra return roller added.

Above: A *PzKpfw* Model B light tank in France in summer 1940. The first model was powered by a Krupp 60hp petrol engine but the Model B had the 100hp Maybach engine. This was a great improvement but the tank was still under-armed.

outer ends of the bogie axles and the rear idler. The drive-sprocket was at the front, which meant that the transmission train ran along the floor of the hull to a differential beside the driver's feet. Both driver and commander shared the same compartment, the driver climbing in through a hull door on the side, the commander using a large hatch in the turret roof. Since his vision was very restricted when the vehicle was closed down, the commander generally spent his time standing up with the upper half of his body well exposed. The little turret was traversed by hand, and the commander fired the two machine-guns, for which there were 1,525 rounds of ammunition.

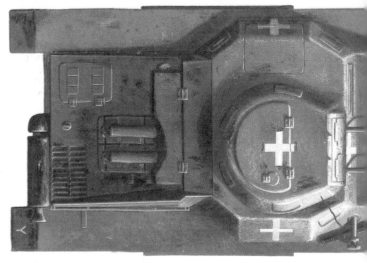

The inadequacies of the Krupp engine became quickly apparent, and it was superseded by a more powerful one of 100bhp. This was a six-cylinder water-cooled inline Maybach, and to fit it in the chassis an extra 1ft 5in (43cm) of length had to be added to the hull. This brought about changes in the suspension, and an extra wheel station was added. In turn this lengthened the track in contact with the ground, and so the rear idler was lifted up. This was designated the *PzKpfw* 1 B, which was altogether a better vehicle, although it suffered from the same failings in armour and armament as did the 1A.

Over 2,000 IBs were built, reflecting the greater use that could be made of the more powerful model, and although only meant as interim vehicles until the proper battle tanks could be introduced, they were in action as early as 1936 in the Spanish Civil War, and after that in Poland, the Low Countries in 1940, Africa, Greece, the Balkans and even in Russia during 1941, though by then they were well out-dated and inadequate for anything except very minor tasks. In their early days these little tanks had survived very largely by virtue of the fact that there was no effective anti-tank armament in service with any army, and tanks were virtually immune to infantry weapons. However, as soon as any light guns could be brought to bear the *PzKpfw* I was doomed, and many were destroyed by British 2pounder fire in the retreat to Dunkirk.

Above: The PzKpfw Model A light tank was used in action for the first time during the Spanish Civil War, and later in Poland, Low Countries in 1940, Africa, Greece, Balkans and even during the early part of the Russian campaign. It was soon phased out of front line service as it lacked both armour and firepower and many were knocked out by the small British 2pounder anti-tank gun during the retreat to Dunkirk.

Left and above left: Top and front views of the PzKpfw 1 light tank which entered service with the German Army in 1934. Its two-man crew consisted of the driver and commander/gunner. Armament was of two 7.92mm MG 34 machine guns in a turret, offset to the right of the hull. Variants of the tank included a command vehicle and an ammunition carrier. A few were fitted with a 4.7cm anti-tank gun or a 15cm gun, but these conversions were not a great success as the chassis was overloaded.

Several experiments were tried on the type, one such being the introduction of radio. This was only fitted to the 1B version, and judging from photographs there was a sizeable proportion of each unit which could communicate by this means. The other vehicles watched for hand signals from their sub-unit leader. A successful variant to the basic tank was the conversion to a small command vehicle, an idea which started in 1936. By 1938 200 had been completed. The turret was replaced by a square full-width superstructure with a low square cupola on top. A single machine-gun was fitted for self-defence, and could be removed and set up on its ground mount. The crew was increased to three, and two radio sets were fitted. These vehicles were allotted to armoured units of all kinds, and altogether 96 of them saw action in France. Many others went to Russia in the following year, though they must have been terribly vulnerable to any form of effective fire.

A very small number of redundant *PzKpfw Is* were converted to other roles. A few were made into repair tractors, and others became ammunition carriers. About 200 were fitted with a 4.7cm gun and became light SP anti-tank guns; a very few others were fitted with 15cm guns, but in both cases the chassis was overloaded and the idea was dropped after limited use.

PzKpfw II Light Tank

***PzKpfwII*, or *SdKfz* 121 *Ausf* A to F.**
Country of origin: Germany.
Crew: 3.
Armament: One 2cm *KwK* 30 or 38 gun; one 7.92mm MG 34 machine-gun co-axial with main armament.
Armour: 0.39in (10mm) minimum; 1.18in (30mm) maximum in the *Ausf* A, B and C; 0.57in (14.5mm) minimum; 1.38in (35mm) maximum in the *Ausf* F.
Weight: 29,944lb (9,500kg).
Ground pressure: 11.3lb/in^2 (0.8kg/cm^2).
Engine: Maybach HL 62 TR six-cylinder water-cooled inline petrol engine developing 130hp at 2,600rpm.
Performance: Road speed 25mph (40km/h); range 120 miles (192km); vertical obstacle 1ft 5in (0.43m); trench 5ft 8in (1.72m); fording depth 3ft (0.91m); gradient 50 per cent.
History: In service with the German Army from 1936 to 1943. Also used by Spain.

From a 1934 specification, a *PzKpfw* II design by MAN was finally selected. A number of prototypes was built, and some of them were sent to Spain for full-scale trials in action. The first production models appeared in 1935, but deliveries were slow for the next 18 months as changed were made in the design. The armour was increased in thickness, particularly in the front, and some changes were made in the suspension. The weight increased by nearly 1.95 tons (2,000kg), and experiments were made to improve the engine horsepower. An extra 10hp was found by boring out the cylinders of the Maybach engine, though the lower power motor appears to have continued to be fitted to some versions.

The three variants of the *PzKpfw* II, the *Ausf* A, B and C, were all very

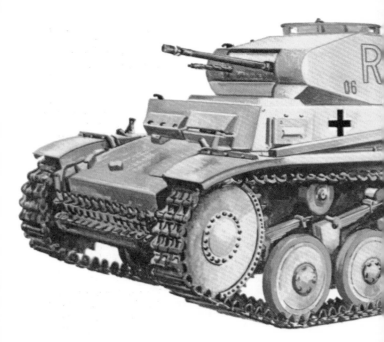

similar, with only minor dimensional differences. The *Ausf* A had the original low power engine and weighed 16,105lb (7,305kg). About 100 were built in 1935 and 1936. The *Ausf* B featured the higher power engine, new reduction gears and tracks, and again the weight increased. The *Ausf* C appeared in 1937 and carried thicker front armour, bringing the weight up to the final figure of 20,944lb (9,500kg). Issues to units began in earnest in 1937, and by 1939 there were sufficient for over 1,000 to take part in the Polish campaign. Manufacture of the general type continued up to late 1942 or early 1943, by which time the basic tank was well outdated.

The hull was built up from welded heat-treated steel, 1.18in (30mm) thick on the front and 0.39in (10mm) on the sides and rear. The turret was made in a similar way, again 1.18in (30mm) thick on the front and 0.63in (16mm) around the sides and back. The engine was in the rear compartment, driving forward through the fighting compartment to a gearbox and final drive in front. The gearbox was a ZF crash-type with six forward speeds and one reverse, the steering being by clutches and brakes. The driver sat off-centre to the left side. The fighting compartment had the turret above it, again offset slightly to the left. The armament was an improvement on that of the *PzKpfw* I, but still not very effective: the 2cm gun had a maximum range of 656 yards (600m), and only fired armour-piercing ammunition, but I had a reasonably rapid rate of fire. Some 180 2cm and 1,425 7.92mm rounds were carried. However, armour penetration of these 2cm rounds was not impressive. Once again, vision was poor from the turret, and fire-control difficult when fully closed-down. Most vehicles seem to have had radio. The suspension was distinctive. There were five road wheels hung on quarter-elliptic leaf springs, with the rear idler and front drive sprocket both clear of the ground. This suspension was quite effective, and within the limits of its engine power the *PzKpfw* II was

Left: *PzKpfw* II *Ausf* F light tank of a regimental H.Q. (indicated by the letter R on the turret side). The figures 06 identify the tank as part of a reconnaissance *Zug*. This actual tank was captured in North Africa and is now displayed at the Royal Armoured Corps Tank Museum at Bovington Camp, Dorset, England. The specification for the tank was issued in 1934 and prototypes were built by Henschel, Krupp and MAN. The latter was selected for production and first models were completed the following year. By May 1940 the German Army had 955 *PzKpfw* II tanks and this had risen to 1,067 vehicles by the following year.

quite manoeuvrable and agile. The tracks were narrow, but apparently quite strong.

Despite the limitations of the design, the *PzKpfw* II formed the backbone of the armoured divisions of the German Army, and as late as April 1942 860 were still on strength. An attempt to improve the performance was made in late 1940 with the F variant. Thicker armour

Below: A PzKpfw II Ausf B or C of the Afrika Korps advances across the desert with soft-skinned vehicles.

was fitted to the front and sides and a higher velocity gun installed, though its calibre was still only 2cm. However these changes did little to increase the battlefield value of the tank, and the extra 2,204lb (1,000kg) of weight that they entailed put an extra strain on the engine. The basic chassis was used for several different special-purpose vehicles, and also as a test-bed for a variety of ideas, including the use of torsion-bar suspension systems. Some were turned into flamethrower vehicles, capable of about 80 shots of 2 to 3 seconds duration.

Below left and right: Views of a PzKpfw II Ausf F of 6th Panzer Div. after the Polish campaign, with the new black-cross national markings.

PzKpfw III Battle Tank

PzKpfw III, or SdKfz 141, Ausf A to N.
Country of origin: Germany.
Crew: 5.
Armament: *Ausf* A, B, C and D, one 3.7cm *KwK* L/45 gun, two 7.92mm MG 34 machine-guns co-axial with main armament; one 7.92mm MG 34 machine-gun in hull. *Ausf* E, F, G and H, one 5cm *KwK* 39 L/42 fun; one 7.92mm MG 34 machine-gun co-axial with main armament; one 7.92mm MG 34 machine-gun in hull. *Ausf* J and L, one 5cm *KwK* 39 L/60 gun; one 7.92mm MG 34 machine-gun co-axial with main armament; one 7.92mm MG 34 machine-gun in hull. *Ausf* M and N, one 7.5cm *KwK* L/24 gun; one 7.92mm MG 34 machine-gun co-axial with main armament; one 7.92mm MG 34 machine-gun in hull.
Armour: *Ausf* A, B and C, 0.57in (14.5mm) minimum; 3.54in (90mm) maximum. *Ausf* D to G, 1.18in (30mm) minimum; 3.54in (90mm) maximum. *Ausf* H to N, 1.18in (30mm) minimum; 3.15in (80mm) maximum, but often seen with additional plate and spaced armour.
Dimensions: Length *Ausf* A and B 18ft 6in (5.7m); *Ausf* D to G 17ft 8in (5.4m); *Ausf* H 18ft 1in (5.52m); *Ausf* J to N 21ft 1 in (6.4m). Width *Ausf* A to C 9ft 2in (2.8m); *Ausf* D to G 9ft 6in (2.9m); *Ausf* H to N 9ft 8in (2.95m). Height *Ausf* A 7ft 7in (2.35m); *Ausf* B and C 8ft 4in (2.55m); *Ausf* D to G 8ft (2.4m); *Ausf* H to N 9ft 8in (2.95m).
Weight: *Ausf* A to C 33,069lb (15,000kg); *Ausf* D and E 42,769lb (19,400kg); *Ausf* F and G 44,753lb (20,300kg); *Ausf* H 47,619lb (21,600kg); *Ausf* J to N 49,163lb (22,300kg).
Ground pressure: *Ausf* A to C 15.3lb/in² (0.973kg/cm²); *Ausf* D 13.2lb/in² (0.93kg/cm²); *Ausf* E and H to N 13.5lb/in² (0.95kg/cm²); *Ausf* F and G 14.1lb/in² (0.99kg/cm²).
Engine: *Ausf* A to C Maybach HL 108 TR V-12 water-cooled inline petrol engine developing 230hp at 2,600rpm; *Ausf* D Maybach HL 120 TR developing 320hp at 3,000rpm; *Ausf* E to N Maybach HL 120 TRM developing 300hp at 3,000rpm.
Performance: Road speed *Ausf* A to C 20mph (32km/h); *Ausf* E to N 25mph (40km/h). Cross-country speed all models 11mph (18km/h). Range *Ausf* A to C 94 miles (150km); *Ausf* D 103 miles (165km); *Ausf* E to N 109 miles (175km). Vertical obstacles all models 2ft (0.6m). Trench *Ausf* A to G 7ft 6in (2.3m). Fording depth *Ausf* A to J 2ft 7in (0.8m); *Ausf* L to N 4ft 3in (1.3m). Gradient 30 degrees.
History: In service with the German Army from 1939 to 1945. Also used by Spain and Turkey.

Above: A *PzKpfw* III crew member surrenders to British infantry on 29 October 1942, during the North African campaign.

In 1935, having gained some experience with the small tanks of that time, the Germans began to draw up specifications for their main battle tanks. The intention, as stated by General Guderian, was to have two basic types, the first carrying a high velocity gun for anti-tank work, backed up by machine-guns, and the second, a support tank for the first, carrying a large-calibre gun

Right and below: Front, rear and side views of a *PzKpfw* III *Ausf* J of 3rd *Panzer* Division on the Russian Front in 1941. The tank is armed with a 50mm *KwK* L/42 low velocity gun for which 78 rounds of ammunition were carried. On top of the hull rear are two sets of replacement road wheels.

capable of firing a destructive HE shell. The intention was to equip the tank battalions with these in the ratio of three companies of the first type to one company of the support vehicles.

The *PzKpfw* III was the first of these two vehicles, and originally a high-velocity 5cm gun was called for. But the infantry were being equipped with the 3.7cm anti-tank gun, and it was felt that in the interest of standardisation the tanks should carry the same. However, a large turret ring was retained so that the vehicle could be up-gunned later without much difficulty. This was an important consideration and it undoubtedly enabled the *PzKpfw* III to remain in service for at least two years longer than would otherwise have been the case. The specification called for a weight of 14.76 tons (15,000kg), which was never achieved, and the upper limit had to be set at 23.62 tons (24,000kg) in deference to German road bridges.

The first prototypes appeared in 1936, and Daimler-Benz was chosen to be the main contractor. The *Ausf* A, B, C and D all appeared during the development phase, and were only produced in comparatively small numbers, and all were used to try out the different aspects of the design. The *Ausf* E became the production version, and was accepted in September 1939

Right: A feature of the *PzKpfw* III was the prominent cupola at the rear of the turret which gave the commander very good all-round observation. This particular tank has spaced armour added across the front of the superstructure and across the mantlet front. Note the spare track links fixed under the nose.

Below: The PzKpfw III was originally armed with a 37mm gun but it was progressively upgunned to 50mm and finally to 75mm.

as the *Panzerkampfwagen* III (3.7cm) (*SdKfz* 141). Production was spread among several firms, none of whom had had any previous experience of mass-producing vehicles – a fact which was to cause some trouble later on. The *PzKpfw* III *Ausf* E now formed the basis of the armoured divisions of the *Wehrmacht*. Some 98 were available for the invasion of Poland, and 350 took part in the Battle of France in May 1940. These tanks were mainly *Ausf* E, but there was still a number of earlier marks in service.

All versions featured a good crew layout. There was room for every man to do his job, and the prominent "dustbin" cupola at the rear of the turret gave the commander an excellent view. The driver was assisted by a pre-selector gearbox giving him ten forward speeds and one reverse. The gearbox was rather complicated, and maintenance was difficult, but gear changing was easy and driving far less tiring than in many contemporary tanks at that time. The 320hp from the Maybach engine was adequate, if not exactly generous, and cross-country performance reasonably good. However, the tank was not entirely successful in action. The 3.7cm gun was not good enough to penetrate the armour of the British infantry tanks in France, and the 1.18in (30mm) of frontal armour could not keep our 2pounder shot. The same happened in the Western Desert when the *PzKpfw* III first went out with the *Afrika Korps*, but a new Krupp 5cm gun was rushed into production in late 1939 and was fitted to the *Ausf* E to H. This gun was not entirely satisfactory either as it was a low-velocity weapon, but it fired a useful HE shell and could outrange the British 2pounder. Some 99 rounds of 5cm ammunition and 2,000 of 7.92mm ammunition were carried.

A steady programme of improvement and development was now applied to the *PzKpfw* III, The *Ausf* H introduced extra armour bolted on to the hull and turret, and the tracks were widened to carry the extra weight. The complicated ten-speed gearbox was replaced by a simple six-speed manual change, and some of these features were retrofitted to earlier marks.

By 1941 there were nearly 1,500 *PzKpfw* IIIs in service, and the type was very successful in the first stages of the invasion of Russia. But the T-34 and KV tanks were impervious to the 5cm low-velocity gun, and in a crash programme a high-velocity version was introduced, though even this soon proved to be inadequate on the Eastern Front. However, it did well in the desert. Improved versions were now being designed fast. Production of the *PzKpfw* III had never reached the intended numbers (indeed it never did) and the J version, which carried 78 5cm rounds, was meant to be easier to produce and at the same time to provide better protection. The M went a bit further and also cut out many minor items such as hatches and vision ports. Some 2,600 were built in 1942, but already the tank was being outmoded and the N version carried a low-velocity 7.5cm gun to provide HE support to the heavy tank battalions. Some 64 7.5cm and 3,450 7.92mm rounds of ammunition were carried.

Below: A *PzKpfw* III with additional armour to hull front and mantlet, armed with a short-barrelled 7.5cm L/24 gun. Flame-thrower versions of the tank were in service by 1943.

Caption;

Above: Supporting infantry, a *PzKpfw* III *Ausf* J acts as protection against enemy fire during the advance on Moscow in 1942. The *PzKpfw* III was the backbone of the *Panzer* Divisions in the early stages of the Russian campaign but could not seriously trouble the Soviet T-34 and KV tanks. It was replaced by later models of the *PzKpfw* IV.

Below: Apparently in the heat of battle, a *PzKpfw* III, again with additional armour to hull front and mantlet and the short-barrelled 7.5cm L/24 gun.

PzKpfw IV Medium Tank

SdKfz 161.
Country of origin: Germany.
Crew: 5.
Armament: One 7.5cm *KwK* L/24 gun; one 7.92mm MG 34 machine-gun co-axial with main armament; one 7.92mm MG 34 machine-gun in hull.
Armour: 0.79in (20mm) minimum; 3.54in (90mm) maximum.
Dimensions: Length 19ft 5in (5.91m); width 9ft 7in (2.92m); height 8ft 6in (2.59m).
Weight: 43,431lb (19,700kg).
Ground pressure: 10.6lb/in² (0.75kg/cm²).
Engine: Maybach HL 120 TRM V-12 inline diesel developing 300hp at 3,000rpm.
Performance: Road speed 25mph (40km/h); cross-country speed 12.5mph (20km/h); range 125 miles (200km); vertical obstacle 2ft (0.6m); trench 7ft 6in (2.3m); fording depth 2ft 7in (0.8m); gradient 30 degrees.
History: In service with the German Army from 1936 to 1945. Also used by Italy, Spain and Turkey. Last used by Syria in 1967.
(Note: Date relate to the PzKpfw IV Ausf D.)

The *PzKpfw* IV was the only German tank to stay in continuous production throughout World War II, and it was probably in production longer than any other tank from that war, with the exception of the T-34. It began with the German specifications of 1935 in which it was foreseen that the main battle would be fought with two types, the more numerous one carrying a high-velocity gun (the *PzKpfw* III) and a support tank carrying a large-calibre gun firing a good HE shell. This was the *PzKpfw* IV. The gun chosen from the

Below: Front view of a *PzKpfw* IV *Ausf* F2 of the *Afrika Korps* armed with the long barrelled 75mm *KwK* L/43 gun. This was encountered by the British in the Western Desert and called the "Pz IV Special". The fitting of this gun changed the role of the tank from that of a close support vehicle to a tank that could engage and defeat other tanks.

Right: Front view of *PzKpfw* IV *Ausf* A of 1st *Panzer* Division.

Above: *PzKpfw* IV *Ausf* H with long-barrelled L/48 gun, apron armour 5mm thick for the hull and 8mm thick on the turret. *"Zimmerit"* anti-magnetic paste was usually applied to these vehicles to prevent magnetic charges from being attached.

Right: Disabled *PzKpfw* IV *Ausf* H tanks on the Voronezh Front in 1943. Note the skirt armour plates on the front tank; called *Schurzen,* they were 5mm thick and were intended to detonate HEAT projectiles prematurely. The detachable hull plates were often lost in the heat of battle but the turret plates were a permanent fixture. By the end of World War II 8,000 IVs had been built and it was the only German tank to remain in production all through the war. Some were even used as recently as 1967 by the Syrian Army in the static anti-tank role.

beginning was the 7.5cm short-barrelled *KwK,* and the tank was not to exceed 23.62 tons (24,000kg) in overall weight. In fact the specification called for a very similar vehicle to the *PzKpfw* III, and the layout of both was much the same, as were their tasks. Contracts were laid with a variety of firms, and there was the same fairly extended development time while the different designs were refined. It was 1939 before deliveries could be made in any quantity, and by that time the models had progressed to the Type D. This was the model which took part in the Polish and French campaigns, finally advancing into Russia in 1941, when its deficiencies became too apparent to be ignored further.

The Type D was slightly larger than the *PzKpfw* III, but had the same thin hull form and general shape. There were three compartments for the crew, the driver and radio operator occupying the front, with the hull machine-gun on the right side and set slightly back from the driver. In the fighting compartment the turret contained the commander, gunner and loader. The turret itself was traversed by an electric motor, whereas that of the *PzKpfw* III was hand-operated. The commander had a prominent cupola at the rear of the turret, and good all-round vision. There were escape hatches in the turret sides. The engine was in the rear compartment, and was the same as that of the *PzKpfw* III, although the layout of the ancillaries was slightly different. The drive ran forward to a front gearbox and sprocket. Suspension was by four coupled bogies on each side, sprung by leaf springs. There was a large idler wheel at the back and four small return rollers. There was room enough in the hull for 80 rounds of ammunition for the gun, and 2,800 rounds in belts for the machine-guns.

Battle experience soon showed that in this form the tank was a sound

design and well laid out, but the armour was too thin for it to be able to perform its proper task of supporting the *PzKpfw* IIIs as it had scarcely any advantage over any other tank. There followed a steady programme of improvement which was to continue until t he end of the war. The next model, the E, was given thicker armour on the nose and turret, and a new cupola. Older models were retrofitted, which confuses precise identification of many photographs today. The F model was intended to be the main production version, tough it too was soon overtaken, and a long-barrelled version of the 7.5cm gun was fitted. This long gun completely changed the role of the vehicle as it now became a fighting tank and began to take over that duty from the *PzKpfw* III from about mid-1941 onwards. The F was made in large numbers and fought on all fronts, as did the G which came soon after it, differing outwardly only in respect of its thicker armour and side skirting plates.

In 1943 another lease of life was injected by fitting the more powerful 7.5cm *KwK* 40 L/48 which enabled the *PzKpfw* IV to take on almost any tank in the world, and to give a good account of itself against the T-34. These larger guns had of course changed the turret, which from the G onwards was protected with extra plates, making it appear much longer at the rear. Large 0.2in (5mm) skirting plates hung over the sides and radically altered the look of the tank, making it appear deep and rather clumsy.

The last model was the J, which came out in 1944. By this time many raw materials were scarce and the design had to be simplified, but it was still basically the tank which had started the war five years before. By 1945 over 8,000 had been delivered and many more were built for specialist purposes. A few were still in service with the Syrian Army in the Arab-Israeli War of 1967, and apparently went well.

PzKpfw VI Tiger I Heavy Battle Tank

PzKpfw VI Tiger I, or ***SdKfz*** 181.
Country of origin: Germany.
Crew: 5.
Armament: One 8.8cm *KwK* 36 L/56 gun; one 7.92mm MG 34 machine-gun co-axial with main armament; one 7.92mm MG 34 machine-gun in hull.
Armour: 1.02in (26mm) minimum; 4.33in (100mm) maximum.
Dimensions: Length 27ft (8.25m); width 12ft 3in (3.73m); height 9ft 4in (2.85m).
Weight: 121,253lb (55,000kg).
Ground pressure: 14.8lb/in² (1.04kg/cm²).
Engine: Maybach HL 230 P 45 V-12 water-cooled inline petrol engine developing 700bhp at 3,000rpm.
Performance: Road speed 24mph (38km/h); cross-country speed 12mph (20km/h); range 62 miles (100km); vertical obstacle 2ft 7in (0.8m); trench 5ft 11in (1.8m); fording depth 4ft (1.2m); gradient 35 degrees.
History: In service with the German Army from 1942 to 1945.
(*Note: Data relate to t he Tiger I Ausf E.*)

Below and right: Four views of the *PzKpfw* VI Tiger (Model H) of the 1st *SS Panzer* Division, "Leibstandarte Adolf Hitler", as used on the Russian Front. The bands around the barrel of the 88mm *KwK* L/56 gun indicate the number of enemy tanks killed.

Despite the decision to mass produce the *PzKpfw* III and Iv, and the fair certainty at the time that these two models would be adequate for the expected battles of the future, the German general staff also called for an even heavier tank in 1937. This was to be of 29.53 tons (30,000kg) or more and was to be a heavy "breakthrough" tank to lead the armoured assaults. The design lapsed until 1941, by when it was realised that the *PzKpfw* IIIs and IVs had been less successful than had been expected against the heavily armoured French and British tanks in 1940. This view was fully endorsed when the Soviet T-34s and KV-Is were met later in 1941, and resulted in a specification for a heavy tank capable of mounting the highly successful 8.8cm high-velocity gun in a turret with full traverse and carrying sufficient armour to defeat all present and future anti-tank weapons.

Two firms submitted prototypes, using some of the developments from the 1937 ideas. These were Porsche and Henschel. The turret was common to both and came from Krupp. The Porsche design was unconventional and was not accepted, although it became a self-propelled gun. The Henschel design was relatively conventional, was obviously easier to make, and was

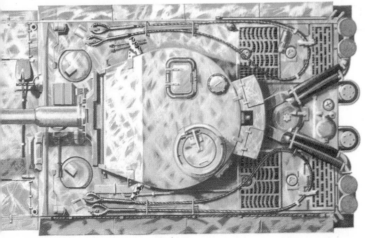

thus accepted. This was given the designation *PzKpfw* VI and the name Tiger. Production began slowly in August 1942.

At the time of its introduction, and for some time afterwards, the Tiger was the most powerful tank in the world. The 8.8cm gun, which had 92 rounds of ammunition, was enormously formidable, and the armour ensured that any frontal shot could not penetrate. So effective was it that the Allies had to evolve special tactics to cope with it, though there were occasions when the tank was used so ineffectively that it never realised its potential. The Tiger was intended to be deployed in special battalions of 30 vehicles under the control of an army or corps headquarters. In general, this was done, tough some armoured divisions were given their own Tiger battalions, particularly those of the *Waffen*-SS. Hitler had taken a personal interest in the Tiger, and he pressed for its u se at the earliest opportunity. They were thrown into battle near Leningrad in the late summer of 1942, well spread out and in small numbers on poor ground. The result was a fiasco, as was the Kursk battle next year. But when used in ambush, where its gun could inflict the most damage, and where the heavy armour allowed a phased withdrawal, the Tiger was supreme. Indeed, in 1944 one solitary Tiger held up an entire division in France, and knocked out 25 Allied tanks before being stalked and destroyed.

The hull of the Tiger was a comparatively simple welded unit with a one-piece superstructure welded on top. The armour was not well sloped, but was thick. At the front it was 3.94in (100mm), around the sides 3.15in (80mm) and 1.02in (26mm) on the decks. To assist production all shapes were kept simple, and a long box-like side pannier ran along the top of the tracks. The turret was also simple, and the sides were almost upright. The mantlet was very heavy, with 4.33in (110mm) of armour, and carried the long and heavy gun. The turret traverse was a very low-geared and driven by a hydraulic motor which took its power from the gearbox. Thus when the main engine was stopped, the turret had to be traversed by hand. The engine was changed in late 1943 to one of slightly greater power, but in general it was reliable and powerful enough.

The difficulty was that the tank's range was always too limited for operations, and top speed was low because of the need to gear down the transmission. The weight was too great for the usual German clutch and

brake steering and Henschel adapted the British Merritt-Brown regenerative unit and coupled it to a pre-selector Maybach gearbox with eight forward speeds. The result was a set of controls which were very light for the driver, but by no means easy to maintain or repair. The suspension was formed by overlapping road wheels; it was the first German tank to carry this distinctive feature, which gave a soft and stable ride. There were no less than eight torsion-bars on each side, and the floor was tightly packed with them. The difficulty with the overlapping wheels was that in the Russian winter nights they froze together and jammed the tracks, and the Russians often timed their attacks for dawn, when they could be sure of the Tigers being immobilised. The tracks were too wide for rail transport, and narrower ones were fitted for normal road and railway transport, when the outer set of road wheels was also removed.

The crew were housed in four compartments in the hull, the driver and hull gunner being separated in front, with the gearbox between them. The turret was fairly normal, though there was little room to spare when 92 rounds of 8.8cm ammunition were fully stowed. The gun was balanced by a heavy spring in a tube on the left of the turret. The 8.8cm shell could penetrate 4.4in (112mm) of armour at 492 yards (450m), which was more than enough for the armoured vehicles of the day. It was much feared by the crews of the comparatively vulnerable Shermans, the main Allied tank.

The Tiger was reasonably compact, but it was very heavy. It could not cross German bridges, and the first 400 models were capable of wading through deep rivers when they came to them. The necessity of fitting and re-fitting special tracks for rail travel was tedious, and the road wheels gave trouble from overloading. More nimble Allied tanks found that they could outmanoeuvre the Tiger and attack it from the rear, and these, together with the other limitations, caused it to be phased out in 1944. By August of that year 1,300 had been made, not many in view of their reputation and effect on Allied morale.

Below: Tiger (Model E) captured by the British in Tunisia. The British first encountered the Tiger in February 1943 near Pont du Fahs in Tunisia, when 6-pounders engaged two Tigers and nine *PzKpfw* IIIs and IVs. Both Tigers were knocked out at 500 yards.

PzKpfw V Panther Battle Tank

***Pzkpfw* V, or *SdKfz* 171.**
Country of origin: Germany.
Crew: 5.
Armament: One 7.5cm *KwK* 42 L/70 gun; two 7.92mm MG 34 machine-guns.
Armour: 0.6in (20mm) minimum; 4.72in (120mm) maximum.
Dimensions: Length 22ft 6in (6.68m); width 10ft 10in (3.3m); height 9ft 8in (2.95m). (Dimensional data relate to the *Ausf* G.)
Weight: 98,766lb (44,800kg).
Ground pressure: 12.5lb/in^2 (0.88kg/cm^2).
Engine: Maybach HL 230 P 30 V-12 water-cooled petrol engine developing 700bhp at 3,000rpm.
Performance: Road speed 29mph (46km/h); cross-country speed 15mph (24km/h); range 110 miles (177km); vertical obstacle 3ft (0.9m); trench 6ft3in (1.9m); fording depth 4ft 7in (1.4m); gradient 35 degrees.
History: In service with the German Army from 1943 to 1945. Also used by the Soviet Union and France after the war.

Left and below: Front, rear and side views of the *PzKpfw* V Panther, one of the best tanks of the World War II. It was designed around the general concept of the Soviet T-34 tank, first seen in 1941.

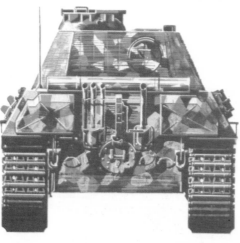

Above: The *PzKpfw* V Panther featured well sloped armour, low turret-mounted 7.5cm *KwK* 42 L/70 gun, two 7.92mm MG 34 MGs and interleaved suspension that caused problems in the winter.

Until the invasion of Soviet Russia, the *PzKpfw* IV had been the heaviest tank in the German Army, and had proved quite adequate. In early October 1941 the new Soviet T-34 (*qv*) appeared and proved the *PzKpfw* IV to be completely out of date. The sloped armour, speed and manoeuvrability of the T-34 brought about a profound change of heart on the part of the Germans, and a new requirement was hurriedly drawn up. At first, to save time, it was even considered that the T-34 should be copied directly, but national pride forbade this approach and the specification issued in January 1942 merely incorporated all the T-34 features.

Designs were submitted in April 1942, and the first trial models appeared in September, the MAN design being chosen for production. There were the usual multitude of modifications called for as a result of the prototype's performance and spurred on by Hitler himself, MAN brought out the first

Above: The Panther tank was first committed to action during the Battle of Kursk in July 1943 and proved to be very unreliable. Many tanks broke down before they reached the front. There were problems with the engine, transmission and suspension, but once these were overcome the Panther became very popular with crews and was equal to the dreaded Soviet T-34 tank.

production tank in January 1943, but Daimler-Benz had to be brought in to help. From then on production forged ahead, but never reached the ambitious target of 600 vehicles a month set by Hitler. There were many difficulties. The engine and transmission were overstressed to cope with the increase in weight, cooling was inadequate, engines caught fire, and the wheel rims gave trouble. When the Panther first went into action at Kursk in July 1943, it was at Hitler's insistence, and it was a failure. Most broke down on the journey from the railhead, and few survived the first day. All that were salvaged had to be sent back to the factory to be rebuilt. Later models corrected the faults, and the Panther soon became a fine tank which was superior to the T-34/76 and very popular with its crews.

The hull was fairly conventional in the German fashion, with a large one-piece glacis plate in which were originally two holes, one for the gunner and one for the driver. The G model had only the gun hole, the driver using a periscope. The turret was well sloped, although rather cramped inside, but the commander was given a good cupola. The mantlet was massive, with tiny holes for the machine-gun and the gunner's binocular sight. From the front the protection was excellent. The suspension was by inter-leaved bogies sprung on torsion bars and it gave the Panther the best arrangement of any German tank of the war. The trouble was that the bogies could freeze up when clogged

Above: Panthers were built by MAN and Daimler-Benz, and by the end of the war over 5,000 had been built. But production never reached the 600 tanks a month demanded by Hitler in 1943.

with snow in Russian winters, and so immobilise the vehicle. Maintenance was also difficult since the outer wheels had to be removed to allow access to the inner ones. Steering was by hydraulically operated disc brakes and epicyclic gears to each track, which allowed the tracks to be stopped separately when required without loss of power. It was an adaption of the Merritt-Brown system, but rather more complicated in design. The long 75mm gun (with 79 rounds) could penetrate 4.72in (120mm) of sloped plate at 1,094 yards (100m) and this, together with the protection of the thick frontal armour, meant that the Panther could stand off from Allied tanks and knock them out without being harmed itself. The US Army reckoned that it took five Shermans to knock out one Panther and over 5,000 Panthers had been built by the end of the war. After 1943 the Germans needed numbers of tanks rather than improved designs, and the Panther was simplified to ease production. The hull sides were sloped more, the mantlet was thickened to prevent shot being deflected into the decking, and the gearbox was improved to cope with the weight problem.

Despite its complexity and high manufacturing cost, the Panther was a successful design and many consider it to have been one of the best tanks produced during the war. Towards the end of the war its petrol engine and complications were distinct disadvantages, but it was a powerful supplement to the *PzKpfw* IVs of the armoured formations, and it was really only defeated by the overwhelming Allied air strength.

PzKpfw VI Tiger II Heavy Battle Tank

PzKpfw VI Tiger II, or **SdKfz** 182.
Country of origin: Germany.
Crew: 5.
Armament: One 8.8cm KwK 43 L/71 gun; two 7.92mm MG 34 machine-guns.
Armour: 1.57in (40mm) minimum; 7.28in (185mm) maximum.
Dimensions: Length 23ft 9in (7.25m); width 12ft 3in (4.27m); height 10ft 1in (3.27m).
Weight: 153,000lb (69,400kg).
Ground pressure: 15.2lb/in² (1.07kg/cm²).
Engine: Maybach HL 230 P 30 V-12 water-cooled inline petrol engine developing 600bhp at 3,000rpm.
Performance: Road speed 24mph (38km/h); cross-country speed 11mph (17km/h); range 68 miles (110km); vertical obstacle 2ft 9in (0.85m); trench 8ft 2 in (2.5m); fording depth 5ft 3in (1.6m); gradient 35 degrees.
History: In service with the German Army from 1944 to 1945.

Right: The PzKpfw **Tiger II, or Royal Tiger as it was often called, fitted with Porsche-built turret for its 88mm** KwK **43 L/71 gun, for which 80 rounds of APCBC and HE were carried.**

Above: The *PzKpfw* Tiger II with Henschel turret which was easier to build and also offered better protection than the Porsche turret fitted to the first 50 Tiger II tanks.

The Tiger I had hardly entered service before the German general staff requested a bigger and better successor, superior in armour and hitting power to anything that the Soviet Army was likely to produce. Once again Porsche and Henschel were asked for designs which were to incorporate the latest sloped armour and the longer 71-calibre 8.8cm gun. Porsche updated its Tiger I design and this time was so sure of an order that it started work on the turret and actually put casting in hand. Unfortunately the Porsche ideas of electric transmission were once more rejected, supplies of copper being too small, and the contract went

to Henschel for the second time. However, 50 Porsche turrets were made and fitted to the first models. Henschel then fitted its own turret, which was simpler and had better protection. Another requirement of the specification was to liaise with MAN in order to standardise as many parts as possible with the Panther II, which never appeared, and the subsequent delays meant that production did not get under way until December 1943.

The Tiger II, known to its own side as the *Königstiger* and to the Allies as the Royal Tiger, was a massive and formidable vehicle. It was intended to dominate the battlefield, and that it could do, providing that its crew used it sensibly. It was the heaviest, best protected and most powerfully armed tank to go into production during World War II, and its armour and gun would do justice to a main battle tank today. The price paid for all this superiority was size, weight and low performance. Manoeuvrability, ground pressure and that subtle thing "agility" all suffered, and inevitably the reliability of the over-stressed engine and transmission decreased.

The hull was welded, as was that of the Tiger I, but the armour was better sloped, using the experience of the T-34. Hull layout was similar to that of the Panther, and the large turret was roomy although the gun came right back to the rear wall and made a complete partition longitudinally. Some 80 rounds of ammunition were stowed round the turret sides and floor and there were plenty of racks and shelves for the minor equipment. The commander's cupola allowed an excellent view, though he usually chose to have his head out of the top. The long and

powerful 8.8cm gun could outrange and out-shoot the main armament of nearly all Allied tanks, and this allowed the Tiger II to stand off and engage targets as it chose. Barrel wear was a difficulty with this high-velocity gun, and the later models had a two-piece barrel which allowed the faster-wearing part to be changed easily.

Only one model was built, and altogether no more than 485 examples were completed. Production never suffered despite the heaviest Allied bombing, and Henschel always had at least 60 vehicles in construction on its shop floors at any one time. At the peak it was taking only 14 days to complete a Tiger II. Severe fuel shortages forced the factory to use bottled gas for testing, though petrol was supplied for operations.

The Tiger II was introduced into service in the autumn of 1944, on the same distribution as the Tiger I, and again in small units of four or five. Its enormous size and weight made it a ponderous vehicle, often difficult to conceal; in a fast moving battle it was quickly left behind, and this fate did occur to several in Russia. But when used properly it was enormously effective and could engage many times its own numbers of enemy, and knock them all out without damage to itself.

Below: *PzKpfw* VI Tiger IIs drawn up in line abreast. The *Königstiger* ("King Tiger"), called "Royal Tiger" by the Allies, was reckoned to be so formidable that these tanks were often deployed in groups of five or less in order to engage and halt or delay the advance of much larger numbers of Allied tanks.

Maus Heavy Tank

Country of origin: Germany.
Crew: 6.
Armament: One 12.8cm *KwK* L/55 gun; one 7.5cm L/36.5 gun co-axial with main armament; one 2cm cannon.
Armour: 1.57in (40mm) minimum; 13.78in (350mm) maximum.
Dimensions: Length (including gun) 30ft 10in (10.1m); width 11ft 2 in (3.67m); height 11ft 9in (3.63m).
Weight: 414,465lb (188,000kg).
Ground pressure: 20.6lb/in^2 (1.45kg/cm^2).
Engine: Daimler-Benz MB 509 V-12 water-cooled inline petrol engine developing 1,080hp at 2,400rpm.
Performance: Road speed 12.5mph (20km/h); range 116 miles (186km); vertical obstacle 2ft 2in (0.72m); trench 13ft 9in (4.5m); gradient 30 degrees.
History: Built only in prototype forms.

During the course of World War II the Germans directed a great amount of effort and resources to the development of super-heavy AFVs. There were two tank models under development (the *Maus* (Mouse) and the E-100) but neither of these was ever taken into service. On 8 June 1942, Dr. Ferdinand Porsche (the famous car designer) was approached concerning the possibility of producing a tank type vehicle mounting a 12.8cm or 15cm gun in a revolving turret. A co-axial 7.5cm gun was also to be incorporated. At this time Porsche was head of the German Tank Commission and had a great deal of influence with Hitler, on whom he urged the development of super-heavy tanks. The majority of German tank designers and the leading theoreticians of tank warfare, however, were opposed to the use of such super-heavy tanks. When the project was first suggested, the vehicle was referred to as the *Mammut* (Mammoth), and allocated the project Number 205. The Alkett firm began assembly of the first tank on 1 August 1943.

Above: *Maus* heavy tank. It was planned to build 150 of these, but by May 1945 only two had been built with nine more partially completed.

Krupp supplied the hull in mid-September and the new tank, now referred to as the *Maus* made its first trial run at Alkett on 23 December 1943. On 10 January 1944 the tank was sent to Böblingen near Stuttgart for extensive trials. Apart from slight trouble with the suspension the trials were fairly successful. At this time instructions were given to Porsche by Hitler that the completed tank, with turret and guns, was to be ready by June. By 9 June the turret had been assembled and fitted to the tank and further trials were commenced. These were very satisfactory, and at the beginning of October orders were received to send the tank to the proving ground at Kummersdorf. A second prototype (Mouse II) was sent to Kummersdorf without trials. This model had a different engine, which gave considerable trouble. By the end of the war a further nine prototypes were in various stages of construction, and production plans had been made for 150. The vehicles at Kummersdorf were blown up by the Germans prior to the arrival of the Russians.

Left: The *Maus* I heavy tank, complete with turret and armament. It was powered by a Daimler-Benz MB 509 petrol engine giving a road speed of 12.5mph (20km/h) and mounted a 128mm *KwK* L/55 gun, co-axial 75mm L/36 and a 20mm cannon.

Leopard 1 Main Battle Tank

Leopard 1, 1A1, 1A1A2, 1A2, 1A3, 1A4, 1A5, 1A5(BE), and 1A5(IT).
Country of origin: Germany.
Crew: 4.
Armament: One 105mm gun; one 7.62mm machine-gun co-axial with main gun; one 7.62mm machine-gun on turret roof; four smoke grenade dischargers on each side of the turret.
Armour: 10mm-70mm (0.4in-2.8in).
Dimensions: Length (including main armament) 31ft 4in (9.54m); length (hull) 23ft 3in (7.1m); width 10ft 8in (3.25m); height 8ft 8in (2.64m).
Weight: Combat 93,394lb (42,400kg).
Ground pressure: 12.23lb/in² (0.86kg/cm²).
Engine: MTU MB 838Ca M-500 10-cylinder multi-fuel engine; 830hp at 2,200rpm.
Performance: Road speed 40mph (65km/h); range 373 miles (600km); vertical obstacle 3ft 9in (1.15m); trench 9ft 10in (3.0m); gradient 60 per cent.
History: Entered service with West German Army in 1967. Orders for MBT version were: Australia (90); Belgium (334); Canada (114); Denmark (120); Germany (2,437); Greece (106); Italy (920); Netherlands (468); Turkey (77). Current (early 2000) in-service position is: Australia (90); Belgium (132, all Leopard 1A5(BE)); Brazil (87); Canada (114); Denmark (330, all Leopard 1A5); Germany (724): Greece (335); Italy (920); Netherlands (0); Norway (172); Turkey (307).

The German Leopard 1 MBT is the most successful European tank of the post-World War II era, with some 4,800 MBTs and 1,722 other versions being ordered by 10 armies. Indeed, for some years during the Cold War it appeared that Leopard 1 was NATO's *de facto* standard MBT, being used by nine of the 15 Alliance's armies. The Leopard 1's origins lay in a 1950s Franco-German-Italian collaborative programme for a new common MBT, but then, as has happened with every MBT collaborative project, there were disagreements and the

Below: Leopard 1A3 with infra-red/white searchlight mounted over the 105mm gun that was developed for the Centurion tank.

Above: Early production Leopard 1 MBT of the German Army being recovered by a Leopard armoured recovery vehicle built by MaK.

partners split up: the French bought the national AMX-30, while the Italians bought a number of US M60s (although they later bought a much larger number of Leopard 1s). The German Army placed a contract for Leopard 1 with Krauss-Maffei in 1963 and the first production vehicle was delivered in September 1965. Thereafter, Krauss-Maffei produced most of the MBTs and some of the specialised versions, while MaK of Kiel produced some MBTs and the majority of the armoured engineer vehicles, bridgelayers and recovery vehicles. The German production lines closed in 1979 but reopened in 1981 to meet orders from Greece and Turkey. A third production line was established by OTO Melara in Italy to meet most of the Italian order.

The Leopard 1 has a crew of four, with the driver in the front of the hull and to the right, while the other three crew are located in the turret. The main

Below: The Leopard 1A3 has a number of improvements including a new all-welded steel turret which gives increased protection.

Above: A dramatic study of a Leopard 1 MBT at full speed. It can reach a top speed of 40mph (65km/h) on made-up roads, a little slower than the Leopard 2 MBT.

armament of all versions of the Leopard is the British L7A3 105mm gun manufactured by Royal Ordnance at Nottingham, for which 55 rounds are carried, 13 in the turret and 42 in the hull. There are two Rheinmetall MG3 7.62mm machine-guns, one mounted co-axially with the main armament, the other in a flexible mounting on the turret roof.

Standard equipment includes night vision devices, an NBC system and a crew heater. The vehicle can ford to a maximum depth of 7ft 5in (2.25m) with minimum preparation using a short tower fitted over the commander s hatch, and to 13ft 2in (4m) with a taller tower. Such equipment is, however, rarely used and, except in the most unusual circumstances, rivers are crossed by bridge or ferry.

The first 1,845 Leopard 1s were built for the *Bundesheer* in four production batches and all were subsequently modified with the installation of a thermal sleeve on the main armament, gun stabilisation system, new tracks and skirts. They were then further modified with applique armour on the turret and gun mantlet, after which they were re-designated Leopard 1A1. Some of these were later fitted with a low-light television (LLTV) system to become Leopard 1A1A2.

The fifth production batch consisted of 342 tanks, of which 232 were built to Leopard 1A1 standard, but instead of applique armour they had a cast turret of thicker steel, as well as a better NBC system and passive image intensification

equipment for the commander and driver. These were designated Leopard 1A2.

The remaining 110 tanks of the fifth batch were built with all the improvements of Leopard 1A1 and 1A2, but with a welded turret and a new mantlet. This was designated Leopard 1A3 and was the version sold to Greece and Turkey in the early 1980s. The final production batch for the *Bundesheer* consisted of 250 Leopard 1A4s, which were essentially Leopard 1A3s with an integrated fire-control system.

The German Army then instigated an upgrading programme for most of its fleet of Leopard 1s. This involved installing the STN Atlas Elektronik EMES-18 fire-control system. Designated Leopard 1A5, 1,300 were converted between 1986 and 1992, some 75 being diverted to Greece. The Belgian Army had its own, separate programme for a new integrated fire-control system, which was installed in 132 of its fleet. These then received the designation Leopard 1A5(BE). There is yet another version, developed by OTO Breda for the Italian Army, which is designated Leopard 1A5(IT); 120 are being converted.

Since the end of the Cold War and the entry into service of more advanced tanks, the overall stock of surviving Leopard 1s has been moved, particularly under the NATO policy of cascading surplus equipment from wealthier to less-wealthy nations. Germany, still retains 724 Leopard 1A5s, but has cascaded 507 to other NATO countries: Denmark (110); Greece (75); Norway (92); and Turkey (320). Belgium is retaining 132, all of which have been upgraded to Leopard 1A5 (BE) standard; the remaining 115 are surplus, of which 87 have been sold to Brazil and the others await a buyer. The Netherlands wishes to retain none of its Leopard 1s: 170 have been cascaded to Greece and all the remainder are for sale.

Leopard 2 Main Battle Tank

Country of origin: Germany.
Crew: 4.
Armament: One Rheinmetall 120mm smoothbore gun; one MG3 7.62mm co-axial machine-gun; one MG3 7.62mm anti-aircraft machine-gun; 16 smoke dischargers (eight on each side of turret).
Armour: Spaced, multi-layer.
Dimensions: Length (including main armament) 31ft 9in (9.67m); length (hull) 25ft 4in (7.72m); width 12ft 2in (3.7m); height 8ft 2in (2.48m).
Weight: Combat 121,475lb (55,150kg).
Ground pressure: 11.80lb/in^2 (0.83kg/cm^2).
Engine: MTU MB-873 Ka-501 12-cylinder liquid-cooled diesel engine developing 1,500bhp at 2,600rpm.
Performance: Road speed 45mph (72km/h); range 600 miles (550km); vertical obstacle 3ft 7in (1.1m); trench 9ft 10in (3m); gradient 60 per cent.
History: Entered service with German Army in 1980. Ordered by: Germany (1,800), the Netherlands (445) and Switzerland (380).

The development of the Leopard 2 MBT can be traced back to a national project started in the 1960s. At this time the Germans and the Americans were still working on the MBT-70 programme, so the project had a very low priority. Once the MBT-70 (*qv*) was cancelled, the Germans pushed ahead with the Leopard 2, and 17 prototypes were completed in 1974. These prototypes were built by the manufacturers of the Leopard 1, Krauss-Maffei of Munich, with the assistance of many other German companies. Without doubt, the Leopard 2 is one of the most advanced tanks in the world and the Germans have succeeded in designing a tank with high success in all three areas of tank design: mobility; firepower and armour protection. In the past, most tanks have only been able to achieve two of these objectives at once.

A good example was the British Chieftain, which had an excellent gun and good armour, but poor mobility; the French AMX-30 was at the other end of the scale with good mobility, an adequate gun but rather thin armour.

The layout of the Leopard 2 is conventional, with the driver at the front, turret with commander, gunner and loader in the centre, and the engine and transmission at the rear. The engine was in fact originally developed for the MBT-70. The complete powerpack can be removed in about 15 minutes for repair or

Above: A German Army Leopard 2 comes to an abrupt halt on a training track. The slab sides of the turret set a fashion followed by a number of other designs, such as the Japanese Type 90.

Left: Main armament of the Leopard 2 is a 120mm Rhein-Metall smoothbore gun which fires two types of fixed ammunition, APFSDS (Armour-Piercing Fin-Stabilised Discarding Sabot) and HEAT-MP (High-Explosive Anti-Tank Multi-Purpose). A total of 42 rounds of 120mm ammunition are carried.

141

Leopard 2 was the first tank to be armed with the Rheinmetall 120mm smoothbore gun, which has since been adopted by a large number of other armies.

Above: Two Leopard 2s on a night-firing range, with one firing its 120mm smoothbore gun. Hiding such an enormous flash would be an impossibility in battle.

replacement. At first it was widely believed that the Leopard 2's armour was of the spaced type, but late in 1976 it was revealed that it used the British-developed Chobham armour. This gives superior protection against attack from all known projectiles. It is of the laminate type, and consists of layers of steel and ceramics. The suspension system is of the torsion-bar type with dampers. It has seven road wheels, with the drive sprocket at the rear and the idler at the front, and there are four track return rollers.

The first prototypes were armed with a 105mm gun of the smoothbore type developed by Rheinmetall, but later prototypes had the 120mm smoothbore gun. The 120mm gun fires two basic types of fin-stabilised ammunition (in which small fins unfold from the rear of the round just after it has left the barrel), and this means that the barrel does not need to be rifled. The anti-tank round is of the Armour-Piercing Discarding Sabot type, and has an effective range of well over 2,405 yards (2,200m); at this range it will penetrate a standard NATO heavy tank target. The second round is also fin-stabilised and is designed for use against field fortifications and other battlefield targets. The cartridge case is semi combustible and only the cartridge stub, which is made of conventional steel, remains after the round has been fired. The job of the loader is eased by the use of the hydraulically-assisted loading mechanism. The gun has an elevation of +20° and a depression of –9°. A standard 7.62mm MG3 machine-gun is mounted co-axially with the main armament. A 7.62mm MG3 machine-gun is installed on the loader's hatch for use in the anti-aircraft role. 42 rounds of 120mm and 2,000 rounds of 7.62mm ammunition are carried. Eight smoke dischargers are mounted each side of the turret. A very advanced fire-control system is fitted which includes a combined laser and stereoscopic rangefinder, and the gun is fully stabilised, enabling it to be laid and fired on the move with a high probability

of the round hitting the target.

Standard equipment includes infra-red and passive night-vision equipment, an NBC system and heaters for both the driver's and fighting compartments. The Leopard 2 can ford streams to a depth of 2ft 7in (0.8m) without preparation, and with the aid of a schnorkel can deep ford to a depth of 13ft 1in (4m).

The Leopard 2 has established an enviable reputation and has been tested by a number of armies. The US Army evaluated a special tank designated "Leopard 2 Austere Version" against the US-designed XM1, from which the latter emerged victorious. In the late 1980s the British also examined a different version known as Leopard 2 (Improved), but again this failed to win an order against the national rival, in this case the Challenger 2.

The German tank has won four major foreign orders and a fifth at second-hand. The first foreign customer was the Netherlands, purchasing 445, which were delivered between 1981 and 1986. Of these, 114 were sold to Austria in the mid-1990s and the rest are being upgraded to Leopard 2A5 standard (with one possibly being scrapped) . Sweden purchased 280 tanks from Germany, of which 160 were early model Leopard 2s from German Army stocks and are designated Stridsvagn 121 in Sweden. The remaining 160 are new-build Leopard 2A5s, assembled in Sweden from components supplied by Germany; this model is designated *Stridsvagn* 122 (*Strv*-122). Spain has ordered 219 Leopard 2A5s (see separate entry), but has obtained 108 Leopard 2A4s from the German Army on a five year lease; these were delivered in 1995-1996. Switzerland took delivery of 350 Leopard 2s between 1987 and 1993, where it is known as *Pz87 Leo* and it is anticipated that most, if not all, will be upgraded the Leopard 2A5 standard.

The most important variant is the Leopard 2A5, which is described in the next entry. Other variants include a bridging vehicle, an armoured recovery vehicle and a driver training vehicle, all of which have been ordered by both the Dutch and German Armies. Known trials versions include one with a 55-calibre 120mm gun and another with a 140mm gun.

Leopard 2A5 Main Battle Tank

Leopard 2A5, Strv-122/Leopard 2(S), and Leopard 2A5E.
Country of origin: Germany.
Crew: 4.
Armament: One Rheinmetall smoothbore 120mm/L44 gun; one MG3 7.62mm machine-gun coaxial with the main armament; one MG3 7.62mm machine-gun on turret roof; eight single-barrelled smoke grenade launchers on each side of turret.
Armour: Classified.
Dimensions: Length (including main armament) 32ft 8in (9.97m); length (hull) 23ft 7in (7.72m); width 12ft 3in (3.74m); height 8ft 8in (2.64m).
Weight: Combat 131,614lb (59,700kg).
Ground pressure: 12.6lb/in^2 (0.89kg/cm^2).
Engine: MTU MB-873 Ka-501 4-stroke, 12-cylinder, liquid cooled, exhaust supercharged diesel, 1,500bhp at 2,600rpm.
Performance: Road speed 45mph (72km/h); range 310 miles (500km); vertical obstacle 3ft 7in (1.1m); trench 9ft 10in (3.0m); gradient 60 per cent.
History: Prototypes 1990; upgrading programme started 1995; in service with Germany (225), Netherlands (180). New builds to 2A5 standard on order for Sweden (120) and Spain (219).

Below: Spain has ordered 219 Leopard 2A5E (E = España) and to fill the gap until they become available 108 Leopard 2A4s have been leased from the German Army.

Above: The characteristic arrowhead shape of the Leopard 2A5 turret is formed by removable plates, which increase protection against both kinetic energy and chemical rounds.

The Leopard 2 (*qv*) entered service in 1978 and various improvements have been either incorporated into the design or retrofitted into service vehicles since that time. In the late 1980s, however, a major improvement programme was set in train, consisting of two elements. The first, designated KWS I, involves installing a new 120mm 52-calibre weapon; this programme, which as of early in year 2000 had not yet been approved, is described in more detail below.

The other programme – KWS II – has been approved and involves a number of modifications, the most obvious external sign of which is the reshaping of the front of the turret, giving it unique > (arrowhead) profile. This is the result of fitting new, removable panels to increase protection against both kinetic energy (ie, APFSDS/APDS) and chemical (ie, HEAT) rounds. Additional armoured panels are also fitted to the skirts to improve protection of the suspension and the side of the hull. The interior of the turret has been lined with a spall inhibitor. The tank's electronic and electrical systems are considerably improved. This includes a new all-electric gun-control system, new navigation system, a modified laser ranging system, a thermal sight for the commander, and a television camera at the rear feeding a monitor on the driver's

Above: The Swedish Strv-122 is a new-build Leopard 2A5 with additional Swedish-developed, armour on the front, sides and turret roof, and a Celsius Command and Control System (TCCS).

console, enabling him to see where he is going when reversing.

The new gun in the KWS I programme is the Rheinmetall smoothbore 120mm, but with a barrel lengthened from 44 calibres (ie, 17ft 4in/5.28m) to 55 calibres (21ft 7in/6.60m). This extra length results in an increase in muzzle velocity and the gun can also fire the new range of APFSDS-T, as well as all existing 120mm ammunition. Despite its extra length and weight, the new gun fits into the existing cradle. A 140mm tank gun is also under development, which, in combination with a bustle-mounted autoloader, would reduce the turret crew to two.

The current status of these programmes is as follows. In 1994 the KWS II package was approved for installation in 225 of the current German fleet of 1,857 Leopard 2s. This was completed by the end of 1998 and the 225 Leopard 2A5s equip six tank battalions in the Crisis Reaction Force. Also in 1994, the Royal Netherlands Army started a programme to modify all 330 of its Leopard 2s to Leopard 2A5 standard; this will be completed by late 2000.

Sweden has ordered 120 new-build Leopard 2A5s under the national designation *Strv*-122 (*Stridsvagn* = battle tank), also known as Leopard 2(S). These not only have all the improvements of the German/Dutch programme, but also have yet further, Swedish-developed, armour protection on the front, sides and turret roof, a modular Celsius tech Tank Command and Control System (TCCS) and a new, eye-safe laser ranging device. These *Strv*-122s are in addition to the 160 ex-German Army Leopard

2A4s delivered in 1995; Sweden has an option on a further 90 *Strv*-122s.

Spain has ordered 219 Leopard 2A5s which are being built under licence, under the designation Leopard 2A5E (E = *Espana*). To fill the gap before these become available, the Spanish Army has obtained 108 Leopard 2A4s from the German Army on a five year lease.

Below: Some 225 Leopard 2s of the German Army have been upgraded to Leopard 2A5 standard and equip six armoured battalions of the Bundesheer's Crisis Reaction Force.

Arjun Main Battle Tank

Country of origin: India.
Crew: 4.
Armament: One 120mm rifled gun; one 7.62mm machine-gun co-axial with main armament; one 12.7mm heavy anti-aircraft machine-gun on turret roof; nine single-barrelled smoke dischargers on each side of the turret.
Armour: Composite
Dimensions: Length (including main armament) 33ft 5in (10.20m); width 12ft 7in (3.85m); height (to turret roof) 7ft 7in (2.32m).
Weight: Combat 128,970lb (58,500kg).
Ground pressure: 11.9lb/in^2 (0.84kg/cm^2).
Engine: MTU 838 Ka-501 10-cylinder, liquid-cooled diesel, 1,400hp at 2,500rpm
Performance: Road speed 45mph (72km/h); range 280 miles (450km); vertical obstacle 3ft 0in (0.9m); trench 8ft 0in (2.43m); gradient 77 per cent.
History: First prototypes in 1984; in low-rate production for Indian Army; less than 100 currently in service.

The Indian Army's armoured corps is huge: 60 armoured regiments, each with 45 tanks, which, together with reserves, makes a requirement for a fleet of well over 3,000 MBTs. Following independence in 1947, the Indian Army was equipped with British tanks left over from the days of the British Indian Army, but it was then decided to establish national tank production facilities. The first tank to be produced was the Vickers MBT, some 2,200 of which were built under licence at the Heavy Vehicles Factory at Avadi, near Madras under the name *Vijayanta* (Victorious). It was then intended to develop a wholly Indian tank, for which the operational requirement was issued in 1972. Design work started in 1974 and the first prototype was running in 1984.

The new project was originally known as MBT-90, after its intended year of fielding, but this proved to be hopelessly optimistic, and the tank was designated *Arjun*, instead. Indeed, the programme soon became so far behind schedule that an assembly line was established to produce the Russian T-72M1 (*Ajeya* in Indian service), initially from kits supplied from Russia, but later using a progressively greater proportion of Indian-built components. Some 1,100 were delivered to the Indian Army

Below: *The Arjun* has a 120mm main armament, which is rifled, due to the Indian Army's continuing requirement for HESH rounds, which cannot be fired from a smoothbore barrel.

Above: An *Arjun* at speed on desert terrain. The programme has suffered great delays (it was once known as MBT-90) but is now back on course, with the tank in production for the Indian Army.

between 1988 and 1994, and there are some officials in India who claim that it would be more cost-effective to produce an improved *Ajeya* rather than continue work on the ever more costly *Arjun*.

Meanwhile, work has continued on the *Arjun*, which was planned to be a particularly ambitious project, with the great majority of components designed and manufactured in India, including a gas-turbine power pack, 120mm rifled gun, hydropneumatic suspension, composite armour and a fully integrated command and fire control system. Such an ambitious programme would have taxed the resources of a country with a long-standing tank and component design and development capabilities, and not surprisingly the Indians over-stretched themselves in some areas.

The *Arjun* is armed with an Indian-designed, rifled 120mm gun. The reason it is rifled is that, like the British, the Indian Army sees a continuing need for using HESH (High Explosive Squash Head) ammunition. The tube is made from electro-slag-refined steel fitted with a fume extractor and is surrounded by a thermal sleeve, but, as far as is known, is not fitted with a muzzle reference system. It fires APFSDS, using a new, high-energy propellant to achieve a significant increase in muzzle velocity, as well as HESH, HEAT, HE and smoke rounds. A total of 39 120mm rounds are carried and these are fired by separate charges using a semi-combustible case. Both gun and ammunition are reported to be a success and are in production.

The propulsion system has, however, been a less satisfactory story. At the time that work started on the *Arjun* it appeared that gas-turbines offered the way-ahead, with such units powering the US Army's M1 and the Russian T-80, and the plan was for the *Arjun* to be similarly powered. But this was discontinued after only a few years of development and replaced by a project for an Indian-designed air-cooled diesel. This proved to take much longer than expected and in the interim the well-proven German Leopard 2 power train (MTU 838 Ka-501 and Renk transmission) was installed in the prototypes, although it is still planned to install the Indian engine in due course.

The tracks are constructed of aluminium alloy with rubber inserts and track pins. There are seven rubber-rimmed road wheels on each side using a hydropneumatic suspension system.

Production of the *Arjun* got under way slowly in the mid- and late-1990s. Early production versions have been issued to the Indian Army but full production is not likely until the early 2000s. The *Arjun* has proved to be a valiant attempt to create a fully fledged Indian national tank and component design, development and production capability and will probably be successful in the longer term, but this is being achieved at the cost of considerable financial outlay and lengthy delays.

153

Merkava Main Battle Tank

Marks 1 to 3.
Country of origin: Israel.
Armament: One M68 105mm rifled gun; one co-axial 7.62mm machine-gun; two 7.62mm anti-aircraft machine-guns; one 60mm mortar.
Armour: See text.
Dimensions: Length (gun forward) 28ft 5in (8.65m); length (hull) 24ft 5in (7.54m); width 12ft 2in (3.70m); height (to turret roof) 8ft 9in (2.66m).
Weight: Combat 132,160lb (60,000kg).
Engine: Teledyne Continental AVDS-1790-6A V-12 diesel developing 900hp.
Performance: Road speed 29mph (46km/h); range 250 miles (400km); vertical obstacle 3ft 1in (0.95m); trench 9ft 10in (3.0m); gradient 70 per cent.
History: In service with the Israeli Army (c1,000).
(*Data are for Mark 1.*)

Since the State of Israel was established in 1949 its Army has had more experience of armoured warfare than any other in the world. The Israeli Armoured Corps has always been forced by circumstances to use a mixture of tank types, some bought overseas and others captured during one of the numerous Arab-Israeli wars. Thus, in 1991 the foreign tanks in service came from three principle sources: British-supplied Centurions (1,080), US-supplied M48A5s (550) and M60s (1,400), and Soviet tanks captured from Arab armies, comprising T-54/T-55s (488) and T-62s (110).

The Israelis began to develop their own armoured warfare doctrines based on their increasingly extensive combat experiences and quickly integrated these disparate

Below: The Merkava MBT was designed after decades of practical experience in the Arab-Israeli wars and incorporates a number of ideas since followed by other tank designers.

tank designs into their overall scheme. Nevertheless, the aim was to design their own tank, which would be tailored to their own needs. Being a small country with much less of a manpower base than their larger neighbours, the Israelis cannot afford large losses and it became particularly evident to them in the 1967 campaign that they needed to give armoured protection top priority in any future MBT design. This left firepower as the second priority and mobility third. The outcome was the Merkava (*Chariot*), the first prototype of which was completed in 1974, although it was not revealed publicly until 1977. The first production vehicles were issued to the Army in 1979 and the type saw initial combat in Lebanon in 1982. Following these early experiences a modified vehicle was developed, designated the Mark 2, and all Mark 1s are being gradually brought up to this standard, with some 600 Merkavas of both marks currently in service with the Israeli Army.

The majority of modern MBTs have the engine at the rear, but the layout of the Merkava is unusual, with the engine and transmission at the front of the tank. This is intended to increase the protection for the crew, since the Israeli Army would much rather save the crew and lose the tank. The hull is made of an outer layer of cast armour, with a welded inside layer, the space between the two being filled by diesel fuel. The driver is seated forward and on the left, with the engine to his right. The engine is a Teledyne Continental AVDS-1790-6A, a more powerful version of that fitted in the US Army's M60, which is also used by the Israeli Army. The Mark 1 used the standard Allison CD-850-6BX semi-automatic transmission, but this has been replaced in the Mark 2 by an Israeli-designed Ashot system whose efficiency is such, it is claimed, that it results in a substantial increase in range. The suspension and road wheels are similar to those used by the Israeli Army's Centurions and there are six road wheels with the drive sprockets at the front and idlers at the rear. There are return rollers and the tops of the tracks have steel covers backed by plates of "special" armour to protect them and the suspension from damage by HEAT weapons.

The turret has an exceptionally small cross-section and a well-sloped front, presenting an extremely small target when the tank is in a hull-down position. There is a layer of "special" armour on the turret front and sides.

The commander and gunner are seated on the right of the turret, with the loader on the left. The main armament is an Israeli-produced version of the M68 105mm gun, which is itself a licence-produced version of the British L7. The barrel is fitted with a thermal sleeve and a fume extractor. The gun is also mounted in the Israeli Centurion, M48 and M60 MBTs, as well as on most of the captured T-54/-55 and T-62s.

The gun has an elevation of +20° and a depression of –8.5°. There is a travelling

Above: A view inside the turret of a Merkava Mark 1, with the gunner's station, offset to the right side of the turret, in view. The peritelescope includes a moving mirror head and electro-optical laser-type rangefinder, magnifications ranging from x8 to x1.

Left: Putting the Merkava's suspension through its paces, a pair of tanks advance over rough terrain on the Golan Heights to take up position in a wood. Visible in the vertical hull rear is a most interesting feature – a rear entry/exit hatch, enabling the crew to escape from the tank and also bestowing the tank with a transport role.

Above: A factory-fresh Merkava Mark 3, the latest variant to enter service with the Israeli Army. Note the entry/exit door.

lock for the gun on the right forward engine deck. The gun fires all the standard 105mm projectiles, as well as the specially-developed M111 APFSDS-T projectile developed by Israel Military Industries and the more recent M413 which has a maximum effective range of about 6,500 yards (5,950m). No fewer than 85 rounds are carried, significantly more than in any other modern MBT.

There is one co-axial 7.62mm machine-gun and two 7.62mm anti-aircraft machine-guns (AAMGs) on flexible mounts on the turret roof; all are of the MAG type, built under licence from FN in Belgium. It is reported that some Merkavas have been fitted with a remotely operated 12.7mm machine-gun in place of one of the two AAMGs. A unique feature is a 60mm mortar, which is loaded and fired from within the turret. Capable of firing HE, smoke and illuminating rounds, this is intended to save valuable 105mm ammunition, and, again, is an interesting result of Israeli combat experience.

Placing the engine at the front creates considerable space at the rear of the tank. This is normally used to house ammunition and the Merkava carries a normal load of 62 rounds, although this can be increased to 85, if required. The space can also be used to accommodate infantrymen or commandos, however, although this is done in exceptional circumstances only. Additional communications facilities can also be installed in place of some of the ammunition to enable the tank to be used as a command post.

The Merkava Mark 3 entered service in 1989, armed with a 120mm smoothbore gun, for which 50 rounds are carried. Other improvements include all-electrical controls and a new series of laser rangefinder. The armour is of a modular design which is not only more effective than that on the Marks 1 and 2 but can also be changed in the field. A new suspension is also fitted, which, in combination with the uprated engine and improved transmission, give enhanced cross-country mobility.

A new MBT is under development. This, it is believed, will be armed with a 140mm smoothbore gun.

Below: A Merkava Mark 3 in side elevation, revealing the 120mm smoothbore gun adopted in place of the M68 105mm rifled gun.

Fiat 3000 Light Tank

Fiat 3000 Model 21, and Model 30 (3000B).
Country of origin: Italy.
Crew: 2.
Armament: Twin SIA or FIAT Model 29 6.5mm machine-guns.
Armour: 6mm (0.24in) minimum, 16mm (0.63in) maximum.
Dimensions: Length (without tail) 11ft 9in (3.61m); length (with tail) 13ft 8in (4.17m); width 5ft 5in (1.64m); height 7ft (2.19m).
Weight: Combat 12,125lb (5,500kg).
Engine: FIAT four-cylinder petrol engine developing 50hp at 1.700rpm.
Performance: Road speed 15mph (24km/h); range 59 miles (95km); vertical obstacle 2ft (0.6m); trench 4ft 11in (1.5m); gradient 60 per cent.
History: Entered service with the Italian Army in 1923 and remained in service until 1943. Also exported to Albania, Ethiopia and Latvia.

In 1918 France supplied Italy with a Schneider tank and a few Renault FT-17 light tanks. Italy requested additional tanks but at that time France could not even meet her own requirements, let alone export orders. FIAT, assisted by Ansaldo and Breda, then started to design a vehicle similar to the FT-17 but using Italian components. FIAT received an order for 1,400 tanks but this was reduced to 100 when World War I ended in 1918. The first prototype was completed in 1920 but it was not until 1923 that it entered service with the Italian Army. Compared with the French Renault FT-17, the Italian FIAT 3000 (or *Carro d'Assalto* FIAT 3000 Model 21) was lighter and much faster.

First models were armed with turret-mounted twin 6.5mm machine-guns with an elevation of +24° and a depression of −17°, 2,000 rounds of machine-gun ammunition being carried. In 1929 a FIAT 3000 was fitted with a 37mm gun in place of the machine-guns, and most surviving examples were rebuilt as the FIAT 3000 Model 30 (or FIAT 3000B). In addition to the new armament the suspension was improved and a more powerful engine, which developed 63hp, was fitted. The 37mm gun was offset to the right and had an elevation of +20° and a depression of −10°, 68 rounds of 37mm ammunition being carried. Some FIAT 3000s were fitted with a radio for use in the command role, and trials versions included a 105mm self-propelled howitzer and another with twin 37mm guns.

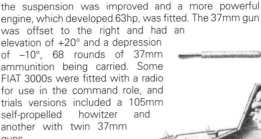
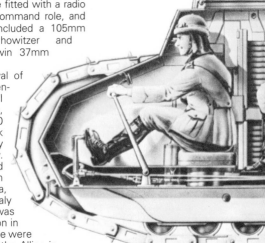

Until the arrival of the British Carden-Loyd Mark VI vehicles in 1929, the FIAT 3000 was the only tank the Italian Army had in quantity. The Italians used the tank in action in Abyssinia, Libya and in Italy itself. The type was last used in action in 1943, when some were encountered by the Allies in their invasion of Sicily.

Above: The Fiat *Carro d'Assalto* Model 30 (3000B), mounting a 37mm gun. Variants included a command vehicle and an experimental 105mm SP gun.

Below: Cut-away view of the Fiat *Carro d'Assalto* Model 21, production version of the Fiat 3000A with turret-mounted twin 6.5mm machine-guns. Later versions mounted a 37mm gun. The vehicle was based on the French Renault FT-17 light tank.

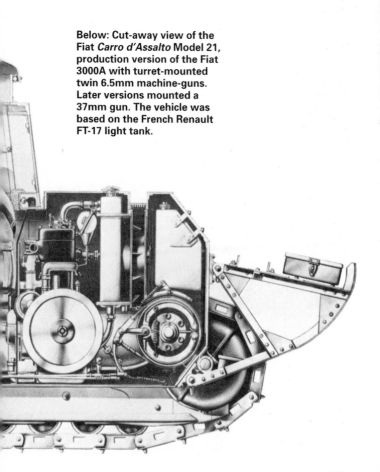

Fiat 2000 Heavy Tank

Country of origin: Italy.
Crew: 10.
Armament: One turret-mounted 65mm gun; seven FIAT 6.5mm machine-guns.
Armour: 20mm (0.79in) maximum; 15mm (0.59in) minimum.
Dimensions: Length 24ft 3in (7.4m); width 10ft 2in (3.1m); height 12ft 6in (3.8m).
Weight: Combat 88,185lb (40,000kg).
Engine: Fiat A12 six-cylinder petrol engine developing 240hp.
Performance: Maximum road speed 3.7mph (6km/h): range 47 miles (75km); vertical obstacle 3ft 3in (1m); trench 9ft 10in (3m).
History: Entered service with Italian Army in 1919–20 and phased out of service in early 1930s.

Whilst the Italian Army took an early interest in armoured cars, it was not until the appearance of Allied tanks on the battlefields of France in 1916 that Italy took any real interest in tracked armoured vehicles. In 1915, however, a Captain Luigi Cassali had designed a tank-type vehicle, a prototype of which was built by the Pavesi company, well known for its cross-country articulated vehicles. This vehicle had two turrets, each fitted with a single machine-gun, but after unsuccessful trials the project was dropped. It should be remembered that the conditions under which the Italian Army fought were not comparable with conditions on the Western Front, and many of the Italian actions were fought in terrain unsuitable for armoured operations. Italy did obtain a French Renault light tank and a Schneider medium tank for trials purposes, but as the French could not supply large numbers it was at first hoped that these types would be built in Italy. In the end, however, the Italians built an improved version of the Renault FT-17, the FIAT 3000, and built their own heavy tank, the FIAT 2000.

Design work on the FIAT 2000 had in fact started in 1916 before the army even issued a requirement. The first two prototypes were completed at the end of 1918 but did not see any action. Most sources have stated that these were followed by four further vehicles in 1920. These remained in service with the Italian Army until at least 1934, when they were finally phased out of service. In many respects the FIAT 2000 was an advanced vehicle, especially when one considers that the FIAT company had no experience of building tracked vehicles of this type.

The driver was seated at the very front of the hull and had excellent vision: a periscope was provided for observation when in action, and a hatch could be opened up at the front when the vehicle was moving up to the front line. The engine was at the rear of the hull with the transmission at the front under the driver's position. Compared with those of other tanks of the period, the interior of the FIAT 2000 was quite roomy as most of the mechanical components were under the floor.

Main armament consisted of a turret-mounted 65mm gun which could be traversed through 360°. The FIAT 2000 was in fact the first tank to mount such a heavy armament in a turret, rather than in the front or side of the hull with limited traverse. In each side of the hull were three machine-guns, and there was a single machine-gun in the rear of the hull. These covered almost every angle of approach to the tank except the front, and most of this angle was in fact covered by the forward machine-guns on each side, which could be traversed through 100°. In the 1930s it is believed that some of the FIAT 2000s had their forward machine-guns replaced by 37mm guns. The suspension consisted of 10 road wheels, of which eight were grouped in pairs on bogie units, these being sprung on leaf springs. The other two road wheels were located between each end bogie and the idler or drive sprocket. Although the FIAT 2000 did not have the cross-country capability of the British tanks of this period, it was superior to the French Saint Chamond and Schneider tanks in this respect, and was also very well armed.

Left: The Fiat 2000 heavy tank, mounting a 65mm gun and six 6.5mm machine-guns.

Carro Veloce CV33 Tankette

Country of origin: Italy.
Crew: 2.
Armament: Twin 8mm FIAT Model 18/35 machine-guns.
Armour: 15mm (0.6in) maximum; 5mm (0.2in) minimum.
Dimensions: Length 10ft 5in (3.16m); width 4ft 7in (1.4m); height 4ft 2in (1.28m).
Weight: Combat 7.571lb (3,435kg).
Ground pressure: 7.1lb/in² (0.5kg/cm²).
Engine: SPA CV3 four-cylinder petrol engine developing 43bhp at 2,400rpm.
Performance: Road speed 26mph (42km/h); range 78 miles (125km); vertical obstacle 2ft 2in (0.65m); trench 4ft 9in (1.45m); gradient 100 per cent.
History: Entered service with the Italian Army in 1933 and phased out of service in 1943. Also used by Afghanistan, Albania, Austria, Bolivia, Brazil, Bulgaria, China, Germany (a few in 1943–44), Greece, Hungary, Iraq and Spain (Civil War).

In 1929 the Italians purchased some British Carden-Loyd Mark VI tankettes and also obtained a licence to manufacture the type in Italy. Twenty-five of these vehicles were built in Italy under the designation CV 29, production being undertaken by Ansaldo with automative components being supplied by FIAT. The CV 29 was armed with a 6.5mm water-cooled machine-gun, later replaced by an air-cooled weapon of the same calibre. Further development resulted in the CV 3, which was tested by the

Right: Heavily-camouflaged L3/33 tankettes of the Italian Army travel through wooded country.

Below: Side view of L3/33 tankette. This was in extensive service with the Italian Army during the initial campaigns in North Africa.

Italian Army in 1931–32, and with modifications this was placed in production as the *Carro Veloce* CV 33.

The original production order was for some 1,300 vehicles, 1,200 armed with machine-guns and 200 (CV 33 special) armed with a 37mm gun. In the end only 300 or so were built, and these were known as the Series I, production being undertaken by FIAT/Ansaldo. these were armed with a single 6.5mm machine-gun. The Series I was followed in production in 1935 by the Series II, and at a later date most Series I vehicles were brought up to Series II standard. Armament consisted of twin FIAT Model 18/35 machine-guns with an elevation of +15° and a depression of –12°, traverse being limited to 12° left and 12° right. A total of 3,200 rounds of machine-gun ammunition was carried.

The hull of the CV 33 was of all-riveted/welded construction with a minimum thickness of 6.5mm (0.256in) and a maximum thickness of 13.5mm (0.53in). The commander/gunner was seated on the left of the hull and the driver on the right. The engine was mounted transversely at the rear of the hull, and power was transmitted to the gearbox in the forward part of the hull by a shaft. The suspension consisted of six small road wheels, with the drive sprocket at the front and the idler at the rear, although there was also an adjustable idler wheel to the rear of the sixth road wheel. There were no track-return rollers. Of the six road wheels, the four centre ones were mounted on two sprung bogies, two wheels to a bogie.

There were a number of variants of the CV 33. The flamethrower was called the *Carro Lancia Fiamme* and had the machine-guns replaced by a flamethrower. Some 109 gallons (500 litres) of flame fuel were carried in a two-wheeled trailer towed behind the tankette. Alternatively, a tank could be mounted on the rear of the hull, the tank holding 13 gallons (60 litres) of flame fuel. The maximum range of the flamethrower was about 110 yards (100m). The vehicle was used in North Africa. The radio model was called the *Carro Radio* and had a loop-type radio aerial on the rear of the hull. The command model was similar but had no armament. An armoured recovery vehicle known as the *Carro Veloce Recupero* was developed to the prototype stage but was not placed in production. This model was unarmed and was provided with a tow bar at the rear of the hull. The bridgelayer was known as he *Passerella* and towed a trailer on which was a bridge 23ft (7m) in length and in four components. The crew had to leave the tankette to assemble the bridge, but this took

less than 10 minutes. The CV 33 could also two a tracked trailer carrying ammunition and supplies, and some vehicles had an 8mm machine-gun over the roof of the fighting compartment for use in the anti-aircraft role. A few vehicles had their machine-guns replaced by the Swiss Solothurn s18–1000 20mm anti-tank gun, which fired an armour-piercing round with a muzzle velocity of 2,460fps (750m/s).

A Sovoia-Marchetti SM82 aircraft was modified to carry a CV 33 recessed under its fuselage, but this was for experimental purposes only. In 1933–34 the CV 33 was followed in production by the CV 35. This had a redesigned hull of bolted construction, and was armed with a single Breda 13.2mm machine-gun. At least one CV 35 had its superstructure removed and a 47mm anti-tank gun mounted on the forward part of the hull, the vehicle being known as the *Semovente* L 3 *da* 47/32. The type did not enter service. The last model to enter service was the L 3/38, which had a new suspension. In 1937 FIAT/Ansaldo built a light tank based on a CV 33 chassis, the L3. This had a redesigned hull and a turret-mounted 20mm gun, but was not placed in production. In 1938 the designation of the CV 33 was changed to L–3–33, and the CV 35 became the L–3–35.

About 2,500 of the CV 33/CV 35 were built both for the Italian Army and for export, although some of the latter were fitted with different armament. The CV 33 was used in the Spanish Civil War, where its short-comings soon became apparent when it encountered the Russian tanks used by the Spanish Republican forces. It saw combat with the Italian Army in Albania, Ethiopia, France, North Africa, Russia and Yugoslavia. The tankette still formed a major part of the Italian armoured forces in North Africa when World War II started, but by that time the design was obsolete and the British had no trouble dealing with the vehicle as its armour was so thin.

Below: The L3/33 (LF) *Carro Lancia Fiamme*. This flame-thrower variant of the tankette had a long-barrelled hooded flame-thrower replacing the machine-guns, with 500 litres of fuel towed in the wheeled trailer.

Carro Armato L 6/40 Light Tank

Country of origin: Italy.
Crew: 2.
Armament: One Breda Model 35 20mm gun; one Breda Model 38 8mm machine-gun co-axial with main armament.
Armour: 30mm (1.26in) maximum; 6mm (0.24in) minimum.
Dimensions: Length 12ft 5in (3.78m); width 6ft 4in (1.92m); height 6ft 8in (2.03m).
Weight: 14,991lb (6,800kg).
Ground pressure: 6.87lb/in^2 (0.61kg/cm^2).
Engine: SPA 180 four-cylinder inline petrol engine developing 70hp.
Performance: Road speed 26mph (42km/h); road range 124 miles (200km); vertical obstacle 2ft 4in (0.7m); trench 5ft 7in (1.7m); gradient 60 per cent.
History: Entered service with the Italian Army in 1941 and used in small quantities by German Army in 1944. In service until the early 1950s.

The L 6/40 was developed from a series of 4.92ton (5,000kg) tracked vehicles developed by FIAT-Ansaldo mainly for the export market. The first prototypes were completed in 1936, one being armed with twin 8mm Breda machine-guns whilst another had a 37mm gun and a co-axial 8mm machine-gun. The Italian Army ordered 283 L 6/40s and these were delivered between 1941 and

1942. From the information available it would appear that a number of these were in fact completed as *Semovente* L40 47mm self-propelled anti-tank guns.

The hull of the L 6/40 was of riveted construction with a minimum thickness of 0.24in (6mm) and a maximum thickness of 1.26in (30mm). The driver was seated at the front of the hull on the right; the turret was offset to the left, and the engine was located at the rear. The suspension consisted of two bogies each with two road wheels, with the drive sprocket at the front and the idler at the rear, and three track-return rollers were provided. The main armament consisted of a 20mm cannon with an elevation of +20° and a depression of −12°, and an 8mm machine-gun was mounted co-axial with the main armament. Some 296 rounds of 20mm and 1,560 rounds of 8mm machine gun ammunition were carried.

The L 6/40 was designed to replace the CV 33 tankette, but it was already obsolete by the time it entered service with the Italian Army in 1941. It was used in Italy, North Africa and Russia. A flamethrower model was developed but this did not enter service. The command model was fitted with radios and had an open roof. The *Semovente* L40 was armed with a 47mm anti-tank gun mounted in the front of the superstructure to the left of the driver. This model had a crew of three, and 49 rounds of 47mm ammunition were carried.

Left: The L 6/40 light tank, with turret-mounted 20mm gun and co-axial 8mm machine-gun. More than 280 L 6/40s were delivered in 1941–42, but it was not employed in significant quantity until 1943–43, when the tank was issued to the armoured groups of Italian cavalry divisions and to reconnaissance units. A number of these tanks were used by Italian forces on the Russian front – the heaviest tanks sent to that theatre by the Italian high command. The tank was also produced in small numbers as a flamethrower, without the 20mm gun. This variant, which never entered service, was some 441lb (200kg) heavier and carried 44 gal (200 litres) of flame fuel. A light assault and support vehicle was based on the chassis of the L 6. This was designated the *Semovente* L40, and mounted a 47mm anti-tank gun.

Carro Armato M 13/40 Medium Tank

M 13/40, M 14/41, M 15/42, P40 (P26), and *Semovente* **M 42M, M 42T.**
Country of origin: Italy.
Crew: 4.
Armament: One 47mm gun; one 8mm machine-gun co-axial with main armament; one 8mm anti-aircraft machine-gun; twin 8mm machine-guns in hull front.
Armour: 42mm (1.65in) maximum; 6mm (0.24in) minimum.
Dimensions: Length 16ft 2in (4.92m); width 7ft 3in (2.2m); height 7ft 10in (2.38m).
Weight: Combat 30,865lb (14,000kg).
Ground pressure: 13.2lb/in² (0.92kg/cm²).
Engine: SPA 8 TMO40 eight-cylinder diesel developing 125hp.
Performance: Road speed 20mph (32km/h); road range 125 miles (200km); vertical obstacle 2ft 8in (0.8m); trench 6ft 11in (2.1m); gradient 70 per cent.
History: Entered service with Italian Army in 1940 and phased out of service in 1942.

The *Carro Armato* M 11/39 was designed in 1936 with the first prototype being completed the following year. This used some suspension components of the L3 tankette. Armament consisted of twin turret-mounted Breda 8mm machine-guns and a 37mm mounted in the right side of the hull. The 37mm gun could be traversed through 30° and had an elevation of +12° and a

Below: A *Carro Armato* **M 13/40 medium tank (No. 1, 3 Ptn, 2 Coy, XI Bn) now preserved as a memorial to Italians killed at El Alamein. The tank was armed with an effective high-velocity 47mm gun but its thin armour made it vulnerable to many anti-tank weapons on the battlefield. At least two Allied units, the British 6th Royal Tank Regiment and the Australian 6th Cavalry, were equipped with captured M 13/40s in 1941.**

depression of –8°, and 84 rounds of 37mm and 2,808 rounds of 8mm ammunition were carried.

The M 11/39, of which only 100 were built, weighed 10.83 tons (11,000kg) and had a crew of three, and saw action in North Africa in 1940–41. It soon became apparent that the main armament would have to be mounted in a turret rather than in the hull front with a limited traverse. The chassis of the M 11/39 was retained, but the hull was redesigned, to form the first prototype of the M 13/40, completed in 1940, with first production tanks being completed in the same year. Main armament consisted of a turret-mounted 47mm gun with an elevation of +20° and a depression of –10°. An 8mm machine-gun was mounted co-axial with the main armament and there was a similar weapon for the anti-aircraft role. Two 8mm machine-guns were mounted in the hull front on the right. Some 104 rounds of 47mm and 3,048 rounds of 8mm ammunition were carried.

The hull was of bolted construction with a minimum thickness of 0.24in (6mm) and a maximum thickness of 1.65in (42mm). The driver and bow machine-gunner were seated in the front of the hull, and the loader and commander in the turret. The commander had to aim and fire the main armament in addition to his other duties. The suspension on each side consisted of four double-wheeled articulated bogies, mounted in two assemblies, each of the latter being carried on semi-elliptic springs. The drive

Above: US Army personnel inspect a captured M 13/40 tank. The type saw service in North Africa, Greece and Yugoslavia. The chassis was also used for a number of self-propelled guns.

sprocket was at the front and the idler at the rear, and there were three track-return rollers.

The M 13/40 was used in North Africa in 1941 and was found to be very prone to breakdowns as it was not designed to operate in desert conditions. The M 13/40 was followed in production by the M 14/41 which had a more powerful engine developing 145hp and fitted with filters to allow it to operate in the desert. The last model in the series was the M 15/42, which entered service in 1943. This had a slightly longer hull than the earlier models and was powered by an eight-cylinder petrol engine which developed 192hp, this giving the tank a top road speed of 25mph (40km/h). Other modifications including the re-siting of the hull escape door on the right of the hull, a longer gun barrel, power-operated turret traverse and heavier armour.

Production of the tanks was undertaken by Ansaldo-Fossati and the following quantities were built: M 13/40 799, M 14/41 1,203 and M 15/42 between 82 and 90. The M 13/40 and M 14/41 were the most important Italian tanks of World War II and were used in North Africa, Greece and Yugoslavia. Many were captured when they ran out of fuel and at least two Allied units, the British 6th Royal Tank Regiment and the Australian 6th Cavalry, were equipped with these tanks for a brief time when British tanks were in short supply in 1941.

The Italians developed a variety of self-propelled artillery based on these

chassis. The *Semovente* M 40, M 41 and M 42 were based respectively on the M 13, M 14 and M 15 chassis. Armament consisted of a Model 35 75mm gun/howitzer with an elevation of +22° and a depression of −12°, traverse being 20° left and 18° right. There was also a command model with the main armament removed. This was armed with a hull-mounted 13.2mm machine-gun and an 8mm anti-aircraft machine-gun. The *Semovente* M42M (75/14) self-propelled gun was to have been based on the P 40 tank chassis but as a result of delays less than 100 were built, and these were based on the M 15/42 chassis. Armament consisted of a 75mm gun with 42 rounds of ammunition. This was followed by the M 42L which had a 105mm gun. When the Germans took over the Ansaldo works they built a model known as the M 42T which had a 75mm gun.

The M 13/30, M 14/41 and M 15/42 were to have been replaced by a new tank designated the P 40 (or P 26). Although design work on this tank started as early as 1940, it was not until 1942 that the first prototype was ready for trials. The delays were caused by changes in the main armament and the difficulty in finding a suitable engine for the tank. The tank entered production in 1943 but did not enter service with the Italian Army, although a few appear to have been used in the static defence role by the Germans in Italy. The P 40 weighed 25.59 tons (26,000kg) and was armed with a 75mm gun and an 8mm co-axial machine-gun. The P 40 was itself to have been followed by the P 43, but this latter only reached the mock-up stage. The Italians also designed a tank called the *Carro Armato Celere Sahariano*, which had a Christie suspension and resembled the Crusader which the Italians encountered in North Africa, but this never entered production.

OF-40 Main Battle Tank

Marks 1 and 2, and OF-40/120.
Country of origin: Italy.
Crew: 4.
Armament: One OTOBreda 105mm rifled gun; one 7.62mm machine-gun co-axial with main armament; one 7.62mm anti-aircraft machine-gun on turret roof (12.7mm machine-gun optional); four single-barrelled smoke launchers on each side of turret.
Armour: All-welded.
Dimensions: Length (including main armament) 30ft 3in (9.22m); width 11ft 6in (3.51m); height (to turret roof) 8ft 0in (2.45m).
Weight: Combat 100,100lb (45,500kg).
Ground pressure: 13.1lb/in^2 (0.92kg/cm^2).
Engine: MTU 10-cylinder, 4-stroke, multi-fuel engine, 830hp at 2,200rpm.
Performance: Road speed 37mph (60km/h); range 370 miles (600km); vertical obstacle 3ft 6in (1.1m); trench 9ft 10in (3m); gradient 60 per cent.
History: First prototype completed 1980; in service with Dubai (36).

Following the end of World War II, the Italian Army used American MBTs for many years. They ordered the M60A1, of which 100 were supplied from US arsenals and a further 200 were produced in Italy by OTOMelara. The Italians were, however, interested in a European tank and had some contact with France and Germany during the European Tank Project. As described in more detail elsewhere in this book, the partners failed to agree; Italy never joined fully, while France and Germany were eventually unable to agree on the other's interpretation of the operational requirement. This led to Germany producing the Leopard 1, for which the Italian Army placed a large order in 1970.

Below: OF-40 on a company test track. It could climb a 3ft 6in (1.1m) vertical obstacle, cross a 9ft 10in (3m) trench, or, as shown here, climb a 60 per cent slope.

Above: The OF-40 (OF = OTOBreda/Fiat) was produced in Italy for export, but only 36 (plus 3 ARVs) were ever sold, all to Dubai. It weighed 40 tons and was armed with a 105mm rifled gun.

The Italian Army eventually received 920 of the MBT version, of which the first 200 were produced by Krauss-Maffei in Germany and the remaining 720 by OTOBreda in Italy, with production ending in 1978. The Italian Army also took delivery of 241 specialized versions (AVLB, 64; ARV, 137; and AEV, 40), of which 81 were produced in Germany and the remaining 160 in Italy. Having gained such experience, OTOBreda decided to develop a new tank specifically for export and combined with Fiat to design and develop the OF-40 (O = OTOBreda; F = Fiat; 40 = 40 tons all up weight), with the first prototype running in 1980.

Outwardly, the OF-40 bears some resemblance to the Leopard 1A4. The hull is of all-welded construction, with the driver at the front right and the engine compartment at the rear. The remaining three men are in the all-welded turret with the commander and gunner on the right and the loader on the left. The gun is a 105mm 52-calibre weapon, which was designed and built by OTOBreda, but fires all types of NATO standard 105mm ammunition. The tube is rifled, has a bore evacuator and is surrounded by a thermal jacket. As built, the gun was not fitted with a stabilizer, although this was an optional extra. A total of 57 rounds are carried. Secondary armament consisted of two 7.62mm machine-guns, one co-axial with the main gun and one on a flexible-mounting on the turret roof, but either or both could be replaced by 12.7mm machine-guns if required by the operator. The fire control system was designed specifically for the OF-40 by Officine Gallileo. The power train was the responsibility of Fiat, who produced a power-pack built around an MTU multi-fuel, liquid-cooled engine with a power output of 830bhp at 2,300rpm. The transmission system was produced by ZF (Zahnradfabrik), with four forward and two reverse gears.

A total of 18 Mark 1 tanks was completed and delivered between 1981 and 1984. Meanwhile, the manufacturers had developed a Mark 2 version, which differed from the Mark 1 in incorporating a Galileo fire-control system, day/night periscope for the commander and a low-light television camera. Some 18 Mark 2s were produced and delivered to Dubai between 1984 and 1985, and all Mark 1s were then upgraded to the new standard. Three ARVs (armoured recovery vehicles) were also produced for Dubai on the OF-40 chassis. The OF-40 was offered to various other countries, including Egypt, Greece, Spain and Thailand, but Dubai remains the only purchaser and the OF-40 is no longer being marketed. A further development the OF-40/120 armed with a 120mm smoothbore gun was also developed but no orders were placed.

C1 Ariete Main Battle Tank

Country of origin: Italy.
Armament: One OTO Melara 120mm smoothbore gun; one 7.62mm co-axial machine-gun; one 7.62mm anti-aircraft machine-gun.
Armour: See text.
Dimensions: Length (gun forward) 31ft 3in (9.52m); length (hull) 24ft 11in (7.60m); width 11ft 10in (3.6m); height (commander's cupola) 8ft 0in (2.45m).
Weight: Combat 119,000lb (54,000kg).
Engine: One IVECO V-12 MTCA turbo-charged inter-cooler 12-cylinder diesel developing 1,300hp at 2,300rpm.
Performance: Road speed +40mph (+65km/h); range +342 miles (+550km); vertical obstacle 6ft 10in (2.1m); trench 9ft 10in (3.0m); gradient 60 per cent.
History: First prototype 1986; Italian Army ordered 200; entered service 1995; production complete by 2002.

Following the end of World War II the Italian Army used American MBTs for many years. They ordered the M60A1, of which 100 were supplied from US arsenals and a further 200 were locally-built by OTO Melara. The Italians were, however, interested in a European tank and had some contact with France and Germany during the European Tank project which resulted, after the nations had agreed to split, in the AMX-30 and Leopard 1. In 1970 the Italian Army ordered Leopard 1s from Germany. The initial order was for 200 Leopard A1 MBTs, which were delivered from Krupp-MaK in 1971/72, followed by 69 ARVs and 12 AEVs. A further 720 MBTs, 68 ARVs, 28 AEVs and 64 AVLBs were built by OTO-Melara under a licence agreement.

OTO-Melara, in conjunction with Fiat then designed the first Italian post-

Below: The Italian-designed and built C1 *Ariete* represents a major step forward in the country's indigenous tank-building programme. It entered service in 1995.

war MBT, the OF-40 (O = OTO-Melara, F = Fiat, 40 = approximate combat weight in tons). This neat and powerful-looking tank was designed specifically for export (see separate entry); sales amounted to 36 MBTs and 3 ARVs, all for the United Arab Emirates.

The Italian Army issued a requirement for a new MBT in 1982, for which one of the criteria was that it must be manufactured in Italy. Design work started in 1984 and the OTO-Melara/Iveco Fiat consortium had the first prototype up and running in 1986, with the remaining five prototypes completed by 1988.

The C1 has a combat weight of 105,725lb (48,000kg) and is armed with a 120mm smoothbore gun, which has been designed and manufactured in Italy by OTO Melara. Like other such weapons, the tube is fitted with a muzzle reference system and fume extractor, and is covered by a thermal sleeve. The chamber is identical with that on the Rheinmetall 120mm smoothbore, thus ensuring that the same ammunition can be used in both types of weapon. The gun fires APFSDS and HEAT-MP rounds, together with smoke and illuminating rounds, a total of 42 being carried, 15 in the bustle and 27 in the hull. The gun is mounted in a fixed mantlet and has a maximum elevation of 20° and depression of –9°. A two-axis stabilization system is fitted. There are also eight smoke dischargers, four on each side of the turret.

The layout of the four-man crew is conventional. The driver sits under the glacis plate forward and to the right. The remainder of the crew are in the turret with the commander and the gunner on the right of the main gun and the loader to its left. The hull is of all-welded steel construction and there is a layer of "advanced armour" on the nose and glacis plate. The turret is well-shaped with a well-angled face, unlike some modern tanks (such as early Leopard 2s) which have a vertical face. .

The torsion-bar suspension system has seven roadwheels with four return rollers. The suspension and upper part of the track are protected by skirts.

Type 89B Medium Tank

Country of origin: Japan.
Armament: One type 90 57mm gun; one 6.5mm machine-gun in turret rear
one 6.5mm machine-gun in hull front.
Armour: 17mm (0.67in) maximum; 10mm (0.39in) minimum.
Dimensions: Length 14ft 1in (4.3m); width 7ft (2.15m); height 7ft 2in (2.2m)
Weight: Combat 25.353lb (11,500kg).
Engine: Mitsubishi six-cylinder inline diesel developing 120hp at 1,800rpm.
Performance: Road speed 17mph (27km/h); range 100 miles (160km)
vertical obstacle 3ft (0.914m); trench 6ft 7in (2m); gradient 60 per cent.
History: Entered service with the Japanese Army in 1934 and remained in
service until at least 1943.

After the end of World War I, the Japanese purchased in Europe a number of
tanks for experimental purposes. The first tank of Japanese design and
construction was the Type 87, or Experimental Tank Number 1, built in 1927
at the Osaka Arsenal. This tank had a crew of five and was powered by an
eight-cylinder water-cooled petrol engine which developed 140hp, giving the
tank a top speed of 12.5mph (20km/h). Armament consisted of a turret-
mounted 57mm gun, a single 7.2mm machine-gun in a turret at the front of
the hull, and another machine-gun in a similar turret at the rear of the hull. This
was followed in 1929 but the Type 89 Experimental Tank Number 2. This
weighed 9.84 tons (10,000kg) and was armed with a turret-mounted 37mm
gun, a machine-gun in the turret rear and another machine-gun in the hull
front. Its Daimler six-cylinder petrol engine gave it a top speed of 15mph
(25km/h). This was then placed in production by Mitsubishi as the Type 89
medium tank. The Type 89 was powered by a petrol engine, although later
models had a diesel, the petrol-engined model then becoming known as the
Type 89A.

The Type 89B, sometimes called the Type 94 as it first appeared in 1934,
replaced the Type 89A in production: the most significant improvement was
the installation of a six-cylinder air-cooled diesel which offered a number of
advantages over the earlier petrol engines, including improved safety and
easier starting in cold climates. Other changes included a new turret and a
one-piece glacis plate rather than the two-piece glacis plate of the earlier
model. Armament consisted of a turret-mounted Type 90 57mm gun, a Type
91 6.5mm machine-gun mounted in the rear of the turret and a similar
weapon in the hull front on the left. Some 100 rounds of 57mm and 2,745

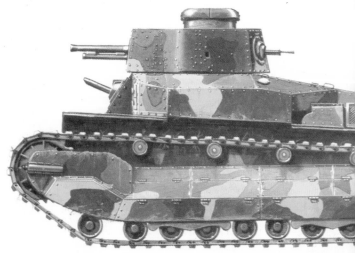

Above: The Japanese Type 89B medium tank, seen here in China where it was in extensive operational use, was the standard medium tank throughout the 1930s. The Japanese flags are for aerial recognition.

rounds of machine-gun ammunition were carried. The hull was of all-riveted construction with the driver at the front on the right and the bow machine-gunner to his left. The turret was in the centre of the hull and was provided with a cupola for the commander. The engine and transmission were at the rear of the hull. The suspension consisted of nine small wheels with the idler at the front and the drive sprocket at the rear. Four track-return rollers were fitted. An unditching tail was provided at the rear of the hull. The Type 89 saw action in China from 1932, and was also employed in the early stages of World War II, some being used in the Philippines campaign.

Further development of the Type 87 Experimental Tank Number 1 resulted in the Type 91 heavy tank, which was not completed until 1932 weighing some 18 tons (18,290kg) and powered by a six-cylinder BMW aircraft engine developing 224hp. This gave the tank a top road speed of 15mph (25km/h) and an operating range of about 100 miles (160km). Armament consisted of a 70mm turret-mounted gun with a machine-gun in the turret rear. There was also a machine-gun turret at the front of the hull and a similar turret at the rear. The Type 91 was followed by the 26-ton 5-crew Type 95 heavy tank, although it would appear that few of these were built. This had a turret with a 70mm gun and a machine-gun in the main turret rear, whilst the front turret had a 37mm gun and the rear turret a machine-gun. There were a number of further heavy tank projects, but none of these ever reached service. It is even believed that the Japanese were building a 98.4 ton (100,000kg) tank at one time.

Left: A Type 89B tank as used in Manchuria. Note the special tail to assist in trench crossing. The tank entered service in 1934 and served into World War II.

179

Type 95 HA-GO Light Tank

Country of origin: Japan.
Crew: 3.
Armament: One Type 94 37mm gun; Type 91 6.5mm machine-gun in hull front (see text).
Armour: 12mm (0.47in) maximum; 6mm (0.25in) minimum.
Dimensions: Length 14ft 4in (4.38m); width 6ft 9in (2.057m); height 7ft 2in (2.184m).
Weight: Combat 16,314lb (7,400kg).
Ground pressure: 8.7lb/in² (0.61kg/cm²).
Engine: Mitsubishi Model NVD 6120 six-cylinder air-cooled diesel developing 120hp at 1,800rpm.
Performance: Road speed 28mph (45km/h); range 156 miles (250km); vertical obstacle 2ft 8in (0.812m); trench 6ft 7in (2m); gradient 60 per cent.
History: Entered service with Japanese Army in 1935 and remained in service until 1945.

In 1934 Mitsubishi Heavy Industries built the prototype of a new light tank, which was tested in both China and Japan, and followed by a second prototype the following year. This was standardised as the Type 95 light tank but was also known as the *HA-GO* (this being the Mitsubishi name) or the *KE-GO* (this being its official Japanese Army name). Although most sources state that Mitsubishi built the prototype, others claim that these were built at the Sagami Arsenal.

The Type 95 was used by the cavalry and the infantry, and saw action in both China and throughout the World War II (or the Great East Asia War as the Japanese call it). Production amounted to about 1,250 tanks, most of which were built by Mitsubishi although numerous other companies and arsenals were also involved in component manufacture. When it was originally built the Type 95 compared well with other light tanks of that period, but by the early part of World War II it had become outdated, as indeed had most Japanese armoured vehicles. The Japanese used the Type 95 in small units or wasted them in the static defence role in many of the islands that they overran in the Pacific area.

The hull of the tank was of riveted and welded construction varying in thickness from 0.35in (9mm) to 0.55in (14mm). The driver was seated at the front of the hull on the right, with the bow machine-gunner to his left. The commander, who also had to load, aim and fire the gun, was seated in the

turret, which was offset to the left of the hull. The engine and transmission were at the rear of the hull, and the crew could reach the engine from within the hull. The inside of the tank was provided with a layer of asbestos padding in an effort to keep the temperature as low as possible, and this also gave the crew some protection against personal injury when the tank was travelling across very rough country. There was a space between the asbestos and the hull to allow air to circulate. The suspension was of the well-tried bellcrank type and consisted of four road wheels (two per bogie), with the drive sprocket at the front and the idler at the rear. There were two track-return rollers. Some of the Type 95s used in Manchuria had their suspensions modified as it was found that severe pitching occurred when the tank was crossing the local terrain, and these were redesignated the Type 35 (Special).

Armament consisted of a turret-mounted 37mm tank gun which could fire both HE and AP rounds, and a Type 61 6.5mm machine-gun mounted in the

Right and below: Front, rear and top views of Type 95 *HA-GO* light tank. This entered service with the Japanese Army in 1935 and remained in service until 1945, although by this time it was hopelessly out of date by any standard. One of the many disadvantages of the tank was that the commander had to load, aim and fire the 37mm gun. Some 1,250 HA-GO tanks were built.

front of the hull with a traverse of 35° left and right. Later the Type 61 gun was replaced by a Type 97 7.7mm machine-gun and a similar weapon was mounted in the turret in the 5 o'clock position, this being operated by the commander/gunner. Later in the war the 37mm Type 94 tank gun was replaced by a Type 98 tank gun, which had a higher muzzle velocity. Some 119 rounds of 37mm and 2,970 rounds of machine-gun ammunition were carried. A number of tanks were also fitted with smoke dischargers on the sides of the hull, towards the rear.

There were a number of variants of the Type 95 light tank, including an amphibious version. In 1943 some Type 95s had their 37mm guns replaced by a 57mm gun as fitted to the Type 97 medium tank, and these vehicles then became the Type 3 light tank. The Type 3 was followed by the Type 4 light tank in 1944: this was a Type 95 with the standard turret removed and replaced by the complete Type 97 medium tank turret with its 47mm gun. The Type 95 was to have been replaced by the Type 98 light tank, and prototypes of this were completed as early as 1938 by both Hino Motors and Mitsubishi Heavy Industries. This did not enter production until 1942, and only 100 seem to have been built (some sources state that 200 were built) before production was stopped in 1943. This model had a more powerful engine, which gave it a higher road speed, and thicker armour. Its suspension consisted of six road wheels wit the drive sprocket at the front and the idler at the rear, there being three return rollers. The driver was seated at the front of the hull in the centre. Armament consisted of a 37mm Type 100 tank gun and two Type 97 7.7mm machine-guns.

Other light tanks developed by Japan included the Improved Model 98 which had four road wheels, idler at the front and drive sprocket at the rear. No return rollers were fitted as the top of the track rested on the road wheels. Finally, there were the Type 2 (less than 30 built) and the Type 5, only one of which was built by Hino Motors before the end of the war.

Below: Type 95 *HA-GO* tank in typical operating environment. The inside of the tank was provided with a layer of asbestos padding in an effort to keep the temperature as low as possible, as well as giving the crew some protection against personal injury when the tank was crossing very rough country. Air was allowed to circulate between this and the hull.

Above: A column of Type 95 *HA-GO* light tanks with their main and secondary armament removed. These were probably being used for carrying ammunition or other supplies.

Below: A column of Type 95 light tanks moves forward during the Japanese invasion of Luzon in the Philippines in 1941/42.

Type 97 CHI-HA Medium Tank

Country of origin: Japan.
Crew: 4.
Armament: One type 90 57mm gun; one 7.7mm Type 97 machine-gun in turret rear; one 7.7mm Type 97 machine-gun in bow.
Armour: 25mm (0.98in) maximum; 8mm (0.3in) minimum.
Dimensions: Length 18ft 1 in (5.516m); width 7ft 8in (2.33m); height 7ft 4in (2.23m).
Weight: Combat 33,069lb (15,000kg).
Engine: Mitsubishi 12-cylinder air-cooled diesel developing 170hp at 2,000rpm.
Performance: Road speed 24mph (38km/h); range 130 miles (210km); vertical obstacle 2ft 6in (0.812m); trench 8ft 3in (2.514m); gradient 57 per cent.
History: Entered service with the Japanese Army in 1938 and continued in service until 1945. Also used by China after World War II.

The standard Japanese medium tank in the 1930s was the Type 89, but by 1936 it had become apparent that this would have to be replaced by a more modern vehicle. The General Staff Office and the Engineering Department could not agree on the best design, so two different prototypes were built. Osaka Arsenal built a prototype to the design of the General Staff, called the *CHI-NI*, whilst Mitsubishi built the model of the Engineering Department, called the *CHI-HA*.

The *CHI-NI* weighed just under 9.84 tons (10,000kg) and was powered by a six-cylinder air-cooled diesel developing 135hp, which gave the tank a top

speed of 18.5mph (30km/h). The *CHI-NI* had a three-man crew, and was armed with a 57mm type 90 tank gun and a 6.5mm Type 91 machine-gun.

The Mitsubishi design was much heavier and weighed 15 tons (15,241kg). It was powered by a Mitsubishi 12-cylinder air-cooled diesel which developed 170hp and gave the tank a top road speed of 24mph (38km/h). Armament consisted of a 57mm gun and two 7.7mm machine-guns. The *CHI-HA* had a crew of four, of whom two were in the turret. Both of these prototypes were completed in 1937 and were subjected to comparative trials. Both tanks had good and bad points, however, and it was not until war broke out in China that it was decided to place the Mitsubishi tank in production as the Type 97 (*CHI-HA*) medium tank. Even today, many feel that the *CHI-NI* could have been developed into a first-class light tank.

Most Type 97s were built by Mitsubishi, although other companies, including Hitachi, also built the tank. The hull was of riveted and welded construction. The driver was seated at the front of the hull on the right, with the bow machine-gunner to his left. The two-man turret was in the centre of the hull and offset to the right. The engine was at the rear of the hull, and

Left and below: Front and rear views of the Type 97 medium tank clearly showing the turret offset to the right of the hull and the 7.7mm Type 97 machine gun in the rear of the turret. Main armament was a 57mm Type 90 gun with another 7.7mm Type 97 machine-gun in the bow to left of the driver's position.

Left: A Type 97 tank of 3rd Company, 7th Tank Regiment, advances through the jungle on the Bataan peninsula during the invasion of the Philippines in 1942. Note the smoke dischargers above the 57mm gun and the radio frame aerial circumscribing the turret which was a characteristic feature of Japanese tanks.

power was transmitted to the gearbox in the front of the hull by a propeller-shaft which ran down the centreline of the hull. The suspension consisted of six dual rubber-tired road wheels, with the drive sprocket at the front and the idler at the rear. There were three track-return rollers, although the centre one supported the inside of the track only. The four central bogie wheels were paired and mounted on bellcranks resisted by armoured compression springs. Each end road wheel was independently bellcrank-mounted to the hull in a similar fashion.

Armament consisted of a short-barrelled 57mm Model 97 tank gun, firing HE and AP rounds, a 7.7mm Model 97 machine-gun in the rear of the turret and a machine-gun of the same type in the bow of the tank. The main armament had an elevation of +11° and a depression of –9°, turret traverse being 360°. Two sets of trunnions allowed the gun to be traversed independently of the turret. The inner vertical trunnions, set in a heavy steel bracket fitted to the cradle, permitted a 5° left and right traverse. Some 120 rounds (80 HE and 40 AP) of 57mm and 2,350 rounds of machine-gun ammunition were carried. The large provision of HE ammunition compared to other tanks of this period was because the Japanese believed that the role of the tank was to support the infantry rather than to destroy enemy armour.

Compared with those of earlier Japanese tanks, the turret of the Type 97 was a great improvement: at last the tank commander could command the tank rather than operate the main armament. In late years, the large-diameter turret-ring fitted enabled the tank to be up-armed as more powerful weapons became available. As a result of combat experience gained against Soviet forces during the Nomonhan incident of 1939, it was decided that a gun with a higher muzzle velocity was required. A new turret was designed by Mitsubishi and when installed on the Type 97 it raised the tank's weight to 15.75 tons (16,000kg). These tanks were known as the Type 97 (Special). The gun fitted was the 47mm Type 1 (1941), which had a long barrel by Japanese standards and could fire both HE and AP rounds. The latter had a muzzle velocity of 2,700fps (823m/s) and would penetrate 2.76in (70mm) of armour at a range of 500 yards (457m). The breech-block was of the semi-automatic vertical sliding type. Some 104 rounds of 47mm and 2,575 rounds of machine-gun ammunition were carried.

There were many variants of the Type 97 medium tank: flail type mine-clearing tank, bulldozer tank, a variety of self-propelled guns, an anti-aircraft tank with a 20mm gun, bridge laying tank and a number of different engineer

Above left: Japanese Type 97 tanks drive down a road at Bukit Timah, Singapore. The main role of these was infantry support.

Above: Type 97 *CHI-HA* medium tanks in Singapore. One of the major improvements of this tank over earlier Japanese tanks was the provision of a two-man turret which enabled the commander to command the tank rather than operating the main armament.

and recovery models, to name a few. One of the most unusual models was the ram tank (*HO-K*), which had its turret removed and a steel prow mounted at the front of the hull, developed for clearing a path through forests in Manchuria.

The Type 97 medium tank was followed by the Type 1 medium tank, or *CHI-NE*. This weighed 17.2 tons (17,476kg) and its armour was increased to a maximum of 2in (50mm). It was powered by a Mitsubishi Type 100 12-cylinder air-cooled diesel which developed 240hp at 2,000rpm. Armament consisted of a type 1 47mm gun and two type 97 7.7mm machine-guns, one in the turret rear and one in the hull front. This was followed by the Type 3 (*CHI-NU*) medium tank in 1943. This had the same hull as the Type 1, but a new turret was fitted, increasing weight to 18.8 tons (19,100kg), which reduced top speed to 24mph (38km/h). Armament consisted of a 75mm Type 3 tank gun with a 7.7mm machine-gun in the hull front, there being no machine-gun in the turret rear. Production of the Type 3 commenced in 1944 but only some 50 or 60 examples were built. The Type 4 (*CHI-TO*) had a longer chassis and weighed 30 tons (30,480kg). This was armed with a turret-mounted 75mm gun and a bow-mounted 7.7mm machine-gun, and only a few of these were built.

The final Japanese medium tank was the Type 5 (*CHI-RI*). This weighed 37 tons (37,594kg) and was armed with a turret-mounted 75mm gun and a bow-mounted 37mm gun. Its armour had a maximum thickness of 3in (75mm) and it was powered by a BMW aircraft engine developing 550hp at 1,500rpm. This gave the tank a top road speed of 28mph (45km/h). The suspension consisted of eight road wheels with the drive sprocket at the front and the idler at the rear, and there were three track-return rollers. This tank did not reach the production stage, however. If it had, it would have been a difficult tank for the Americans to destroy, although by the end of the war, the superior M26 Pershing had been deployed to the Pacific area.

Type 97 (2597) Te-ke/Ke-ke Tankette

Country of origin: Japan.
Crew: 2.
Armament: One 37mm type 94 gun (see text).
Armour: 12mm (0.47in) maximum.
Dimensions: Length 12ft 1in (3.682m); width 5ft 11in (1.803m); height 5ft 10in (1.773m).
Weight: Combat 10,469lb (4,748kg).
Engine: Ikega four-cylinder inline air-cooled diesel developing 65hp at 2,300rpm.
Performance: Maximum road speed 26mph (42km/h); range 155 miles (250km); trench 5ft 7in (1.701m); gradient 60 per cent.
History: Entered service with the Japanese Army in 1938 and remained in service up to 1945.

The Type 97 tankette (or *Te-ke/Ke-ke*) was developed to replace the earlier Type 94 tankette which had proved rather unreliable in service. Two different prototypes of the Type 97 were built by the Tokyo Motor Industry (later known as Hino Motors), with engines supplies by Ikega. The first prototypes were completed in 1937. The initial model had the engine and driver at the front, with the turret at the rear, whilst the later model had the engine moved to the rear to facilitate communication between the driver and the gunner. After trials the second model was standardised as the Type 97 tankette, and this entered service with the Japanese Army in 1938.

The Type 97 was the last tankette to be adopted by the Japanese Army as by the start of World War II this type of vehicle had become obsolete. Production of the vehicle continued well into the war, however, and the type was built in larger numbers than any other Japanese tankette. The vehicle had a hull of riveted

construction, with the driver at the front of the vehicle on the left and the commander, who had to load, aim and fire the gun, in the turret located in the centre of the hull. The engine and transmission were at the rear. The suspension consisted of two bogies, each with two wheels, with the drive sprocket at the front and the idler at the rear, and there were two track-return rollers. Armament consisted of a 37mm gun with a total of 96 rounds of ammunition. Some models were armed with a single 7.7mm machine-gun in place of the 37mm gun.

There were a number of variants of the Type 97 tankette including one with the turret removed, engine moved forward and a fully enclosed cargo area at the rear. This model was used for a wide variety of roles including those of ammunition carrier, observation post vehicle, barrage balloon mooring vehicle and self-propelled gun with a 37mm or 47mm anti-tank gun mounted at the rear of the hull.

Above and left: Japanese Type 97 tankette as examined by the British School of Tank Technology. In addition to commanding the tank the commander also had to operate the turret-mounted 37mm gun (or a 7.7mm MG).

Type 94/Type 92 Tankette

Country of origin: Japan.
Crew: 2.
Armament: One 6.5mm machine-gun.
Armour: 12mm (0.47in) maximum; 4mm (0.16in) minimum.
Dimensions: Length 10ft 1in (3.08m); width 5ft 4in (1.62m); height 5ft 4in (1.62m).
Weight: Combat 7,496lb (3,400kg).
Engine: Four-cylinder air-cooled petrol engine developing 32hp at 2,500rpm.
Performance: Road speed 25mph (40km/h); range 130 miles (208km); vertical obstacle 1ft 8in (0.508m); trench 4ft 7in (1.4m); gradient 60 per cent.
History: Entered service in 1934 and still in service in 1943 at least.

In the late 1920s the Japanese purchased six British Carden-Loyd Mark VI machine-gun carriers, and some time subsequently two Mark VIb carriers. As a result of trials with these vehicles the Japanese decided to develop a similar vehicle. The prototype was built in 1933–34 by the Tokyo Gas and Electric Industry (later to become Hino Motors) and after trials in both China and Japan it was standardised as the Type 94 tankette, although American sources have always referred to it as the Type 92 tankette.

The hull of the tankette was of riveted construction, with the engine and driver at the front and the small turret at the rear of the hull. A large door was provided in the rear of the hull so that stores could be loaded quickly. Armament consisted of a single 6.5mm machine-gun in a turret with manual traverse. The suspension was designed by Tomio Hara and was similar to that used on most Japanese tanks. It consisted of four bogies (two on each side), these being suspended by bellcranks resisted by armoured compression springs placed horizontally one ach side of the hull, externally. Each bogie had two small rubber-tired road wheels with the drive sprocket at the front and the idler at the rear, and there were two track-return rollers. When in service, the Type 94 was found to be very prone to throwing its tracks when it made a high speed turn. Further redesign work was carried out on the suspension and the small idler was replaced by a bigger idler, which was now on the ground, but it did not solve the basic problem. This model was powered by an air-cooled petrol engine which developed 35hp at 2,500rpm. Armament initially consisted of a single Type 91 6.5mm machine-gun, although in later models this was replaced by a single 7.7mm machine-gun. Some are reported to have been fitted with a 37mm gun.

The primary role of the Type 94 was to carry supplies in the battlefield area, but it was often used in the reconnaissance role for which it was totally unsuited as its armour could be penetrated by ordinary rifle bullets. It was often used to tow a tracked ammunition trailer in a fashion similar to the British and French tankettes of this period. The Type 92 was replaced in service by the Type 97.

Another interesting vehicle of this period was the so-called Type 92 combat car developed for the cavalry. The first prototype was completed by the Ishikawajima Motor Works in 1932, and after trials the vehicle was standardised as the Type 92 and was used in China in the 1930s. The vehicle weighed 3.45 tons (3,500kg) and was powered by a six-cylinder air-cooled petrol engine. This gave it a top road speed of 25mph (40km/h) and an operational range of about 124 miles (200km). The Type 92's hull was of all-welded construction with some of its components riveted into position. The driver was seated at the front of the hull on the left with the 12.7mm machine-gun and gunner to his right. This weapon could also be used against low-flying aircraft, although its lack of full traverse was a disadvantage. The commander's turret had a traverse of 360° and was armed with a 6.5mm machine-gun. The engine and

Above: A convoy of Type 94 tankettes. These were also known as the Type 92 in Western sources. In 1936, each Japanese Infantry Division had a Tankette Company which had 6 Type 94s, for use in reconnaissance role.

transmission were at the rear of the hull. The suspension consisted of six small road wheels with the drive sprocket at the front and the idler at the rear, there being three track-return rollers. Some Type 92s were later rebuilt with four larger road wheels and two return rollers as the earlier Type 92's suspension had proved rather weak. There was also an amphibious model of the Type 92 combat car driven in the water by a propeller, but this was not adopted for service. The Type 92 was not built in very large numbers and was replaced by 1940.

Below: Side elevation of the Japanese Type 94/92 tankette which was based on the British Carden-Loyd Mk VI MG carrier acquired in the late 1920s.

Type 2 KA-MI Amphibious Tank

Country of origin: Japan.
Crew: 4–5.
Armament: On 37mm gun; one 7.7mm machine-gun co-axial with main armament; one 7.7mm machine-gun in bow of tank.
Armour: 13mm (0.51in) maximum; 9mm (0.35in) minimum.
Dimensions: Length 24ft 4in (7.416m); width 9ft 2in (2.794m); height 7ft 8in (2.336m).
Weight: Combat (with pontoons) 24,915lb (11,300kg).
Engine: Six-cylinder air-cooled diesel developing 120hp.
Performance: Road speed 23mph (37km/h); water speed 6mph (9.6km/h); road range 124 miles (200km); water range 93 miles (150km); vertical obstacle 2ft 5in (0.736m); trench 6ft 7in (2.006m); gradient 50 per cent.
History: Entered service with the Japanese Marines in 1942 and remained in service until 1945.

The Japanese started experimenting with amphibious armoured vehicles as early as 1928, and up to 1940 most work was undertaken by the Japanese Army. Then the Japanese Navy took over the development of amphibious vehicles as these were to be used by the Marines. A whole series of vehicles was developed, including the *KA-MI-SHA* (Type 1), *KA-MI-SHA* (Type 2), *KA-CHI-SHA* (Type 3), *KA-TSU-SHA* (Type 4), *KA-TSU-SHA* II (also known as the Type 4) and finally the *TO-KU-SHA* (Type 5).

The Type 2 used many components of the Type 95 light tank. The hull

was redesigned, and was of all-welded construction and fully sealed. Large pontoons were fitted front and rear to give the vehicle additional buoyancy. These were constructed of 0.12in (3mm) steel plate. The front pontoon was divided into eight compartments to minimise the effects of damage from shell fire. In the water the tank was propelled by two propellers driven by the main engine via transfer case. The Type 2 was steered in the water by two rudders, which were operated by the tank commander from his turret. Once ashore the pontoons were released by operating hand-wheels which controlled split-finger type pincer-clamps. The tank was armed with a 37mm gun in a turret with a traverse of 360°, a 7.7mm machine-gun mounted co-axially with the main armament, and a similar weapon in the bow of the tank on the left. Some 132 rounds of 37mm and 3,500 rounds of 7.7mm machine-gun ammunition were carried.

These tanks were normally launched from ships or landing-craft offshore, and they would then head for the shore, cross the reef and, once ashore, discard their pontoons and head inland to their objectives. Some of the Japanese amphibious vehicles were designed to be carried on the decks of submarines whilst others could carry a naval torpedo on each side of the hull!

Below: The Japanese Type 2 *KA-MI* light amphibious tank. The end pontoons could be removed for land operation.

Type 61 Main Battle Tank

Country of origin: Japan.
Crew: 4.
Armament: One 90mm gun; one M1919A4 .3in machine-gun co-axial with main armament; one M2 .5in anti-aircraft machine-gun.
Armour: 2.52in (60mm) maximum.
Dimensions: Length (overall) 26ft 10 1/2in (8.19m); length (hull) 20ft 8in (6.3m); width 9ft 8in (2.95m); height 10ft 4in (3.16m).
Weight: Combat 77,162lb (35,000kg).
Ground pressure: 13.5lb/in^2 (0.95kg/cm^2).
Engine: Mitsubishi Type 12 HM 21 WT 12-cylinder diesel developing 600hp at 2,100rpm.
Performance: Road speed 28mph (45km/h); range 124 miles (200km); vertical obstacle 2ft 3in (0.685m); trench 8ft 2in (2.489m); gradient 60 per cent.
History: Entered service with the Japanese Ground Self-Defence Force (JGSDF) in 1962. Being phased out of service, with some 100 remaining in 1999.

Right: The Type 61 was the first tank to be developed in Japan after the end of World War II and entered service with the Japanese Ground Self-Defence Force in 1962. A small number remain in service.

In appearance the Type 61 has a number of features of the American M47 medium tank, which the Japanese tested in small numbers in the early 1950s. The hull of the Type 61 is of all-welded construction, but the glacis plate can be removed for maintenance purposes. The driver is seated at the front of the hull on the right. The turret is cast, with the commander and gunner on the right and the loader on the left. A stowage box is mounted at the rear of the turret bustle. The engine and transmission are at the rear of the hull. The Japanese have always favoured diesel engines as these have a number of advantages over petrol engines, including low fuel consumption and much-reduced fire hazard. The engine is air-cooled and turbocharged. The suspension is of the torsion-bar type and consists of six road wheels, with the drive sprocket at the front and the idler at the rear. There are three track-return rollers. The Type 61 is armed with a 90mm gun built in Japan, and there is a .3in machine-gun mounted co-axially with the main armament. The gun is elevated and traversed hydraulically, with manual controls for use in an emergency. An M2 Browning machine-gun is mounted on the commander's cupola for anti-aircraft defence and this can be aimed and fired from within the cupola. The tank can ford to a depth of 3ft 3in (0.99m) without preparation, but there is no provision for the installation of a schnorkel for deep fording operations. Some tanks have been provided with both infra-red driving lights and an infra-red searchlight for night operations.

Compared with other tanks of the early 1960s, such as the Leopard and AMX-30, the Type 61 is undergunned, but it should be remembered that it was designed to meet Japanese rather than European requirements. The weight and size of the tank had to be kept within certain dimensions as the tank has to be able to be carried on Japanese railways, which pass through numerous narrow tunnels.

There are three basic variants of the Type 61 MBT. The bridgelayer is called the Type 67 Armoured Vehicle-Launched Bridge, and has

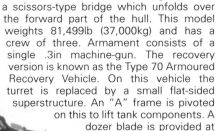

a scissors-type bridge which unfolds over the forward part of the hull. This model weights 81,499lb (37,000kg) and has a crew of three. Armament consists of a single .3in machine-gun. The recovery version is known as the Type 70 Armoured Recovery Vehicle. On this vehicle the turret is replaced by a small flat-sided superstructure. An "A" frame is pivoted on this to lift tank components. A dozer blade is provided at the front of the hull. The ARV has a crew of four and a loaded weight of 77,094lb (35,000kg). Armament consists of a .3in and a .5in machine-gun and an 81mm mortar. Finally there is an Armoured Engineer Vehicle known as the Type 67. This weighs 77,094lb (35,000kg) and has a crew of four.

Type 74 Main Battle Tank

STB-1, Type 74 and Type 78 ARCV.
Country of origin: Japan.
Crew: 4.
Armament: One L7 series 105mm gun; one 7.62mm machine-gun co-axial with main armament; one .5in anti-aircraft machine-gun, six smoke dischargers.
Armour: Classified.
Dimensions: Length (gun forward) 30ft 10in (9.41m); length (hull) 22ft 6in (6.85m); width 10ft 5in (3.18m); height (with anti-aircraft machine-gun) 8ft 10in (2.67m) at a ground clearance of 2ft 2in (0.65m).
Weight: Combat 83,776lb (38,000kg).
Ground pressure: 12lb/in² (0.85kg/cm²).
Engine: Mitsubishi 10ZF Model 21 WT 10-cylinder air-cooled diesel developing 750bhp at 2,200rpm.
Performance: Maximum road speed 33mph (53km/h); range 186 miles (300km); vertical obstacle 3ft 3in (1m); trench 8ft 10in (2.7m); gradient 60 per cent.
History: In service with Japanese Ground Self-Defence Force (JGSDF) in 1973. Production completed, with some 850 in service.

Right: The first example of the Type 74 was called the STB-1. Features included an automatic loader for the 105mm main gun and a 12.7mm anti-aircraft machine-gun which could be aimed and fired by the commander from within the tank's turret.

Above: The Type 74 main battle tank is manufactured by Mitsubishi Heavy Industries near Tokyo and is armed with the British-designed 105mm L7 type rifled tank gun which is manufactured in Japan under licence.

The Japanese realised in the early 1960s that the Type 61 would not meet its requirements for the 1980s, so in 1962 design work commenced on a new main battle tank. The first two prototypes, known as STB-1s, were completed at the Maruko works of Mitsubishi Heavy Industries in late 1969. Further prototypes, the STB-3 and the STB-6, were built before the type was considered ready for production. The vehicle entered production at the new tank plant run by Mitsubishi Heavy Industries at Sagamihara in 1973, and the first order was for 280 tanks. The Type 74 has not been exported since at the present time it is the policy of the Japanese government not to export arms of any type.

The layout of the tank is conventional, with the driver at the front of the hull on the left and the other three crew members in the turret. The commander and gunner are on the right and the loader is on the left. The engine and transmission are at the rear of the hull. The suspension is of the hydro-pneumatic type and consists of five road wheels, with the drive sprocket at the rear and the idler at the front. There are no track-return rollers. The suspension can be adjusted by the driver to suit the type of ground being crossed. When crossing a rocky, broken area, for example, the suspension would be adjusted to give maximum ground clearance. This clearance can be adjusted from a minimum of 8in (20cm) to a maximum of 2ft 1½in (65cm). It can also be used to give the tank a tactical advantage: when the tank is on a reverse slope, the suspension can be lowered at the front and increased at the rear so that the main armament is depressed further than normal. The only other tank in service with this type of suspension is the Swedish S-tank, which has to have this type of suspension as the gun is fixed to the hull. This type of suspension was also used on the American T95 and the German/American MBT-70 tanks, but both these projects were cancelled.

The Type 74 is armed with the British L7 series 105mm rifled tank gun, built under licence in Japan. A 7.62mm machine-gun is mounted co-axial with the main armament. The main gun has an elevation of +9° and a depression of –6° and using the hydropneumatic suspension an elevation of +15° and a

Above: One of the more interesting features of the Type 74 MBT is its hydro-pneumatic suspension which enables the driver to adjust the ground clearance to suit the type of terrain being crossed. In addition, when the tank is firing on a reverse slope the suspension can be raised at the front and lowered at the rear to give the 105mm gun a depression angle of –12.5° (normal depression angle is –6°). Principal armament is an L7 series 105mm gun, backed up by a co-axial 7.62mm machine-gun. A 12.7mm machine-gun is mounted adopt the turret for anti-aircraft purposes.

depression of –12.5° can be obtained. The fire control system includes a laser rangefinder and a ballistic computer, both of which are produced in Japan. Some 151 rounds of 105mm ammunition are carried. Prototypes had an automatic loader, but this would have cost too much to install in production tanks. A .5in M2 anti-aircraft machine-gun is mounted on the roof. On the prototypes this could be aimed and fired from within the turret, but this was also found to be too expensive for production vehicles. Three smoke dischargers are mounted on each side of the turret.

The tank is provided with infra-red driving lights and there is also an infra-red searchlight to the left of the main armament. The Type 74 can ford to a maximum depth of 3ft 3in (1m) without preparation, although a schnorkel enabling it to ford to a depth of 6ft 6in (2m) can be fitted. All tanks are provide with an NBC system.

In designing the Type 74 MBT the Japanese sought, and managed, to combine the best features of contemporary tank design within a weight limit of 83,702lb (38,000kg). There is only one variant of the Type 74 at the present time, which is the Type 78 Armoured Recovery Vehicle; this is provided with a hydraulically-operated crane, winch and a dozer blade at the front of the hull. It has been produced in small numbers. The Type 74 chassis has also been used for the Type 87 35mm SP anti-aircraft gun, of which 12 have been produced.

Mitsubishi Type 90 Main Battle Tank

Country of origin: Japan.
Crew: 3.
Armament: One Rheinmetall smoothbore 120mm main gun; one 7.62mm machine-gun co-axial with main gun; one 12.7mm heavy machine-gun on turret roof; one triple-barrelled smoke discharger on each side of turret.
Armour: Composite.
Dimensions: Length (including main gun) 32ft 0in (9.76m), length (hull) 24ft 7in (7.5m); width 11ft 3in (3.43m); height (to turret roof) 7ft 8in (2.34m).
Weight: Combat 110,000lb (50,000kg).
Ground pressure: 12.6lb/in² (0.89 kg/cm²).
Engine: Mitsubishi 10ZG 10-cylinder, water-cooled diesel, 1,500hp at 2,400rpm.
Performance: Road speed 43mph (70km/h); range 250 miles (400km); vertical obstacle 3ft 2in (1m); trench 8ft 10in (2.7m); gradient 60 per cent.
History: Prototypes started trials in 1982; type-classified in 1991; production commenced 1991; entered service with Japanese Ground Self-Defense Force in 1992; about 180 in service by 2000.

The operational requirement for the new Japanese main battle tank was finalized in 1980 and two prototypes of the first version began running trials two years later. Both were armed with a Japanese-designed 120mm main gun firing Japanese ammunition, and it must be assumed that these were less than satisfactory since the next group of prototypes were armed with the German Rheinmetall smoothbore 120mm gun. Following further trials this new version was accepted and entered production in 1991.

 The Type 90 is armed with the standard Rheinmetall 120mm smoothbore gun, which is manufactured under licence in Japan. The tube, breech, fume extractor and thermal sleeve are identical to the German original, but the

mount and recoil system are of Japanese design, as is the automatic loader. This loader is mounted in the bustle and the gun returns automatically to 0 degrees for the loading to take place, and then returns, also automatically, to the firing position, ready to fire the next round. Rounds fired are APFSDS-T (Armour-Piercing, Fin-Stabilized; Discarding Sabot) and HEAT-MP (High-Explosive Anti-Tank, Multi-Purpose), both of which use a semi-combustible cartridge case. There is also a co-axial 7.62mm machine-gun and a roof-mounted, manually controlled 12.7mm machine-gun.

The tank is fitted with six road wheels on each side, with a hybrid suspension system, in which the first and last pairs are mounted on hydropneumatic units, while the centre pair are mounted on torsion bars. The hydropneumatic units enable the tank to be tilted longitudinally to increase the elevation or depression of the gun, but cannot be used to vary the transverse attitude, to compensate for trunnion tilt. The power unit is a Mitsubishi 10ZG supercharged two-stroke, water-cooled diesel, using direct fuel injection and an electronic fuel control system

The hull is of conventional layout but is fabricated from Japanese designed and manufactured composite armour. The glacis plate is well sloped, with the driver on the left and reserve ammunition on the right. The turret has vertical front and sides, with a large, overhanging bustle. As is to be expected from a Japanese system, the Type 90 is equipped with the most advanced, domestically designed electronic systems, which include a fully integrated fire-control system, thermal imaging sights and a computer which takes account of ambient factors such as temperature, wind strength and direction, muzzle droop (using a permanently mounted muzzle reference system) and the angle of the gun relative to the horizontal (trunnion tilt or cant angle).

Production of the Type 90 was still under way in early 2000. Japanese laws prevent the export of defence equipment such as this.

Left: The Japanese Type 90 is armed with the Rheinmetall 120mm smoothbore gun, but the mount, recoil system and the bustle-mounted autoloader are all of Japanese design.

Hyundai K1 Main Battle Tank

K1, K1A1 and K1(M).
Country of origin: Republic of Korea (South Korea).
Crew: 4.
Armament: One M68A1 105mm rifled gun; one 7.62mm co-axial machine-gun, one 12.7 anti-aircraft machine-gun (gunner) and one 7.62mm machine-gun (loader); 12 smoke dischargers (six on each side of turret).
Armour: Composite.
Dimensions: Length (including main armament) 31ft 9in (9.67m); length (hull) 24ft 6in (7.48m); width 11ft 10in (3.60m); height (to turret top) 7ft 5in (2.25m).
Weight: Combat 112,335lb (51,000kg).
Ground pressure: 12.23lb/in^2 (0.86kg/cm^2).
Engine: MTU MB 871 Ka-501 12-cylinder water-cooled diesel engine developing 1,200hp at 2,600 rpm.
Performance: Road speed 40mph (65km/h); range 310 miles (500km); vertical obstacle 3ft 4in (1.0m); trench 9ft 0in (2.74m), gradient 60 per cent.
History: Entered production for the Republic of Korea Army in 1985. Some 800 in service in late 1999 out of an initial order for 1,000-plus.

The Republic of Korea (RoK) Army has traditionally used American equipment and its tank corps was equipped with a succession of such tanks, including the M47 and M48A5. It came, therefore, as something of a surprise when the RoK Army issued invitations in the mid-1970s for proposals for a new MBT,

Above: The K1A1 differs from the K1-M in being armed with the M268 120mm smoothbore gun. The M60E2 co-axial MG is retained, but is moved to a higher position in the mantlet.

Left: The South Korean K1-M is armed with the M68A1 105mm rifled gun firing the full range of NATO-standardized ammunition, with a co-axial 7.62mm M60E2 machinegun.

which was to be designed to South Korean specifications, with a view to production in South Korea. Several manufacturers submitted proposals and the Chrysler Defense (later General Dynamics Land Systems Division) design was selected in 1980. Two prototypes, designated XK-1, were built in considerable secrecy and sent to the Aberdeen Proving Grounds in Maryland, USA, for testing in 1983. Production started in 1984 at the Hyundai factory at Changwon under the designation K1 MBT and several tank battalions had been equipped with the new MBT by the time it was revealed to the public in late 1987. The total RoK Army requirement is believed to be well over 1,000.

The tank is of conventional design with the vulnerable parts of the hull constructed of British-designed and American-manufactured Chobham armour. There is a four-man crew, with the driver sitting in the front compartment on the left. The commander is seated in the turret on the right of the gun with the gunner in front of and below him, and the loader on the left of the gun.

The main armament is an M68A1 105mm rifled gun, another British design built in the USA. The great majority of Western MBTs currently in production are armed with 120mm guns and it is a little surprising that the South Koreans should have opted for the older and smaller calibre weapon. However, the 105mm is well-proven, very accurate and quite capable of defeating any tank operated by the North Koreans. In addition, the RoK Army's M48A5s are

armed with the same weapon and there is an ammunition production facility in the country, producing all natures of 105mm ammunition including APFSDS.

There is the usual co-axial 7.62mm machine-gun. There are also two machine-guns mounted on the turret roof: the gunner has a 12.7mm weapon, while the loader's is of 7.62mm calibre. There are also 12 smoke grenade dischargers.

The rear-mounted engine is a German MTU 871 Ka-501, developing 1,200hp and giving the tank a power : weight ratio of 23.5hp/ton. The hybrid suspension is similar to that used in modern Japanese tanks, with the centre pair of road wheels having torsion bars and the front and rear pairs having hydropneumatic suspension. As with the Japanese tanks this enabled the K1 to elevate its main gun to +20° and to depress it to–10°.

Two prototypes of a new version, K1A1, started testing in 1996. These are armed with a 120mm smoothbore gun and it is probable that many K1s will be modified in due course. A lighter version, K1(M), was developed for the Malaysian Army's MBT competition, the outcome of which is still not known.

Below: Specialist versions of the K1-M include this Armoured Vehicle Launched Bridge (AVLB), which carries a 72ft (22m) British No 8 bridge that can span a 67ft (20.5m) gap.

Developed in cooperation with MaK, the K1-M armoured recovery vehicle (ARV) has a jib with a straight lift of 25 tons and a 35-ton (70 tons with pulley) recovery winch.

7TP Light Tank

7TP, 7TP Improved, 10TP and 14TP.
Country of origin: Poland.
Crew: 3.
Armament: One 37mm gun; one 7.92mm machine-gun co-axial with main armament.
Armour: 40mm (1.57in) maximum.
Dimensions: Length 15ft 1in (4.997m); width 7ft 11in (2.413m); height 7ft 0½in (2.159m).
Weight: 24,251lb (11,000kg).
Engine: Saurer diesel developing 110hp.
Performance: Maximum road speed 20mph (32km/h); range 100 miles (160km); vertical obstacle 2ft (0.609m); trench 6ft (1.828m); gradient 60 per cent.
History: In service with the Polish Army from 1934 to 1939.

In the early 1930s Poland purchased between 40 and 50 Vickers 6 ton tanks. Further development of this by the PKI resulted in the 7TP light tank, in production from 1934 to 1939. The first model had two turrets, each fitted with a single machine-gun, and weighed 8.86 tons (9,000kg). It was powered by a 110hp Saurer diesel. This was followed by the second model which had a Swedish turret armed with a Bofors 37mm gun and a co-axial 7.92mm machine-gun. As a result of difficulties in obtaining the turrets from Sweden this model was not built in large numbers. The final

model (the 7TP Improved) had heavier armour, a redesigned turret with an overhanging rear, and stronger suspension. This did not enter production.

The 7TP was to have been replaced by the 10TP, the first prototype of which was completed in 1937. This had a Christie type suspension and was powered by an American La France 210hp 12-cylinder engine. This gave the vehicle a top road speed of 31mph (50km/h). Like some of the American Christie tanks, the 10TP could also be run on its road wheels, top speed without its tracks being 44mph (70km/h). The 10TP had the same turret as the 7TP, but in addition had a hull-mounted machine-gun. The 14TP was a medium tank which also had Christie type suspension, although this model could run only on its tracks. The tank had a top road speed of 31mph (50km/h) and was powered by a German Maybach 12-cylinder engine. Combat weight was 13.78 tons (14,000kg). Like the 10TP, this never entered production. The Poles ordered two American Christie tanks in 1935, but as they never paid for them the tanks were never delivered and were taken over by the US Army.

When the Germans invaded Poland in 1939 the Polish-Army had 169 7TP tanks on strength as well as 50 Vickers 6 ton tanks, 67 World War I Renault FT-17 light tanks, 53 French Renault R-35s (these were withdrawn to Romania and were not committed to action), some 700 TK/TKS tankettes and 100 assorted armoured cars. These were pitted against over 3,000 German tanks and most were soon destroyed or captured.

Left: The final model of the 7TP light tank, mounting the 37mm Bofors. The 7TP was developed from the Vickers 6-tonner.

PT-91 Twardy Main Battle Tank

Country of origin: Poland.
Crew: 3.
Armament: One D81T 125mm smoothbore gun; one PKT 7.62mm machine-gun co-axial with main armament; one 12.7mm NSV machine-gun on turret roof; six single-barrelled smoke grenade dischargers on each side of turret.
Armour: Standard T-72 armour plus ERA on glacis and turret front.
Dimensions: Length (9.53m); width (3.59m); height (2.2m).
Weight: Combat 99,886lb (45,300kg).
Ground pressure: 13.4lb/in^2 (0.94 kg/cm^2).
Engine: Type S-12U, 4-stroke, multi-fuel diesel, 850hp at 2,300rpm.
Performance: Road speed 37mph (60km/h); range 400 miles (650km); vertical obstacle 2ft 10in (0.85m); trench 9ft 2in (2.8m); gradient 60 per cent.
History: Prototype in 1992; in production and in service with Polish Army in 1995.

The Polish armaments industry has produced large numbers of Russian-designed tanks under licence, starting with the T-54/55 and then progressing to the T-72M1, as well as derivatives for specialized roles, such as bridgelaying, recovery, engineering and

Below: PT-91 prototype being put through its paces on a Polish Army test track. Note the many plates of explosive reactive armour (ERA) on the glacis plate, turret sides and roof.

Above: Polish PT-91 is a development of the Russian T-72M1. This is a good view of the front skirts, designed to minimise dust, which is usually a certain give-away for an armoured column.

driver training. The Polish Army has also produced an increasing number of individual enhancements to the basic T-72M1, including explosive reactive armour (ERA) packages and new fire-control systems, but with the PT-91 *Twardy* (= strong) it has gone much further to produce a much improved version of the Russian T-72.

The basic vehicle is still the T-72M1 (see Russian T-72 entry), which was placed in production in Poland at the time of the Cold War, with the same 2A46 125mm smoothbore main gun. The overall weapons effectiveness has, however, been considerably improved by the introduction of a new fire-control computer, enhanced stabilization system, a laser rangefinder and improved sights including a new night observation device (NOD) for the driver and commander. Protection has also been improved by applying a covering of Polish-designed ERA blocks to the glacis plate, the front and roof of the turret, and the forward part of the skirts. There is also a laser-warning system, with four antennas spaced equally around the turret. There are also 12 smoke grenade dischargers, mounted in groups of six on a base attached to the turret.

Other improvements include an uprated engine; hull escape hatch; rubber blocks in the tracks; new radios; nose skirts to keep down dust, and a new fire warning and suppression system for both the engine and crew compartments.

KS Light Infantry Tank

Country of origin: Russia.
Crew: 2.
Armament: One 37mm gun; one 7.62mm machine-gun.
Armour: 16mm (0.63in) maximum; 8mm (0.31in) minimum.
Dimensions: Length (with tail) 16ft 5in (5m); length (without tail) 13ft 1in (4m); width 5ft 9in (1.75m); height 7ft 5in (2.25m).
Weight: Combat 15,432lb (7,000kg).
Ground pressure: 5.68lb/in² (0.4kg/cm²).
Engine: One Fiat four-cylinder water-cooled petrol engine developing 33.5hp at 1,500rpm.
Performance: Road speed 5.3mph (8.5km/h); range 37.5 miles (60km); vertical obstacle 1ft 10in (0.6m); trench 5ft 11in (1.8m); gradient 38 degrees.
History: In service with the Russian Army from 1921 to 1941.

During the Russian Civil War the Soviets made their first attempts to provide the new Red Army with a serviceable tank. This was no easy task: at that time Russia had virtually no indigenous automobile and scarcely any established heavy industries. What scant facilities that had been developed by the Tsarist governments had been almost totally destroyed during the Civil War. Despite this, during September 1919 the Soviets established a special Military Industrial Council (*SVP*) to direct the native manufacture of heavy military technology, and this was headed by P.A. Bagdanov. During the spring of 1919 two small Renault FT tanks were captured by the Soviet 2nd Ukrainian Army from the White forces at Zakhvacheni. One of these was shipped back to the Krasny Sormovo Machine-Building Plant for investigation. The Military Industrial Council received a personal request from Lenin himself to undertake the production of a new Soviet light tank based on the captured Renault FT.

Below: An early KS tank with short-barrelled 37mm gun. Built by command of Lenin, the first production model bore his name.

Above: The KS "Russkiy-Renault" light tank of 1920 was modelled on the French Renault FT. The final production model, seen here, mounted a long-barrelled 37mm gun.

This new light tank was intended purely for the accompaniment of infantry. It was, at that time, impossible for the Krasny Sormovo plant to manufacture the whole of the tank, so two other factories were drawn into the programme. The armour was to be produced by the Izhorskiy Factory in Petrograd and the power plant by AMO (later called ZIS and then ZIL). Production of the first tank began in February, and the armour was delivered to Sormovo in June, followed by the automotive components in July. Assembly of the tank was completed in August. The first preliminary trials showed up a number of faults in both design and manufacture, and these had to be corrected by September-October. By November 1920 the first completed tank, designated KS (Krasny Sormovo), had been subjected to extensive military and automotive tests.

On 1 December 1920, the Military Industrial Council was able to inform Lenin that the first Soviet tank had been successfully completed. On the same day Lenin sent a directive to the Military Industrial Council ordering the production of a further 14 such tanks, to be completed by the following spring. Delivery of the first tank was scheduled for 15 December and completion of the fifteenth tank between October 1919 and March 1920. The original vehicle was christened "Comrade Lenin, the Freedom Fighter". Subsequent vehicles were nicknamed Paris Commune", "Red Fighter", "Ilya Muromets", "Proletariat", "Tempest" and "Victory".

These Sormovo tanks, which were also referred to as "Russian Renaults", could be considered to be quite good for that time with respect to their combat characteristics and performance. The very first vehicles produced had either a machine-gun (with 3,000 rounds) or a 37mm gun (with 250 rounds) as their main armament, but subsequent vehicles had both – a substantial improvement over the original French tank which also had one or the other. As the Red Army captured more and more Renault tanks, they reworked them to the KS standard. KS tanks were used operationally against the Interventionist forces and during the Russo-Polish War. Up until the time of their removal from service with the Red Army, they received several modifications and were finally handed over to the *"Ossoaviakhim"*, the Red Army's civilian para-military training organisation.

MS Light Infantry Tank

MS-1 and T-18M
Country of origin: Russia.
Crew: 2.
Armament: One 37mm Hotchkiss gun; one 7.62mm Fiodorov or Degtarov machine-gun.
Armour: 16mm (0.63in) maximum; 8mm (0.31in) minimum.
Dimensions: Length (with tail) 14ft 4in (4.38m); (without tail) 11ft 6in (3.50m); width 5ft 9in (1.76m); height 6ft 11in (2.12m)
Weight: Combat 12,125lb (5,500kg) to 14,770lb (6,700kg) depending on model.
Ground pressure: 4,76lb/in² (0.335kg/cm²).
Engine: One modified Fiat four-cylinder air-cooled petrol engine developing 35 to 40hp, depending on model.
Performance: Road speed 10.3mph (16.5km/h) to 13.8mph (22km/h) depending on model; range 37.5 miles (60km) to 41.3 miles (66km) depending on model; vertical obstacle 1ft 10in (0.6m); trench 4ft 3in (1.3m); gradient 40 degrees.
History: In service with the Russian Army from 1928 to 1942.

Following the adoption of the KS tank, much experimental work was carried out to evolve a better light infantry accompanying tank. Towards the end of 1924, following the establishment of a special Tank Bureau on 6 May, the tactical-technical specifications were issued for a light tank weight: 2.95 tons (3,000kg), speed 7.5mph (12km/h), armament one 37mm gun or a machine-gun, armour 0.63in (16mm) and crew 2 men. During the spring of 1925 the Red Army staff reviewed the project and recommended that the weight be increased to 4.92 tons (5,000kg) and that both artillery and machine-gun

**Right: The MS-1 (T-18)
light tank, the first tank
of entirely Russian
design, entered service
in 1928.**

armament be included.

The first vehicle of this type to be completed successfully, in May 1927, was the five-ton T-16 tank. After extensive tests changes were made to the engine, and the length of the tank increased to reduce the bad pitching effect. Work on improving the light tank was completed in November 1927, the final model being designated T-18. Without awaiting completion of design work and tests, on 6 July the Revolutionary Military Council accepted the T-18 as standard. It was officially designated Small Accompanying – One (*MS*-1). Production of the tank, which began in 1928, was entrusted to the Leningrad "Bolshevik" plant which built the first batch of 30 utilising the resources of the *Ossoaviakhim* (the para-military training organisation) by May 1929.

The *MS*-1 was the first Soviet tank to be placed in serial production. Some 960 were manufactured between 1928 and 1931, the tank being withdrawn from service in 1932 and relegated to the *Ossoaviakhim*. The tank had both artillery and machine-gun armament (with 109 and 2,016 rounds of ammunition respectively) and a special air-cooled engine. The use of rubber-tyred bogies was a novelty. The designers had attempted to make the vehicle more compact and to reduce its weight, and for this reason the engine, which was built integral with the transmission, was mounted transversely at the rear of the hull. The improved layout made it possible to keep the tank weight down to 5.4 tons. Several improved models appeared, the final service model having a modified turret with overhang. By October-November 1929 a quantity of *MS*-1 tanks had been sent to the Special Far-Eastern Army and, on 20 November, units of this army used these tanks to put down the Chinese attempt to seize the Far-Eastern Railway. At the beginning of the Russo-German War, in mid-1941, some 200 *MS*-1 tanks were reworked into T-18*M*s mounting 45mm guns.

T-26 Light Tank

T-26, T-26/*TU*, T-26s and variants.
Country of origin: Russia.
Crew: 3.
Armament: Various (see text).
Armour: Between 6mm (0.24in) and 25mm (0.98in) according to model.
Dimensions: Length between 15ft 2in (4.62m) and 16ft (4.88m); width between 8ft (2.44m) and 7ft 11in (2.41m); height between 7ft 8in (2.33m) and 6ft 10in (2.08m).
Weight: Between 17.637lb (8,000kg) and 20.944lb (9,500kg) according to model.
Ground pressure: Between 8.96lb/in² (0.55kg/cm²) and 9.96lb/in² (0.72kg/cm²) according to model.
Engine: Model T-26 four-cylinder air-cooled petrol engine developing 91hp at 2,200rpm.
Performance: Road speed between 17.5mph (28km/h) and 20mph (32km/h) according to model; range between 63 miles (100km) and 140 miles (225km) according to model; vertical obstacle 2ft 5in (0.79m); trench 5ft 10in (1.90m); gradient 40 degrees.
History: In service with the Russian Army from 1932 to 1945.

As was the case with many other Soviet tanks of the early 1930s the T-26 light tank was developed from a British model purchased from the Vickers-Armstrong company. In this instance the basic British model was the famous 6-ton twin-turreted tank. The Soviets developed it into their basic light infantry support tank to replace the obsolescent *MS* model, and it remained in mass production throughout the period between 1931 and 1940. Altogether more than 12,000 of these vehicles, in a multiplicity of models, were manufactured. During 1930 a group of engineers in the Experimental Design department (*OKMO*) at the Bolshevik factory in Leningrad, directed by N. V. Barikov and S. A. Ginzbury, manufactured 20 similar vehicles under the designations *TMM-1* and *TMM-2*. Following comparison trials with Soviet-designed models (T-19 and T-20), on 13 February 1931 the Vickers design was accepted by the Revolutionary Military Council for adoption by the Red Army. After minor alterations by the engineer Zigelya, the vehicle was standardised as the T-26.

The production vehicle was practically identical to the British original apart from a few alterations to the shape of the hull front and the shape of the two independently rotating machine-gun turrets. During the following year, mass production of the T-26 tank began at several factories, including the Kirov factory in Leningrad. Tanks of the original series had two turrets in juxtaposition, and these could mount a multiplicity of armament combinations. For commanders a special version, fitted with radio and rail aerial circumscribing the hull. A companion version of this model, with one turret removed and the other mounting a new long-barrelled 37mm gun, was scheduled for adoption by the Red Army. Only a small number of these were produced, however, as a result of the decision to adopt a single-turreted model with larger turret. Mass production of this single-turreted model was carried out in 1933. Original models mounted the new 37mm gun, but eventually the

Above: The T-26A-4V command version of the T-26 series, identifiable by its all-round "handrail" frame radio aerial. Most T-26As had the twin turrets of the Vickers prototype: the T-26B and later models had a single turret mounting a 45mm gun.

tank received the new 45mm gun. During 1938 reports were received from General Blyukher, commander of the Special Far-Eastern Army, stating that the riveted T-26 tanks had proved ineffective against Japanese fire. It was therefore decided to adopt a new version with welded armour, designated T-26s. Some of the earlier models were retrofitted with the turret of this tank.

Below: More than 12,000 light tanks of the T-26 series, based on the British Vickers Models A and B, were built in 1931-1940.

Prior to World War II, the T-26 saw action in the two main battles with the Japanese in Manchuria, in Spain in the Russo-Finnish War. The T-26 underwent many alterations and modifications, and several special-purpose vehicles were developed around its chassis; these included self-propelled guns, flame-throwers, bridge-layers, smoke and chemical tanks, artillery tractors, remote-controlled tank mines, and many others.

Below: T-26B tanks pass infantry positions. Russo-Japanese conflict in Manchuria in 1938 revealed weaknesses in the T-26's riveted armour; the final production model, the T-26s, had armour of 10 to 25mm and was welded throughout. Even so, losses in the first few months of World War II were enormous, but by that time the Russians had designed two new tanks that were to turn the tide – the T-34 medium and the KV-1.

T-28 Medium Tank

T-28, T-28 06 1938, T-28 06 1940, T-28M, IT-28 and T-29-5.
Country of origin: Russia.
Crew: 6.
Armament: One 76.2mm gun; three DT machine-guns.
Armour: 20mm to 80mm (0.79in to 3.15in) depending on model.
Dimensions: Length 24ft 5in (7.44m); width 9ft 3in (2.82m); height 9ft 3in (2.82m).
Weight: 61.729lb (28,000kg) to 70,547lb (32,000kg) depending on model.
Ground pressure: 10.25lb/in² (0.73kg/cm²) to 10.95lb/in² (0.78kg/cm²) depending on model.
Engine: One M-17L 12-cylinder water-cooled petrol engine developing 500hp at 1,450rpm.
Performance: Road speed 23mph (37km/h); range 140 miles (220km); vertical obstacle 3ft 5in (1.04m); trench 9ft 6in (2.9m); gradient 80 per cent.
History: Served with the Russian Army from 1933 to 1941.

Work on building a suitable type of medium tank was undertaken during the early 1930s. After trials with numerous prototypes in this tank class (including the T12, T24 and TG), which for a multiplicity of reasons proved unsuitable for mass production, in 1932 the Leningrad Kirov plant built a new prototype medium tank based on the general design of the British A6E1 16 ton (16,257kg) tank. A specimen of this vehicle was not purchased (being still secret at the time), but it is believed that much information was obtained on it through espionage.

The first Soviet specification for a multi-turreted 16 ton medium tank, intended for breaking through strongly fortified defensive zones and for exploitation by mechanised brigades, was issued to the Kirov plant in 1931. The specification demanded a crew of five men, 20mm to 30mm (0.79in to 1.18in) armour, a 500hp engine and a maximum speed of 37mph (60km/h). The armament was to comprise one 45mm gun and a machine-gun in the main turret, and one machine-gun in each of the two forward subsidiary turrets. Some 7,938 rounds of machine-gun ammunition were to be carried. A prototype, which weighed 17.3 tons (17,575kg), was completed during 1932. After trials with the prototype vehicle, it was requested that heavier armour be applied and that the main armament be increased to 76.2mm (with 70 rounds).

A specification was then laid down for a 27.56 ton (28,000kg) medium tank, designated T-28. The final model was accepted for adoption by the Red Army on 11 August 1933. All tanks of this type were provided with two-way radio equipment, having the characteristic frame aerial around the top of the main turret. They were also fitted with smoke-emitters. In later production vehicles a device was employed to stabilise the main turret. Designed by A. A. Prokofiev, this greatly improved accuracy of fire while on the move. The T-28 was noted for its quiet, smooth motion and abnormal capability for crossing trenches and other terrain obstacles. During 1938 this tank was subjected to extreme modification (now called T-28 06 1938). The existing armament (16.5 calibres long) was replaced by the 76.2mm L-10 gun of 26 calibres length.

T-28 tanks were employed against the Japanese in 1939 and also during the Russo-Finnish War. In the course of this war, it was discovered that the armour was inadequate and, as a result, modification of the armour was carried out. This was achieved by "screening" (yekpanirovki) suitable parts of the existing armour. The turret and hull frontal plates were increased from 50mm to 80mm (1.97in to 3.15in), the sides and rear to 40mm. Consequently, the weight of this new model (called T-28 06 1940 or T-28M) rose to 31.5 tons (32,000kg). Despite the increase in weight the speed was not significantly impaired. This up-armoured tank gained much acclaim during the break-through of the Mannerheim Line in 1940. Its mass production was terminated soon after the conclusion of hostilities between the USSR and Finland, when the type was replaced in production by the new T-34 medium tank.

The chassis of the T-28 was used for several types of experimental self-propelled gun as well as special-purpose tanks (eg bridgelayer IT-28 and a mine-clearing tank). During 1934 the design bureau at the Kirov Factory developed a wheel/track variant of the T-28, called the T-29-5. Although this never passed beyond the prototype stage, it formed the first link in the eventual development of the T-34.

Top of the page: The T-28 was the first medium tank to enter service with the Soviet Army in 1933. Its design owed a lot to the British A6E1 16 ton tank which was designed by Vickers Armstrongs in the late 1920s but did not enter service with British Army.

Left: Prototype of the T-28 was completed in 1932 and following trials it was decided to increase both armour and firepower. The T-28 was used during the war against Finland, when again it was found to be under-armoured. It was improved with special plating and the tank then gave a good account of itself, despite the extra weight. The T-28 also served against Japan in 1939.

T-35 Heavy Tank

T-35 and *SU*-14.
Country of origin: Russia
Crew: 11 (when provided with all turrets; some models had some of the turrets removed).
Armament: Basic model – One 76.2mm gun; two 45mm guns; six 7.62mm DT machine-guns; one P-40 AA machine-gun. (Some later models had a few of the subsidiary weapons removed.)
Armour: 30mm (1.18in) maximum; 10mm (0.39in) minimum.
Dimensions: Length 31ft 10in (9.72m); width 10ft 6in (3.2m); height 11ft 3in (3.43m).
Weight: Combat 110,230lb (50,000kg). (Some models were lighter.)
Ground pressure: 11.08lb/in^2 (0.78kg/cm^2).
Engine: One Model M-17T V-12 12-cylinder water-cooled petrol engine developing 500hp at 2.200rpm.
Performance: Road speed 19mph (30km/h); range 94 miles (150km); vertical obstacle 4ft (1.2m); trench 11ft 6in (3.5m); gradient 20 degrees.
History: The T-35 heavy tank was approved for adoption by the Red Army on 11 August 1933. It remained in production until 1939.

At the beginning of the 1930s, when widespread investigation into the field of AFVs was being carried out in the Soviet Union, the Red Army staff intended vehicles of the heavy, multi-turreted type to operate as a shock force when breaking through enemy defensive positions. This required the use of "*Bronenoster*" (Ironclads) of immense dimensions and having extraordinary firepower. Based on the general philosophy of the British A-1 "Independent" tank (a specimen was never actually purchased), the 36.4 ton (37,000kg) prototype of the T-35 was manufactured. This vehicle had five turrets – a main one mounting a 76.2mm gun (with 90 rounds), two diagonally placed subsidiary turrets each mounting one 37mm gun (front and rear of the main turret) and two further small turrets each mounting one 7.62mm machine-gun and placed on the opposite diagonals to the 37mm turrets. To man this massive firepower the tank required a crew of 11 men. Subsequent production vehicles dispensed with some of these turrets, and a few had 45mm guns (with 113

Above: The multi-turreted T-35 mounted a 76.2mm gun, two 45mm and six machine-guns.

rounds each) in place of the 37mm type. The final model had sloping welded armour.

The T-35 was a typical member of the multi-turreted heavy tank family which prevailed in the 1920s and 1930s and was considered to be a highly promising weapon. About the middle of the 1930s, however, the appearance of a multiplicity of anti-tank weapons made it necessary to up-armour the heavy tank. Because of the excessive weight increases involved, this could not be achieved with a multi-turreted design. Two experimental tanks – the SMK and the T-100 were produced with only two turrets, but at the same time there appeared the experimental single-turreted KV tank, designed by Zh. Kotin. All three vehicles were tried out during the breakthrough of the Mannerheim Line (in Russo-Finnish War of 1939-40), and the KV proved the most successful. Even though the T-35 was outmoded at the beginning of the Russo-German War, it was retained in service until its final action during the Battle of Moscow (December 1941).

The T-35 appeared in several variants and about 60 were produced and issued to the tank bridges of the High Command Reserve. Apart from changes to the armour layout and weapon availability there were differences to the number of wheels and types of suspension. All vehicles were fitted with radio equipment and had the characteristic frame aerial around the top of the man turret. On this tank chassis several experimental self-propelled artillery mountings were developed, particularly the heavy SU-14 series which had interchangeable armament. When finally phased out, towards the end of 1941, the armoured hulls of the later T-35 tanks were removed from their chassis and, after slight modification, attached to railway flatcars. In this manner they comprised armoured train units used through the entire war.

Left: The T-35 heavy tank replaced the T-32 from 1933. A notable feature was radio, with a frame aerial on the main turret.

T-37 Light Amphibious Tank

T-37, T-37A, T-37 _U_ and T-37 _TU_.
Country of origin: Russia.
Crew: 2.
Armament: One 7.62mm Degtarov machine-gun.
Armour: 9mm (0.35in) maximum; 4mm (0.16in) minimum.
Dimensions: Length 12ft 4in (3.75m); width 6ft 7in (2m); height 5ft 11in (1.82m).
Weight: Combat 7,055lb (3,200kg).
Ground pressure: 7.5lb/in^2 (0.5kg/cm^2).
Engine: One GAZ-AA four-cylinder water-cooled petrol engine developing 40hp at 3,000rpm.
Performance: Road speed 21.9mph (35km/h); water speed 2.5mph (4km/h); land range 116 miles (185km); vertical obstacle 1ft 7in (0.5m); trench 5ft 3in (1.6m); gradient 40 degrees.
History: Served with the Russian Army from 1934 to 1942.

During 1930 some examples of the Carden-Loyd Light Amphibious Tank (A4E11) were purchased from the British Vickers-Armstrong company. Soviet designers and engineers at Factory No 37 in memory of S. Ordzhonikidz in Moscow, directed by N. A. Astrov, developed a series of experimental vehicles of this type. The first of these, the T-33 (often referred to as MT-33), was completed in prototype form in 1932 and subjected to extensive tests. This tank was not accepted for mass production, however, because of the many limitations revealed during the trials. A subsequent vehicle of this type, the T-41, was then produced during 1932 and tested. This also failed to meet the requirements. These tanks, however, did serve as the basis for developing a further model, designated T-37. On 11 August 1933, following the successful completion of trials with the Red Army, the T-37 light amphibious tank was accepted for service. Production began at Factory No 37. Prior to this, however, improvement of the vehicle had been effected by another group of engineers under N. N. Koziryev, resulting in the variant designated T-37A. Since the original vehicle never entered

Right: A T-37A light amphibious tank, in Russian service from 1939 to 1942. Derived from the British Carden-Loyd A4E11, the T-37 replaced the T-27 tankette.

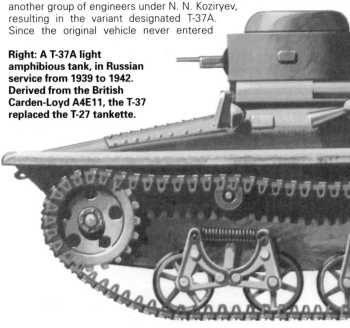

Above: the early model T-37 had a flush turret. Production began in 1933.

service, however, the suffix A was dropped and the improved variant became referred to purely as T-37.

Mass production of the tank began towards the end of 1933 and continued until the end of 1936 when the improved T-38 type was adopted. Altogether about 1,200 vehicles of this type were built in various models, successive production series incorporating various improvements. The most noticeable of these were the adoption of a turret having a cupola and the use of die-formed armour on the hull.

Platoon and company commander's tanks, designated T-37*U* or T-37*TU* (*TU* standing for Command Tank) were provided with radio equipment and had the characteristic hand-rail aerial running round the hull. All vehicles were armed with one 7.62mm DT machine-gun, with 585 rounds, mounted in a rotary turret.

T-37 tanks were issued to sub-units of armoured reconnaissance formations as well as organic tank battalions of infantry and cavalry units, where they replaced the obsolescent T-27 tankette in the reconnaissance role. During 1935 T-37 tanks were successfully transported by air, carried by TB-1 and TB-3 bombers. They were later deployed in this manner during the Soviet occupation of Bessarabia in 1940. Several trials were also carried out in which these tanks were launched into the water direct from their aircraft. In the course of production individual tanks underwent progressive alteration, and the chassis was also used to construct various experimental light self-propelled guns.

225

BT-7 Fast Tank

BT-7 BT-7A, BT-7M, BT-7U, BT-7TU and variants, plus BT-1, BT-S, BT-5.
Country of origin: Russia
Crew: 3
Armament: One 45mm M1935 gun; one co-axial 7.62mm DT machine-gun. (Some vehicles had an additional 7.62mm DT machine-gun in turret rear and a P.40 machine-gun.)
Armour: 22mm (0.87in) maximum; 10mm (0.39in) minimum.
Dimensions: Length 18ft 7in (5.66m); width 7ft 6in (2.29m); height 7ft 11in (2.42m).
Weight: 30.644lb (13,900kg).
Ground pressure: 11.25lb/in² (0.79kg/cm²).
Engine: One Model M17T 12-cyliner water-cooled petrol engine developing 500hp at 1,650hp/ton.
Performance: Road speed on wheels 46mph (73km/h); road speed on tracks 33mph (53km/h); range on wheels 450 miles (730km/h); range on tracks 270 miles (430km); vertical obstacle 1ft 10 in (0.55m); trench 6ft 7n (2m); gradient 60 per cent.
History: In service with the Russian Army from 1935 to 1945.

Next to the T-26 light infantry-accompanying tank, the *BT* fast tank was the most prolific AFV in the Red Army during the 1930s. The initials *BT* form an acronym for *Bistrokhodny Tank,* or Fast Tank. It was known among Soviet tankmen as the *Betka* (Beetle) or as the *Tri-Tankista* (Three Tanker – as the result of its three-men crew).

As distinct from most of the other Soviet vehicles at that time, which were based on British Vickers models, the *BT* tank was derived from an American design by J. W. Christie. This design was also later taken up by the British to develop their famous Cruiser tank range, the most famous member being the Crusader. The basic Christie vehicle was purchased by Soviet officials in America during 1930 and one vehicle was shipped back to Russia during that

Right: Front view of late model of *BT*-7 with conical turret and twin horn periscopes. The gun is a modification of the standard M-1935 firing an armour piercing round with a muzzle velocity of 820 metres a second. One of the features of the *BT*-7 was that its tracks could be removed, so enabling it to run at high speed on roads.

year and delivered to the Kharkhov Locomotive Works. After extensive tests of the Christie vehicle, on 23 May 1931 the Revolutionary Military Council of the USSR authorised the tank for Red Army use and requested its mass production. The drawings for the *BT* tank prototype were delivered to the *Komintem* Factory in Kharkhov during August 1931.

On 3 September 1931, the first two prototypes, designated *BT-1*, left the factory gates and were delivered to the Red Army for trials. This first vehicle was provided with machine-gun armament only, and the Red Army test commission which investigated the tank requested that the production model be armed with an artillery weapon. In the meantime the *BT-2* model, still with machine-gun armament, was developed in limited quantities. After the production of a small number of vehicles, however, the *BT-2* tank

Below: A *BT*-7-I(V), the command version of the early *BT*-7. It has the cylindrical turret of the *BT*-5 command tank with all-round frame radio aerial. These were used to control BT-7 units.

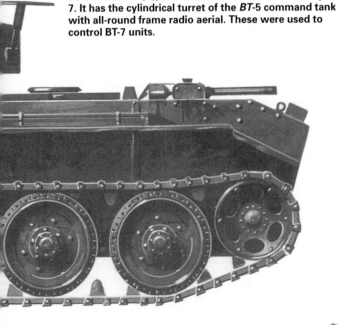

received a 37mm Model 1930 tank gun mounted in the original machine-gun turret. During 1932 the Red Army requested that the *BT* tank be armed with a more powerful weapon, in the form of the 45mm gun. After various prototypes had been tested, the *BT-S* model was accepted. This mounted a 45mm gun in a turret almost identical to that fitted to the T-26 light tank. A co-axial 7.62mm DT machine-gun was also installed. Commanders' vehicles, which received the suffix *U* or *TU* (*BT-5U* or *BT-5TU*), were provided with two-way radio equipment, which was mounted in the turret overhang, thereby displacing some of the 45mm ammunition. As in the case of the T-26 commander's model, the turret was fitted with the characteristic frame aerial.

The *BT* tank was intended for large, independent long-range armoured and mechanised units (called *DD* groups). These were to act in the rear of enemy positions and take out nerve centres such as headquarters, supply bases, airfields, etc. Under such circumstances high speed was a great advantage. One of the basic attributes of the Christie design was the ability of the tank to run on either tracks or the road wheels. Track drive was used when moving across country or along poor roads, whilst wheel drive was used for long strategic road drives. The time taken to change from one mode to the other was put at between 10 and 15 minutes. This ability to run on wheels, however, was never actually exploited by the Red Army in military operations. When the tank was operated in the wheeled mode, the tracks were attached along the track guards, and engine power was transmitted to the rear pair of wheels. The two front road wheels could be turned to provide steering. In contrast to most other tanks, where two steering levers were employed, the *BT* was controlled by a steering wheel.

As the result of large-scale exercises carried out by the Red Army during the early 1930s, it was realised that the long-range *DD* groups required some form of accompanying artillery to provide artillery fire-support during the attack. For this reason, special artillery support tanks, which received the suffix *A*, were developed. The first of these, the *BT5A*, was introduced in 1935. It mounted a short-barrelled 76.2mm gun in a turret very similar to that used as the main one on the T-28 medium tank. As a result of combat experience, the Red Army requested that the *BT* be redesigned with welded armour and that the armour be sloped to increase its immunity. Thus there emerged the *BT-7* model, a vast improvement over the previous models.

Ammunition stowage comprised 188 45mm rounds and 2,142 7.62mm rounds.

As in the case of the *BT*-5, a commander's model was developed, designated *BT-7U* or *BT-7TU*. The first series of this vehicle still retained the original cylindrical turret of the T-26 tank, however. In 1938, following experience against the Japanese in Manchuria, the new turret which had been designed for the T-26 light tank was also fitted to the *BT-7*. A commander's version of this model was also produced. To provide artillery fire-support the *BT-7A* version was developed. This had the same turret as the *BT-5A*. Other alterations to the *BT-7* were the use of a more powerful engine and an improved transmission system. During 1938 the new V-2 diesel engine had been developed specifically for tank use, and this was installed in all subsequent *BT-7* tanks. To distinguish it from previous models, the vehicle was designated *BT-7M*; it has, however, also been referred to as the *BT-8*. This new engine developed 500hp at 1,800rpm, and being a diesel power-plant allowed the *DD* groups a much greater range of operation than had been possible previously. It also reduced the fire risk, since diesel fuel is not so volatile as petrol.

Several specialised and experimental vehicles were developed from the *BT* tank. During 1936 the experimental *BT-IS* (investigator tank) was developed. This had heavily sloped armour that shrouded the tracks. This vehicle contributed greatly to the eventual development of the T-34 tank. During 1937 several *BT* tanks were equipped with schnorkels, enabling them to deepford water obstacles. Such vehicles were designed *BT-5PH*. As the *BT-5* and *BT-7* models gained numerical significance in the Red Army, the older *BT* models were used to develop special-purpose vehicles such as the *BT* bridgelayer, smoke tank and chemical tank.

Below left: *BT*-7 tanks accompany infantry in an attack on Japanese units in the Khalkin-Gol area of Manchuria/Mongolia in 1939. The Russians deployed 3 divisions of 5 armoured brigades, commanded by General Zhukov (of WWII fame).

Below: Late production *BT*-7 tanks move through Gorky Street, Moscow, in November 1941. The *BT*-7 chassis was also used for specialised versions such as bridgelayer and smoke tank.

KV-1 Heavy Tank

KV-1, KV-1s, KV-2, KV-3 and KV-85
Country of origin: Russia.
Crew: 5.
Armament: One 76.2mm gun (various types); three 7.62mm DT machine-guns. (Some vehicles had an additional machine-gun in the turret rear and a P-40 AA machine-gun.)
Armour: 100mm (3.94in) to 75mm (2.95in), varying with model.
Dimensions: Length 20ft 7in (6.273m); width 10ft 2in (3.098m); height 7ft 11in (2.413m). (Dimensions varied slightly according to models.)
Weight: 104,719lb (47,500kg), varying slightly with model.
Ground pressure: 10,68lb/in² (0.75kg/cm²).
Engine: One Model V-2-K 12-cylinder water-cooled diesel developing 600hp at 2,000rpm.
Performance: Road speed 22mph (35km/h); range 156 miles (250km); vertical obstacle 3ft 8in (1.2m); trench 8ft 6in (2.8m); gradient 70 per cent.
History: Served with the Russian Army from 1940 to 1945.

At the outbreak of World War II, the Russian Army was practically the only armed force in the world to be equipped with production heavy tanks. The first of these, the KV-1 (Klim Voroshilov) was designed by a group of engineers at the Kirov Factory in Leningrad, under the direction of Zh. Kotin. Work began in February 1939 and the State Defence Committee approved a mock-up in April. The completed tank was demonstrated to the Red Army staff in September. It was accepted as standard at the same time as the T-34 medium, on 19 December 1939.

Production began in February 1940 and in that year 243 vehicles of the type were produced. A platoon of these, meanwhile, was sent to Finland for combat tests, and in February 1940 the tanks took part in the breakthrough of the Finnish main position. Not one of them was destroyed, although companion multi-turreted models were knocked out. Subsequent production was undertaken at the Chelyabinsk Tractor Factory to where in September 1941, as a result of the imminent German threat to Leningrad, the Kirov Factory was evacuated. By June 1941, however, when the Germans attacked, 636 had been built. In Chelyabinsk the Kirov Factory was amalgamated with the Chelyabinsk Tractor Factory, and other industry transferred there, to form the immense complex called "Tankograd". This became the sole Soviet industrial establishment producing heavy tanks and heavy self-propelled guns for the remainder of the war. By the time of the Battle of Moscow, 1,364 KVs had been built; of course, many of these had been destroyed or captured in the

Above: KV-1 heavy tank production line at the Leningrad defence plant in October 1942. This plant worked throughout the 900 day siege. The KV-1 was designed at the Kirov Factory under the direction of Kotin in February 1939 and was accepted for service in December 1939 with production commencing in 1940.

Right and below: A KV-1A heavy tank showing 7.62mm DT machine gun in the turret rear. The KV-1 was first used in action against Finland in 1940 and aquitted itself well. The 76.2mm gun of the KV-1 was the same as that fitted to the T-34/76.

Above: KV-1s built with funds donated by farmers in the Moscow area are presented to representatives of the Red Army by a group of patriotic donars. Such presentations were common among many countries during World War II.

Above right: A KV-2 heavy tank armed with a 152mm howitzer. It was first used by the Red Army against the Mannerheim line defence in 1940 during the Russo-Finnish War, but it had such poor performance that production was stopped.

Right: KV-1s, armed with the same 76mm gun as installed in the T-34/76 tank, on their way to the front at Leningrad in 1942.

meantime. Throughout the war, Tankograd supplied the Red Army with some 13,500 heavy tanks and self-propelled guns on this chassis.

Alongside the KV-1 tank, which was armed with the same gun as the T-34 (76mm), a special artillery fire-support version, the KV-2, was adopted. This had a massive box-shaped turret mounting a 152mm howitzer. Immediately after the start of production of the KV-1 and KV-2, the Kirov Factory received orders to design an even heavier tank with more powerful armament (107mm gun) and thicker armour. A prototype, designated KV-3, was built at the beginning of 1941 but the German attack interrupted plans for its mass production. During the period 1941-42, therefore, production of the KV-1 continued. The KV-2 was dropped as the result of its poor performance. Successive models of the KV-1 received thicker armour and some had castings in place of welded components. A new longer-barrelled gun was also introduced.

Experience at the front showed that the KV was now becoming too slow, so a lighter, faster version, the KV-1s, was introduced during the second half of 1942. As the need arose for more powerful armament, an 85mm gun was adopted in autumn 1943 for a model designated KV-85. In subsequent attempts to improve the KV tank a whole range of experimental vehicles was produced, but eventually the tank was replaced by the new IS (Iosef Stalin) series which was equipped with much better armament and also represented a radical approach to armour protection.

T-40 Light Amphibious Tank

T-40, T-40A and T-40S.
Country of origin: Russia.
Crew: 2.
Armament: One 12.7mm DShK heavy machine-gun; one 7.62mm DT machine-gun.
Armour: 6mm to 13mm (0.24in 0.51in).
Dimensions: Length (overall) 13ft 6in (4.43m); width 7ft 8in (2.51m); height 6ft 6in (2.12m).
Weight: 12,324lb (5,590kg).
Ground pressure: 6.55lb/in^2 (0.5kg/cm^2).
Engine: GAZ-202 six-cylinder water-cooled petrol engine developing 85hp at 3,600rpm.
Performance: Road speed 28mph (45km/h); range 220 miles (350km); vertical obstacle 2ft 2in (0.7m); trench 5ft 8in (1.85m); gradient 34 degrees.
History: In service with Russian Army from 1941 to 1946.

Following the adoption of the KV heavy and the T-34 medium tanks, the Red Army was supplied with a new light amphibious tank, designated T-40. This was intended as a replacement for the older T-37 and T-38 amphibious tanks. It was introduced into the Red Army to equip reconnaissance and armoured liaison units at the beginning of 1941. It is interesting that this tank was a complete departure from previous Soviet light tank designs, utilising independent torsion-bar suspension, welded armour throughout, and a new turret design. The turret

Below: Side view of a T-40 light amphibious tank used by Russian reconnaissance units in the armoured battles of 1941-42.

and mantlet were very similar to those currently fitted to Swedish tanks, but no vehicles had ever been purchased by the Soviets from Sweden. It is thought that the Russians may have been influenced by investigation of captured Polish 7TP tanks, which they obtained during the occupation of eastern Poland'in 1939; these tanks utilised Swedish Bofors gun mountings. The T-40 was armed with machine-guns only (one 12.7mm heavy machine-gun with 550 rounds and a 7.62mm machine-gun with 2,016 rounds) and was relatively thinly armoured. About the time of the introduction of the T-60 light tank, some T-40s were rearmed with the 20mm ShVAK-20 gun.

As with previous light tank models, to simplify production, conventional automobile components were employed. The T-40A, introduced during late 1941, differed from the original tank in having the bow top faired away at the sides where originally it had been flat. The T-40A also had a trim vane which unfolded from the bow. During 1942 the T-40S was placed in limited production as a successor to the T-40 and T-40A. Since the thin armour on the previous models became a considerable handicap during operations, this new model had the armour increased on certain parts of the hull and turret. With the increase in weight, however, the tank lost its amphibious capability, so the water-propulsion and water-steering devices were removed during production. The hull of this series of tank was very original, slightly resembling a boat, with a large squat front, and the turret mounted slightly to the rear on the left-hand side. Flotation tanks were built into the hull to assist buoyancy, and in the water the T-40 was driven by a single four-bladed propeller at the rear and steered by two rudders.

T-60 Light Tank

T-60 and T-60A.
Country of origin: Russia.
Crew: 2.
Armament: One 20mm ShVAK cannon; one 7.62mm DT machine-gun.
Armour: 7mm to 20mm (0.28in to 0.79in).
Dimensions: Length (overall) 14ft 1in (4.3m); width 8ft 1in (2.46m); height 6ft 2in (1.89m).
Weight: 11,354lb (5,150kg).
Ground pressure: 6.55lb/in^2 (0.46kg/cm^2).
Engine: GAZ-202 six-cylinder water-cooled petrol engine developing 70hp at 2,800rpm.
Performance: Road speed 28mph (45km/h); range 382 miles (615km); vertical obstacle 1ft 9in (0.54m); trench 6ft 1in (1.85m); gradient 60 per cent.
History: In service with the Russian Army from 1941 to 1945.

In 1941 the T-60 light tank appeared as a replacement for the T-40 light amphibious tank. In this case, however, because of the need for much heavier armour, the tank was a purely land-based vehicle. Experience gained during the first months of the Russo-German War had shown that high mobility and an amphibious capability were not all that were needed in battle. Designers in Soviet tank factories therefore took steps to increase the armour and fire-power on the light tank. As a result they developed the T-60 light tank with 20mm (0.79in) armour on the front.

The greatest stumbling block, however, was the provision of more powerful armament. Soviet engineers attempted to mount a 37mm gun but, even with a reduced charge round, the turret ring was incapable of absorbing the recoil of this weapon. The Soviet armament designer B. Shpital'n was therefore given the task of developing a special high-powered weapon for the tank. He developed the rapid-firing 20mm ShVAK-20 gun. Despite the reduced calibre, the armour-piercing incendiary round of this gun possessed the same armour-penetration qualities as the original 37mm gun. It fired a heavy soft-core round incorporating a sub-calibre slug. In comparison with previous light-tank models, the hull front and turret had improved protection against heavy-calibre machine-gun rounds, and although cast armour had been adopted for the medium and heavy tank classes and for the turret of the

236

T-50 light tank, both hull and turret of the T-60 were welded throughout.

The T-60 entered production during November 1941 and over 6,000 were produced before the type was supplanted by the successor T-70 light tank. The vehicle was issued to reconnaissance units and also to infantry units for direct infantry support. The turret was offset to the left, with the engine mounted alongside it on the right and the driver was placed centrally in the front. An improved model of the T-60 was produced in late 1941/early 1942, and this was designated T-60A. It had increased armour, but the main external difference lay in the wheels. The T-60 had spoked road-wheels and rollers whilst those on the T-60A were pressed solid. When eventually replaced by the more powerful T-70 light tank, the T-60 chassis were employed as mountings for M-8 and M-13 (Katyusha) rocket-launchers, and also as artillery tractors for 57mm anti-tank guns.

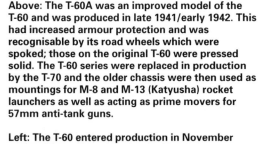

Above: The T-60A was an improved model of the T-60 and was produced in late 1941/early 1942. This had increased armour protection and was recognisable by its road wheels which were spoked; those on the original T-60 were pressed solid. The T-60 series were replaced in production by the T-70 and the older chassis were then used as mountings for M-8 and M-13 (Katyusha) rocket launchers as well as acting as prime movers for 57mm anti-tank guns.

Left: The T-60 entered production in November 1941 as the replacement for the T-40 light amphibious tank and over 6,000 were eventually built. The T-60 was not amphibious, as experience during the first few months of the Russo-German War had shown that high mobility and an amphibious capability were not all that were needed in battle. The T-60 was armed with a 20mm ShVAK-20 gun which fired an armour piercing round with the same penetration qualities as a 37mm gun – which was quite an achievement.

T-34 Medium Tank

A-20, T-32, T-34, T-34/76 and T-34/85.
Country of origin: Russia.
Crew: 5.
Armament: One 85mm M1944 Z1S S53 L/51 gun; two 7.62mm DT machine-guns.
Armour: 18mm to 60mm (0.71in to 2.36in).
Dimensions: Length (including gun) 24ft 7in (7.5m); width 9ft 7in (2.92m,); height 7ft 10in (2.39m).
Weight: 70,547lb (32,000kg).
Ground pressure: 11.2lb/in² (0.8kg/cm²).
Engine: One V-2-34 12-cylinder water-cooled diesel developing 500hp at 1,800rpm.
Performance: Road speed 31mph (50km/h); range 186 miles (300km); vertical obstacle 2ft 7in (0.79m); trench 8ft 2in (2.49m); gradient 60 per cent.
History: In service with the Russian Army from 1940. Still used by many countries today.

During 1936 the young engineer M. I. Koshkin was transferred to the Komintern Factory in Kharkov as chief designer. The design bureau of the factory had been concerned with the continued modernisation of the *BT* wheel/track tank. At the beginning of 1937 this factory was assigned the task of designing a new medium tank, also a wheel/track design, designated A-20. The design of this tank was completed in November of that year. The 17.7 ton (18,000kg) A-20, armed with a 45mm gun, was the first of the so-called "Shellproof Tanks", having greatly inclined armour, a characteristic feature of the later T-34 tank. The chassis was similar to that used on the *BT* tank but with certain automotive changes. A further version, mounting a 76.2mm gun, was developed and designated A-30.

In the meantime, Koshkin had come to the conclusion that to produce the new medium tank as a wheel/track vehicle was erroneous. The Red Army had seldom if ever used the *BT* tank in the wheeled mode, and to incorporate this facility required complication of design and severe weight penalties. He therefore proposed the development of a purely tracked

Right and below: A T-34/76B which appeared in 1941. It was basically a commander's T-34/76A with a rolled plate turret armed with a more powerful Model 1940 7.62mm L/41.5 gun for which a total of 77 rounds of ammunition were carried. A 76.2mm DT machine gun was mounted co-axial with the main armament and a second 7.62mm mounted in hull to right of the driver. The commander's tank was often the only one in a company with a radio.

variant, designated A-32 (later T-32). The Main Military Council of the USSR accepted this proposal and authorised the construction of a prototype. They had not, however, yet dismissed the wheel/track project and awaited comparison trials at a later date. Prototypes of the A-20 and T-32 tanks were completed at Kharkov at the beginning of 1939, and during that year were exhibited to the Armoured Directorate. The Directorate recommended an increase in armour on the T-32 and the adoption of more powerful

Above: A column of T-34/76s on the way to the front line. By the end of 1940 only 115 T-34s had been completed but by June 1941 when Russia was attacked by Germany a total of 1,225 had been built.

Right: The T-34/85 had a larger turret and was armed with the potent 85mm D-5T gun. It entered production in 1944.

armament. The group under Koshkin achieved this, the final variant being called T-34.

Due to the serious international situation, on 19 December 1939, before the completion of a prototype, the Main Military Council accepted the T-34 project for equipping the armoured units of the Red Army. Towards the end of January 1940, the first production models of the T-34, designated T-34 06 1940, were released from the Komintern Factory. At the beginning of February two of these underwent a trial march, under the personal supervision of Koshkin. During June 1940, the manufacturing drawings were completed and the tank entered mass production. Since Koshkin had been taken ill, his assistant A. A. Morozov had taken over the final design.

The T-34 (called *Prinadlezhit-Chetverki* or "Thirty-Four" by the troops) was noted for its excellently shaped armour, which considerably increased its resistance to shell penetration. The armament, a 76.2mm long-barrelled high-velocity gun, was also an innovation for tanks of this class. The use of the new 500hp V-2 diesel engine (already in service on the *BT-7M* tank) reduced the fire risk and greatly increased the operational range of the tank. The modified Christie suspension permitted high speeds, even on rough terrain, and the wide tracks reduced the ground pressure to a minimum. The overall design of the tank facilitated rapid mass production and lent itself to simple maintenance and repair in the field.

By the end of 1940 115 T-34s had been produced. Some were dispatched to Finland for combat tests but arrived too late to participate in operations. By June 1941, when the Germans attacked, a total of 1,225 had been

produced. By the Battle of Moscow, 1,853 had been delivered to units, but of course many of these had since been destroyed. The T-34 made its combat debut on 22 June 1941, in the vicinity of Grondno (Belorussia). It was a complete surprise to the German Army, who learned to treat this tank with the greatest respect. The question was raised of manufacturing a copy of it in Germany, but this proved impracticable. As a result, the Germans developed their famous Panther tank, whose general design was greatly influenced by that of the T-34. With the evacuation of the Soviet tank industry to the east, subsequent production of the T-34 was carried out at the *Uralmashzavod* (Ural Machine-Building Plant) in the Urals, as well as a number of subsidiary plants generally safe from German bombing.

The T-34 tank was originally armed with the 76.2mm Model 1939 L-11 gun mounted in a welded turret of rolled plate. In order to accelerate production, a new cast turret was soon introduced. During mid-1941 a new Model 40 F-34 gun was adopted. This had a longer barrel and higher muzzle velocity. A multiplicity of minor and major changes were made to the T-34 during production, but the most significant took place in autumn 1943, when the 85mm 215 S-53 or D-5T gun, with 55 rounds, was adopted. Some 2,394 rounds of 7.62mm ammunition were also carried. This new tank was called T-34/85 and was approved for mass production on 15 December 1943. By the end of the year 283 had been built, and in the following year a further 11,000 were produced. The T-34/85 remained in production until the mid-1950s, when the T-54 was adopted. In the 1970s China used the T-34 chassis for an SPAA weapon.

T-70 Light Tank

T-70 and T-70A.
Country of origin: Russia.
Crew: 2.
Armament: One 45mm L/46 gun; one 7.62mm DT machine-gun.
Armour: 0.39in (10mm) minimum; 2.36in (60mm) maximum.
Dimensions: Length 15ft 3in (6m); width 7ft 8in (2.52m); height 6ft 9in (2.22m).
Weight: 21,958lb (9,960kg).
Ground pressure: 9.53lb/in² (0.67kg/cm²).
Engine: Two Z1S-202 six-cylinder water-cooled petrol engines each developing 70hp at 2,800rpm.
Performance: Road speed 32mph (51km/h); range 279 miles (446km); vertical obstacle 2ft 2in (0.71m); trench 9ft 6in (3.12m); gradient 70 per cent.
History: In service with the Red Army from 1942 to 1948.

During late January 1942 the T-70 light tank began to replace the T-60 model in Russian service. Despite the fact that it had been shown that the light tank was not an effective vehicle. It was cheaper and easier to mass produce and this meant that units could receive tanks where they would otherwise had none. With the tremendous losses suffered by the Soviet tank parks during the first six months of the war (put at over 18,000 vehicles) and the fact that most of the Soviet tank industry had to be transferred to the central regions of the USSR, thereby delaying production, any tank production was imperative. As the war progressed, however, the production of medium and heavy tanks soon reached the desired level and the final light tank model to enter service remained the T-70. The T-70 light tank was mass produced at the Gorki Automobile Works. It replaced the T-60 in light tank units.

The T-70 had the same chassis as the T-60 (with the drive taken to the front, instead of the rear), slightly reinforced to take the extra weight, but mounted a 45mm gun (with 70 rounds) and co-axial 7.62mm DT machine-gun (with 945 rounds) in a new welded turret. The hull armour was also modified to give a cleaner outline and better protection, and the driver was provided with an armoured visor. The engine power was doubled by providing two engines of the type used in the T-60.

During mid-1943 the T-70A was produced. This was an improved version with increased armour and slightly more powerful engines. The turret, which was more heavily armoured, had a squared-off rear, as distinct from the rounded type of the T-70. Production of the T-70 and T-70A light tanks was discontinued in the autumn of 1943 as the result of increased medium tank output. Altogether, 8,226 of the T-70 light tank were turned out. In 1944 the surviving chassis were modified (an extra bogie wheel on each side) and converted to self-propelled gun mountings.

Right: The T-70 was introduced as the successor to the T-60 light tank and had the same chassis but with drive sprocket at the front instead of the rear. It was armed with a 45mm gun in place of the 20mm cannon. To cope with the increased weight the T-70 was powered by two ZIS-202 petrol engines developing 70hp each. By the time it was introduced the Soviets had realised that the value of the light tank was limited compared to that of the medium tank such as the T-34 but as there were insufficient of these to equip all tank units production of the T-70 was allowed to continue for a few years. Many of the surviving T-70s were subsequently converted into Su-76 SPGs.

Above: The T-70A was introduced in 1942 and differed from the T-70 in having a more heavily armoured turret with squared off rear, as distinct from the rounded type of the original model, and more powerful engines. Production of the T-70 was completed in 1944 after some 8,226 had been built.

Above: The T-70A was introduced in 1942 and differed from the T-70 in having a more heavily armoured turret with squared off rear, as distinct from the rounded type of the original model, and more powerful engines. Production of the T-70 was completed in 1944 after some 8,226 had been built.

IS-2 Heavy Tank

IS-1, IS-2 and IS-3.
Country of origin: Russia.
Crew: 4.
Armament: One 122mm M1943 (D-25) L/43 tank gun; one 12.7mm M1938 DShK machine-gun; one 7.62mm DT or DTM machine-gun.
Armour: 132mm (5.2in) maximum; 19mm (0.75in) minimum.
Dimensions: Length (including gun) 32ft 9in (10.74m); width 10ft 6in (3.44m); height 8ft 11in (2.93m).
Weight: 101,963lb (46,250kg).
Ground pressure: 11.25lb/in^2 (0.79kg/cm^2).
Engine: One Model V-2 IS 12-cylinder water-cooled diesel developing 520hp at 2,000rpm.
Performance: Road speed 23mph (37km/h); range 94 miles (150km); vertical obstacle 3ft 3in (1m); trench 8ft 2in (2.86m); gradient 70 per cent.
History: In service with the Russian Army from 1943 to late 1970s.

In August 1942 the Soviet high command was well aware of the fact that Germany was developing new heavy tanks with more powerful armament and thicker armour. Work on a new heavy tank was therefore begun. Based on the experience gained so far in the design of experimental KV models (KV-3 and KV-13), in 1943 the design bureau investigated a new project designated IS (Iosef Stalin). Early in autumn 1943 the first three prototypes of the IS-1 (also called IS-85 because of its 85mm gun) were completed. After demonstrated before the special commission from the Main Defence Commissariat and the completion of general factory trials, the IS design was approved. Directions were given to begin mass-production in October 1943.

The new tank, weighing little more than the KV (and for that matter, the German Panther medium tank) had thicker, better shaped armour which provided excellent protection. In addition, the weight was kept low by the use of more compact component design. The tank had a new cast turret mounting an 85mm gun specially designed by General F. Petrov (the same turret as fitted to the KV-85 as an expedient).

Soon after the start of production of the IS-1 tank, the need arose for a more powerfully armed vehicle. At that time the 85mm gun was being used in the T-34 medium (T-34/85) and it was considered inappropriate that a heavy tank should have the same armament. A few prototypes were therefore fitted with a new 100mm gun (IS-100), but were not accepted for production. This was because another group, under General Petrov, had within two weeks conceived a scheme for mounting a 122mm gun (with 28 rounds). Towards the end of October 1943 factory and proving ground tests were concluded for the IS tank fitted with this weapon. On 31 October the tank was accepted as standard and designated IS-2. By the end of the year the Kirov Factory had produced 102 IS-2 tanks.

The IS tank was used for the first time during February 1944 at Korsun Shevkenskovsky. During this battle General Kotin personally observed the performance of the IS-2 tank and gained vital information as to its performance and short-comings. After producing several other experimental vehicles of this type, work on a further improvement to the armour layout led, towards the end of 1944, to the new IS-3 model. The design of this tank, carried out by a group under N. Dukhov, was conceived around the armour philosophy of the T-34. Armour plate of even greater thickness and better ballistic shape was heavily inclined to give maximum protection. In contrast to its predecessors, the IS-3 hull was made of rolled plate and the turret was carapace-shaped. Despite all these improvements, the overall weight of the new tank still did not exceed that of the contemporary German medium tank. The final model of this heavy tank, T-10, was the tenth model to be produced. The prefix "IS" was discontinued as a result of the general de-Stalinisation policy adopted in the Soviet Union during the mid-1950s.

Below: IS-2 heavy tank on the Leningrad front. The IS-2 was accepted for service on 31 October 1943 and by the end of that year the Kirov factory had built 102. By the end of 1944 a total of 2,250 had been completed. Further development resulted in the IS-3 which entered service in January 1945.

PT-76 Light Amphibious Tank

Country of origin: Russia.
Crew: 3.
Armament: One 76.2mm gun; one SGMT 7.62mm machine-gun co-axial with main armament.
Armour: 14mm (0.55in) maximum.
Dimensions: Length (gun forward) 25ft (7.62m); length (hull) 22ft 8in (6.91m); width 10ft 4in (3.14m); height 7ft 2in (2.19m).
Weight: Combat 30,865lb (15,000kg).
Ground pressure: 6.8lb/in^2 (0.48kg/cm^2).
Performance: Maximum road speed 27.34mph (44km/h); water speed 6.2mph (10km/h); range 162 miles (260km); vertical obstacle 3ft 8in (1.1m); trench 9ft 2in (2.8m); gradient 60 per cent.
History: Entered service with Soviet Army in 1952; some 12,000 produced between 1952 and 1967. In service with Afghanistan (60), Belarus (8), Benin (20), Cambodia (10), Congo (3), Croatia (5), Cuba (50), Guinea (20), Guinea-Bissau (20), Indonesia (130), Iraq (100), North Korea (number not known), Laos (25), Madagascar (12), Nicaragua (10), Russia (200), Uganda (20), Vietnam (300), Yugoslavia (5), Zambia (30).

The PT-76 (*Plavaushiy Tank*) was based on the *Pinguin* cross-country vehicle. Since it entered service with the Soviet Army in 1952, it has been exported to many countries and has seen combat in Africa, the Middle East and the Far East. It has a hull of all-welded steel construction. The driver is seated at the front of the hull, with the commander/gunner and loader in the turret, and the engine and transmission at the rear of the hull. The PT-76 is armed with a 76.2mm gun, this having an elevation of +30° and a depression of –4°. A 7.62mm SGMT machine-gun is mounted co-axially with the main armament. 40 rounds of 76.2mm and 1,000 rounds of 7.62mm ammunition are carried.

The most outstanding feature of the PT-76 is its amphibious capability. It is propelled in the water by two water-jets, one in each side of the hull, with their exits in the hull rear. Before entering the water a trim vane is erected at the front of the hull and the driver's centre periscope is raised so that he can see over the top of the trim vane.

The PT-76 has been built in large numbers and its basic chassis has been used for a whole family of other armoured vehicles. A modified version has

Below: Side and rear drawings of a PT-76 Model 2 showing covered waterjet outlets at rear of hull and inlets on hull sides towards rear.

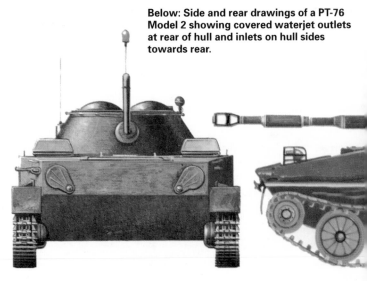

Above: PT-76 Model 2s show their amphibious capabilities: note trim vane erected, driver's periscope extended and schnorkel on the rear of the turret.

Above: PT-76 and motorcycle combination team being used in the reconnaissance role receive their orders by hand from "Hoplite" helicopter (many Soviet AFVs are not fitted with radios).

been built in China as the Type 63. This has a similar hull to the PT-76, but has a new turret mounting an 85mm gun and a co-axial 7.62mm machine-gun; there is also a 12.7mm anti-aircraft machine-gun on the roof. Although now some 40 years old, the PT-76 is still a useful vehicle in the reconnaissance role.

Right: The chassis of the PT-76 light tank is used for many other applications such as launcher/transporter for the Frog 3 surface-to-surface missile system. This missile has a nuclear warhead and a maximum range of some 40km.

Above: In addition to being used by the Soviet Army the PT-76 is also used by the Soviet Marines and some 20 other countries.

T-10 Heavy Tank

T-10, T-10M.
Country of origin: Russia.
Crew: 4.
Armament: One 122mm gun; one 14.5mm machine-gun co-axial with main armament; one 14.5mm anti-aircraft machine-gun.
Armour: 20mm-250mm (0.79-10.8in)
Dimensions: Length (gun forward) 34ft 9in (10.6m); length (hull) 23ft 1in (7.04m); width 11ft 8in (3.566m); height 8ft (2.43m) without anti-aircraft machine-gun.
Weight: Combat 114,640lb (52,000kg).
Ground pressure: 11.09lb/in² (0.78kg/cm²).
Engine: V-2-IS (V2K), 12-cylinder water-cooled diesel developing 700hp at 2,000rpm.
Performance: Road speed 26mph (42km/h); range 155 miles (250km); vertical obstacle 2ft 11in (0.9m); trench 9ft 10in (3m); gradient 60 per cent.
History: Entered service in 1957. In service with East Germany, Egypt, Soviet Union, Syria and Vietnam. Production completed in early 1960s.
(*Note: data above relate to T-10M.*)

The standard Russian heavy tanks during the closing years of World War II were the IS series. The IS-4 entered service in small numbers in 1946-7 and further development resulted in the IS-5, IS-6, IS-7, IS-8, IS-9 and finally the IS-10. The last was placed in production in 1956 as the T-10. The tank has the same engine as the IS-3, but a more powerful gun and much improved armour layout.

Today T-10s do not form a part of the normal equipment of Russian tank regiments or divisions, but are instead formed into special battalions and attached to divisions as required. The T-10 has a crew of four (commander, gunner, loader and driver). The driver is seated at the front of the vehicle with the other three crew members in the turret, the commander being on the left. The engine and transmission are at the rear of the hull. The suspension consists of seven road wheels (the IS series have six) with the idler at the front and the drive sprocket at the rear; there are three track-return rollers on each side.

The first model to enter service was the T-10. This is armed with a 122mm gun and 12.7mm DShK anti-aircraft and co-axial machine-guns. The 122mm gun has an elevation of +17° and a depression of −3°, and a total of 30 rounds of 122mm ammunition of the separate loading type is carried, as well as

Below: T-10M heavy tank from the rear; this particular tank does not have a sheet metal stowage box on the rear of the turret, but does have extra fuel tanks.

Above: The T-10 was developed in the early 1950s and made its first public appearance at the November 1957 Moscow parade.

1,000 rounds of 12.7mm machine-gun ammunition. The T-10 fires two types of ammunition, an HE projectile which weighs 60lb (27.3kg) and an APHE projectile which weighs 55lb (25kg); both have a muzzle velocity of 2,904ft/s (885m/s). The APHE round will penetrate 7.3in (185mm) of armour at a range of 1,092 yards (1,000m). The 122mm gun has a maximum range of 18,154 yards (16,600m) with the gun at its maximum elevation, and its effective range in the anti-tank role is between 1,312 and 2,187 yards (1,200-2,000m).

The T-10M is a further development of the T-10 and this has a number of major improvements to increase its combat effectiveness. The 12.7mm machine-guns have been replaced by 14.5mm KPVT (Co-axial) and KPV (anti-aircraft) machine guns. The double baffle muzzle-brake on the T-10 has been replaced by a multi-baffle muzzle-brake, but the fume extractor has been retained. The main armament is now stabilised in both planes, eg elevation and traverse. In addition to the HE and APHE rounds the 122mm gun can fire a HEAT round with a muzzle velocity of 2,953ft/s (900m/s), which will penetrate 18in (460mm) of armour. The basic T-10 is provided with infra-red driving lights, but in addition the T-10M has an infra-red searchlight on the commander's cupola; there is another infra-red searchlight mounted to the right of the main armament, and this moves in elevation with the main armament. The T-10 can ford to a depth of 3ft 11in (1.2m) without preparation, but the T-10M can be provided with a schnorkel for deep fording operations. The T-10M is also provided with an NBC system and many have been fitted with a large stowage box of sheet metal welded to the turret rear. Additional fuel tanks can be fitted at the rear of the hull to increase the operating range of the tank.

The T-10 has been used by Egypt and Syria in the 1973 Middle East campaign. It is normally used to provide long-range anti-tank support to the T-55/T-62 tanks. It would also be used to spearhead a breakthrough on a vital sector, where its firepower and armour would prove most useful. The T-10 does have a number of draw-backs. First, it is slightly slower than the T-62 and T-55 MBTs, which could mean that an advance has to slow down to allow the T-10s to keep place. Second, as with most Russian tanks, the T-10's gun has a very limited depression, making it difficult to fire from reverse slopes. And third, its ammunition is of the separate loading type (eg projectile and separate cartridge case), which takes a little longer to lead and therefore reduces the tank's rate of fire to three or four rounds per minute. The T-10 has excellent armour, and is one of the most difficult of Russian tanks to destroy.

T-54/T-55 Main Battle Tanks

Country of origin: Russia.
Crew: 4
Armament: One 100mm gun; one SGMT 7.62mm co-axial machine-gun, two SGMT 7.62mm anti-aircraft machine-guns.
Armour: 150mm (5.9in) maximum.
Dimensions: Length (including main armament) 29ft 6in (9.0m); length (hull) 21ft 2in (6.45m); width 10ft 9in (3.27m); height 7ft 10in (2.4m).
Weight: Combat 91,410lb (41,500kg).
Engine: 12-cylinder four-stroke water-cooled diesel engine developing 630hp at 2,000rpm.
Performance: Road speed 31mph (50km/h); road range with two additional 200l fuel tanks 340 miles (545km); vertical obstacle 2ft 8in (0.8m); trench 8ft 10in (2.7m); gradient 60 per cent.
History: T-54 entered service with Soviet Army in 1947, T-55 in 1960. Over 60,000 T-54/T-55s produced in Soviet Union, 2,000 in Poland and 3,000 in Czechoslovakia, of which some 24,000 are still in service with 59 armies. Production of T-55 ended in Soviet Union in 1981. Copy of T-54 produced in China (see Type 59).
(*Data apply to T-55 AM2B.*)

Over 65,000 T-54/T55 MBTs were produced in the Soviet Union, Czechoslovakia and Poland, plus a further 7,000 Type 59s in China. This beats the 50,000-unit production figures of the Soviet T-34 by a handsome margin, making the T-54/T-55 the most widely-used tank of all time; a record which is unlikely to be broken in the future.

During World War II, the Soviet Army's main tank design was the T-

Below: An Egyptian Army T-55 after the fitment of a 105mm gun in the UK.

34, which mounted an 85mm gun and is generally accepted to have been the best all-round tank in the war. The T-34 was developed into the T-44, which was produced in small numbers, but turned out to be an interim design, as the much improved T-54 appeared in 1947 and became the Warsaw Pact's first standard MBT. The T-54 is armed with the D-10T 100mm gun, firing APHE, HEAT and HE rounds, and is capable of an elevation of +17° and a depression of –4°, the latter being significantly less than in Western MBTs. The turret is virtually hemispherical in shape, which gives good ballistic protection, but makes it somewhat cramped inside by Western standards.

The T-55 appeared in 1960 and incorporated many improvements, including a more powerful engine. It uses the same 100mm main gun and the first production model also retained the bow-mounted machine-gun although this was deleted from the T-55A onwards.

There are many modified versions of the T-54/55 series and sophisticated retrofit programmes have been undertaken by the Israeli Army, the British firm of Royal Ordnance and the US firm of Teledyne Continental. TRussian Federation armies also continue to update versions in service, of which one of the most recent is the T-55 AM2B. This has a new turret, appliqué armour on both turret and hull, a new

Right: Front and rear views of a T-54 tank while serving with the Egyptian Army during the 1967 Middle East War. The 12.7mm DShK AA machine-gun is mounted on the loader's cupola and can be traversed 360°.

and more powerful engine, much improved electronics and vision devices, and the same tracks as used on the T-72.

This new version is designed to fire the 9K116 anti-tank guided missile from its 100mm main gun. This missile has a maximum range of some 4,400 yards (4,023m), using a semi-automatic guidance

system which requires the gunner to keep his sight on the target until impact. The shaped-charge warhead on the missile is small in diameter, which limits its effectiveness against the latest Western tanks which use Chobham-type armour, although it would be very effective against older tanks.

Left: The T-55 entered service in late 1950s and was first seen in public in 1961. Major improvements include a more powerful engine, armament stabilised in both planes and more ammunition carried.

Iraqi T-55s take a rest following their invasion of Kuwait in 1990. Early the following year they fled toward Iraq but were most likely destroyed by Coalition forces.

T-62 Main Battle Tank

T-62, T-62A, T-62K, T-62M and M1977.
Country of origin: Russia.
Crew: 4.
Armament: One U-5TS 115mm gun; one PKT 7.62mm PKT machine-gun co-axial with main armament; one DShK 12.7mm anti-aircraft machine-gun (optical).
Armour: 20mm-242mm (0.79in-9.52in).
Dimensions: Length (overall) 30ft 7in (9.33m); length (hull) 21ft 9in (6.63m); width 11ft (3.35m); height (without anti-aircraft machine-gun) 7ft 10in (2.4m).
Weight: Combat 88,200lb (40,000kg).
Ground pressure: 11.8lb/in² (0.83kg/cm²).
Engine: Model V-55-5 12-cylinder water-cooled diesel engine developing 580hp at 2,000rpm.
Performance: Road speed 31mph (50km/h); range (without additional fuel tanks) 280 miles (450km); vertical obstacle 2ft 8in (0.8m); trench 9ft 2in (2.8m); gradient 60 per cent.
History: Entered service with the Soviet Army in 1963. Produced in Soviet Union (c. 20,000), Czechoslovakia (1,500) and North Korea (c. 2,000). Production has ended. Approximately 8,000 remain in service in 18 armies.

Above: The T-62 can ford to a depth of 1.4m without preparation, and to a depth of 5.5m with a snorkel fitted. Clearly shown in this photograph is the small door in the rear of the turret, through which the spent 115mm cartridge cases are ejected, and the long range fuel tanks at hull rear.

Right: Standard equipment on the T-62 includes an NBC system and night vision equipment including infra-red driving light, infra-red searchlight to the right of the main armament and infra-red searchlight on the commander's cupola that can be operated from within the turret.

Above: A column of T-62s trundles past a Soviet Army motor-cycle reconnaissance team on exercise in the Soviet Union in the 1970s.

The T-62 was developed in the late 1950s as the successor to the earlier T-54/T-55 series, and was first seen in public in May 1965. In appearance it is very similar to the earlier T-54. It does, however, have a longer and wider hull, a new turret and main armament, and can easily be distinguished from the T-54 as the latter has a distinct gap between its first and second road wheels, whereas the T-62's road wheels are more evenly spaced, and the T-62's gun is provided with a bore evacuator. The hull of the T-62 is of all-welded construction with the glacis plate being 4in (10cm) thick. The turret is of cast armour, and this varies in thickness from 6.7in (17cm) at the front to 2.4in (6cm) at the rear. The driver is seated at the front of the hull on the left side, with the other three crew members

Fully closed down
T-62 tanks on the advance.
The 115mm smooth bore gun
can fire APFSDS, HEAT and HE
rounds at a maximum of four
rounds per minute; some 40
rounds of 115mm ammunition
are carried.

in the turret, the commander and gunner on the left and the loader on the right. The engine and transmission are at the rear of the hull. The suspension is of the well-tried torsion bar type, and consists of five road wheels with the idler at the front, and the drive sprocket at the rear.

The U-5TS gun is of the smoothbore type, and has an elevation of +17° and a depression of −4°. A PKT 7.62mm machine-gun is mounted co-axially with the main armament. When the T-62 first entered service it did not have an anti-aircraft machine-gun, but many T-62s have since been provided with the standard DShK 12.7mm weapon which is mounted on the loader's cupola, T-62s thus fitted being designated T-62A. Three types of ammunition are carried – High Explosive, Fin-Stabilised Armour-Piercing

Below: T-62 tank crews "scramble" on exercise. In a real emergency, such a formation would be extremely vulnerable.

Discarding Sabot (FSAPDS) and High Explosive Anti-Tank (HEAT). The FSAPDS round has a muzzle velocity of 5,512ft/s (1,689m/s) and an effective range of 1.749 yards (1,600m). When this round is fired the sabot (the disposable "slipper" round the projectile) drops off after the round has left the barrel and the fins of the projectile unfold to stabilise the round in flight. According to Israeli reports this round will penetrate 11.8in (30cm) of armour at a range of 1,094 yards (1,000m). The 115mm round is manually loaded, but once fired the gun automatically returns to a set angle at which the empty cartridge case is ejected from the breech, after which it moves on to a chute and is then thrown out through a small hatch in the turret rear.

There are three variants of the T-62; the T-62M is an improved MBT, the T-62K is a command tank and the M1977 is an armoured recovery vehicle. Some 8,000 T-62s remain in service around the world and many are being upgraded by the addition of new armour, tracks, sideskirts, and guns.

T-64 Main Battle Tank

T-64, T-64K, T-64A (M1981/1), and T-64B.
Country of origin: Russia.
Crew: 3.
Armament: One 2A26 125mm gun; one PKT 7.62mm co-axial machine-gun; one 12.7mm anti-aircraft machine-gun.
Armour: Classified.
Dimensions: Length (including main armament) 32ft 6in (9.90m); length (hull) 24ft 5in (7.45m); width 15ft 3in (4.64m); height 7ft 3in (2.20m).
Weight: Combat 92,512lb (42,000kg).
Engine: 5DTF, 5-cyclinder opposed piston liquid-cooled diesel engine developing 750hp at 2,000rpm.
Performance: Road speed 47mph (75km/h); road range 250 miles (400km); vertical obstacle 2ft 8in (0.8m); trench 8ft 10in (2.7m); gradient 60 per cent.
History: T-64 entered service with Soviet Army in 1980 and serves only with the armies of the former USSR. Approximately 8,000 produced; production complete.
(Data apply to T-64B).

In the 1960s the Soviet Army built prototypes of a tank known as the M1970 MBT. This tank was similar to the T-62 and was armed with the same 115mm smoothbore gun, but differed in having an entirely new suspension system, with six small roadwheels. The M1970 was not put into production, but a development then appeared, designated the T-64, which entered service with the Soviet Army in the late 1960s. This has a similar hull and suspension to the M1970, but with a new turret mounting a new 125mm smoothbore gun, which is fed from an automatic loader.

The driver of the T-64 sits in the front of the vehicle in the centre. The other two crewmen are in the turret, with the commander on the right of the gun and the gunner on the left. The gun is the 2A266 125mm smoothbore, which has been the largest-calibre tank gun in service in any army since its appearance in the T-64. The 2A26 has a vertical ammunition stowage system

Below: The T-64 preceded the T-72 in production but is used only by the Russian Army. It has the same 125mm gun with an automatic loader as the T-72 but has different suspension and a slightly different turret.

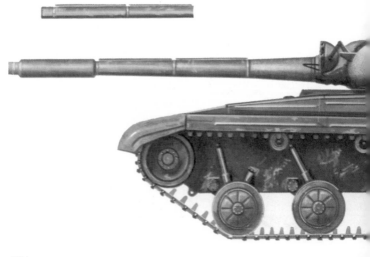

Above: The T-64 MBT entered service in 1980 and has remained exclusive to the armies of the former Soviet Union ever since. Production has ended.

for its automatic loader, which was reported to have given some trouble in its early years of service, with a number of crewmen being seriously injured. There is an infra-red searchlight mounted on the left side of the turret. There are 12 smoke-grenade launchers mounted individually on the forward face of the turret. There is also a thermal sleeve for the main gun, and hinges for track guards which are constructed of thin metal plate.

The suspension has six small, dual roadwheels mounted on hydro-pneumatic arms, a most unusual arrangement in the Russian armies, which have used large roadwheels and torsion bars since the Christie tanks of the 1930s. There are two thin schnorkels for fording operations, one for the gunner's periscope mount, the other for the engine air intake.

The T-64K is a minor variant of the basic T-64 design for use as a command post tank, for which role it carries extra radios, slightly reducing the number

of rounds of 125mm ammunition carried. A telescopic mast is carried on the outside of the hull, which is erected whenever the tank is at the halt.

Three major versions of the T-64 have been identified. The first was the initial production version described above. Next came the T-64A (designated T-64 M1981/1 by the US Army) which had a number of minor modifications. The T-64B then appeared in the early 1980s, fitted with the 2A26M2 125mm smoothbore gun, the same as that fitted to the T-80, although it retained the same type of automatic loader as that in the T-64A. The rounds carried are APFSDS or HEAT-FS, but this tank can also launch an anti-tank guided-weapon, which is designated AT-8 "Songster" by NATO.

The AT-8 is propelled out of the barrel by a boost motor and the main motor then cuts in and powers it to the target at a speed of some 1,640ft/s (500m/s). Maximum effective range is about 4,400 yards (4,00m) and the HEAT warhead will penetrate about 3in (76mm) of steel armour, although its effect against modern ceramic and reactive armours is probably much less.

The T-64B is fitted with a laser rangefinder and additional sensors which are used to acquire helicopter targets prior to engagement with the AT-8 missile. The T-64B is also fitted with mountings for 111 blocks of bolt-on reactive armour, which cover the tank's glacis plate, hull sides and most of the turret. The blocks on the turret necessitate the smoke-grande dischargers being moved to the rear of the turret abreast the commander's hatch.

No T-64s were exported and the type served only with the tank divisions in the Western military districts of the Soviet Union, with the Soviet forces in Hungary and in the group of Soviet Forces Germany. It remains in service with various armies of the former Soviet Union.

Below: Former Soviet chemical troops conduct a decontamination operation on exercise with a T-64, shown without bolt-on reactive armour.

Below: The T-64B's 2A26 125mm smoothbore gun can fire the same ammunition as the T-72, and the AT-8 "Songster" missile.

T-72 Main Battle Tank

T-72, T-72A, T-72AK, T-72AV, T-72B, T-72BK, T-72BM, T-72B1, T-72M, T-72M1, T-72M2, T-72Eh, T-72S, T-72S1, and foreign-produced versions.
Country of origin: Russia.
Crew: 3.
Armament: One 2A46 125mm gun; one PKT 7.62mm co-axial machine-gun; one NSVT 12.7mm anti-aircraft machine-gun.
Armour: Classified.
Dimensions: Length (including main armament) 30ft 4in (9.24m); length (hull) 22ft 10in (6.95m); width 15ft 7in (4.75m); height 7ft 10in (2.37m).
Weight: Combat 90,310lb (41,000kg).
Ground pressure: 11.80lb/in^2 (0.83kg/cm^2)
Engine: V-12 diesel engine developing 780hp at 2,000rpm.
Performance: Road speed 50mph (80km/h); road range 300 miles (483km); vertical obstacle 2ft 8in (0.85m); trench 8ft 10in (2.7m); gradient 60 per cent.
History: Entered service with Soviet Army 1973. Produced in Soviet Union, Czechoslovakia, India, Iran, Iraq, Poland and Former Yugoslavia. Some 18,000

Below: The T-72 MBT is in widespread service with the Russian and a host of other armies around the world. It has a three-man crew and an automatic loader, with each round of ammunition having its charge and projectile loaded separately.

Above: Escorted by APCs, Finnish Army T-72 MBTs press forward, their 2A46 125mm guns firing. The Finnish Army is just one of 14 export customers for the T-72, having acquired 80 examples. Iraqi Army T-72s were heavily used in the Gulf War, but their effectiveness was comprehensively neutralised by the Coalition anti-tank forces.

are in service in 29 armies: Algeria (285); Angola (50); Armenia (100); Azerbaijan (140); Belarus (1,225); Bosnia-Herzegovina (50); Bulgaria (433); Croatia (30); Czech Republic (540); Finland (162); Georgia (31); Hungary (200); India (1,100); Iran (250); Iraq (500); Kazakhstan (600); Kyrgystan (210); Libya (260); Poland (800); Romania (30); Russia (7,000); Sierra Leone (2); Slovakia (270); Syria (1,500); Tajikistan (40); Turkmenistan (570); Ukraine (1,300); Uzbekistan (100); Yugoslavia (300).

Although the T-72 bears an external resemblance in certain respects to the T-64 it was, in fact, developed at a quite different design bureau. It entered production in 1971 and was in wide-scale service by 1973, although it was not reported publicly by Western experts until 1977. As in all recent Russian MBTs the driver is seated centrally under a well-sloped glacis plate, which has transverse ribs and a splashboard. The other two crew members are seated in the turret, the commander on the right and the gunner on the left. All T-72s built for use by armies of the (former) Warsaw Pact have an interior lining of a special synthetic, lead-based material. This is intended to provide some degree of protection against two of the products of a nuclear explosion: for the crew against neutron radiation and for the electronic equipment against electro-magnetic pulses.

There is an automatic loader, which, unlike that in the T-64, has a horizontal feed system. Except in the earliest version, the main gun is the entirely new 2A46 125mm smoothbore, which is fitted with a light alloy thermal sleeve and a fume extractor, and fires three types of ammunition. The kinetic energy APFSDS-T round is fired with a muzzle velocity of 5,900ft/s (1,800m/s) and has a maximum effective range of 2,300 yards (2,100m). The other anti-tank round is the shaped-charged type, which is officially known as HEAT-FS and which has a maximum effective range of 4,400 yards (4,000m). Finally, there is an HE-FRAG(FS) round, which would be used against targets such as bunkers, troops in the open or light vehicles, and which has a maximum range in the indirect fire mode of 10,300 yards (9,400m).

The tank normally carries 39 rounds: 12 APFSDS-T, 21 HE-FRAG-FS and 6 HEAT-FS. All three types of ammunition come in two parts: the projectile and the cartridge case, the latter being entirely combustible apart from a small metal stub. The theoretical rate of fire is 8 rounds per minute, although whether this could be achieved, let alone sustained, on the battlefield is a different matter.

The suspension uses six large-diameter roadwheels mounted on torsion-bars. An unusual feature of the earlier production models is that the tracks are given a degree of protection by four spring-loaded skirt plates, which spring forward at an angle of about 60° when unclipped prior to going into action. This supposedly gives protection against HEAT rounds, but seems of dubious value and has not been repeated on later versions.

There is a single, narrow schnorkel tube for deep-fording rivers, which fits over the gunner's periscope mounting. Such a tube provides no means of escape for the crew in the event of something going wrong whilst underwater and the whole tactic of fording is very unpopular with the soldiers serving in the Russian armoured units.

There have been numerous versions of the MBT since the basic T72 first appeared. There have also been many minor variations within the major types, leading to confusion in the designations. The original version, which was produced in limited numbers and entered service in 1973, was the T-72; this was armed with the same 2A26 smoothbore gun as the T-64. Most of these were subsequently rebuilt to have additional armour on the turret roof and a laser rangefinder. There was also a command version, T-72K, with additional communications.

The next version, which entered service in June 1979, was the T-72A. It incorporated a considerable number of improvements, the most important of which were the definitive 2A46 125mm gun, laser rangefinder and night sights. It also had a new type of diesel engine, improved suspension, a new smoke-grenade launcher system, and greatly increased armoured protection, especially on the forward part of the turret. There was a parallel command version (T-72AK). A number of T-72As were later given additional ERA and were re-designated T-72AV. All this additional armour on the tank's frontal and upper surfaces was a clear response to the increased threat posed by NATO's ever-improving anti-tank weapons, especially the "top attack" munitions, which were starting to enter service at this time.

The T-72B, which was first seen by Western observers in 1985, incorporated yet further improvements, including the 2A46M 125mm gun which could launch the AT-11 Svir missile, a beam-rider with a maximum range of 5,500yd (5,000m). As in the 2A26, the 2A46M was fitted with a thermal jacket and fume extractor, but this was also the first Russian tank gun to use a muzzle reference system. The number of 125mm rounds was increased from 39 to 45, and the fire-control system enhanced. Again, the armoured protection was increased with a 0.8in (20mm) sheet of appliqué armour added to the glacis plate and extra armour on the front and sides of the turret. There was the usual command version, T-72BK, but there was also the parallel T-72B1, which was identical to the T-72B except that it was not equipped to launch the AT-11 Svir missile, resulting in greatly increased stowage for conventional ammunition. Introduced in 1992, the T-72BM was an improved production version for the Russian Army, with a large number of ERA tiles fitted in manufacture (as opposed to retrofits), giving greatly enhanced protection against HEAT and APFSDS rounds.

The T-72s produced for the Soviet/Russian Army had parallel export versions, although these usually appeared somewhat later and frequently did not have all the sophisticated equipment and armour protection of their Soviet equivalents. Thus the T-72Eh, which appeared in 1975, was the export model of the original T-72, and was followed by the T-72M (1980) and T-72M1 (1982), which were export models of the T-72A, the M with decreased armour and the M1 with increased armour. The export versions of the T-72B were the T-72S and T-72S1, both of which appeared in 1987. In both cases, the hull and turret are virtually identical to those of the earlier T-72M1, but both are fitted with 155 ERA boxes.

Above: An excellent study of T-72s on the move, in this case six of the 400 examples acquired by the Polish Army (note the national insignia diamond displayed prominently on each turret). In each case, the tank commander is manning the NSVT 12.7mm machine-gun. Polish T-72s have been seeing carrying the PW-LWD mine-clearing system, this being positioned on the hull top towards the rear.

The main difference is that the T-72S can fire the AT-11 missile (as in T-72B) while T-72S1 fires only gun ammunition (as in T-72B1).

There are a variety of special versions of the T-72, including the BREM-1 armoured recovery and repair vehicle (ARRV); IMR-2 combat engineer vehicle (CEV), and the MTU 72 and MTU-90 armoured vehicle launched bridges (AVLB). All T-72s, with the exception of command tanks, have the mountings necessary for mine-clearing ploughs at the front of the hull, but Polish Army T-72s can also use the PW-LWD rocket-propelled, explosive-filled hose, which is carried in a container mounted atop the engine compartment, and operates in a similar manner to the British Giant Viper system.

With such a large number of the various models of T-72 in service around the world, it is not surprising that there should be a large number of upgrade packages on the market, being supplied by French, Russian, Ukrainian and Yugoslav companies.

Above: The innovative Russian T-72A caused considerable trepidation in the West when it was unveiled at the height of the Cold War, but proved to be less effective in battle than expected.

Production of the T-72 and its variants has now ended, some 20,000 having been produced in four State armaments factories in Russia, as well as in Czechoslovakia, and Poland. The Type 72M1 was produced in India as the *Ajeya* and in Iraq as the *Assad Babyle* (Lion of Babylon). It was also produced in

the former Yugoslavia as the M-84, which differed from the T-72 in a number of respects, mainly in optics and electronics, and a number of these were exported to Kuwait. There were also plans to produce the T-72 in Romania as the TR-125, but after a few had been assembled from Russian-suppled kits, the project was cancelled. Some 19,000 T-72s are in service with at least 29 armies. (It should be noted that the Iranian tank designated Type 72Z is *not* a variant of the Russian T-72 described here, but is a locally upgraded version of Russian-supplied T-54/T-55 and Chinese-supplied Type 59 tanks.)

T-80 Main Battle Tank

T-80, SMT 1989, T-80BV, T-80U and T-80UD.
Country of origin: Soviet Union.
Crew: 3.
Armament: One 2A46 125mm gun/missile launcher; one PKT 7.62mm co-axial machine-gun; one NSVT 12.7mm anti-aircraft machine-gun.
Armour: see texxt.
Dimensions: Length (including main armament) 32ft 6in (9.9m); length (hull) 24ft 3in (7.40m); width 11ft 2in (3.40m); height 7ft 3in (2.20m).
Weight: Combat 94,715lb (43,000kg).
Ground Pressure: 11.80lb/^{2} (0.83kg/cm^2)
Engine: SG-1000 gas turbine engine developing 1,000hp.
Performance: Road speed 47mh (75km/h); road range 250 miles (400km); vertical obstacle 2ft 11in (0.90m); trench 9ft 6in (2.9m); gradient 60 per cent.
History: T-80 entered service with the Soviet Army in 1985. In service with China (2,000), Cyprus (41), Pakistan (320), Russia (3,500), South Korea (80), Ukraine (322).

Design and development of the T-80 was undertaken by the AF Kartsev design bureau, located in the Ural fighting vehicle factory at Nizhni-Tagil, which was also responsible for the T-64 MBT. Development started in the early-1970s, with production starting around 1975 and service introduction around 1977.

The T-80 incorporates numerous advances over the T-64, of which the most significant is the installation of a gas turbine engine, possibly influenced by the use of a similar powerplant in the United States Army's M1 Abrams MBT. The SG-1000 gas turbine develops approximately 1,000hp and is coupled to a manual transmission with five forward and one reverse gears. Two additional jettisonable fuel tanks are mounted on the rear of the T-80 and a third tank can be fitted on the engine covers. A later version of the T-80 (described in more detail below) is powered by

Above: The T-80 is powered by a gas-turbine engine and has achieved some export successes, including China (200), Cyprus (41), Pakistan (320), and South Korea (80).

a diesel engine, so it must be presumed that the Russian Army was not satisfied with either the overall performance of the gas turbine or its high fuel consumption – or, possibly, both!

The hull of the T-80 is of steel, with laminated armour in various crucial areas such as the glacis plate. The turret is of cast steel, but has an inner layer of "special" armour. The inside of the driver's compartment and the turret are lined with a special synthetic, lead-based material, similar to that on the T-72, which provides protection against neutron radiation and electro-magnetic pulses.

The suspension uses six road wheels on each side, mounted on torsion bars. This is a reversion to the more traditional Soviet system, compared to the T-64's small wheels and hydropneumatic

Left: The T-80BV, like the T-64, has been fitted with explosive reactive armour to give a massive increase in protection against the latest generation of anti-tank guided weapons, which carry HEAT warheads.

suspension.

The main weapon is the 2A46 125mm smoothbore gun with a horizontal loader, which is identical to that used in the T-72. It fires the AT-8 "Songster" anti-tank guided-weapon or two types of APFSDS-T, HEAT-FS and HE-FRAG(FS).

As with all Russian tanks the T-80 is fitted for deep wading. A large cylindrical container is mounted across the rear of the turret, which carries two schnorkel tubes. One fits over the gunner's periscope mounting, the other over the radiator grille to provide an air-intake for the gas turbine.

A new version of the T-80 was revealed in 1987, although it had already been in service for some years. Originally known by its US Army designation of T-80 Model 1984 but now designated T-80BV, it has between 185 and 220 explosive reactive armour (ERA) blocks mounted on the glacis plate and turret. These ERA blocks explode when hit by an incoming HEAT round, initiating the high-powered, molten metal jet, which then dissipates its energy in penetrating the block, leaving insufficient energy to then penetrate the main armour of the tank. Such devices provide very significant protection against HEAT rounds fired from guns and missiles fitted with

Right: Russian T-80UM. Note the ERA panels on the glacis, frontal skirts for dust suppression, and extra armour on track skirts. The plates around the turret are part of an ERA package.

HEAT warheads.

Yet a further improved version of the T-80 appeared in 1989, the T-80U originally dubbed Soviet Medium Tank M1989, or SMT 1989 by NATO. The most obvious external change is a new type of additional armour protection on the turret, in which a metal cowl has been fitted over the bank of ERA blocks, resulting in a marked change to the tank's appearance. The ERA blocks on the glacis plate have also been rearranged to give a neater and more comprehensive coverage. There are many other changes, including remote-control firing for the roof-mounted 12.7mm anti-aircraft machine-gun, additional smoke grenade dischargers and an improved on-board fire control system. A further development, the T-80UD, has a 1,100hp diesel engine in place of the gas-turbine.

Left: This rear view of a T-80UM shows the large exhaust filter, the rests for the long-range fuel tanks, and the undstching beam. Note the large array of ERA panels on the turret.

Russian T-80s prepare for a river crossing, an activity intensely unpopular among the crews. Each tank has three tubes: one for people, one for the engine air intake, one for the exhaust.

T-90 Main Battle Tank

T-90, T-90Eh and T-90S.
Country of origin: Russian Federation.
Crew: 3.
Armament: 2A46M 125mm smoothbore gun; one PKT 7.62mm machine-gun co-axial with main gun; one remote-controlled NSVT 12.7mm machine-gun on turret roof; six single-barrelled smoke grenade dischargers on each side of turret.
Armour: Composite, with added ERA.
Dimensions: Length (including main gun) 31ft 3in (9.53m); length (hull) 22ft 6in (6.86m); width 12ft 5in (3.78m); height (to turret roof) 7ft 4in (2.23m).
Weight: Combat 102,513lb (46,500kg).
Ground pressure: 12.9lb/in² (0.91kg/cm²).
Engine: V-84MS 4-stroke, 12-cylinder diesel, 840bhp at 2,000rpm.
Performance: Road speed 37mph (60km/h); range 342 miles (550km); vertical obstacle 2ft 10in (0.85m); trench 9ft 2in (2.8m); gradient 60 per cent.
History: Entered production in 1994; approximately 200 in service with Russian Army in 2000.

Development of the T-90 began at the same design bureau that had been responsible for the T-72B (qv) and prototypes were running in 1990 with first production models being delivered to the Russian Army in 1994. Production has continued since but at a very slow rate compared to previous Soviet/Russian tanks, with only about 200 in service by the year 2000.

The main armament is the 2A46M 125mm smoothbore gun, which is fitted with a fume extractor and surrounded by a thermal jacket. The autoloader holds 22 projectiles and charges, and there are a further 21 stored elsewhere in the tank. The gun, which is the same as that mounted in the T-72 and T-80, fires the same APFSDS, HEAT and HE-FRAG rounds. In addition, however, it has a new type of fragmentation round which can be detonated from the tank as it passes over the target, thus giving a new top-attack capability. As in the earlier tanks, the 125mm gun can launch an anti-tank missile, but in this case

Below: T-90 on its first international demonstration, in Abu Dhabi in 1997. Developed by the design bureau responsible for T-72B, T-90 is in service in small numbers with the Russian Army.

Above: T-90 shows its 2A46M 125mm smoothbore gun, which fires both normal ammunition and laser-guided 9M119M "Refleks" (NATO = AT-11 Sniper) anti-tank missiles.

it is the latest, laser-guided 9M119M Refleks (designated AT-11 Sniper, by NATO) which has a tandem warhead, designed to attack tanks fitted with ERA.

There are six 81mm launcher tubes on each side of the turret, which can be used to launch a variety of grenades, including conventional smoke and a new type of spray, which is intended to defeat incoming missiles using infra-red

homing guidance systems. It is of interest that on T-90 these launchers point at a relatively low angle (about 20 degrees) compared to a much higher angle (about 80 degrees) on earlier Russian tanks, indicating that they are intended to achieve their effect at a greater range from the tank. The T-90, like all Russian MBTs, can also create its own smoke-screen by spraying diesel fuel into the main exhaust outlet. Although T-80 was powered by a gas turbine, the power unit in T-90 is a four-stroke diesel engine, with a multi-fuel capability, enabling it to run on diesel fuel, gasoline, kerosene or benzine.

The T-90 is on offer for export as the T-90Eh and T-90S, but no orders have so far been announced.

Chiormy Oriol (Black Eagle) Main battle Tank

Country of origin: Russian Federation.
Crew: 3.
Armament: One 2A46M 125mm gun; one 7.62mm machine-gun mounted co-axially with main gun.
Armour: Welded steel with Kaktus active defence system.
Dimensions: Length (hull) 23ft 0in (7.0m); width 12ft 0in (3.66m); height 7ft 2in (2.2m).
Weight: Combat 111,772lb (50,700kg).
Ground pressure: 13.6lb/in^2 (0.96kg/cm^2)
Engine: One turbine-supercharge diesel; 1,200hp.
Performance: Road speed 43mph (70km/h; range 210 miles (338km); vertical obstacle 3ft 4in (1.0m); trench 9ft 5in (2.85m); gradient 63 per cent.
History: Prototype running in 1995 and first shown in public in 1997. Production plans not clear.
(*All data are estimates.*)

The *Chiormy Oriol* (Black Eagle) main battle tank was shown briefly at a Russian armoured vehicle demonstration in 1997. It is not confirmed whether this is a one-off prototype, a technology demonstrator or a precursor to a production MBT. Some soruces suggest that it is not intended for the Russian Army but may have been developed at the instigation of a foreign army, but whichever of these it might be, it is a vehicle of considerable interest.

It was originally thought that the Black Eagle was based on the T-80UM hull, but it is now clear that the hull is new, being longer than that of the T-80UM and with a seventh road-wheel. The extra length has allowed the armoured protection to be increased, partly by greater angling of the glacis plate, but also by the addition of a new type of explosive reactive armour (ERA) known as Kaktus.

It is believed that the Black Eagle was originally designed to mount the new

Right: This view of Black Eagle shows the low turret with a large bustle which houses the new autoloader. The large caliber gun is also shrouded for secrecy from Western observers.

Above: Chiorny Oriol (Black Eagle) on its initial demonstration, with the turret carefully shrouded in a camouflage net. The tank has a T-80UM chassis, but with a completely new turret.

152mm gun now under development, but the prototypes mount the same 2A46M 125mm as the T-80UM. The major innovation is the turret, which has a large, overhanging bustle, which has long been a feature of Western tanks such as the US M1 and British Challenger 1 and 2, but has not been used before by Russian designers. One advantage is that such a bustle produces a counter-balance to the ever-increasing weight and length of the gun, thus reducing the mechanical stresses on the turret mounting. A further advantage is that it provides a considerable increase in the internal storage space which can be used to house the autoloader and the ready-use ammunition behind a safety bulkhead. This would overcome the serious disadvantage of current Russian MBTs where the autoloader (and thus the ready-use ammunition) is inside the crew compartment, which has proved dangerous in the event of a hit.

During this new MBT's first exposure to the public the turret was carefully covered in a camouflage net, presumably to conceal features which the Russians were not ready to reveal, but more recent displays have shown the turret uncovered and have thus confirmed that it is much lower and more sloped than in recent MBTs. The Black Eagle is also fitted with the Drozhd active protection system.

Stridsvagn Strv.m/40 Light Tank

Strv.m/40, Strv.m/40L, Strv.m/40K, Strv 74H and Strv 74V.
Country of origin: Sweden.
Crew: 3.
Armament: One 37mm gun; two 8mm machine-guns co-axial with main armament.
Armour: 24mm (0.94in) maximum.
Dimensions: Length 16ft 1in (4.901m); width 6ft 11in (2.108m); height 6ft 10in (2.082m).
Weight: 20,944lb (9,500kg).
Engine: Scania-Vabis six-cylinder water-cooled petrol engine developing 142hp (see text).
Performance: Road speed 30mph (48km/h); vertical obstacle 2ft (0.609m); trench 5ft 6in (1.676m); gradient 60 per cent.
History: Entered service with Swedish Army in 1940 and phased out of service in 1950s. Some were then exported to Dominica and these remained in service until recently.

The first Swedish tank was completed in 1921 and was known as the *Stridsvagn m/21*. Ten of these were built, and they weighed 9.55 tons (9.700kg), were armed with twin 6.5mm machine-guns (female) or one 37mm gun (male) and were powered by 55hp Daimler engines giving them a road speed of 13mph (21km/h). They were designed by the German tank designer Joseph Vollmer, who had also designed the German A7V, K-*Wagen* and LKI/LKII tanks. In appearance the m/21 owed a lot to the last German design. In 1929 these were fitted with more powerful 85hp engines and then became known under the designation m/21-29. Sweden also purchased some British Carden-Loyd carriers and French Renault NC 27 light tanks.

In the late 1920s the Landsverk company was formed, and this concern developed a

number of tracked and tracked/wheeled vehicles. Their first tracked vehicle was the L-5, and this was followed by the L-10 (some of which were purchased by the Swedish Army as the m/31), L-30 (wheel/track), L-80 (wheel/track), L-60 (a type not adopted by Swedish Army, but of which some were sold to Eire and others were built under licence in Hungary), L-100 and L-101. Further development of the L-60 resulted in the Strv m/38, which was built for the Swedish Army. This weighed 8.37 tons (8,500kg), had a crew of three and was armed with a 37mm gun and an 8mm machine-gun. The m/38 was followed by the similar m/39, which had a twin rather than a single 8mm machine-gun, but retained the 37mm gun.

The first tank to be built in large numbers for the Swedish Army was the Strv m/40. The first production model was known as the Strv m/40L, and had a 142hp engine. This was followed by the Strv m/40K, which had heavier armour, which increased weight to 10.73 tons (10,900kg), and was powered by a 160hp engine. In 1944 the Strv m/42 entered service. This had a longer chassis than the earlier m/40, and had six rather than four road wheels. It had a crew of four, and was armed with a 75mm gun and twin 8mm co-axial machine-guns. There was also a 8mm machine-gun mounted in the front of the hull. Combat weight was 22.14 tons (22,500kg) and top road speed 28mph (45km/h). Between 1956 and 1958 these were rebuilt with a revised turret armed with a new 75mm gun, and were designated Strv 74H or 74V. These were replaced by the Ikv 91 light tank/tank destroyer. There was also a 105mm self-propelled gun called the m/43, which used a hull similar to that of the m/42.

Below: An Strv m/40L light tank (also known as the Strv 33) produced in 1941 for the Swedish Army. Mounting a 37mm gun, it was an improvement on the m/38 tank of 1935. On the m/40L the front glacis ventilator was removed and a door was provided in the centre of the glacis.

Stridsvagn Strv.m/41 Light Tank

Strv 41 SI and SII, Strv m/43 SPG, and Pbv 301.
Country of origin: Sweden.
Crew: 3.
Armament: One 37mm gun; one 8mm machine-gun co-axial with main armament; one 8mm machine-gun in hull front.
Armour: 25mm (1in) maximum.
Dimensions: Length 15ft (4.572m); width 7ft (2,133m); height 7ft 8in (2.336m).
Weight: Combat 23,148lb (10.500kg).
Engine: Scania-Vabis six-cylinder water-cooled petrol engine developing 145 or 160hp.
Performance: Road speed 26mph (45km/h); range 125 miles (201km); vertical obstacle 2ft 7in (0.787m); trench 6ft 2in (1.879m); gradient 60 per cent.
History: Entered service with the Swedish Army in 1942 and phased out of service in 1950s (see text).

Shortly before World War II, the Swedish Jungner company assembled 50 Czech AN-IV-S (or TNHS) light tanks for the Swedish Army, these being designated Strv m/37. The m/37 weighed 4.43 tons (4,500kg), had a crew of two and was armed with twin 8mm machine-guns. Its 80hp engine gave it a top road speed of 37mph (60km/h). The Swedish Army then placed an order for the Czech TNHP tank, but World War II broke out before these could be delivered. Sweden was able to obtain a licence to build the type of Sweden, however, and 238 were built by Scania Vabis between 1942 and 1944.

Two basic models were built, the SI with a 145hp engine, and the SII with a more powerful 160hp engine. There was also a self-propelled gun model built in 1944, this being known as the *Stormartillerivagn* m/43. The m/43 SPG had a crew of four and was armed with a 105mm gun in a ball-type mount in

Right: The m/41 light tank, a licence-built version of the Czechoslovakian-designed TNHP light tank with an improved engine. The m/41s served until the 1950s, when they were rebuilt as Pbv 301 armoured personnel carriers mounting a 20mm cannon. The Pbv 301 was phased out of service with the Swedish Army in 1971.

Above: Side view of the Strv m/42 light tank which entered Swedish service in 1944. In the late 1950s m/42s were rebuilt as the Strv 74H or 74V, which differed in the number of rounds carried for the new 75mm gun and in what type of gearbox was installed.

the front of the superstructure. Loaded weight was 11.8 tons (12,000kg), and a 140hp engine gave the weapon a top road speed of 27mph (43km/h). The m/41 served in the Swedish Army until the 1950s when they were withdrawn from service and rebuilt by Hägglund and Söner to become the *Pansarbandvagn* 301 armoured personnel carrier. These were the first full tracked APCs of the Swedish Army but have now been replaced by the Pbv 302 APC.

Infanterikanonvagn 91 Light Tank/Tank Destroyer

Country of origin: Sweden.
Crew: 4.
Armament: One 90mm gun; one 7.62mm machine-gun co-axial with main armament; one 7.62mm anti-aircraft machine-gun; 12 smoke dischargers.
Armour: Classified.
Dimensions: Length (with gun forward) 29ft (8.85m); length (hull) 21ft 0in (6.41m); width 9ft 10in (3m); height 7ft 7in (2.32m).
Weight: Combat 35,934lb (16,000kg)
Ground pressure: 6.97lb/in² (0.49kg/cm²).
Engine: Volvo-Penta TD 120A 6-cylinder turbo-charged diesel developing 330hp at 2,200rpm.
Performance: Road speed 40mph (65km/h); range 310 miles (500km); vertical obstacle 2ft 8in (0.8m); trench 9ft 2in (2.8m); gradient 60 per cent.
History: Entered service with the Swedish Army in 1965. In service in Sweden (210). Production complete.

The Swedish Army is required to be able to fight a potential enemy in the forests and among the many lakes of its native country, in temperatures which can be as low as –35°C (–31°F). Further, as a neutral country, it must be prepared to fight any enemy and without the aid of allies. It is thus not surprising that, faced with these unusual requirements, the Swedish Army should produce some unusual military equipment.

The Ikv-91 is the outcome of a contract placed with Hägglund Vehicle AB in 1968 for a new combat vehicle to replace the Strv 74 light tank, Ikv-102 and Ikv-103 infantry cannon, and the Pansarvarnskanonvagn m/63 then in service. The result was the Ikv-91, which is a cross between a light tank and a self-propelled anti-tank gun. Some 210 were produced for the Swedish Army, production having started in 1975 and been completed in 1978. The Ikv-91 and a new version with a

Above: The Ikv-91 fires its L/54 90mm gun from cover. The low-pressure gun is claimed to create less recoil loads and reduce muzzle effects (flash, smoke, thrown-up dust) than others.

Below: Sweden's Ikv-91, which is designed to operate with anti-tank units in almost any terrain. It has good cross-country performance, and operates well in regions where there is marshy ground and water obstacles, such as rivers and lakes.

Above: In water the Ikv-91 is propelled by its tracks, giving it a speed of 4.36mph (7km/h), sufficient to cross moderately fast-flowing rivers. For amphibious operations a trim vane is erected and low screens are raised for air inlets, outlets and exhaust.

Below: The Ikv-91's low silhouette, well profiled glacis plate and turret front are intended to afford protection, although priority has been given to high mobility.

105mm gun (Ikv-105) have both been offered for export, but no orders have been received.

The hull of the Ikv-91 is of all-welded steel construction and is divided into three compartments: driver's at the front, fighting compartment in the centre and the engine at the rear. The driver is seated on the left at the front of the tank, with the other three crew members seated in the all-welded turret, with the commander and gunner on the right and loader on the left. The main armament is a Bofors-designed low-pressure gun, firing fin-stabilised, high-explosive and high-explosive anti-tank rounds. 59 rounds are carried, 18 of which are stowed forward, beside the driver. Elevation limits for the gun are +15°/–10°. The barrel is fitted with a fume extractor and has recently been retofitted with a thermal sleeve. The 360° turret traverse is powered by an electro-hydraulic system, with manual reversion. The gunner's optical sight incorporates a laser rangefinder, which gives a high probability of a first-round hit. There is a co-axial 7.62mm machine-gun, with a second 7.62mm anti-aircraft machine-gun on a flexible mount above the loader's hatch. There are also 12 smoke-grenade dischargers, six on each side of the turret.

The engine is a Volvo-Penta four-stroke, 6-cylinder diesel, which produces 360hp at 2,200rpm; it is mounted diagonally to conserve space. The fully automatic transmission system is provided by Allison and gives four forward and one reverse gears. To cope with starting conditions in the severe winters met in the north of the country there is a built-in blow-torch to pre-heat the engine, a feature not found on many tanks!

The torsion-bar suspension utilises six large, rubber-tyred road wheels and the track has been specially designed by Hägglund for use in snow conditions; there are no return rollers. Studs or 2in (50mm) long conical spikes can be fitted to enhance the performance in deep snow – a valuable asset given the harsh Scandinavian climate.

There are many lakes in Sweden and it was thus essential that the Ikv-91 should be fully amphibious, which is part of the reason for its somewhat bulky appearance. There is a trim vane on the glacis plate which is erected before entering the water and low screens are raised around the air inlets and the exhausts. When swimming, the Ikv-91 is propelled by its tracks, which give a maximum speed of 4.3mph (7km/h).

A new version appeared in the 1980s, armed with a Bofors 105mm low recoil gun: designated the Ikv-105, this vehicle was tested by various countries. In the 1990s another new version armed with a 120mm gun was also developed and tested. No orders for either 105mm or 120mm versions were forthcoming.

Stridsvagn Strv-103C
Main Battle Tank

S-103A, S-103B, Strv-103C.
Country of origin: Sweden.
Crew: 3.
Armament: One L74 105mm rifled gun; two 7.62mm co-axial machine-guns, one 7.62mm anti-aircraft machine-gun (commander); eight smoke dischargers (four on each side of turret).
Armour: All-welded steel.
Dimensions: Length (including main armament) 29ft 6in (8.99m); length (hull) 23ft 1in (7.04m); width 11ft 11in (3.63m); height 7ft 11in (2.43m).
Weight: Combat 93,712lb (42,500kg).
Engine: Detroit Diesel 6V-53T 6-cylinder, water-cooled, diesel engine developing 290hp at 2,800rpm; Boeing 553 gas turbine, 490shp at 38,000rpm.
Performance: Road speed 31mph (50km/h); range 242 miles (390km); vertical obstacle 2ft 11in (0.9m); trench 7ft 6in (2.3m); gradient 60 per cent.
History: Entered service with the Swedish Army in 1966; being phased out as Leopard 2(S) enters service.

At the time it entered service, the Swedish Stridsvagn Strv-103 (popularly known

Above: Although never tested in battle, the highly unconventional nature of the S-tank's design and appearance led to a general re-appraisal of MBT design philosophies. In reality, however, it has proved somewhat ineffective.

Right: A graphic illustration of the Strv-103C's peculiar hydropneumatic suspension, at its maximum elevation of +12°. This side profile also highlights the unique outline of this Swedish design, due to the singular lack of any conventional turret.

as the "S-tank") caused great interest as it appeared to provide a new way forward for tank design, leading to lighter and more mobile three-man MBTs. Its design originated in the 1950s, with the Swedish firm of Bofors being awarded the development contract in 1958. The first two prototypes were completed in 1961 followed by 300 production tanks produced between 1966 and 1971.

The S-tank's crew are all located in a central fighting compartment. The driver/gunner is on the left, facing forwards; behind him sits the radio operator, who faces to the rear and who drives the tank backwards, when required. The commander sits on the right of the gun and also has an accelerator and brake to control the vehicle, if required.

Main armament is the L74 105mm rifled gun, a lengthened version of the British L7 gun, produced in Sweden. The barrel is mounted rigidly in the glacis plate thus doing away with the need for a turret. This results in reduced overall height for the tank and reduced weight, since there is no turret or recoil mechanism, and also enables an automatic loader to be installed. This device holds 50 rounds, a mix, as required by the tactical situation, of APDS, HESH, HE and smoke. The tank can fire 10-15 rounds per minute and empty cases are automatically ejected through a hatch in the rear of the hull.

The power pack in the S-103A and S-103B versions was a Rolls-Royce K60 diesel, which was used for normal operations, and a Boeing gas-turbine which was brought in to provide additional power for combat or when crossing difficult terrain. In the Strv-103C, however, the Rolls-Royce engine has been replaced by a more powerful Detroit Diesel 6V-53T, although the gas-turbine has been retained unchanged.

The hydropneumatic suspension is used to aim the gun. The gun is laid in elevation by the driver/gunner, who adjusts the suspension to alter the elevation between +12° and –10°. The gun is traversed by slewing the tank in its tracks. When the gun is fired the suspension is locked to provide a stable platform.

The S-tank bristles with innovations, which caused much excitement when it first appeared. It was widely tested, the British Army even leasing sufficient to equip a complete armoured squadron in Germany for a protracted field trial. However it has proved to be less successful than first thought. It must expose a large cross-sectional area when in a hull-down firing position and cannot fire with any accuracy on the move. No further designs of this type have been produced.

The S-tank is being replaced by the Leopard 2(S) (qv), the German tank having won against competition from the French Leclerc (qv) and the US M1 Abrams (qv). The Leopard 2(S) is now being fielded and will replace all S-tanks and all the remaining Centurions (qv) except for a small number on the island of Gotland.

Panzer 1958/Panzer 1961 (Pz58/Pz61) Main Battle Tanks

Pz58 and Pz61.
Country of origin: Switzerland.
Crew: 4.
Armament: One L7 105mm rifled main gun; one 20mm Oerlikon cannon co-axial with main gun; one 7.5mm MG 51 on turret roof.
Armour: Cast steel.
Dimensions: Length (main gun forward) 30ft 11in (9.36m); length (hull) 21ft 11in (6.69m); width 10ft 0in (3.06m); height 8ft 1in (2.47m).
Weight: Combat 83,600lb (38,000kg).
Ground pressure: 12.1lb/in^2 (0.85kg/cm^2).
Engine: Daimler-Benz MB-837 V-8 diesel, 630bhp at 2,200rpm.
Performance: Road speed 34mph (55km/h); range 186 miles (300km); vertical obstacle 2ft 6in (0.75m); trench 8ft 6in (2.6m); gradient 60 per cent.
History: Pz58 – two prototypes completed in 1958/59, followed by 10 pre-production tanks in 1960/61; no full production. Pz61 – 150 delivered 1965/66; phased out of service by 1996.

In 1922, the Swiss Army purchased two Renault FT-17 tanks for trials. This was a type which was in production in France, Italy and the USA, and which represented the peak of tank development in the recently ended war. Nothing more was done about tanks for some ten years, and then, in 1934, four British Carden-Lloyd tankettes were acquired, but, again, they were used just for trials. Finally, however, just before World War II an order was placed for a number of Czech LTH light tanks, which were required to equip reconnaissance companies, and would be assembled in Switzerland from kits supplied by Czechoslovakia, but powered by Swiss Saurer 125hp diesel engines and armed with an Oerlikon

20mm cannon. Designated Pz39 (*Panzer 1939*) just 24 had been completed when Czechoslovakia was overrun by Germany and the supply of kits stopped abruptly.

In 1944 the Swiss built a prototype self-propelled 75mm, 10-ton anti-tank gun designated NK I, followed in 1945 by the NK II turretless tank, but neither entered production. Between 1947 and 1952 the Swiss purchased 158 self-propelled anti-tank guns from Czechoslovakia; these had been built as *Jagdpanzer 38(t)* for the German *Wehrmacht* but in Swiss service were designated *G.13 Panzerjager* and these remained in service for some years. As a result of the start of the Cold War Switzerland decided to strengthen its defences and placed its first major orders for modern tanks: 200 AMX-13 light tanks from France (*Leichtes Panzer 51*) and 300 Centurions from the United Kingdom, which were designated *Panzer 55* (Centurion Mk 3) and *Panzer 57* (Centurion Mks 5 and 7). All were delivered with 20-pounder (83.4mm) guns, but most were later re-armed with L7 105mm guns.

Meanwhile, the Swiss General Staff had determined that they should become

Above: An Entp Pz65 armoured recovery vehicle changes the power pack of a second Entp Pz65. The 'A'-frame mounted at the front of the hull lifts a load of 33,040lb (15,000kg), and the vehicle has two winches and one dozer blade.

Left: The Pz61 is armed with an L7 105mm gun designed in the UK and made under licence in Switzerland. Unlike most other tanks, the single 7.62mm machine-gun is used by the loader rather than by the tank commander.

self-sufficient in tank design and production; as a result design work started in the early 1950s. Two prototypes of the national design – *Panzer 1958* (Pz58) – were built; the first, completed in 1958, was armed with the Swiss-designed 90mm gun and the second, completed in 1959, was armed with the British 83.4mm (20-pounder) gun, as mounted in the recently purchased Centurions. Ten pre-production Pz58s were built between 1960 and 1961, all armed with the Swiss 90mm gun, but by then the General Staff had decided to adopt the newly developed British 105mm gun mounted in an improved hull, which was designated *Panzer 1961* (Pz61) and it was this version that went into production, 150 being completed between January 1965 and December 1966.

The Pz61 was an excellent design, especially when it is considered that it was

Right: The second prototype of the Swiss Pz58 was armed with a British 20-pounder gun with a co-axial Oerlikon 20mm cannon; later versions mounted the British L7 105mm gun.

Below : The Pz58 was a major undertaking for Swiss industry, which had never before produced such a sophisticated and up-to-date tank design, but it proved very successful.

Switzerland's first. The hull was a single-piece steel casting, which offered major advantages in production time and costs, and also eliminated the need to import armour plate from abroad. The turret was also a single-piece casting, and was virtually hemispherical in shape. The engine was a Daimler-Benz water-cooled, eight-cylinder diesel with a power output of 630bhp at 2,200rpm. One unusual feature was the 20mm cannon, an unusually large calibre for a co-axial weapon, although it should be noted that some early British Centurion tanks had a co-axial Polden 20mm cannon; the weapon did, however, cause problems, particularly with fumes in the fighting compartment. The Swiss also managed to keep the weight of the vehicle under control, producing a tank with a combat weight of 38.0 tons.

Panzer 1968 (Pz68) Main Battle Tank

Series 1 to 4.
Country of origin: Switzerland.
Crew: 4.
Armament: One 105mm L7A1 rifled gun; one SIG MG51 7.5mm machine-gun co-axial with main armament; one SIG MG51 7.5mm machine-gun on turret roof; three single-barrelled smoke grenade launchers on each side of turret.
Armour: Single-piece cast hull and turret.
Dimensions: Length (gun forward) 31.14ft (9.49m); width 10.30ft (3.14m); height 9.02ft (2.75m).
Weight: Combat 89,743lb (40,700kg).
Ground pressure: 12.2lb/in^2 (0.86 kg/cm^2).
Engine: MTU MB 837 Ba-500 8-cylinder diesel, 660bhp at 2,200rpm.
Performance: Road speed 34.4mph (55km/h); range 219 miles (350km); vertical obstacle 2.46ft (0.75m); trench 8.5ft (2.6m); gradient 60 per cent.
History: Entered service with Swiss Army in 1971. Total production: Series 1 – 170; Series 2 – 50; Series 3 – 110; Series 4 – 60. Some 195 are being upgraded to Pz68/88 standard and will remain in service for some years; unmodified tanks will be phased out by the end of 2000.

Following the success of the Pz 61 the Swiss General Staff decided to procure more, but to an improved standard, which was designated Pz 68. This tank was armed with the same British L7 105mm main gun, but with an improved fire-control system and full stabilization to enable the tank to fire while on the move. The tank also had a slightly more powerful MTU diesel engine and a modified gearbox. As with Pz 61, the Pz 68 hull was a one-piece casting with the driver seated in the front at the centre, under a rear-hinged hatch. The other three crewmen were in the turret, which was also a single-piece casting, with the commander and gunner on the right and the loader on the left. The suspension consisted of six road wheels, with the drive sprocket at the

Below: The Pz 68 had a particularly well-designed, cast hull and turret, both of which made maximum use of sloping to maximise their resistance to the anti-tank projectiles of the day.

Above: Main armament of the Pz 68 was the British L7 105mm gun, which became the virtual standard Western tank gun of the 1950s and 1960s, used by most countries except France.

rear and idler at the front, and three return rollers. Each road wheel was independently located and sprung by layers of Belleville washers, a system developed in Germany towards the end of World War II, but employed on an operational tank for the first time in the Pz61 and Pz 68. This system can not only absorb a large amount of energy in proportion to its size and weight, but can also be installed outside the hull.

The main armament was the British L7 105mm manufactured under licence in Switzerland, for which 52 rounds were carried and whose elevation limits were +21 degrees and -10 degrees. Two Swiss-made SIG MG 51 7.5mm machine-guns were also mounted: one co-axially with the main gun, the other on the turret roof, where it was fired by the loader rather than the commander. The replacement of the 20mm cannon by a 7.5mm machine-gun had two advantages: it created more space within the turret and also removed the problems of a fume build-up. The tank had an NBC system and could ford streams up to maximum depth of 3ft 8in (1.1m).

The Pz 68 was produced in four discrete versions. The original model, Pz 68 Series 1, consisted of 170 tanks, delivered between 1971 and 1974. These were followed by 50 Series 2, all delivered in 1977, which had an alternator, a thermal sleeve for the gun and a fume scavenging system for the fighting compartment. Next to appear was Series 3, with 110 delivered between 1978 and 1979, which differed basically in having a larger turret, and finally the virtually identical Series 4, of which 60 were delivered in 1983-1984.

It was then decided to upgrade the majority of the fleet, starting in 1988, which involved installing an improved fire control system, a new fire suppression system for the fighting and engine compartments, an upgraded suspension, a muzzle reference system, and GRP fuel tanks. This involved 25 Series 2 and all the Series 3 (110) and Series 4 (60) tanks, a total of 195. When the work was completed these were designated Pz68/88 and they will remain in service for at least another decade. A 120mm smoothbore gun has been developed in Switzerland, which has been successfully tested in a Pz68/88 (which also featured upgraded armour), but no production plans have been announced.

The latest Swiss Army tank is the German Leopard 2, 380 of which were delivered between 1987 and 1993. It is designated the Pz 87 Leo (*Panzer 1987 Leopard*) and includes several extra features required by the Swiss Army, including a digital computer, Swiss radios, an exhaust muffling system and enhanced NBC protection. It is anticipated that at least a proportion of the Pz 87 fleet will be upgraded to a standard at least equivalent to the German Leopard 2A5 in due course.

Mk I Tank

Mk 1 (male), Mk 1 (female).
Country of origin: United Kingdom.
Crew: 8.
Armament: (Male) two 6pounder QF guns; four 8mm Hotchkiss machine-guns. (Female) four .303in (7.7mm) Vickers machine-guns; one 8mm Hotchkiss machine-gun.
Armour: 6mm-12mm (0.23-0.47in).
Dimensions: Length 32ft 6in (0.75m); male width 13ft 9in (4.12m); female width 14ft 4in (4.3m); height 8ft 0½in (2.41m).
Weight: Combat 62,720lb (28,450kg) for male; 60,480lb (27,434kg) for female.
Ground pressure: 26lb/in² (1.8kg/cm²) at 1in (25.4mm) sinkage.
Engine: Daimler six-cylinder inline water-cooled petrol engine developing 105hp at 1,000rpm.
Performance: Speed 3.7mph (5.95km/h); range 23½ miles (37.8km); vertical obstacle 4ft 6in (1.35m); trench 11ft 6in (3.45m); gradient 24 per cent.
History: A total of 150 Mk.I tanks was built in 1916 by William Foster of Lincoln and the Metropolitan Carriage. Wagon and Finance Company of Wednesbury. Some 49 of these vehicles, the first tanks to see action, took part in the Battle of Flers-Courcelette in September 1916, and Mk.I vehicles were in use for various purposes right to the end of the war.

During the building of "Little Willie" at Fosters in 1915, Lieutenant Wilson produced a second design to meet the revised War Office requirement of crossing an 8ft (2.44m) trench and surmounting a 4ft 6in (1.37m) parapet. The high prow that this requirement dictated resulted in the characteristic rhombodial shape that remained virtually unaltered to the end of the war. The Landship Committee authorised Fosters to proceed with this machine, and on January 16, 1916 the prototype, known as "Mother" (also as the Wilson Machine or Big Willie) ran for the first time. It lived up to every expectation and dealt with a specimen "battle-field obstacle course" with ease. As a result of the success of Mother, a firm order was placed for 100 Mk.I "tanks", split between Fosters and the Metropolitan Carriage, Wagon and Finance Co. The order was later increased to 150. In May 1916 a new unit, known for security as the Heavy Section, Machine Gun Corps, was formed to man these vehicles. Its commanding officer was Colonel Swinton, one of the earliest exponents of the "landship" concept.

The hull of the Mk.I tank was basically the rectangular box structure used on Little Willie, though made of armour plate this time. In place of pivoting track frames, the Mk.I Tank (and all subsequent heavy tanks of the war) had two large track frames, rhombodial in outline, fixed to the sides of the hull. These frames had the high prows and large radius curves along their bottom edges that contributed to the machine's incredible performance over obstacles. The return of the track was carried up inclines at the rear and then ran forward along skidways on each side of the hull roof.

Internally, the Daimler engine and Foster transmission were the same as those used in Little Willie, though in this case the engine was at the front, driving back to the gearbox and differential. Secondary gearboxes were built into the side of each track frame, and through these different ratios could be selected for each track, producing a form of geared turn. Steerable wheels were once more included at the rear, but proved such a liability in action that they were soon removed.

The high top run of the track precluded the use of the turret for the main armament, and so naval experience was drawn on in the fitting of "sponsons" outside each track frame to carry one 6pounder gun (also provided from naval sources) and one machine-gun on each side. These

Below: Top and side views of Mk I Tank. This retained the original steering principle of "Little Willie", in the form of a rear limber, with two drivers controlling the speed of the tracks through rods and cables to the rear gearbox. This tank is a "male", with two 6-pounder QF guns mounted in side sponsons and a secondary armament of four 8mm Hotchkiss machine-guns.

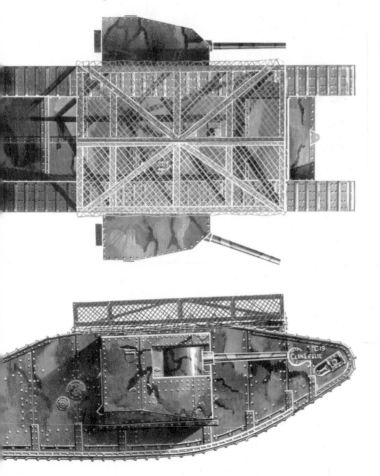

Above: Front and rear views of the Mk.1 Tank, developed from the experimental "Mother". It was built in two basic types, "male" and "female", differing only in armament. A "male" is shown here.

sponsons could, with considerable effort, be removed completely for the tank's rail movement. Some doubt was expressed, during the design stage, of a gun-armed tank's ability to hold off massed infantry, so half the production Mk.I tanks were completed as "females", armed with two Vickers MGs in each sponson in place of the 6pounder guns. Conditions for the crews of these early tanks were incredible. The commander and driver sat high up at the front in the cupola, from which forward vision was very limited by the track horns, the two "gearsmen" crouched on either side of the gearbox, and the gun crews knelt or squatted on tiny seats in the gun sponsons. Right in the middle sat the bellowing unsilenced six-cylinder engine, and right around the crew compartment ran the unsprung tracks! Normal conversation was impossible, and simple instructions were passed by banging on the engine casing, together with hand signals!

Much against the wishes of those who were campaigning for the first mass tank attack to be a surprise action on good ground, the Mk.I tanks were thrown into action at Flers-Courcelette on September 15, 1916. The ill-fated Somme offensive had bogged down, the going was awful, and many crews were inexperienced. Forty-nine tanks started off, but very few reached their objectives. Those that did keep going, however, swept all opposition before them. Army staffs took note and orders for further tanks quickly followed.

Mk IV Tank

Mks IV (male and female) and V.
Country of origin: United Kingdom.
Crew: 8.
Armament: Two 6pounder guns and four .303in Lewis machine-guns (male); six .303in Lewis machine-guns (Female).
Armour: 12mm (0.47in) maximum; 6mm (0.25in minimum.
Dimensions: Length 26ft 5in (8.05m); width 13ft 9in (4.19m); height 8ft 2in (2.48m).
Weight: Combat 62,720lb (28,450kg) for the male; 60,480lb (27,434kg) for the female.
Engine: Daimler six-cylinder water-cooled inline petrol engine developing 100hp or 125hp.
Performance: Speed 3.7mph (5.92km/h); range 35 miles (56km); vertical obstacle 4ft 6in (1.371m); trench 10ft (3.048m).
History: Entered service with the British Army in June 1917 and continued in use until the end of the war. Also used by Eire (one Mk V), Latvia (Mk V), Japan (one Mk IV), Russia, Canada, France and the United States (Mk V).

The Mk IV was the workhorse of the Tank Corps in World War I. It was derived from the Mk I and incorporated the improvements introduced in the Mks II and III, though all three of these early models were built only in comparatively small numbers. The Mk IV was the classic rhombidial shape, and outwardly little different from its predecessors. There were many detailed changes, however: the crew compartment was better ventilated and escape hatches were located in the roof as well as the sides; the fan drew cooling air for the engine from inside the tank and blew it out through the radiator, which was at the back between the rear horns; and a silencer was fitted to the exhaust to

Below: Introduction of tanks took the Germans completely by surprise; at first they were forced to use captured examples, such as these British Mk IVs marked with the Teutonic Cross.

305

reduce some of the deafening noise inside (on the earlier models silencers had been made by the crew from oil drums). The engine was improved, though the tank was still underpowered. Aluminium pistons allowed the revolutions to be increased, and so more power was developed. Twin carburettors improved the induction flow and the vacuum fuel system ensured that petrol reached the engine at all times. With the previous gravity arrangement, it was not uncommon for the engine to be starved of fuel while plunging into deep trenches or on steep slopes.

The armour was the improved type fitted to the Mks II and III, and kept out the German tungsten-cored anti-tank bullets. Closer attention to riveting of the joints reduced much of the bullet splash which had been a hazard on the Mk I. Splash was still a danger, however, and crews were issued with leather face masks and goggles, though few could tolerate wearing them. The track-rollers were strengthened and so were the drive-chains from the gear-shafts. A plain idler wheel was fitted on the front, and wider tracks were tried. The second gear-shaft, which took a great deal of strain in action, had been found to twist, and in the Mk IV it was made from nickel steel. The sponsons were hinged to allow them to be swung in for rail travel. With the earlier marks the sponsons had to be unbolted and stowed inside the tank for shipment, and their removal and replacement was a long and tiring business. An unditching beam was fitted as standard and carried on top of the hull at the rear. Rails carried the beam clear of the cupola when it was used. Chains were provided to attract it to the tracks at each side, and once clear of the obstacle the beam could be recovered and restowed by the crew.

The armament was not a happy story. Because of a shortage of Hotchkiss machine-guns Lewis guns were substituted, and this proved to be a mistake. The Lewis had a large round cooling-jacket and a larger hole had to be made in the armour for it. This allowed splinters and bullet splash to come inside, and the jacket itself was vulnerable to the intense small arms fire which a tank attracted. Later Mk IVs reverted to the Hotchkiss, much to the relief of the crews. The 6pounders were reduced in length from the original 40 calibres to 23 calibres. This had been done on some of the later Mk IIIs, which were virtually identical to the Mk IV. The shorter barrel meant that

Right and below: Some British Mk IV tanks were captured by the Germans. Designated "Beutepanzerwagen" (captured armoured vehicles), they were used by the Germans against the Allies.

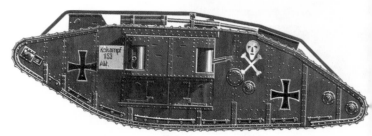

there was no danger of the muzzle being dug into the ground when the tank was crossing wide trenches. This had happened with the Mk Is, and the shortening also made the gun easier for the crew to handle when stowing the sponsons.

The eight-man crew was distributed in the same was as in the Mk I. The driver sat in the cupola in the front and controlled the speed and direction of the vehicle. Beside him was the commander, who also operated the brakes and fired the front machine-gun. At the rear, seated alongside the engine, were the two gearsmen; they changed the secondary gears to each track, and so steered the tank in wide curves; sharp turns were by brakes to each side. These gearsmen were almost totally deafened all the time, and they changed their gears in response to hand signals from the driver. They also acted as gunners mates to the 6pounders. Two men fired the 6pounders, and the last two men fired the machine-guns in the rear of each sponson and generally assisted the 6pounder gunners if necessary. One of them would also be detailed to fire the rear machine-gun, which pointed out between the rear horns. There were no lights inside the tank, and the only illumination came from daylight filtering through the vision slits and hatch covers. The gearsmen would have had to peer hard through the gloom and smoke from the engine to see their signals, and when the guns fired more smoke was added to the inside.

In general, a Mk IV on the move was sheer hell for its crew. The temperature rapidly rose to almost 90° and in summer was well over that. The naked engine and gearbox screamed and shrieked and smoked, the radiator fan roared, the tracks clanged and banged round the hull, and the whole unsprung mass rolled and pitched over the ground, occasionally dropping suddenly into holes or trenches. A speed of 3mph (4.8km/h) was the maximum that any hull and crew could possible stand, and in battle the noise and danger from bullets striking the sides or shells exploding alongside, were enough to drive men almost witless. Few could tolerate the protective helmets or masks provided, and many crewmen were injured by being thrown around inside on rough ground, or falling against the hot engine and gearbox. For the gunners, targets appeared fleetingly in the restricted view of their vision slits, and most shooting was done "on the fly" as the tank rolled on. Few shots were carefully aimed unless the vehicle was stationary.

Nevertheless, the armament was formidable, especially that of the male, and when the first German tanks appeared in April 1918 somefemales were given a male sponson on the right-hand side so that they could protect themselves, the resulting marriage being called an "Hermophrodite". Altogether 420 male and 595 female Mk IVs were produced, and the type was used from the Battle of Flers in September 1917, through Cambrai to the end of the war. Although there were five later marks of rhombodial tank, only the Mk V was made in any quantity and by 1919 these large, slow moving, vulnerable vehicles were obsolete and were replaced by lighter, faster models.

Below: The standard Mk IV tank of World War I. This was one of the most widely-used and most successful British tanks of the 1914-1918 war.

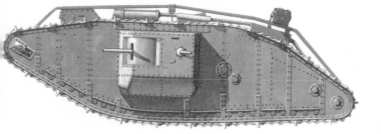

Medium C Tank

Country of origin: United Kingdom.
Crew: 4.
Armament: Four .303in Hotchkiss machine-guns.
Armour: 14mm (0.55in) maximum; 6mm (0.25in) minimum.
Dimensions: Length 25ft 10in (7.856m); width 8ft 11in (2.71m); height 9ft 8in (2.94m).
Weight: Combat 43,680lb (19,813kg).
Engine: Ricardo six-cylinder water-cooled inline petrol engine developing 150bhp at 1,200rpm.
Performance: Speed 7.9mph (12.64km/h); range 75 miles (120km); vertical obstacle 4ft 6in (1.371m); trench 10ft (3.352m); gradient unknown.
History: Designed in December 1917 and intended for the campaigns of 1919. The war ended before more than a small number were built, and these continued in service with the Tank Corps until the Vickers mediums came into service in 1923.

The Medium C would have been the main fighting tank in the proposed breakthrough of the German lines in 1919. It combined the experience of the Mk IV and the Medium A (Whippet) into one machine. The great improvement lay in the conditions for the crew, which was now grouped together in one compartment with voice tubes connecting each position. One man could control the tank, which had been impossible in the Mk IV, and the commander was placed in a small rotating cupola at the back of the turret where he had a good view. The engine was isolated in a compartment at the rear, which to some extent lowered the noise level and reduced the amount of smoke inside the vehicle. Ventilation was also improved, and the post-war Medium C tanks had extra armoured ventilators in the back of the turret.

The suspension was uninspired, and reflected the designers' involvement with the earlier rhomboidal machines. The tracks ran all round the hull and the bogies were unsprung. The Medium C was the last tank to be so designed, and the speed was low as a result. In fact 7.9mph (12.64km/h) could only be achieved on smooth, flat grassland or a good road. Track life was also very short. A good point was the provision of long mud chutes, which kept the bogies clean, and a Wilson gearbox and transmission.

The turret had mountings for five guns, though only four were fitted. Guns could be shifted from one port to another, but this cannot have been easy to do when the tank was moving. Only female tanks were built, but it had originally been intended that there

Above: The Medium C's design represented a great improvement over earlier tanks. It had a greatly-improved transmission, much higher speed, and excellent cross-country capability for its time. It was intended to operate in conjunction with the new Medium D design in the projected advance designated "Plan 1919".

should be a male version with one 6pounder gun. Apparently one was actually made, but never put into service. The 6pounder was mounted in the front of the turret, presumably on a vertical mantlet as in the sponsons of the rhomboidals, and this gun must have cut down space in the fighting compartment even further. A hatch in the roof could be opened and one of the Hotchkiss guns mounted on a pintle for AA fire, though this naturally exposed the gunner completely.

Extravagant plans were made for the production of the Medium C. After the pilot model had been demonstrated 200 were ordered. In October 1918 a further 4,000 females and 2,000 males were ordered, but immediately cancelled. By February 1919 36 of the original 200 had been completed, and all further work stopped, the remaining half-completed hulls being scrapped. One feature of the Medium C design which was in advance of its time was that assemblies and sub-assemblies were intended to be manufactured in different factories, coming together only for final construction. All other tanks had been built wholly under one roof, which was slower and more expensive. Although so few Medium Cs were ever made, the design was a significant step in tank history. It was the truly interim design between the war-time rhomboidals and the latter fully-sprung fast models. The Vickers mediums took the next logical step and laid the basis for all modern tanks.

Left: The Medium C was the final British tank of World War I. It was armed only with four .303in Hotchkiss machine-guns.

Mk A Whippet Medium Tank

Country of origin: United Kingdom.
Crew: 3.
Armament: Four .303in Hotchkiss machine-guns.
Armour: 14mm (0.55in) maximum; 5mm (0.2in) minimum.
Dimensions: Length 20ft (6.09m); width 8ft 7in (2.61m); height 9ft (2.74m).
Weight: Combat 31,360lb (14,225kg).
Engine: Two Tylor six-cylinder water-cooled inline petrol tractor engines, each developing 45hp.
Performance: Speed 8mph (12.8km/h); range 40 miles (64km).
History: In service with the British Army early in 1918, first saw action in March 1918 and then in continuous use until the end of the war. Not used in peace-time. Approximately 200 were produced. Also used by Japan and Russia.

No sooner had the early rhomboidal Mk Is shown their capabilities than the War Office called for a lighter, faster tank capable of carrying out the traditional cavalry task of exploiting a breakthrough and following up a retreating enemy. The idea was for an armoured substitute for the horse and Sir William Tritton, the designer of the Mk I and the managing director of William Foster & Co of Lincoln, set about designing what he called the "Tritton Chaser", a self-explanatory name. It was decided that trench-crossing was less important than with the battle tanks, since it was reasonable to assume that the latter would have done the job of dropping fascines into the wider holes, and so the length of the "Chaser" could be reduced, which would ensure a reduced weight and a generally smaller size.

The layout resembled that of the then-current armoured cars, in that the engine compartment was at the front, the driver looking out over a long bonnet. Behind him was to be a rotating turret containing the commander and gunner. In the production models the rotating turret was unfortunately dropped to simplify manufacture, but this brought about a sharp increase in the crew difficulties since the commander and his gunner now found themselves having to handle no fewer than four machine-guns within the confines of a fighting compartment never intended for such a task.

Sir William Tritton was well aware of the power losses caused through

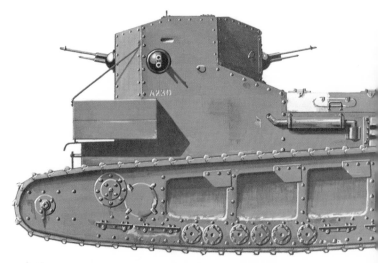

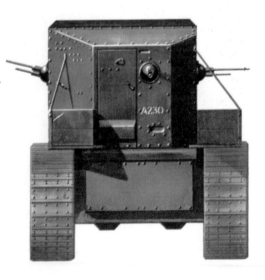

Right: Front and rear views of a medium tank Mk A (Whippet) of 17th Battalion, based in Dublin, June 1919. The tank shown is No. A230, christened "Gofasta" by its crew. About 200 Whippets were built, entering service in 1918.

Left: Side view of a Whippet tank. Notable features include a fixed turret mounted towards the rear and special mudchutes along the tank's side. The crew entered the tank from the rear, through a specially-provided armoured door.

steering by brakes on this final drive-shafts, and in an effort to overcome this, yet not introduce more manufacturing complications, he used an engine for each track. Theoretically this is straightforward, in practice anything but that. In the Whippet, as the new type was officially name, the driver had a steering wheel connected to the two throttles, and movement of the wheel was translated into differential movement of the throttles. For straight ahead driving he could lock both output shafts by a splined sleeve, thus effectively destroying any steering at all. The whole process was fiendishly difficult to manage, and it was common practice for drivers to stall one engine and spin the tank on one track. On soft ground the stalled track was then shed, and the tank was immobile. The idea was revived in a wheeled amphibian of the US Navy in World War II with predictably similar results. The layout of the tracks was the first indication of a break away from the ideas of running them all round the hull, and the concept was quite modern in appearance. The mud chutes were a substantial step forward, helping considerably in clearing the tracks and bogies and so reducing the maintenance load. Unfortunately the bogie were unsprung and high speed was out of the question; in fact the quoted top speed could only be achieved on smooth ground, and on the battlefields of Flanders the Whippet was nowhere near as fast a s a horse.

The range was too short for a vehicle intended to follow up a breakthrough: 40 miles (64km) were just too few and crews carried extra

petrol in tins strapped on the outside of the hull, a suicidal habit in action. The normal petrol tank was in front of the engine, between the front horns, in the best position to receive anti-tank fire, although it was armoured.

Despite the shortcomings, and it is easy to find more, the Whippet was considered a great success and the Germans set about copying it almost exactly, though they wisely tried to mount a 57mm gun in the turret. The Armistice overtook the German design, although it was further developed in Sweden as the m-21 by Bofors (one still exists) to become a much more useful tank. The British abandoned the design in 1919 and scrapped the 200 that had been made. As an experiment the Tank Corps' Central Workshops in France took the Whippet and gave it sprung bogies. This improved the ride considerably and when a 360hp Rolls-Royce Eagle aero engine was taken from a Handley Page bomber and fitted instead of the two Tylors, 30mph (48km/h) was easily obtained. The implications were ignored, however, and British tank thinking turned to the Medium C and its derivatives.

Below: Whippet tanks of 3rd Battalion at Maillet Mailly, France, 30 March 1918, accompany infantry of the New Zealand Division. Unlike the heavier British tanks of WWI, Whippets could operate independently and effectively because of their fairly high speed and manoeuvreability.

Mk II Medium Tank

Country of origin: United Kingdom.
Crew: 5.
Armament: One 3-pounder gun; one .303in Vickers machine-gun mounted co-axially; two .303in Vickers machine-guns mounted in hull.
Armour: 12mm (0.47in) maximum 8mm (0.31in) minimum.
Dimensions: Length 17ft 6in (5.33m); width 9ft 1½in (2.78m); height 9ft 10½in (3.01m).
Weight: Combat 30,128lb (13,666kg).
Engine: Armstrong Siddeley eight-cylinder air-cooled inline developing 90bhp.
Performance: Speed 16mph (25.6km/h); range 120 miles (192km); vertical obstacle unknown; trench 6ft 6in (1.981m); gradient unknown.
History: Entered service with the British Army in 1926 and continued in use as a training vehicle until 1941. Also used by Australia.

The Vickers medium tanks were the first truly post-war models to go into service with the Royal Tank Corps, and they showed a number of advances over war-time designs. The Vickers mediums were also the first fast tanks in British service (the top speed was officially 16mph or 26km/h, but it was actually nearer 30mph or 48km/h), and they were the first with revolving turrets. In other respects their war-time ancestry still showed: they still mounted machine-guns in the hull, and were the last tanks so to do. The entrance hatches were in the sides of the hull above the track guards, and although there was plenty of room inside for the crew, these small hatches were apparently difficult to use when evacuating a wounded man. The hull was built up from flat plates with as few curves as possible, and was very box-like in shape. The turret was

Above: The Vickers medium tank was the first standardized tank to enter British service after World War I. It was a very successful design, remaining in service until shortly before World War II.

large and round and much narrower than the hull.

The engine was in front, on the left with the driver alongside on the right. The driver's view was excellent, if a little vulnerable; he had a large vertical plate in front of him, and could open a large hatch for road driving.

The commander had no cupola, and had to rely on vision blocks in the turret, or put his head out of the top. Of the four men in the turret, one fired the 3pounder; the second loaded for him and handled the co-axial machine-gun; the third was the radio operator, when a radio was fitted, and a machine-gunner for one of the hull guns; and the fourth was the commander, who handled the other gun if necessary, although there was sufficient room for the men to move about and change from one station to another. Ventilation was reasonable, and the great heat of the old rhomboidals was gone. There were some crew comforts such as a fireless cooker, some cooking utensils and rations for three days.

The suspension was multi-roller, and by no means intended for speed. The road wheels were small and sprung by short coils on vertical rods, giving a few inches of movement. The tracks were of steel plates, with a distinctive H-shaped grip indented in each of them.

These tanks, and there were about 160 of them in all, serviced in the Tank Corps throughout the difficult inter-war years and on mobilisation in 1939 they were used for training gun crews and drivers. A few were used in North Africa in the early months of the war, and several ended their days dug into the ground as anti-invasion pill-boxes around Britain.

Left: While the vehicle shown above is a Vickers medium tank Mk II, the one here is a normal medium Mk II. The Vickers medium tank was the first to be adopted with a fully-rotating turret.

Vickers Mk V1 Light Tank

Mks I-IV, VIA, VIB and VIC.
Country of origin: United Kingdom.
Crew: Mks II, III, & IV, 2; Mks V & VI, 3.
Armament: One 0.303in Vickers machine-gun in turret (Mks II-IV); and one 0.5in Vickers and one O.303in Vickers in turret (Mks V & VI).
Armour: Mk II 4mm (0.16in) minimum, 10mm (0.39in) maximum; Mks III-V 12mm (0.47in), and Mk VI 14mm (0.55in).
Dimensions: Length 11ft 9in (3.58m) – Mk II, 12ft 11in (3.99m) – Mk VI; width 6ft 3½in (1.91m) – Mk II, 6ft 9in (2.05m) – Mk VI; and height 6ft 7½in (2.02m) – Mk II, 7ft 4in (2.23m) – Mk VI.
Weight: 11,648lb (5,283kg) Mk VI, 9,520lb (4,318kg) Mk II.
Engine: Mks II & III, Rolls-Royce six-cylinder water-cooled inline petrol engine developing 60hp; Mks IV, V & VI, Meadows six-cylinder water-cooled in line petrol engine developing 88bhp.
Performance: Mks II & III speed 30mph (48km/h), range 150 miles (240km); Mk VI speed 35mph (56km/h), range 130 miles (208km); vertical obstacle 2ft (0.61m); trench 5ft (1.52m); gradient, 60 per cent.
History: Developed from the Carden-Loyd series of light tanks and carriers, the Mk I came into service in 1929. Progressive marks were produced throughout the 1940s until the Mk VI of 1936, which was itself improved and went up to the Mk VIC. Mk VIs remained in service until 1941 and saw service in France, Egypt, Malta and Persia. They were supplied to Australia, Canada, South Africa and India.

The various marks of Light Tank derived directly from the miscellany of Carden-Loyds which had appeared during the 1920s. In 1928 Vickers took over the Carden-Loyd firm and concentrated on one design for both the British Army and for export. The Mk I was the first light tank with a rotating turret that the firm had made, and it went into British service in 1929. This set the pattern for the rest, though there was to be considerable change and modification before the final model was accepted. All the light tank series featured the Horstmann coil-spring suspension with twin and single bogies and one or more return rollers. All had the engine at the front of

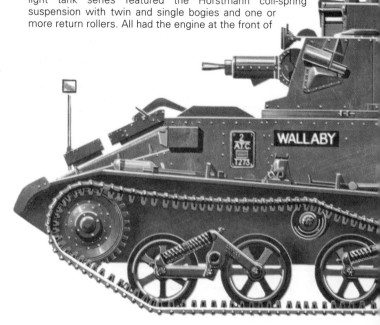

Above: A Mk VI light tank; note the mainly circular turret extended at rear for a No 7 wireless set.

the hull, beside the driver.

The Mk VI was heavier, faster and harder-hitting than its forerunners, though still lightly armoured by 1940 standards and lacking in effective cross-country performance. For the most part they were used for reconnaissance, although a few in Egypt were converted to mobile artillery observation posts. The India Army sent some Mks VIs to Persia when that country was occupied in 1941.

The Mk I (1929 Model) was very similar to the Carden-Loyd Mk VIII. The suspension was by leaf springs and the turret was cylindrical in shape. A Mk IA came in 1930 and had coil springs and the turret off-set from the centre-line.

The Mk II appeared in 1931 and was the first to fit the Rolls engine. The turret was rectangular with sloping sides and mantlet and an armoured sleeve over the gun. There was a square hatch for the commander and another in front for the driver. Vision was through slits and glass blocks. Mk IIs had two sets of twin bogies on each side and a raised rear idler. This was peculiar to that mark and was not repeated on others. The Mk IIA was an improved Mk II with few external differences, and entered service in 1933.

The Mk III came out in 1934, but few were built. The turret was lower and narrower than that of the Mk II and there was a front grille for the radiator.

The Mk IV also appeared in 1934 and was a distinct improvement over the previous

Left: Side view of the Mk VIB light tank. This was the final development of the Carden-Loyd series, mounting one .50in and one .303in Vickers machine-guns.

317

models. It was one of the first British tanks to have the hull built out over tracks to give more internal volume, and the turret was circular once again. The rear idler of the Mk II was dropped, and the suspension reverted to a set of twin bogies and one single one on each side. It was slightly smaller than the Mks II and III and could mount either a 0.5in or 0.303in Vickers.

The Mk V (1936) was the first light tank with a 3-man crew. The hull was lengthened and the track extended by adding a rear idler behind the single road wheel and springing it in the same way. The turret was larger and the sides sloped sharply. Two machine-guns were mounted in the turret, which was cramped for the two men in it, but the commander was given a small cylindrical cupola. A smoke discharger, fired by a bowden cable, was mounted on the right hand side of the turret. The driver's hatch became smaller, and the deck in front of the turret was larger than previously. Only 22 Mk Vs were built, but they formed the basis for the Mk VI, and several ideas tried out on the Mk Vs later became standard.

The Mk VI (19836 onwards) was the last in the series and the largest and heaviest. The turret was enlarged to accommodate a No 7 wireless set and cupola was hexagonal. The Mk VIA changed the position of the return rollers and the VIB reverted to a cylindrical cupola. Many carried an external mounting for a Bren gun for AA defence. The Mk VIC mounted a BESA 15mm heavy machine-gun and a coaxial 7.9mm BESA. The cupola was abandoned and two domed hatches have a little more head-room for the crew, though at the expense of the commander's view. The Mk VI had a Wilson pre-selector gearbox and there were steady improvements to the Meadows engine. The twin radiator inlet louvres on the front of the engine cover were reduced to one on this mark and most versions had deflector plates in front of the driver's vision block to reduce bullet splash.

The great majority of the light tanks were used for training after 1940, when it was realised that none of them were a match for the German *Panzers*; there was no hope of mounting a larger gun in the tiny turret, and in any case the armour protection was quite inadequate for modern warfare. As they wore out they were scrapped and armoured cars took over the reconnaissance role.

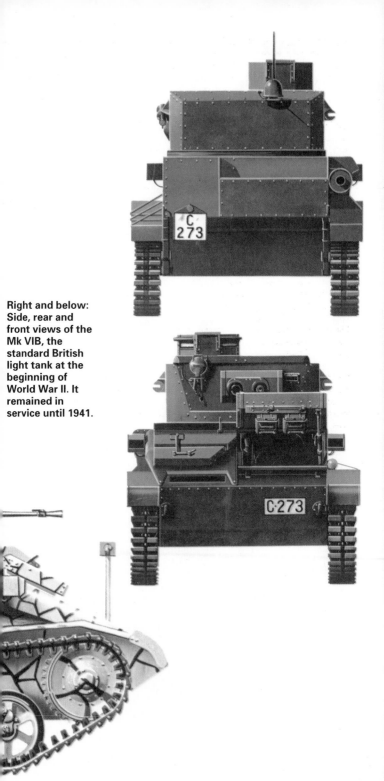

**Right and below:
Side, rear and
front views of the
Mk VIB, the
standard British
light tank at the
beginning of
World War II. It
remained in
service until 1941.**

C
273

C·273

A11 Matilda I Infantry Tank

Country of origin: United Kingdom.
Crew: 2.
Armament: One .3in or .5in Vickers machine-gun.
Armour: 60mm (2.36in) maximum, 10mm (0.39in) minimum.
Dimensions: Length 15ft 11in (4.85m); width 7ft 6in (2.28m); height 6ft 1½in (1.86m).
Weight: Combat 24,640lb (11,161kg).
Engine: Ford eight-cylinder petrol engine developing 70bhp at 3,500rpm.
Performance: Road speed 8mph (12.8km/h), range 80 miles (128km); vertical obstacle 2ft 1in (0.63m); trench 7ft (2.133m).
History: Served with the British Army only between 1938 and 1940.

The origin of the Matilda I lay in a request from General Sir Hugh Elles to Vickers for a tank to be built down to a price. Sir John Carden led the design team and the result was probably the most unfortunate one of his career. The concept of the infantry tank called for good protection, low speed to keep pace with infantry assaulting on foot, and only limited offensive power. It was thought to be sufficient to give the tank an armament of machine-guns and no more. These limits were bad enough, but the price limit was equally daunting at £6,000 for the complete vehicle. Not surprisingly the Matilda I was reduced to the barest essentials, and perpetuated a number of mistakes which had already been well aired.

The first was the crew. Two-man tanks had been shown to be scarcely workable in the 1920s and early 1930s, but Carden was forced to return to a one-man turret because he could not afford the space for two. One machine-gun made a mock of the whole idea of fire-power, and to have a complete tank to carry one gun was a great waste of manufacturing effort and money. Finally, to give the vehicle a top speed scarcely better than that of a running man was quite ludicrous. Those were the limitations, however, and the General Staff accepted the design and the first production order was placed in April 1937. The first models were delivered in 1938 and issued to the 1st Army Tank Brigade, who took them to France in 1939. By 1940 139 had been built and they formed the greater part of the vehicle strength of the 1st

Above: An A11 Matilda I infantry tank. Clearly seen is the single smoke-bomb turret discharger mounted on the side of the turret. The frontal armour was almost impenetrable by any anti-tank gun of the time, but the vehicle had many faults which made it ineffective and expensive. A total of 139 were completed by August 1940 after which time the tank was relegated to training.

Brigade. Their severe limitations showed up with frightening clarity in the *Blitzkreig*, and all were finally lost on the way to, or at, Dunkirk. Their crews fought valiantly, and they had one small success, but the tank was hopeless in battle.

Carden had built the smallest vehicle that he reasonably could and used as many existing components as possible. Since protection was important he put thick armour on the front and used a cast turret. The armour was more than satisfactory and was comfortably invulnerable to the German anti-tank guns in France. The suspension was a less happy story. It was the same as had been fitted to the Vickers 6ton (6,096kg) tank of 1928, and it could only cope with low speeds and moderate power outputs when carrying twice the weight it was designed for. The final drawback lay in the engine, which was the well-proved but low-powered Ford V-8. In order to drive the Matilda it had to be well geared down and the power was taken through a simple transmission to a rear sprocket. When the armament limitations became clear the turret was up-gunned by fitting the Vickers 0.5in machine-gun. This was some improvement, but it took more space in the small turret, and was tiring to use.

Left: Main drawback of the Matilda I was that it was armed only with a .303 Vickers machine-gun operated by the commander/gunner. This was later replaced by a .50 machine-gun, but when this was installed the turret became even more cramped.

Cruiser Tank Mk IV

Mks IV, IVA and VC; A13MkII.
Country of origin: United Kingdom.
Crew: 4.
Armament: One 2pounder gun and one Vickers machine-gun (Mk IVA mounted a 7.92mm BESA).
Armour: 6mm (0.24in) minimum, 38mm (1.5in) maximum.
Dimensions: Length 19ft 9in (6.02m); width 8ft 4in (2.54m); height 8ft 6in (2.59).
Weight: 33,040lb (14,987kg).
Engine: Nuffield Liberty V-12 water-cooled petrol engine developing 340bhp.
Performance: Speed 30mph (48km/h), range 90 miles (144km); vertical obstacle 2ft (0.61m); trench 7ft 6in (2.29m); gradient, 60 per cent.
History: Deliveries began in December 1938 and were completed in late 1939. Some tanks were made and were issued to units of 1st Armoured Division in France in 1939/40. Some

Right: Cruiser Mk IVA
was the designation given to
later production vehicles which had the
Vickers .303in co-axial machine gun
replaced by the 7.82mm BESA weapon, and
additional armour.

Below: A Cruiser Mk IV, officially designated
the A13 Mk II. This tank was developed
from an American Christie tank purchased
in 1936 and entered production in 1938. It
was issued to the 1st and 7th Armoured
Divisions by 1940.

also went to the Western Desert where they were used by the 7th Armoured Division. Withdrawn from service during 1942.

The Cruiser Mk IV derived directly from a Christie tank bought in the USA in 1936. Morris Motors were given the task of redesigning the Christie to make it battle-worthy, and to do this they had to build a new hull and a better turret. The Christie could reach 50mph (80km/h) on roads, and very high speeds across country, but these had to be reduced since it was quickly found that the crew were injured by being thrown about.

The only engine available which gave the necessary power was the American Liberty aero-engine of World War I, and this was de-rated to 340hp to improve torque and reliability. The later Mk IVA had a Wilson combined speed change and steering gearbox and a BESA rather than Vickers coaxial machine-gun. The Mk IV CS was the close support model. The Christie suspension was a great success and gave the Cruiser a very good performance in the desert. It was retained on all British cruiser tanks for the rest of the war.

The turret had undercut sides and sloped upper plates, but the hull was still much of a box and had many sharp angles in which shot could lodge. Some extra plates were added to the desert Cruisers, but they were always under-armoured and after a short while in service various mechanical weaknesses became apparent and reliability was not as good as it should have been. Despite the shortcomings of the Cruiser it was a step forward for British tank design and it set the pattern for the later wartime cruisers.

Left: Cruiser Tank Mk IV of 1st Armoured Division in 1940. This particular tank has been fitted with additional armour plate over the mantlet. A total of 655 were built by Nuffield, LMS, Leyland and English Electric. The tank was essentially an up-armoured version of the earlier Mk II. Some were fitted with a 3.7in mortar for use in the close support role.

A9 Mk I Cruiser Tank

Country of origin: United Kingdom.
Crew: 6.
Armament: One 2pounder gun; three .303in Vickers machine-guns. (CS version had one 3.7in howitzer in place of the 2pounder.)
Armour: 14mm (0.55in) maximum, 6mm (0.25in) minimum.
Dimensions: Length 19ft (5.79m); width 8ft 2in (2.49m); height 8ft 8in (2.64).
Weight: Combat 28,728lb (13,013kg).
Engine: AEC Type 179 six-cylinder water-cooled inline petrol engine developing 150bhp.
Performance: Road speed 25mph (40km/h), cross-country speed 15mph (24km/h); range 150 miles (240km); vertical obstacle 3ft (0.92m); trench 8ft (2.43m).
History: Used by the British Army between 1938 and 1941.

The main British tank throughout the 1920s and the first half of the 1930s was made from the Vickers Medium Mk II, with the scouting (or reconnaissance) role being undertaken by light tanks of various kinds, ultimately types coming after the Carden-Loyd models. This combination was becoming out of date by 1934, quite plainly, and new designs were needed. In particular, it was becoming apparent to the General Staff that better medium tanks were required for the tank-to-tank confrontations which it was foreseen might occur on future battlefields. 1934 was not a good time to be planning major expenditure on military equipment, however; the depression was at its height, and money was almost unobtainable.

Sir John Carden set to work in 1934 to design a tank to meet a General Staff specification for a successor to the Vickers mediums, but with a slightly

Below: The A9 Mk I cruiser tank was designed by Sir John Carden from 1934, the first prototype being built in 1936. In 1937 125 were ordered, 50 from Vickers and 75 from Harland and Wolff.

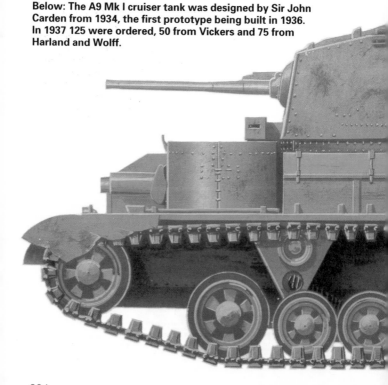

different role to fulfil. The difficulty with the tank specifications of the 1930s was that nobody had any clear idea what they wanted the vehicles to do in the next war. The old ideas of crossing trenches had not entirely died out, yet it was realised that tanks would be needed to act on their own, much in the way that cavalry had done, and also there was a need for armoured reconnaissance. The result of this somewhat baffled thinking was to stipulate a family of three types: cruisers, which were meant to be the cavalry type of machine, yet able to fight it out with other tanks if called upon to do so;

Above: Main armament of the A9 was a turret mounted 2pounder gun with a .303 Vickers MG coaxial to the right. Each side of the driver was a turret armed with a single .303 MG. A few A9s were built for the close support role; these had their 2pounders replaced by a 3.7 inch howitzer. The A-9 was the first British tank to have a power-operated turret and an auxiliary engine.

Above: A9 Mk I from front clearly showing position of .303 hull machine gun turrets.

Right: The A9 was followed by the A10 Mk II cruiser with increased armour but no hull machine gun turrets. A total of 175 A10 cruisers were completed by late 1940.

infantry tanks which moved at slow speeds with the assaulting infantry, and only had to knock out machine-gun nests (a throwback to 1918); and light tanks for the reconnaissance role. Nobody thought out the armament requirement to cope with these different tasks, and the cruisers were particularly badly served since they were given either the 3pounder, which was feeble, or the later 2pounder, which had good armour penetration for its day, but could not fire HE shells. All medium tanks were well supplied with machine-guns, which were quite useless against other armoured vehicles.

With these crippling restrictions around him Sir John Carden produced the first A9 early in 1936. It epitomised all that had served to restrict the design. It was lighter than the mediums so that it could be powered by a commercial engine. At the same time it tried to incorporate all the best features of the Medium Mk III, and to a great extent succeeded, but only by making everything so much lighter that the armour protection was largely negated. The overall weight was only two-thirds that of the Medium Mk III, and the design weight was even less than this. The general layout was reasonable for its day, with a central turret, engine at the rear and acceptable cross-country performance from the suspension. One of the features which spoiled the A9 was the vertical armour, all of it too thin, and the multitude of angles and corners in which armour-piercing shot could lodge, instead of being glanced off.

A point in the A9's favour, however, was the fact that it was the first British tank to have power (hydraulic) traverse for the turret. This was a substantial step forward, and was to be followed on all succeeding designs. Another notable first was the carriage of an auxiliary engine for starting, battery charging, and driving a fan for the fighting compartment. These were sensible innovations, and went some way to offsetting the failings of the A9 as a fighting tank. The crew was a generous allowance of six men, split into a commander, gunner, loader, driver and two hull machine-gunners. The driving and fighting compartments were combined into one, hence the need for a fan to clear the fumes from three machine-guns and a 3pounder. The two hull machine-guns were mounted in small sub-turrets in front, one on each side of the driver. The gunners were cramped, and so

was the driver, and the whole concept was strongly reminiscent of World War I. The arcs of fire of the machine-guns were limited, and their use was therefore doubtful.

The engine was originally meant to be the Rolls-Royce car engine from the Phantom series. The pilot model, however, showed that the vehicle was under-powered and an AEC bus engine was substituted. This just managed to give the tank a speed of 25mph (40km/h) on the road, but had to be geared down considerably to do it. The suspension could manage the cross-country speed of 15mph (24km/h) but the pilot model at first shed its tracks at these speeds. Trials started in 1936 and at the same time the War Office was changing its policy on tanks generally.

The A9 had begun as a medium tank replacement, but now the cruiser idea was born, and the vehicle became the Cruiser Tank Mk I. The first contract for a limited number was placed in August 1937 with Vickers, which was to build 50. Another contract with Harland and Wolff of Belfast specified a further 75, and these constituted the total production. The limitations of the design were soon obvious and the A13 was put in hand as the next model. The intrinsic limitations of the 2pounder meant that tanks could not deal with strongpoints or pillboxes, and this brought about the concept of the Close Support tank. CS tanks carried large-calibre guns for firing HE and other types of ammunition, and a few CS models of the A9, mounting a short-barrelled 3.7in howitzer, were built. The three machine-guns remained. The suspension was a Vickers refinement of the popular multi-bogie system, and it was successful enough to be incorporated into the later Valentine almost without alteration. The steering brakes were mounted externally on the rear sprockets, where they cooled easily, but were perhaps a little exposed to damage. The tracks were narrow, and none too strong, but the low power output of the engine and the relatively gentle gearbox gave them a reasonably long life.

A9s were issued to 1st Armoured Division, which took them to France in 1939 and 1940, and left practically all of them at Dunkirk. The 2nd and 7th Armoured Divisions took the type to Egypt and used it until 1941, by when it was clearly well out of date and out-gunned.

A12 Matilda II Infantry Tank

Country of origin: United Kingdom.
Crew: 4.
Armament: One 2pounder gun; one .303in Vickers machine-gun (Mk I); one 2pounder gun; one 7.92mm BESA machine-gun (Mk II); one 3in howitzer; one 7.92mm BESA machine-gun (Mk II CS).
Armour: 0.55in (14mm) minimum; 3in (78mm) maximum,
Dimensions: Length 18ft 5in (5.61m); width 8ft 6in (2.59m); height 8ft 3in (2.51m).
Weight: 59,360lb (26,926kg).
Engine: Two AEC six-cylinder inline diesels developing a total of 174bhp (Mks I and II); two Leyland six-cylinder inline diesels developing a total of 190bhp (Mk III).
Performance: Road speed 15mph (24km/h), cross-country speed 8mph (12.8km/h); range 160 miles (256km); vertical obstacle 2ft (0.61m); trench 7ft (2.13m); fording depth 3ft (0.91m).
History: Served with the British Army from 1939 to 1945. Also used by Australia and Russia.

When the Matilda I was still in the prototype stage the War Office was already debating whether it could be up-armoured and up-gunned to meet a revised General Staff specification which said in effect that if tanks were to survive while supporting infantry on foot they must be able to withstand the fire of anti-tank guns, yet carry sufficiently heavy armament to cope with enemy infantry, gun positions and tanks. This brought about a fundamental change in approach to the design of infantry tanks. Previously it had been considered that machine-guns were sufficient armament, but the new specification required some sort of shell-firing gun, and a large enough turret in which to pout it. At first it was thought that Matilda I (A11) could be given a two-man turret and a 2pounder gun, but it was soon apparent that there was no hope of this within the narrow hull limits, and in any case the weight of the turret would have defeated the already overloaded Ford engine and another would have to be fitted. The weight of the tank was intended to be kept down to 14 tons (14,225kg), and the A11 could not possibly meet it with the changes

already mentioned, so a new design was called for.

This new tank was entrusted to the Design Department at Woolwich Arsenal and was largely based on the prototype A7 of 1932. The same suspension was used, suitably strengthened, and the same powerplant of twin commercial diesels was put in. The requirement for thick armour meant that a cast turret and bow plate would be the most satisfactory solution, but British industry in the mid-1930s had only a very limited capacity for large castings, and this severely restricted the firms who could be given contracts for this work. It also meant that riveted and welded hulls and turrets were retained on British tanks long after other countries had gone over to castings. However, the contract for Matilda II was given to the Vulcan Foundry of

Right and below: A12 Matilda II infantry tank which entered service in 1939 and was first used by the 7th Royal Tank Regiment during the retreat to Dunkirk. Just under 3,000 Matilda IIs were built before production stopped in August 1943. The Matilda formed a major part of the British armoured forces during the 8th Army's battles in the Western Desert.

Left: The Matilda II was last used in North Africa during the battle of El Alamein in July 1942. After this date it was used for special roles such as clearing mines. The Australian Army continued to use the Matilda in the Far East and also developed more specialised models for their own use including a dozer and a flamethrower. The latter was called the Frog and was followed by the Matilda Murray.

Above: The Matilda III was the close support model and had the 2pounder gun replaced by a 3inch howitzer. It was powered by two Leyland 95hp diesels instead of two 87hp AEC diesels.

Warrington in November 1936 and they produced a wooden mock-up by April 1937. Another year elapsed before the pilot model (made in mild steel) was ready, the delay mainly being occasioned by difficulties in the supply of the Wilson gearbox. Trials with this model were carried out during 1938, but an initial order for 65 tanks was given even before the pilot model appeared, and shortly afterwards this was increased by a further 100. Luckily the trials showed the design to be satisfactory, the only changes being minor ones to the suspension and engine cooling.

Re-armament started in earnest during 1938 and tanks were in desperately short supply, so further orders were given, which were more than Vulcan could manage. Other firms were called in, and contracts were let to Fowler, Ruston & Hornsby, LMS Railway Works, Harland & Wolff and North British Locomotive Works. Vulcan were the main contractor, and undertook most of the casting work. The Matilda was not easy to put into mass production, mainly because of the castings, and certain features of the design were quite difficult. For some reason the side skirts were in one piece, involving another large casting, and an immediate easement to production was to reduce the number of mud chutes from six to five. By September 1939 only two Matildas were in service, but by the spring of 1940 at least one battalion (7th Royal Tank Regiment) was equipped and the tank gave a good account of itself in the retreat to Dunkirk and the subsequent fighting around the port. At the same time several units in Egypt had received it, and used it in the early campaigns against the Italians.

After Dunkirk the Matilda I was dropped altogether and the Matilda II became the Matilda, by which name it was known for the rest of the war. In Libya in 1940 and 1941 the Matilda was virtually immune to any anti-tank gun or tank that the Italians could deploy. This happy state of affairs continued until about mid-1941 when the first units of the German *Afrika Korps* appeared and brought their 8.8cm *Flak* guns into action in the ground role against tanks. This gun could knock out the Matildas at ranges beyond the 2pounder's ability to reply, and the Matilda began to fade from the battle. Attempts to up-gun it to carry a 6pounder were failures because the turret ring was too small to take a larger gun, and the last action when Matilda was used as a gun tank was the first battle of El Alamein in July 1942.

The Matilda was a conventional British tank with the usual three compartments in the hull, the driver sitting centrally behind the nose plate. There was no hull gun, an unusual departure for the time, but sensible, for they were rarely effective in battle. The heavy cast turret was small, and the three men in it were cramped. In the CS version with a 3in howitzer, space was even scarcer. The commander had a circular cupola, but it gave him only limited vision and this lack of good vision was the worst feature of the vehicle, though it was no worse than many other designs of that time. The turret was rotated by hydraulic power, and was one of the first to use this system developed by the Frazer Nash Company, who also developed the turret controls for aircraft. Some 67 rounds of 2pounder and 4,000 of .303in ammunition were carried.

Above: Matilda Baron III mine clearing vehicle. The flail was powered by two Bedford engines mounted in boxes at the hull rear.

The twin AEC diesels were coupled together and drove to a Wilson epicyclic gearbox and a rear sprocket. The suspension was derived from the A7 and was either known as the "scissors" or "Japanese" type. It originated with the Vickers Medium C, though a similar type also appeared on the French tanks of the 1920s and 1930s. It consisted of sets of bogies linked together and working against horizontal compression springs. Each bogie had four rollers, arranged in pairs so that to each suspension point there were four pairs of rollers, two links units, and two springs; the whole was supported by one vertical bracket attached to the hull. On each side there were two of these complete units, one four-roller unit and one large road wheel at the front. The track ran back along return rollers at the top of the side skirt. This apparently complicated arrangement worked well, though it inevitably limited the top speed. Mk III Matildas, and later marks, were fitted with Leyland diesels which gave slightly more power and were made in larger numbers than the AECs. The Mk V fitted an air servo on top of the gearbox to ease gear changing, but apart from these minor modifications, the Matilda stayed very much as it had been designed.

Up to the first battle of El Alamein the Matilda had gained the somewhat high-blown title of "Queen of the Battlefield", or at least some people called it that. After El Alamein it was apparent that the type was well past its best, and it was replaced by the increasing quantities of Grants and Shermans. The problem was to know what to do with the Matildas, most of which were still in good running order. The thick armour and reasonable protection made it an attractive vehicle of special applications, and it was the first British tank to be equipped as a flail mine-clearer, some of which were used at El Alamein. The flail was followed by a host of other devices, including anti-mine rollers, large demolition charges, bridge-layers, dozer blades, Canal Defence Lights (CDL) to illuminate the battlefields at night, gap-closing devices and flamethrowers. One was even used as an experimental radio-controlled vehicle.

Matildas were supplied to the Australian Army, which used them in the Pacific campaign and still had it in service for driver training as late as 1953. The Australians paid particular attention to developing flamethrowing variants which were useful against Japanese infantry positions in the jungle, and a dozer version was also frequently used in that theatre, mainly to improve tracks for wheeled vehicles to follow the tanks. Some Matildas went to Russia, where the thickness of armour was admired, but as in the Churchill later on, the 2pounder gun was politely dismissed as near useless. There are also some reports that the suspension clogged in the winter snow, though the Russians were not particularly communicative about the equipment provided to them.

After four or five years continuous use the Matildas were worn out, and it was not worth rebuilding them. A few were still in service at the end of the war, though not as gun tanks. However, the Matilda can claim to be the only British tank which served right through World War II and there are very few others which can approach that record, whatever their nationality.

Crusader Cruiser Tank

Crusaders I to III.
Country of origin: United Kingdom.
Crew: 5 in the Mark I; 4 or 5 in the Mark II; 3 in the Mark III.
Armament: Crusader I one 2pounder gun and two 7.92mm BESA machine-guns; Crusader II one 2pounder gun and one or two 7.92mm BESA machine-guns; Crusader III one 6pounder gun and one 7.92mm BESA machine-gun.
Armour: Crusader II 40mm (1.57in) maximum and 7mm (0.28in) minimum; Crusader II 49mm (1.93in) maximum and 7mm (0.28in) minimum; Crusader III 51mm (2in) maximum and 7mm (0.28in) minimum.
Dimensions: Length 19ft 8in (5.99m); width 8ft 8in (2.64m); height 7ft 4in (2.23m).
Weight: Combat Crusader I and II 42,560lb (19,279kg); Crusader III 44,240lb (20,040kg).
Ground pressure: 14.7lb/in² (1.04kg/cm²).
Engine: Nuffield Liberty 12-cylinder water-cooled inline petrol engine developing 340bhp.
Performance: Road speed 27mph (43.2km/h), range 100 miles (160km); vertical obstacle 2ft 3in (0.685m); trench 8ft 2in (2.59m); gradient 60 per cent.
History: In service with the British Army from 1939 to 1943.

The Crusader was to a great extent developed from the Covenanter, which it outwardly resembled. The Covenanter was a pre-war design which started in 1937 and was similar to the Cruiser Mark IV, or A13. The Crusader followed in the design pattern of these cruisers, but was designated to be a heavy cruiser, which was a difficult specification to fulfil within the weight and size limitations. It was equally difficult to fulfil when the main armament was only a 2pounder gun. The specification did show, however, that the limitations of the previous models had been appreciated. They were too lightly armoured, but were also too lightly armed, and nothing could be done about this in 1939.
The Crusader was built by a consortium of firms under the leadership of Nuffield Mechanisations Ltd, and 5,300 were made before production ceased.

The hull was similar to that of the Covenanter, with a long flat deck and a well raked glacis plate. The Christie suspension was very similar, except for an extra wheel station and the spring units, which were contained inside the hull. This suspension was the strong point of the Crusader and enabled it to move much faster than the official top speed or 27mph (43.2km/h). In the Western Desert Crusader drivers and fitters opened up the engine governors

to let the Liberty engine go as fast as it could, and the result was sometimes a speed as high as 40mph (64km/h). The Christie wheels could cope with this quite well and still give the crew a tolerable ride, the casualty usually being the engine. The hull was divided into the usual three compartments, with the driver sharing the front one with a hull machine-gunner in the first two marks. The Crusaders I and II had a 7.92mm BESA machine-gun mounted in a small auxiliary turret on the left front deck. This turret was subsequently removed, and omitted from later marks, thus allowing more space for storage, particularly of ammunition. The fighting compartment had the turret above it, and was none too large. It was not ideal for the commander either since he had to combine the tasks of commanding, gun loading, and often wireless operating as well: the usual drawbacks to a two-man turret.

The engine was the elderly but well tried Nuffield Liberty, basically an aero-engine from World War I de-rated from 400 to 240hp. The early Crusader had considerable trouble with their engines, mainly from the cooling arrangements. The large fan often broke its drive shafts, and the aircleaners

Right and below: The Crusader I (Cruiser MkVI) as it appeared in North Africa with the 9th (Queen's Royal) Lancers, 1st Armoured Division. Plagued by mechanical failure and weak armour, Crusaders nevertheless served in all the major North African campaigns. There were 5,300 built but they were out-dated and were generally withdrawn by 1943. A few versions served on in Italy.

were difficult to keep clean, but after some experience and modification the engine went very well.

Undoubtedly the tank was rushed into service before all its development troubles had been ironed out, and in its first engagement in June 1941, Operation "Battleaxe", more Crusaders fell into enemy hands through mechanical failure than through battle damage. Nevertheless the tank went on to fight in all the major actions throughout the Desert Campaign, and by Alamein the Crusader III with a 6pounder gun had arrived. The 6pounder required a larger mantlet, which was flatter than that for the 2pounder and rather ugly. The same mantlet could also be fitted with a 3in Close Support howitzer, though not many were so modified. The Crusader was outdated by the end of the North African campaign. A few went to Italy and some hulls fought in North-West Europe adapted to such uses as AA vehicles and gun-towers. In the desert the Crusader became popular, and its speed was liked, but the armour was too thin, and the armament always too weak.

Right: Crusader (Cruiser Tank Mk VI) advances during the North African campaign. The driver's hatches are in the open position and the 7.92mm turret-mounted BESA MG has been removed.

Below: The final production version of the Crusader was the Mk III of which 144 were built between May and July 1942. This model has a 6pounder in place of the standard 2pounder gun and increased armour protection. Variants of the Crusader included command tanks, gun tractors, dozers, ARVs, mine clearing tanks and various anti-aircraft tanks. The latter were armed with a 40mm gun, twin 20mm or triple 20mm Oerlikon cannon.

Valentine Infantry Tank Mark III

Marks I-XI.
Country of origin: United Kingdom.
Crew: 3 (4 in Mks III and IV).
Armament: One 2pdr and one 7.92mm BESA machine-gun (Mks I-VII); one 6prd and one 7.92mm BESA machine-gun (Mks VIII-X); and one 75mm gun and one 7.92mm BESA machine-gun (Mk XI).
Armour: 8mm (0.31in) minimum; 65mm (2.56in) maximum.
Dimensions: Length (overall) 17ft 9in (5.41m); width 8ft 7½in (2.63m); height 7ft 5½in (2.27m).
Weight: 35,840lb (16,257kg).
Engine: AEC petrol engine developing 135hp (Mk I); AEC diesel developing 131hp (Mks II, III, VIII); GM diesel developing 138hp (Mks IV, IX); and GM diesel developing 165hp (Mks X, XI).
Performance: Road speed 15mph (24km/h), range 90 miles (144km); vertical obstacle 3ft (0.91m); trench 7ft 9in (2.36m); gradient 60 per cent.
History: Entered service with the British Army in May 1940; obsolete by May 1945. Also used by Canada, France and the Soviet Union. Also built in Canada.

The Valentine tank was a private venture by Vickers-Armstrong Ltd and built to the prewar concept of the British Army that there should be two types of tank, a cruiser for the open warfare as practised by cavalry, and a heavy support tank for the infantry. These latter were required to be heavily armoured and performance was a secondary consideration. In designing the Valentine, however, Vickers took several mechanical components from existing cruisers which they were building for the War Office, and so saved both time and effort in trials and production. In fact, the Valentine was more of a well armoured cruiser than a pure infantry tank, but its low speed was always a handicap to its use in open warfare.

The name of Valentine derived from the date when the design was submitted to the War Office, 14 February 1938. An order was not placed until July 1939, when 275 were demanded in the shortest possible time. The first ones were issued to service in May 1940 and several were given to the cavalry to make up for the losses of the Dunkirk evacuation and only later found their way to the

tank brigades for their proper role of infantry support. By the time production ceased in early 1944 8,275 Valentines of all marks had been built. Some 1,420 were made in Canada and 1,390 of these, together with 1,300 from UK, were sent to Soviet Russia. The Russians put them into action straight away and admired the simplicity and reliability of the engine and transmission, but they disliked the small gun which was of little use on the Eastern Front. In some cases they replaced it with their own 76.2mm tank gun.

In British service the Valentine first saw action in the Western Desert in 1941 and successive marks of it continued in the desert right through until the end of the campaign. Some were also landed with the 1st Army in Tunisia. These desert Valentines gained a great reputation for reliability and it is reported that after El Alamein some motored over 3,000 miles (4,830km) on their own tracks following the 8th Army. A squadron was landed with the assault force on Madagascar in 1942 and the 3rd New Zealand Division had Valentines in the Pacific campaign. Some of these tanks had their 2pdr guns replaced by 3in howitzers for close support work. A very small number went to Burma and were used in the Arakan, and a few were put into Gibraltar. By 1944, when the invasion of North-West Europe was mounted, the Valentine had been superseded as a gun tank, but the hull and chassis had already been utilised in a wide variety of different roles, and in these guises many Valentines were taken to France.

Probably no other tank has had so many changes built on to the basic structure. In addition to going through 11 marks as a gun tank, the Valentine was converted for DD drive (amphibious), bridgelaying, flamethrowing and more than one type of minefield clearing. It was an invaluable experimental vehicle for all manner of strange ideas: in one case a stripped chassis was fitted with rockets in an attempt to create that Jules Verne concept – the flying tank. It failed spectacularly.

As with most tanks the hull was divided into three compartments, driving, fighting and engine. The driver sat on the centre line of the vehicle and was rather cramped. He got in and out by a hatch above his head, and when closed down his vision was restricted to a small visor and two episcopes.

The fighting compartment had the turret mounted on it, and the turret was

Left: Valentine I of A Squadron, 17/21st Lancers, 6th Armoured Division, in 1941. A total of 8,275 were built in Britain. Another 1,420 were built in Canada, all but 30 of which were supplied to Russia under Lend-Lease.

Left: Valentine tank captured by the Germans in North Africa and subsequently used by the *Afrika Korps*, only to be knocked out by its original owners in a latter battle. Both the Germans and the British made considerable use of captured vehicles in campaigns in North Africa to supplement their own vehicles.

Left: Valentine II of 50th Royal Tank Regiment. This tank was similar to the Mk I but had an AEC 131hp diesel in place of the AEC 135hp petrol engine. Valentine IIs used in North Africa were fitted with sand shields each side and a jettisonable long range fuel tank at the rear.

Left: Valentine XI used as a command vehicle in 30 Corps Anti-tank Regiment, Royal Artillery, in North-West Europe during 1944/45. The Valentine XI had improved (but still poor) armour protection and a 75mm gun in place of the 6pounder of the Valentine X, and a 165hp General Motors diesel engine.

the worst feature of the whole tank. It was always too small, no matter which mark is considered, an no amount of redesign ever cured this trouble. In the marks which had a three-man crew the two in the turret were overworked, or at least the commander was. He had to load the main armament, command the vehicle, select targets for the gunner, and operate the wireless. His vision was extremely restricted because there was no cupola for him and he had to rely on a single episcope when closed down. This naturally meant that he rarely did close down properly, and left his hatch open so that he could bob up to get a view. This led to casualties as soon as the fighting started. In the back of the turret was the No 19 radio set, which also had a short range set built into it for infantry co-operation. The commander operated these two sets, and also gave instructions to his crew through an RT set. Not surprisingly the Mks III and V, with a four-man crew, were popular with commanders, though the space in the turret was no better and the vision just as bad.

The gun was as poor as the turret. The 2pdr was an accurate little weapon but it was already outdated in 1938 though it survived in the early desert battles because it could just defeat the Italian and lighter German tanks at its maximum range. However, 1,000 yards (915m) was the most that it could do and another drawback was the lack of an HE shell for general targets. Some 79 rounds were carried, and about 2,000 rounds for the coaxial BESA. The Mks VIII, IX and X were fitted with a 6pdr though even that was nearly out of date by the time it appeared and, incredibly, the Mks VIII and IX had no coaxial machine-gun with their 6pdr, so the crew were quite incapable of engaging infantry except with the main armament. The Mk X had the BESA installed, but this cut down the space left for the crew. Most marks carried a Bren LMG inside the turret and this gun could be mounted on the roof, though of course it could only be fired by the commander fully exposing himself through his hatch. The Canadian-built Valentines were equipped with Browning 0.3in machine-guns in place of the BESA and some, but not all, of the later marks were fitted with smoke dischargers on the turret sides.

The turret was traversed with a hydraulic motor controlled by a spade grip. This gave a good lay, but the final touches were done by handwheel. With the 2prd the gun's elevation was laid by the gunner's shoulder-piece, there being no gearing involved at all. The later guns were laid in elevation by a hand gear wheel.

In contrast with the fighting compartment, the engine was well housed and easy to get at. Maintenance was easy for a tank, and the entire unit was most reliable. The Mk I had the AEC petrol engine, but all successive marks used diesels, which appear to have given little trouble. The power went through a five-speed Meadows gearbox to steering clutches and steering brakes, the latter being prominently mounted on the outside of the drive sprockets.

All the marks were built with riveted plate armour and virtually no curves anywhere. Canadian Valentines and some of the British-built Mks X and XI were given cast nose plates which were both stronger and cheaper than the built-up versions, but in general the armour was uninspired. The maximum thickness of 65mm (2.56in) was naturally in front, but at the rear and on top it was down to 8mm (0.31in) and by 1944 this was too thin.

The suspension was typical of its period and is usually described as being a slow-motion type. It consisted of two three-wheeled bogies on each side, the wheels being sprung by horizontal coils in linked bogies. The front and rear wheels were bigger than the others, giving a distinctive appearance to the side view, and the hull was carried well above ground level. The track was returned on three top rollers and was built up from cast track links. These worked very well in all conditions except the Russian winter, when apparently they collected packed snow and stopped the tank altogether.

The Valentine DD version was used mainly for training, but a few were landed during the Italian campaign. None went to Normandy. The basic Valentine was carefully waterproofed and fitted with a collapsible screen which suspended the hull below water level. An external screw was fitted and this had to be hinged up when the vehicle beached.

Below: Bishop was a Valentine II tank fitted with new open-topped turret armed with 25pounder gun. The first 100 were ordered in 1941 from Birmingham Carriage and Wagon Centre.

Light Tank Mark VII (Tetrarch)

Country of origin: United Kingdom.

Crew: 3.

Armament: One 2pounder gun and one 7.92mm BESA machine-gun coaxially mounted in the turret; the Tetrarch I CS mounted a 3in howitzer in place of the 2pounder.

Armour: 16mm (0.63in) maximum; 4mm (0.16in) minimum.

Dimensions: Length 13ft 3in (4.04m); width 7ft 7in (2.31m); height 6ft 11in (2.10m).

Weight: Combat 16,800lb (7,620kg).

Engine: Meadows MAT 12-cylinder horizontally opposed petrol engine developing 165hp at 2,700rpm.

Performance: Speed 40mph (64km/h), range 140 miles (224km); vertical obstacle 1ft 8in (0.508m); trench 5ft (1.524m); gradient 60 per cent.

History: Designed in 1937 and first prototype completed December 1937. Production not ordered until 1940. By 1942 171 completed and manufacture ceased. Intended as a fast light tank, but used by Airborne Forces as a gliderborne support vehicle. Half-squadron took part in Madagascar landings, one squadron in Normandy airborne assault, and a few in the Rhine crossing. In service until 1950. Some 20 sent to Soviet Russia in 1941.

The Light Tank Mark VII was a marked change from the previous Vickers models and incorporated several interesting and radical ideas. The inadequate armament of the Mk VI light tanks had been appreciated, and the Mark VII was given a 2pounder (40mm), the same type as that being carried by the British medium tanks of the time. The Tetrarch's armour was too light, but the chief intention was speed, and much thought had been put into the

Below: Three-quarter off-side front view of the basic Tetrarch Mk I, mounting a 2-pounder anti-tank gun. A unique feature of this tank was that both the sprocket and the idler were positioned in line with the road wheels. It was steered by warping the tracks through alignment of the road wheels to form the arc of a circle. The turret on this tank is the same as that of the Daimler armoured car.

Above: A Mk ICS (Close-Support) version of the Tetrarch light airborne tank is driven from a Hamilcar glider. Unlike the conventional model, this Tetrarch mounts a 3inch howitzer firing either smoke of HE rounds. The vehicle seen here, on trials, is debarking with the aid of sand-bags. Under operational conditions, a special ramp would be used. The Tetrarch remained in British service until 1950.

suspension. The four large road wheels on each side represented a reversion to one of Walter Christie's earliest ideas, that of the fast duel-purpose armoured vehicle. The tracks were meant to be removable so that the Tetrarch could run on roads like an armoured car if it chose so to do, and thick solid rubber tires, together with soft Christie springing, gave a tolerable ride. Maximum speed was very high for its day, and the Tetrarch was meant to be a fast-moving, hard-hitting reconnaissance tank, capable of dashing over the battlefield and fighting for its information when it had to.

The War Office was having second thoughts about this idea just as the prototype appeared, for the Spanish Civil War had not shown light tanks to be as effective as everyone had hoped, and it was not until 1940, when tanks of all kinds were desperately short, that a production order was given. Production was slow, partly because of difficulties with the unusual suspension, and partly because the factory was bombed. Some of the first production models went to Russia, and others took part in the Madagascar operations; the remainder were put in reserve straight from the factory to be kept as airborne tanks. The Hamilcar glider was specifically designed to carry the Tetrarch, but only one squadron flew to Normandy in 1944. One Hamilcar broke up while crossing the English Channel as a result of flying into the slipstream of the towing plane, and its Tetrarch and crew plunged into the sea. A few more Tetrarchs were used in the Rhine crossing in May 1945, but after that they were never used again, although a dwindling number remained on strength until the gliders disappeared in 1950.

The hull was a light box, with vertical sides and within the track width (not built out over the tracks, that is). In front was a large sloping glacis plate marred by a central square box which covered the driver's head and shoulders. The entire front of this box could be swung open to allow the driver to see, but when it was closed down the driver had only a small vision block in the middle of it. The glacis plate was 0.63in (16mm) thick, as was the front of the turret, but the remaining armour was only 0.24in (6mm) thick and highly vulnerable. The turret was built up from plate, much like that of the Mk VI light tank, and had a big square mantlet housing the 2pounder gun. The turret was reasonably roomy, but the view was poor and there was no cupola for the commander. He was in any case very busy since he acted as loader for the 2pounder. It may be no accident that on the few occasions when the Tetrarch was in action it was generally used as a static gun, where the commander would have been able to give all his attention to controlling his gunner. There was a smoke discharger on each side of the turret, and most Tetrarchs had a spare petrol tank in a frighteningly vulnerable position on the rear decking.

The Meadows engine drove to a gearbox which gave five forward speeds and drove through the rear road wheel. The two centre wheels could be moved out or in, to bow the track for steering gentle curves. The idea was derived from the Bren Carrier, but was greatly improved on the Tetrarch and worked very well. Track bowing was controlled by a steering wheel, but sharper turns required the driver to use two levers and apply brakes to the final drive-shafts.

By the time the Tetrarch was ready for service, the 2pounder was already well out-classed, and in an attempt to improve its performance a Littlejohn adaptor was fitted. This gave a higher muzzle velocity, but it could not be used with HE shell, and so was only a marginal improvement.

It seems extraordinary that with the known failings of the Tetrarch the War Office should have ordered a successor on the same pattern, but they did and 102 were built by 1944. This tank was the Mark VIII, or Harry Hopkins as it was felicitously named. Mechanically it was very similar to the Tetrarch, but the hull was simplified in outline and had a long flat top deck with a steeply sloping plate. This last was in one piece and 1.5in (38mm) thick. The turret was lower and had sloped sides, though the front plate was still flat, but a better mantlet was fitted. The armament was unchanged, and the weight went up to 19.040lb (8,636kg). This tank was never used in action (few were even issued for service use), and it could be described as a waste of factory

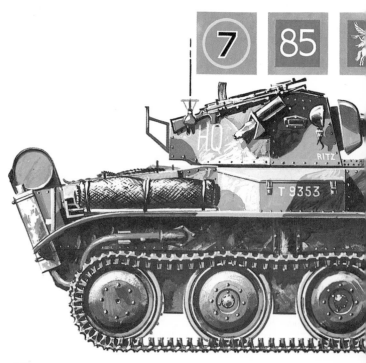

effort at a time when such effort was badly needed for other things.

A derivation of the Harry Hopkins was the Alecto self-propelled gun, developed in response to a General Staff requirement of April 1942 for a light self-propelled gun for infantry support, using the 95mm howitzer. The Alecto used a totally redesigned hull from the Harry Hopkins, with the gun mounted low down in the front. The crew was four, the height reduced by nearly 9in (227mm) and the speed reduced to 30mph (48km/h). In order to keep the weight down as much as possible, the armour was only 0.4in (10mm) at its thickest, but it was all-welded, a new technique at that time. Had the Alecto gone into action it seems quite likely that it would not have survived for long, for all SP guns were the target for the heaviest retaliation that could be fired at them, and 10mm of armour would not have kept out any AP projectiles. As it happened, few were built and none saw action. After the war a very small number were tried as reconnaissance vehicles, with limited success.

Right and below: Rear, front and side views of a typical service-used Tetrarch light airborne tank Mk ICS, with detailed enlargements of its unit markings. This tank was used by Headquarters Squadron, 6th Airborne Reconnaissance Regiment, 6th Airborne Division, which was flown into Normandy on the evening of the D-Day landings, 6 June 1944, to help secure the River Orne crossings.

A39 Tortoise Heavy Assault Tank

Country of origin: United Kingdom.
Crew: 7.
Armament: One 32pounder gun; three 7.92mm BESA machine-guns.
Armour: 225mm (8.86in) maximum; 35mm (1.38in) minimum.
Dimensions: Length (hull) 23ft 9in (7.24m); length (over gun) 33ft (10.1m); width 12ft 10in (3.91m); height 10ft (3.05m).
Weight: Combat 174,720lb (79,252kg).
Engine: Rolls-Royce Meteor 12-cylinder liquid-cooled petrol engine developing 600hp.
Performance: Speed 12mph (19.2km/h).
History: Designed in 1942, the project was not pushed hard, and the first six prototypes were not completed until 1947, whereupon the idea was abandoned.

This monster tank epitomises the triumph of armour protection over all other considerations. It was really an assault gun, but the very restricted traverse, 20 degrees to each side, would have severely limited it even in that role. It could never have been a battle tank in any sense of the word, and how it was meant to be moved to and from the battlefield is problematical, since it was incapable of being carried on the tank transporters known in 1942.

The 32pounder was another name for the 3.7in AA gun, and it was a powerful weapon, well able to penetrate all known armour of World War II. If it had been put into a proper tank chassis, and there is no reason why it should not have been, it would have been a world-beater. In the Tortoise it never stood a chance. The three secondary Besa machine-guns were mounted one in front of the hull and the other two in a small turret on top of the hull roof. The only other weapons were 12 smoke dischargers.

The tracks were massive, as they needed to be, and were carried on multi-wheeled bogies with heavy skirting plates which also acted as carriers for the outward ends of the axles. The geared-down Meteor could offer a top speed of only 12mph (19.2km/h), which was virtually useless. The entire exercise was a great waste of effort and talent, but did not detract greatly from the British war effort.

Above: The Tortoise was developed from 1942 as an assault tank, but it would have been very difficult to deploy on the battlefield.

Below: Side view of the Tortoise. The 32-pounder gun, with a limited traverse of 20° left and right, was the largest fitted with any British AFV during World War II.

A22 Churchill Infantry Tank

Churchills I to VIII.
Country of origin: United Kingdom.
Crew: 5.
Armament: Churchill I one 2pounder gun; one 7.92mm BESA machine-gun and one 3in howitzer in the hull; Churchill II one 2pounder gun and two 7.92mm BESA machine-guns; Churchill III-IV one 6pounder gun and two 7.92mm BESA machine-guns; Churchill IV NA 75 one 75mm gun, one .3in Browning machine-gun and one 7.92mm BESA machine-gun; Churchill V and VIII one 95mm howitzer and two 7.92mm BESA machine-guns; Churchill VI and VII one 75mm gun and two 7.92mm BESA machine-guns; Churchill I CS two 3in howitzers and one 7.92mm BESA machine-gun.
Armour: Churchill I-VI 102mm (4in) maximum and 16mm (0.63in) minimum; Churchill VII and VIII 152mm (6in) maximum and 25mm (1in) minimum.
Dimensions: Length 24ft 5in (7.44m); width 10ft 8in (3.25m); height 8ft 2in (2.49m).
Weight: Combat Churchill III 87,360lb (39,574kg).
Engine: Two 6-cylinder Bedford water-cooled inline developing 350bhp.
Performance: Road speed 15.5mph (24.8km/h); cross-country speed 8mph (12.8km/h); range 90 miles (144km); vertical obstacle 2ft 6in (0.812m); trench 10ft (3.048m).
History: In service with the British Army from 1941 to 1952. Also used by Eire, India and Jordan.

The Churchill was the replacement for the Matilda II. The specification having been drawn up with that in mind it was to the project number A20 that the new tank was first assigned, and design work started in September 1939 by Harland and Wolff of Belfast. The A20 went as far as four prototypes in June 1940, but no further. It was to have been rather like a World War I rhomboidal with side sponsons mounting 2pounder guns. Vauxhall Motors took over the contract for the next infantry tank, the A22, and were able to use the A20 as a starting base. The beginnings were not auspicious with Dunkirk just over, and virtually no armour force in the UK at all. Vauxhall were given one year in which to design, test and produce the tank, the stipulation being that the production lines had to be assembling the type within 12 months. With this extraordinary time limit to constrain them, the design team set to work and

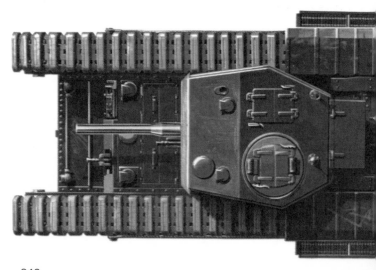

the first pilot model was actually running within seven months. The first 14 production tanks were off the line by June 1941, within 11 months of design starting, and volume production followed on quickly after that.

Such a rush was bound to bring its problems, and the early marks of Churchill had no lack of them. The engine was a purpose-built "twin six", not unlike two Bedford lorry engines laid on their sides and joined to a common crankcase. The idea was to make an engine that was both compact and accessible. Compact it certainly was, but it was scarcely accessible. The petrol pump was driven by a flexible shaft underneath the engine, and had an unfortunate habit of snapping. The hydraulic tappets, copied from American engines, were meant to run without adjustment, but frequently broke, necessitating a change of engine. The carburettor controls were also hydraulic, and also got out of adjustment. The power input was low for the weight of the hull, and the overall response sluggish. In fact the tank was rushed into service before it was ready. After a year of use most of the troubles were ironed out and it became quite reliable, but the first 12 months saw it gain a reputation for fragility and unreliability which it never completely

Right and below: A Churchill III armed with a 6pounder gun, co-axial 7.92mm BESA MG and another 7.92mm BESA mounted in the hull. The Churchill was used in action for the first time during the Dieppe landing in August 1942 when a number of Mk I and II tanks were used fitted with wading equipment. 5,600 Churchills were built.

Above: Churchill armed with 6pounder gun. The tank gave a very good account of itself in the mountainous terrain of Tunisia.

Above right: A post-war view of a Churchill AVRE Mk VII (FV 3903) which was armed with a 165mm breech-loaded low velocity gun and is shown here carrying a 10-ton fascine which it would drop into anti-tank ditches and other obstacles.

Right: Churchill AVRE with deep wading equipment and Standard Box Girder bridge attachment at the front of the hull during the D-Day landings; in the background is a Sherman flail tank.

lived down. The A22 specification was more modern than any that had gone before, and it called for a low silhouette and thick armour, both requirements for survival on the battlefield.

Unfortunately the first Vauxhall design perpetuated the worst features of the armament stagnation that had blighted British tanks since 1918. The turret carried only a 2pounder gun, and by 1940 it was becoming clear that this size was a complete anachronism. The difficulty was that there was none other. The 6pounder design was in being, but the Ordnance Factories were tooled up for 2pounders, and in the desperate days after Dunkirk there was no time to change over, so 2pounders it had to be for another year or more. A 3in Close Support howitzer was mounted low down in the front of the hull, alongside the driver. This was much like the arrangement in the French Char B, and there was little enough faith in that idea; but again, the designers had little option but to use the weapons available to them. A very few Close Support Churchills I were built, and these had the unusual armament of two 3in howitzers, the second one replacing the 2pounder gun in the turret, but the idea was not pursued further. The Churchill II and later marks dropped the hull gun in favour of a BESA machine-gun. By March 1942 the 6pounder was available and was fitted to the turret of the Churchill III in that month. Improvement followed and the Mark VII had a 75mm gun, the Mark VIII a 95mm Close Support howitzer, and some North African Mark IVs were re-

worked in Egypt to accommodate a 75mm gun and 0.3in Browning machine-gun in the turret, both these weapons being taken from Shermans and perhaps Grants.

The armour of the Churchill was probably the best part of the vehicle, and was very heavy for the time. The thickness of the frontal plates went up with successive marks, and most of the earlier marks were re-worked, as time and supplies permitted, to be given extra "appliqué" plates welded on. Turrets increased in size and complexity and the Mark VII was given the first commander's cupola in a British tank to have all-round vision when closed down – a great step forward, though it was common enough in German tanks by that time. The hull was roomy, which was fortunate in view of the amount of development which was done on it, and the ammunition stowage was particularly generous. The Mark I was able to carry 150 rounds of 2pounder and 58 of 3in howitzer ammunition, still leaving room for five men. The hull was sufficiently wide to allow the Mark III's 6pounder turret to be fitted without too much trouble, through the 75mm and 95mm weapons caused a little difficulty and had a rather smaller turret-ring than was ideal. These latter turrets looked a little slab-sided, as a result of the fact that some were built up with welding, rather than cast as complete units.

The Churchill was the first British tank with the Merritt-Brown regenerative steering, which had been tried out in the A6 10 years before. This system not only saved a great deal of power when turning, but also enabled the driver to make much sharper turns, until in neutral he could turn the tank on its own axis. This system, or some variant of it, is now universally used by all tank designers. Another innovation, for British AFVs at least, was the use of hydraulics in the steering and clutch controls, so that driving was far less tiring than it had been on previous designs, and the driver could exercise finer judgement in his use of the controls. The suspension was by 11 small road wheels on each side. Each of these wheels, or more properly bogies, was sprung separately on vertical coil springs, and the amount of movement was limited so that the ride was fairly harsh. However, such a system had the merits of simplicity, cheapness, and relative invulnerability to damage; each side could tolerate the loss of several bogies and still support the chassis, and the manufacture and fitting of bogies was not too difficult.

Churchills were used on most of the European battlefronts. The first time they were in action was the Dieppe raid of August 1942, in which several Mark Is and IIs took part, together with a few Mark IIIs. Few got over the harbour wall, and most were either sunk when disembarking, or captured. A number of Mark I, II and III examples were sent to Russia, and a few Mark IIIs were tried at Alamein. Thereafter they were used in Tunisia and Italy in ever-increasing numbers until the end of the war. Several brigades of Churchills were deployed in North-West Europe, where their thick armour proved very useful, but throughout the campaign the Churchill was hampered by being

outgunned by German armour.

There were many variants on the Churchill chassis as it was quickly found that it was well suited to such tasks as bridging, mineclearing, armoured recovery, and (probably best of all) flamethrowing. The Churchill was also a particularly successful Armoured Vehicle Royal Engineers (AVRE) and fulfilled several different RE roles until replaced by the Centurion AVRE in the early 1960s. Altogether 5,460 Churchills were produced, and they remained in service in varying numbers until the 1950s. The lack of adequate gun power was realised quite early in the Churchill's life, however, and in 1943 Vauxhall developed an improved version carrying a 17 pounder in the turret. The turret-ring had to be enlarged, and so the hull was widened. The armour remained the same thickness, and weight went up to 50 tons – 112,000lb (50,736kg). To support this extra load the tracks were widened, new bogies fitted, and the Bedford engine geared down. Top speed was only 11mph (17,6km/h) and although the prototypes were still being tried in 1945, the idea came to nothing, and the Black Prince, as it was to have been called, was scrapped.

Below: Following trials with a flamethrower installed in a Valentine tank in 1942 it was decided the following year to install the system in a Churchill, with the fuel being carried in a trailer towed behind the tank. This became known as the Churchill Crocodile and entered very successful service in 1944.

A27M Cromwell Infantry Tank

Cromwell Marks I to VIII.
Country of origin: United Kingdom.
Crew: 5.
Armament: One 6pounder gun; one 7.92mm BESA machine-gun to co-axial with main armament; one 7.92mm BESA machine-gun in hull (Marks 1 to III); one 75mm QF Mark V or VA gun; two 7.92mm machine-guns (Marks IV, V and VII); one 95mm howitzer; two 7.92mm BESA machine-guns (Marks VI and VIII).
Armour: 0.31in (8mm) minimum; 3in (76mm) maximum; 0.4in (10mm) minimum; 3in (76mm) maximum in welded variants; 4in (102mm) appliqué armour.
Dimensions: Length 20ft 10in (6.35m); width 10ft (3.04m); height 9ft 3¾in (2.84m).
Weight: 61,600lb (27,942kg).
Ground pressure: 14.7lb/in² (1kg/cm²).
Engine: Rolls-Royce Meteor V-12 water-cooled petrol engine developing 600hp at 2.250rpm.
Performance: Road speed 40mph (64km/h); cross-country speed 18mph (29km/h); range 173 miles (277km); vertical obstacle 3ft (0.92m); trench 7ft 6in (2.28m).
History: Served with the British Army from 1942 to 1950.

The Cromwell emerged from a General Staff specification drawn up in late 1940 and early 1941 for a "heavy cruiser". The cruisers built to the traditional ideas of a light fast vehicle capable of fulfilling the cavalry role of pursuit and exploitation had proved to be unequal to the modern battlefield in two vital areas, protection and gun power. The 1941 specification called for cruiser tanks with an all-up weight of around 25 tons (25,401kg), front armour of 2.75in (70mm) thickness, and a 6pounder gun on a 60in (1.52m) turret ring. Nuffield produced the first model, designated the A24 and originally called the Cromwell. This was an improved Crusader and used several of its components, among which was the Liberty engine which quickly proved itself incapable of performing satisfactorily in a tank weighing nearly 60,000lb (27,216kg). The name was soon changed to Cavalier, and the unsuccessful vehicle was used only for training and a few specialist roles.

Early in 1941 Leyland had collaborated with Rolls-Royce in looking for a satisfactory tank engine, and hit upon the Meteor, a de-rated Merlin aircraft engine. With 600hp this gave more than enough power for the heavy cruiser tanks, and since the main components were already well developed it seemed likely that it would be both robust and reliable. Leyland therefore began work on a tank which came to be called the Centaur, but this was really a Cromwell

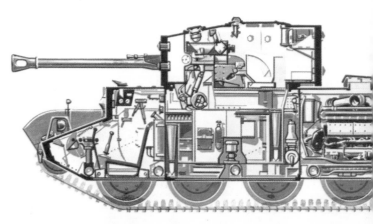

with a Liberty engine. There were no Meteors to be had when the Centaur was first produced, so it was fitted with the available Liberty engines, and was a bit more successful than the unfortunate Cavalier. A particular feature was the fact that the engine compartment could accept the Meteor when it became available, and many óf the production run were so converted after 1943. Meanwhile the Birmingham Railway Carriage and Wagon Company had taken on the design of the final version of Cromwell and produced the first pilot version in January 1942. At this date the name was still causing confusion, and it was variously known as the A27M (M for Meteor), Cromwell M, or Cromwell III. The nomenclature was only finally cleared up when Cavalier and Centaur were confirmed as names.

Because of the failures from too few trials, the Cromwell was exhaustively tested, a luxury at that time of the war, and the first production models did not appear until January 1943; which was far too long. The Meteor engine gave little trouble, and amply demonstrated that power was a necessary feature of tank design. The first engines were built by Rolls-Royce themselves in order to get the design right, but production was switched away from them as soon as possible, to leave them free to concentrate on aircraft engines, and the Meteor was put out to contract.

Just as the first Cromwells appeared, the General Staff changed its policy towards tank armament. Up till then the main armament gun had been required to be used in an anti-tank role, but experience in the desert and North

Right and below: Front and rear views of Cromwell IV cruiser. Frontal insignia are, from left to right, the unit number, the squadron number, and sign of the Guards Armoured Division.

Below left: Cutaway side view of Cromwell IV with 75mm QF Mk V gun and co-axial 7.92mm BESA MG.

Africa showed that after a breakthrough the main targets were not tanks at all, but dug-in infantry and anti-tank guns. What was needed was not an AP-firing gun but one that could fire a substantial HE shell against these softer targets. The Shermans and Grants carried a 75mm gun with such a performance and there was a demand for these to be mounted on British vehicles. The new General Staff specification reflected this approach, though it was also agreed that the need for a Close Support (CS) tank had not yet vanished. The fitting of a 75mm gun inserted some further delay into the programme, and there was also a need to retrofit 75mm guns into tanks that had been produced with the 6pounder. The first 75mm guns were delivered in late 1943, and by this time they were probably already close to the end of their time, though they had to be used until the end of the war. The 75mm was a new gun, developed from the 6pounder and using several components from that gun. The barrel was the same, bored out and shortened and fitted with a muzzle brake. The breech

Right: A Cromwell Mk III, formerly known as Centaur or Cromwell X, powered by Rolls-Royce Meteor engine. A total of 64 rounds of ammunition were carried for the 6pounder gun. To increase the operational range an auxiliary fuel tank was fitted at the rear.

mechanism was also similar, and not surprisingly there were several initial defects, not fully overcome until May 1944. The ammunition was American, taken from Lease-Lend supplies without modification, and gave no trouble. The American gun was interesting in that it had been directly derived from the French 75mm (*soixante-quinze*) of World War I. In 1933 these 75s were adapted for tank use by fitting a sliding breech and different buffer and recuperator, but the ammunition was still the same original French design, and indeed French ammunition could be fired. After Syria was taken from the Vichy French in late 1941, a quantity of French field gun ammunition was shipped to the Western Desert and used in Grant tanks. The gunner used a normal telescope for sighting the 75mm, but he could also use a range drum and clinometer for long range shooting. The two BESA machine-guns were mounted in the turret and hull, the latter displaying the last surviving remnant of the idea of mounting machine-guns all round the hull, which went back to the first tanks of World War I. Later on in the war many Cromwell crews were sceptical of the value of the hull gun, and it was frequently left out on the variants.

The hull conformed to the standard British design of three compartments, and was built of single armour plate, either welded or riveted. In the front compartment were the driver and hull gunner, separated from the turret by a bulkhead with an access hole in it. The commander, gunner and loader were in the turret in the centre compartment, contained in a rotating basket, the right. The turret traversed by hydraulic power and was extremely accurate in fine laying. The turret could be fully rotated through 360 degrees in 15 seconds. The commander had a cupola, the early models having only two episcopes, the later ones with eight, thereby providing all-round vision. Twenty-three rounds of 75mm ammunition were stowed ready for use in the turret and the balance of a full load of 64 rounds was stowed around the walls of the compartment. Some 4,950 rounds of BESA ammunition were carried. The No 19 wireless set

Above: Canadian-crewed Cromwell tanks in action in France in 1944. In the armoured regiments the Cromwells were usually employed with Sherman Fireflies (Sherman armed with the potent 17pounder gun), in the troop ratio of three Cromwells to one Firefly. Close support models had a 95mm howitzer. Generally out-gunned by the heavier German tanks, the Cromwell squadrons nevertheless succeeded with speed and manoeuvrability.

was in the back of the turret behind the loader, who listened in on the net. In the rear compartment the engine was placed between two fuel tanks and two large air cleaners. The radiators were right at the back, mounted upright. Transmission was through a Merritt-Brown regenerative gearbox, which had proved successful in the Churchill tank in 1941. It was used in a cruiser for the first time in the Cromwell, but the combination of Meteor and Merritt-Brown was to be the mainstay of British tank designers for years to come. The suspension was Christie-type, adapted from the A13 and strengthened. Even so it could not tolerate the top speed of 40mph (64km/h) and after the Mark IV the maximum speed was reduced to 32mph (52km/h) by gearing down the final drive. The track was wider than that of the A13, and the ride it gave was remarkably good.

The Cromwell proved itself to be both fast and agile, and was popular with its crews. Maintenance was not too difficult, and the reliability of the Meteor was a blessing to those who had had to cope with the vagaries of overstrained Liberty engines in other designs. A possible drawback for the crew was the difficulty of getting out in a hurry, especially for the driver and hull gunner. Later marks were given side doors to the front compartment so that the two men could climb out whatever the position of the turret and gun. In allowing for these doors some stowage space was lost on the track guards, and there was only a small bin behind the turret. Local enterprise often fitted extra bins, for

T 121801 W

space was tight for five men.

Cromwells were used for training throughout 1943 and 1944, and the opportunity for action did not come until the Normandy invasion. It was then the main equipment of the 7th Armoured Division and a number of armoured reconnaissance regiments. After the breakout from Caen, the Cromwell was able to do the job it was designed for, and exploit the assault. Supported by 95mm Howitzer CS versions, the Cromwell squadrons out-manoeuvred and outran the heavier German tanks, but they were always outgunned, even by the comparatively light Panthers. Attempts to fit the 17pounder gun were a failure, and the Cromwell crews relied for their success on superior training and manoeuvrability when in action. The attempt to fit the 17pounder gun resulted in a tank called the Challenger, built to the specification A30. The first model appeared in August 1942, based on a lengthened Cromwell with an extra wheel station. Performance was poor because the hull was too narrow for the large turret, and the extra weight and longer track base reduced speed and

Above: Cromwell VII armed with 75mm gun; this was a Cromwell re-worked with appliqué armour welded on to the hull front, wider tracks, stronger suspension and reduced final drive ratio.

agility. Nevertheless it was approved for service early in 1943 and 260 were built. A later attempt to improve on the Challenger produced the Avenger, a Challenger with a better turret, but only thin sheet metal on the roof.

The final step in trying to make Cromwell into an SP gun was in 1950, when the Centurion 20pounder was put into a two-man turret on the normal Cromwell hull. This just about worked, and it was issued to the Territorial Army and sold in small numbers to Austria and Jordan. As a gun tank Cromwell was numerically the most important British cruiser of the war, and though never the main battle tank of the army, it supplemented the Shermans in all British tank formations by 1945. Its speed and power were the best ever seen in British tanks till that time, and there was plenty of scope for development in the basic design.

A34 Comet Cruiser Tank

Country of origin: United Kingdom.
Crew: 5.
Armament: One 77mm gun; one 7.92mm BESA machine-gun co-axial with main armament; one 7.92mm BESA machine-gun.
Armour: 102mm (4in) maximum; 14mm (0.55in) minimum.
Dimensions: Length 25ft 1½in (7.66m); width 10ft (3.04m); height 8ft 9½in (2.98m).
Weight: Combat 78,800lb (35,696kg).
Ground pressure: 13.85lb/in² (0.88kg/cm²).
Engine: Rolls-Royce Meteor Mark 3 V-12 water-cooled petrol engine developing 600bhp at 2,550rpm.
Performance: Road speed 32mph (51km/h), range 123 miles (196km); vertical obstacle 3ft (0.92m); trench 8ft (2.43m); gradient 35 per cent.
History: In service with the British Army from 1944 to 1958. Still used by Burma and South Africa.

The requirement for the Comet was first seen during the tank battles in the Western Desert in late 1941 and early 1942, when it was apparent that British tanks had no gun capable of defeating the Germans. The Cromwell, whilst an excellent tank, had been given too small a gun, which could not fire HE. Nor was its 6pounder very powerful against armour. An attempt to upgun it to carry the 17pounder met with little success (the Challenger), and by late 1943 there was an urgent need for a fast cruiser with reasonable protection and a gun capable of taking on the later marks of German tank.

Leyland was given the task of developing the new tank early in 1943, the first priority being to decide upon a suitable gun. The criterion chosen was to look for the most powerful gun that could be mounted on Cromwell, and then a tank would be built using as many Cromwell components as possible. After much searching and deliberation Vickers-Armstrong designed a lighter and more compact version of the 17pounder, the Vickers HV 75mm. This gun fired the same shell as the 17pounder but used a shorter and wider cartridge case which was easier to handle in a turret. It was slightly less powerful, and had a shorter barrel and lower muzzle velocity, but it was still far ahead of any gun carried on Allied AFVs at that time, except the SP tank destroyers. To avoid confusion in

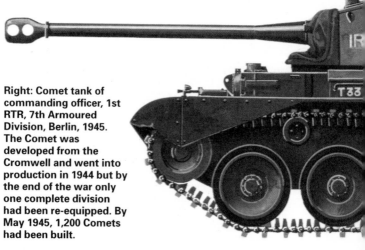

Right: Comet tank of commanding officer, 1st RTR, 7th Armoured Division, Berlin, 1945. The Comet was developed from the Cromwell and went into production in 1944 but by the end of the war only one complete division had been re-equipped. By May 1945, 1,200 Comets had been built.

Above: Comet cruiser tank showing 77mm high velocity gun and bow-mounted 7.92mm BESA machine gun during closing stages of the war. Infantry are riding on deck and track guards.

names and ammunition supply, the new gun was called the 77mm.

The first mock-up of the Comet was ready in late September 1943, and production was planned to be under way in mid-1944. The need for the Comet had become pressing. The first prototypes were delivered early in 1944, but there was a good deal of redesign to be done, and what had started as an up-gunned Cromwell soon reached the point where 60 per cent of the vehicle was a complete redesign, albeit a similar design. The hull was largely untouched, and there was criticism of the retention of the hull gun and the vertical front plate it required. The Cromwell's belly armour was also kept,

Above: Front view of a Comet cruiser tank showing position of the hull-mounted 7.92mm BESA machine-gun.

Right: The Comet was designed under the parentage of Leyland Motors Limited as the A34 cruiser tank. Main armament consisted of an Ordnance Quick Firing 77mm Mk 2 which in fact had a calibre of 76.2mm but was called the 77mm to avoid confusion with the 17pounder gun. This fired an APCBC projectile weighing 7.7kg which would penetrate 109mm of armour at a range of 500 yards (457m), it could also fire a high explosive round. The Comet tank was still in operational service with both Burma and South Africa in the 1980s.

although this had been shown to be too light. But there was no time to do more, and despite front line pressures continual changes and modifications meant that the first production models were not delivered until September 1944, and did not reach the first units until just before Christmas. The 11th Armoured Division was re-equipped with Comets in the first months of 1945, and was the only division to have a complete stock by the end of the war. Other divisions were issued with Comets as the year went by, though more slowly. In early 1949 the Centurion replaced the Comet, although Comets were still in Berlin and Hong Kong until the late 1950s.

Although practically a new tank, the Comet was easily recognisable as a Cromwell successor, and it was in essence an up-gunned and up-armoured version. The hull was welded, with side doors at the front for the driver and hull gunner. The turret was also welded, with a cast mantlet and front armour. The space inside was good, and access was fairly easy. The commander was given all-round vision with the same cupola as the Cromwell, and ammunition was stowed in armoured bins, a distinct step forward. The turret was electrically traversed, a development of the excellent system tried out in the Churchill, and to provide adequate electricity a generator was driven by the main engine. As with the later marks of the Cromwell, there were only two stowage bins over the tracks, and there was a prominent bin at the back of the turret. This to some extent counter-balanced the overhang of the gun. The suspension was meant to be identical with that of the Cromwell, but it was quickly found that this was not adequate for the extra weight so it was strengthened and given return

rollers. With this suspension the Comet was remarkably agile and tough, and its cross-country speed could often be more than the crew could tolerate with comfort. The Meteor engine had adequate power for all needs and on a cross-country training course a good driver could handle a Comet like a sports car – and frequently did. It was sufficiently strong to stand up impressively to high jumps at full speed.

The Comet only went to one variant on its solitary mark, surely a record for any British tank: the main feature of the variant was a change in the exhaust cowls, a modification found necessary after the Normandy fighting. These helped to hide the tank at night, and as also at that time it was usual to lift infantry into battle on the decks and track guards, the cowls protected them from the exhaust.

The Comet was the last of the cruisers, and also the last properly developed British tank to take part in the war. It was not universally popular, and met strong criticism at first, mainly because its detractors believed that it perpetuated the faults of the Cromwell, which in some minor respects it did. This was particularly so in the case of the nose plates and the hull gun. However, to remove them would have involved an extensive redesign and the building of new jigs for the factory. This was out of the question in 1943. The disappointment at the lack of effective belly armour is less easy to refute, since it should have been foreseen, but it was only appreciated too late. Perhaps most of the exasperation of the users sprang from the fact that it was such a good tank and came so late that it was never given a chance to prove itself properly.

Centurion Main Battle Tank

Country of origin: United Kingdom.
Crew: 4.
Armament: One L7 series 105mm gun; one .3in machine-gun co-axial with main armament; one .5in ranging machine-gun; one .3in machine-gun on commander's cupola, six smoke dischargers on each side of the turret.
Armour: 19mm-152mm (0.67in-6.08in) maximum.
Dimensions: Length (gun forward) 32ft 4in (9.85m); length (hull) 25ft 8in (7.82m); width (including skirts) 11ft 1½in (3.39m); height 9ft 10½in (3.01m).
Weight: Combat 114,250lb (51,820kg).
Ground pressure: 13.5lb/in^2 (0.95kg/cm^2).
Engine: Rolls-Royce Meteor Mark IVB 12-cylinder liquid-cooled petrol engine developing 650bhp at 2,550rpm.
Performance: Road speed 21.5mph (34.6km/h), range 118 miles (190km); vertical obstacle 3ft (0.91m); trench 11ft (3.35m); gradient 60 per cent.
History: Entered service with the British Army in 1949. Centurions remain in service with the armies of Israel (1,000 approx); Jordan (293); Singapore (12 approx); South Africa (224); and Sweden (150 approx).

The A41 Centurion tank was developed at the end of World War II and entered service with the British Army in 1949. A total of 4,423 were produced, some 2,500 for export. Those which entered service with the British Army were withdrawn when Chieftain (*qv*) entered service and were sold abroad. Many of those bought by foreign armies have now been withdrawn and scrapped, but well over 1,000 remain in service around the world.

The Centurion proved to be a successful, battleworthy and popular tank, and has also proved capable of accepting many improvements. The original model was armed with a 17-pounder (76.2mm) gun, which was later replaced by the 20-pounder (83.8mm) model; virtually all those still in service, however, are armed with the British-designed

Top: A Centurion AVRE (Armoured Vehicle Royal Engineers) armed with a 165mm demolition gun for destroying fortifications. An hydraulically-operated dozer blade is mounted on the hull front and a fascine can be carried to fill an anti-tank

Above: A Centurion FV4002 armoured vehicle launched bridge begins to swing its bridge into position. The bridge takes two minutes to lay and four minutes to recover and can span up to 13.716m. It is based on the Mk 5 hull.

Left: As with most MBT designs, the Centurion has lent itself well to adaptation, as illustrated in this view of an Armoured Engineering Vehicle. Atop the glacis plate is a length of rolled aluminium roadway, while behind the vehicle is a towed trailer.

L7 105mm gun. The original Centurion was powered by the Rolls-Royce Meteor petrol engine, a modified version of the Merlin which powered the Spitfire fighter. This gave a poor power/weight ratio and also had a very high fuel consumption, resulting in poor mobility and range. All modern users have replaced this by a more economical diesel engine.

The major user of Centurions continues to be the Israeli Army, the latest MBT version being the *Sh'ot*, which is armed with an L7

105mm gun, powered by a General Dynamics AVDS-1790-2A diesel, and has a bolt-on explosive reactive armour (ERA) package. Some may also have a new integrated fire-control system. *Sh'ot* can also be fitted for mine-clearing using either plough or mine-clearing rollers. Surplus Centurion hulls have also been converted for use as armoured personnel carriers (APCs): *Puma* for the armoured engineers, and the *Nagmash'ot* for use by infantry.

All 293 Jordanian Army Centurions have been upgraded, to the new *Tariq* standard. New equipments includes a General Dynamics AVDS-1970 diesel, Belgian fire-control system, hydropneumatic suspension, turret drive and crew-compartment fire suppression system.

During the years of the UN defence equipment embargo, South Africa upgraded its Centurion fleet to produce the *Olifant* Mk 1A. This involved installing a V-12 diesel, a South African version of the British

**Above: A Swedish Army Centurion mounting
a 105mm gun. The Swedish Army has 350
Centurions of three basic marks.**

L7 105mm gun, and other improvements. The later *Olifant* Mk 1B
was a complete rebuild, and included a new suspension system,
power pack and electronics, together with appliqué armour on the
glacis plate and turret.

Swedish Centurions are designated *Strv*-101 and -102 and all have
been upgraded over the years. A reducing number remain in service,
with the last scheduled to remain on the island of Gotland for some
years. A few Centurions are in service with the Singapore Army, while
the Austrian Army has scrapped its Centurion hulls, but retained the
turrets, which are used in the static defence role.

Above: Mounting 105mm guns, British-built Centurions of the Israeli Armoured Corps advance on the Golan heights during the 1973 Yom

Kippur War. Developed in 1944-45, the Centurion has proved one of the most successful tanks of all time, and more than 4,000 have been built.

FV200 Conqueror Heavy Tank

Country of origin: United Kingdom.
Crew: 4.
Armament: One 120mm gun; one .3in machine-gun co-axial with main armament; one .3in ranging machine-gun on commander's cupola, six smoke dischargers on each side of the turret.
Armour: 178mm (7.12in) maximum.
Dimensions: Length (overall) 38ft (11.58m); length (hull) 25ft 4in (7.721m); width 13ft 1in (3.987m); height (overall) 11ft (3.353m).
Weight: Combat 145,600lb (66,044kg).
Ground pressure: 12lb/in² (0.84kg/cm²).
Engine: M.120 No.2 Mk.1A 12-cylinder petrol engine with fuel injection system developing 810bhp at 2,800rpm.
Performance: Road speed 21.3mph (34km/h), range 95 miles (153km); vertical obstacle 3ft (0.914m); trench 11ft (3.352m); gradient 60 per cent.
History: Entered service with the British Army in 1956 and phased out of service in 1966. At least five are still in existence, four in Britain and one in France.

In 1944 development of a new tank, designated the A34, was started. The vehicle was to have been an infantry support tank and would have worked with the A41 heavy cruiser (later known as the Centurion). After the war this became known as the FV200 Series or Universal Tank. The basic idea was to build a tank which could be quickly adopted to carry out the roles of flamethrower tank, dozer tank and amphibious tank. The first prototype was completed in 1948; this had a remote-controlled machine-gun on the left track guard and a Centurion turret with a 17pounder gun. The following year the project was cancelled as it was found that the Centurion tank could undertake many of the roles projected for the FV200 series. The FV201 chassis was then used as the basis for a new heavy tank to compete with the Russian IS-3 which appeared in 1945, and this became known as the FV214 or Conqueror. For trials purposes a model known as the Caernarvon (FV221) was built, this being a Conqueror chassis with a Centurion turret. The first prototype of the FV214 was completed in 1950, with production being carried out from 1956 to 1959. A total of 180 Conqueror Mk.1s and Mk.2s was built, plus some armoured recovery vehicles designated FV219.

The FV200 series included the following projected variants: Armoured Vehicle Royal Engineers (AVRE) in two different models, flail tank for clearing mines, self-propelled anti-tank gun (medium), self-propelled anti-tank gun (heavy), self-propelled artillery (medium), self-propelled artillery (heavy), bridgelayer, Beach Armoured Recovery Vehicle (BARV), artillery tractor and assault personnel carrier. It was lucky for the British Army that these were not built as some of them would have proved a liability on the battlefield!

The Conqueror was issued to armoured regiments in Germany on a maximum scale of nine per regiment, with the task of providing long-range

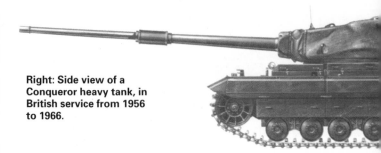

Right: Side view of a Conqueror heavy tank, in British service from 1956 to 1966.

Above: The Conqueror was developed as a counter to the Russian IS-3 tank, but was replaced by the 105mm-gunned Centurion.

anti-tank support for the Centurion. The Conqueror proved difficult to maintain and its electrical system was always giving trouble. It had a very small range of action and was difficult to move about the battlefield because of its weight of 65 tons (66,044kg). By the time it was phased out of service in 1966 the Centurion with the 105mm gun was in service in large numbers.

The hull of the Conqueror was of all-welded construction. The driver was seated at the front of the hull on the right, with some ammunition stowed to his left. The cast turret was in the centre of the hull with the gunner on the right and the loader on the left, both these crew members having their own hatches. The commander had his own cupola, which could be traversed through 360°. The engine, a modified version of the Meteor used in the Centurion, and transmission (five forward and two reverse gears) were mounted at the rear of the hull and separated from the fighting compartment by a fireproof bulkhead. The suspension, of the Horstmann type, consisted of four units each side, each of these having two road wheels, these in turn being supported by three concentric springs. The drive sprocket was at the rear and the idler at the front, and there were four track-return rollers.

The main armament of the Conqueror was a 120mm gun. This had an elevation of +15° and a depression of −7° (not over the rear part of the hull), traverse being a full 360°. Elevation and traverse were powered. The ammunition was of the separate-loading type (that is, separate projectile and cartridge case). A total of 35 rounds of HESH and APDS were carried. A .3in machine-gun was mounted coaxially to the left of the main armament and there was a similar weapon on the commander's cupola which could be laid and fired from within the turret. The only other version to enter service was the FV219 ARV.

369

FV4201 Chieftain Main Battle Tank

Country of origin: United Kingdom.
Crew: 4.
Armament: One L11 series 120mm gun; one 7.62mm machine-gun co-axial with main armament; one 7.62mm machine-gun in commander's cupola, one .5in ranging machine-gun; six smoke dischargers on each side of the turret.
Armour: Classified.
Dimensions: Length (gun forward) 35ft 5in (10.79m); length (hull) 24ft 8in (7.52m); width overall (including searchlight) 12ft (3.66m); height overall 9ft 6in (2.89m).
Weight: Combat 121,250lb (55,000kg).
Ground pressure: 14.22lb/in^2 (0.90kg/cm^2).
Engine: Leyland L.60 No 4 Mk 8A 12-cylinder multi-fuel engine developing 750bhp at 2,100rpm.
Performance: Road speed 30mph (48km/h), road range 280 miles (450km); vertical obstacle 3ft (0.91m); trench 10ft 4in (3.15m); gradient 60 per cent.
History: Entered service with the British Army in 1967. Remains in service with the following armies: Iran (200); Iraq (150); Jordan (90); Kuwait (approx 20); Oman (15).

Following its experiences against German tanks in World War II the British Army has always given top priority to protection and firepower at the expense of mobility. Thus, when a requirement was issued in the 1950s for an MBT to replace the Centurion, the result was the best armoured tank of its generation, with the most powerful main gun. Seven prototypes of the new FV4201 Chieftain were completed between 1959 and 1962, and following protracted development problems with the engine, transmission and suspension, the first of some 900 Chieftains entered service with the British Army in 1967.

The Chieftain has a hull front of cast construction and the rest of the hull is welded; the turret is cast. The driver is placed centrally in the front of the hull in a semi-reclined position, which enables the overall

Below: A Chieftain Mk 5 MBT with a thermal sleeve for its 120mm gun. Chieftains remaining in British Army service are now fitted with the GEC-Marconi Integrated Fire Control System which gives them an enhanced "kill" probability.

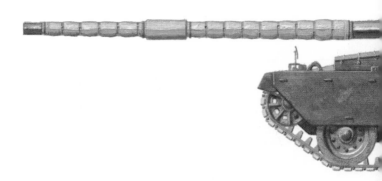

Above: A Chieftain MBT negotiating rough ground with relative ease.

height of the tank to be kept to a minimum. In the turret, the commander and gunner are on the right and the loader on the left. When originally introduced the gunner was provided with a 12.7mm ranging machine-gun, which fired rounds ballistically matched to the 120mm rounds, and was thus able to obtain precise ranging information for the main gun. This was simple and effective compared to the contemporary cross-turret optical rangefinders, but it was replaced by an even more effective method of range-taking in the 1970s, using the Barr & Stroud laser rangefinder. Later still, the Marconi Integrated Fire Control System was installed. Over 300

Main armament of the Chieftain MBT consists of a 120mm rifled tank gun designed by the Royal Armament Research and Development Establishment at Fort Halstead. This fires a wide range of separate loading ammunition (eg, projectile and bagged charge) including Armour Piercing Discarding Sabot Tracer (APDS-T), High Explosive Squash Head (HESH), and Smoke, plus training rounds.

British Army Chieftains have also been fitted with the Thermal Observation and Gunnery Sight, which was developed for the Challenger MBT.

The L11A5 120mm rifled gun is fitted with a muzzle reference system, fume extractor and a thermal sleeve. The main rounds fired are Armour-Piercing Discarding Sabot, Armour-Piercing Fin-Stabilised Discarding Sabot and High Explosive Squash Head.

Chieftain is fitted with a full range of night vision devices. All now have an infra-red (IR) detector, which can localise an IR source to within 62°. Various other devices have been developed for the tank, but are only fitted when the tactical situation requires it. These include a dozer blade and a deep fording kit.

In 1986, the British Army fitted appliqué armour, codenamed *Stillbrew*, which enhanced armour protection at comparatively small cost and with only a small effect on mobility. Other versions of the Chieftain included armoured repair and recovery vehicles, armoured recovery vehicles and the armoured vehicle-launched bridge. Part of the British Army's Chieftain fleet was replaced in the 1980s by the Challenger 1 and the remainder in the 1990s by the Challenger 2 (*qv*).

The Iranian Army placed an order for 700 Chieftains in 1971,

followed by another order for 125 of an improved version called the *Shir* 1 and 1,225 of an even more advanced version called the *Shir* 2. The Chieftains all arrived in Iran, but none of either version of the *Shir* were actually delivered, due to the collapse of the Shah's regime. Jordan subsequently ordered 90 *Shir* 1s, which they designated the *Khalid* (qv), while the *Shir* 2 design became the basis of the British Army's Challenger 1 MBT.

Below: A Chieftain Mk 5 MBT with a thermal sleeve for its 120mm gun. Chieftains remaining in British Army service are now fitted with the GEC-Marconi Integrated Fire Control System which gives them an enhanced "kill" probability.

Vickers Defence Systems Khalid Main Battle Tank

Country of origin: United Kingdom.
Crew: 4.
Armament: One 120mm smoothbore L11A5 gun; one L8A2 7.62mm machine-gun co-axial with main gun; one remote-controlled L37A2 12.7mm machine-gun on turret roof; one six-barrelled smoke-grenade launcher on each side of turret.
Armour: Classified.
Dimensions: Length (including main gun) 38ft 0ins (11.6m); hull 27ft 6in (8.4m); width 11ft 6in (3.5m); height (to turret roof) 8ft 0in (2.44m).
Weight: Combat 127,600lb (58,000kg).
Ground pressure: 12.8lb/in^2 (0.9kg/cm^2).
Engine: Perkins Condor V-12 1200 12-cylinder, water-cooled diesel, 1,200bhp at 2,300rpm.
Performance: Road speed 33mph (56km/h); range 250 miles (400km); vertical obstacle 3ft 0in (0.9m); trench 10ft 4in (3.15m); gradient 60 per cent.
History: Original Iranian order cancelled; in service with Jordanian Army (274).

In the early 1970s the Shah of Iran exercised virtually absolute power over his armed forces and during the course of a visit to London in 1971 he personally ordered 700 Chieftains of the same model as the British Army. This was followed by a second order for 125 of an improved version, designated *Shir 1* (British designation FV 4030/2), and then by a third order for 1,225 of an even more advanced version, *Shir 2* (FV 4030/3). All the

Below: In the early 1970s the British developed a new version of the Chieftain, as Shir 1. When the Shah was toppled the order was cancelled and 274 were sold to Jordan as the Khalid.

Above: The Khalid was similar to the British Mk 8 Chieftain, but with a new power train, new fire-control system, different suspension system and a laser sighting system.

Chieftains of the first order were delivered to Iran, but the Shah's regime was overthrown at a point where production of *Shir 1* had started but before any had been delivered, and *Shir 2* was still under development. However, the new government of Ayatollah Khomeini then peremptorily cancelled both orders.

The Jordanian Army then placed an order for 274 of the FV 4030/2, under the new designation, *Khalid*. This was in essence a Mark 8 Chieftain, but with a new power train, new fire-control system, different suspension system and a laser sighting system in place of the ranging machine-gun. The main armament of the *Khalid* is the Royal Ordnance L11A5 120mm rifled gun, and an in-service modification to the sights and internal stowage racks has enabled this to fire the new Royal Ordnance APFSDS-T round. There are two 7.62mm machine-guns, one mounted co-axially with the main gun, the other on the turret roof in a mount which enables it to be fired by remote-control without the firer having to expose his head and shoulders, as on many other tanks.

The original Chieftain power unit was always a problem and the *Khalid* is powered by the same Perkins Condor, 12-cylinder diesel engine as the Challenger 1, giving a power output of 1,200hp at 2,300rpm and a power/weight ratio of 20.7hp/tonne. This is coupled to a David Brown TN37 fully automatic transmission, originally the Mark 2, but later upgraded to Mark 2A. The double-bogie suspension system is similar to that on Chieftain, but with greatly increased travel. Unlike the British Chieftains, the Jordanian *Khalids* were not fitted with the Stillbrew armour (see Chieftain entry).

The Jordanian Army is reported to be considering a variety of upgrading possibilities for its *Khalid* fleet but no firm decision has yet been announced.

FV101 Scorpion Light Tank/Reconnaissance Vehicle

FV 101, FV 102, FV 103, FV 104, FV 105, FV 106, FV 107, Scorpion 90, Sabre, and Streaker.
Country of origin: United Kingdom.
Crew: 3.
Armament: One L23A1 76mm main gun; one L37A2 7.62mm machine-gun co-axial with main gun; three single-barrelled smoke dischargers on each side of turret.
Armour: Aluminium.
Dimensions: Length (hull) 15ft 8in (4.8m); width 7ft 0in (2.13m); height (to turret roof) 6ft 9in (2.1m).
Weight: Combat 17,800lb (8,073kg).
Ground pressure: 5lb/in^2 (0.36 kg/cm^2).
Engine: Jaguar J60 No1 Mk100B, 4.2 litre 6-cylinder petrol engine, 190bhp at 4,750rpm.
Performance: Road speed 50mph (80.5km/h); range 400 miles (644km); vertical obstacle 1ft 7in (0.5m); trench 6ft 10in (2.1m); gradient 60 per cent.
History: Entered service with British Army in 1972. Light tank versions, as follows.
76mm version: Botswana (36); Brunei (19*); Chile (30); Iran (60* approx); Ireland (14); Jordan (10* approx); New Zealand (26); Nigeria (100); Oman (60*); Philippines (41); Spain (17); Tanzania (40); Thailand (154); UAE (76).
90mm version: Indonesia (121); Malaysia (26); Togo (12); Venezuela (80*).
Note: Belgium and UK bought 710 and 1,100, respectively; both still operate large numbers of CVR(T) family but not 76mm gun version. Honduras (15) does not operate 76mm version.
(*Total includes some non-gun versions.)

This very successful family of light fighting vehicles were designated reconnaissance vehicles by the British Army, but the gun-armed versions have been (and still are) frequently used as light tanks. The design originated in the early 1960s with a British Army requirement for a new reconnaissance vehicle, which was eventually met by two separate designs, Combat Vehicle Reconnaissance (Tracked) (CVR(T)) and Combat Vehicle Reconnaissance (Wheeled) (CVR(W)), of which only the former concerns us here. The first prototype CVR(T) was completed by Alvis, of Coventry, England, in 1969 and production started in 1971 with the first

Above: Scorpion CVR(T) followed by an Alvis Saladin armoured car and a Chieftain MBT. Overhead is a Westland-Aérospatiale AH Mk I Lynx general-purpose helicopter, which has proved a superior tank-killer.

examples entering service in 1972.

The Scorpion was the first all-welded aluminium vehicle to be accepted into service by the British Army, and is a very light and compact vehicle, with a front-mounted engine, which drives the tracks through the forward sprocket. The driver sits at the left front of the vehicle with the engine to his right and the transmission to his front. The turret is towards the rear with the commander on the left and the gunner on the right. The suspension uses five cast aluminium road wheels and torsion bars, with the drive sprocket at the front and the idler at the rear. A flotation screen is permanently carried collapsed around the top of hull and when this is erected the Scorpion is propelled in the water by its tracks at speeds (depending on the current) of up to 5mph (8km/h). The vehicle has

Left: Side view of the Scorpion Combat Vehicle Reconnaissance (Tracked), now in service with the British and Belgian armies and in several Middle East countries. The Scorpion has an all-welded aluminium hull and is manufactured at Alvis of Coventry. It mounts a 76mm gun and 7.62mm co-axial machine gun, with six smoke dischargers. It incorporates an NBC system.

379

spectacular performance and the ground pressure is so low that it can frequently cross soft ground on which a man cannot walk.

The L23A1 76mm gun which arms the standard Scorpion was a lightweight development of a gun which has previously armed the British Saladin armoured car. It fires High-Explosive Squash Head (HESH) and High Explosive (HE) rounds with a range of 5,500yd (5,000m), and smoke, which has range of 4,000yd (3,700m); 40 rounds carried. Elevation limits are +35 degrees to -10 degrees with a 360 degree traverse, which was originally manually controlled but latterly was electrical. This was a very effective gun but some users wanted a heavier weapon, and a new version of the vehicle was developed armed with the Belgian Cockerell 90mm Mk III gun, whose main ammunition is a fin-stabilized HEAT round, but it also fires fin-stabilized HESH and HE, as well as smoke and canister rounds. Because the rounds are larger, the number carried is reduced to 36. The Scorpion 90 also has a laser rangefinder, an integrated fire-control system and electrical traversing. Many Scorpion 90 users have also specified diesel engines and the Perkins T6-3544 is about the only one which can be squeezed into the small space available. The Scorpion 90 is somewhat heavier: 19,230lb (8,723kg) compared to 17,800lb (8,073kg).

An L37A2 7.62mm machine-gun is mounted co-axially with the main armament. Forty rounds of 76mm and 3,000 rounds of 7.62mm ammunition are carried. Although not normally fitted, some users have also specified an anti-aircraft machine-gun in a flexible mounting on the turret roof. Three smoke-grenade dischargers are mounted on each side of the turret. Standard equipment includes an NBC pack and night-vision equipment for both the driver and gunner.

The original requirement was to use a commercially off-the-shelf (COTS) engine and the Jaguar J60 engine was selected, a six-cylinder petrol engine, derated from 26hp to 190hp for this application. This engine had powered a number of most successful sports cars in the 1960s and 1970s, and offered a high power output for a small space requirement, which was considered more important than the dangers of using petrol in a fighting vehicle and its relatively high fuel consumption. Most operators purchased the vehicle with the Jaguar engine but some (Malaysia, Indonesia, Venezuela) specified diesel engines.

The basic vehicle was adapted for a large number of roles and the complete family comprised: FV 101 (Scorpion) reconnaissance vehicle with 76mm gun;

Above: The FV103 Spartan is the APC member of the Scorpion family. With a 3-man crew, it can carry 4 fully-equipped infantrymen.

FV 102 (Striker) anti-tank vehicle with five Swingfire missile launchers; FV 103 (Spartan) personnel carrier (AAC); FV 104 (Samaritan) ambulance; FV 105 (Sultan) command vehicle; FV 106 (Samson) recovery vehicle; FV 107 (Scimitar) reconnaissance vehicle with 30mm Rarden cannon; Scorpion 90, as FV 101 but with 90mm cannon; Sabre, with Scorpion hull and Fox turret, armed with 30mm Rarden cannon and 7.62mm Hughes Chain Gun; and Streaker, a high-mobility load carrier.

The CVR(T) family was produced in both the UK and Belgium and approximately 4,000 had been produced by the time production ceased in the mid-1990s.

Left: The FV102 Striker is the anti-tank member of the Scorpion family. The launcher box on the hull top contains 5 Swingfire ATGWs, ranging to 4,375yd (4,000m). Five more missiles are carried inside the hull.

Challenger 1 Main Battle Tank

Country of origin: United Kingdom.
Crew: 4.
Armament: One Royal Ordnance L30 120mm rifled gun; one McDonnell Douglas 7.62mm co-axial Chain-Gun; one L37A2 7.62mm anti-aircraft general-purpose machine-gun; two five-barrel smoke grenade dischargers.
Armour: Chobham.
Dimensions: Length (including armament) 37ft 11in (11.55m); length (gun to rear) 32ft 4in (9.86m); width 11ft 7in (3.52m); height 8ft 2in (2.49m).
Weight: Combat 127,775lb (60,000kg).
Ground pressure: 12.8lb/in² (0.9kg/cm²).
Engine: Perkins CV12 TCA 12-cylinder 60° V direct injection 4-stroke liquid-cooled diesel engine developing 1,200bhp at 2,300rpm. Perkins 4,108 4-stroke diesel auxiliary power unit.
Performance: Road speed 35mph (56km/h), range 340 miles (550km); vertical obstacle 2ft 11in (0.9m); trench 7ft 8in (2.34m); gradient 60 per cent.
History: Entered production in 1982; entered service with British Army in 1984.

With the Chieftain accepted for service in 1963, the thoughts of the British Army turned towards the next generation tank. A national project was started in the late 1960s and this work continued, albeit at a low tempo, during the period of the Anglo-German MBT project. This started in 1970, but, as with every other collaborative MBT project, the partnership ended in 1977, whereupon attention reverted to the

Above: A sight ground forces dread – a Challenger 1 MBT smashing through a defensive sand berm on its way to battle.

Below: The well-sloped front of the Challenger's low profile turret is a deliberate design attempt to decrease the chances of an anti-tank missile team achieving a successful "kill".

While the obvious purpose of a Main Battle Tank is to fire the shells carried within, the ability to use external space for some improvised logistical self-support is known to every good tank crew.
Photographed during Operation *Desert Storm*, this Challenger 1 proves the point, with a pair of auxiliary fuel drums attached to the rear of the hull and a group of "top up" fuel canisters strapped down to the main body immediately behind the turret.

national network. Meanwhile, the Chieftain had attracted orders from the Shah of Iran and a developed version had been produced designated the *Shir* 1. This led in turn to the *Shir* 2, a very much better MBT, whose development was mainly funded by the Iranian order. Unfortunately the Iranian order then fell through, due to the revolution which ousted the Shah, and Vickers then produced a new version of the *Shir* 2, altered to suit British Army requirements. This was ordered into production in 1978 as the Challenger 1, entering service with the British Army in 1984, with a total of 420 delivered by the time production ended in mid-1990.

There was considerable bad publicity for Challenger 1, which reached its peak when the British Army decided to withdraw from the Canadian Army Trophy, an international tank gunnery contest among NATO teams in the Northern and Central Army Groups. Intense speculation about a future MBT for the British Army culminated in the late 1980s with an announcement that there would be an international competition for what was officially termed the "Chieftain Replacement Programme" (CHIP). The four competitors were the Leopard 2 (Improved) from Germany, the M1A1 Abrams from the USA, the Leclerc from France and the Challenger 2 from the UK. After an intensive evaluation of the competing designs the Challenger 2 was selected, subject to passing a series of "milestones" which would demonstrate that it fully met the British Army's requirement.

Meanwhile, the Gulf War broke out and the British Army sent an armoured division to Saudi Arabia, which included 176 Challenger 1s. These performed exceptionally well, showing a high degree of mechanical reliability, the tanks in the forward armoured regiments covering an average of 217 miles (350km) each in the 100-hour ground war, and there were just two breakdowns in the entire force. The 120mm gun proved very accurate and more than half the engagements involved the use of High-Explosive Squash Head (HESH) rounds. During the Gulf War the Challenger 1s destroyed some 300 Iraqi tanks; not one British tank was destroyed in return. Following this great success and the passing of the milestones, all of which was accompanied by some

intense political lobbying, an order was finally placed for Challenger 2s.

The only upgrade to Challenger 1 was CHIP, but no major work was undertaken due to the replacement of Challenger 1 by Challenger 2.

The Challenger 2's hull is similar to that of the Challenger 1. The driver sits centrally, with an unusual trough in the glacis plate to enable him to see. The other three crewmen are in the turret, with the commander and gunner on the right of the gun, and the loader on the left. The hull and turret are constructed of welded steel and Chobham armour, and are of an exceptionally good ballistic shape.

It was originally intended to replace about half the Challenger 1 fleet by Challenger 2s, but it was subsequently decided to replace them all. As a result, Challenger 1s are being taken out of service and will have been completely replaced in the British Army by Challenger 2s by the end of 2001. Some Challenger 1 hulls will be used for specialist vehicles , such as AVLBs or ARVs; the remainder will be either sold or scrapped.

Above: The sole variation on the Challenger 1 MBT theme to date is the Armoured Recovery and Repair Vehicle, complete with dozer blade. A dozen of these vehicles were deployed to the Gulf in support of UK land forces, and proved their worth many times over in very arduous combat conditions.

Left: Challenger 1s performed well in the Gulf War of 1991, destroying around 300 Iraqi tanks and displaying remarkable mechanical reliability.

Vickers Defence Challenger 2 Main Battle Tank

Challenger 2 and 2E.
Country of origin: United Kingdom.
Crew: 4.
Armament: One Royal Ordnance L30A1 rifled gun; one Hughes L94A1 7.62mm Chain Gun co-axial with the main gun; one L37A2 7.62mm remote-controlled machine-gun on turret roof; five single-barrelled smoke grenade launchers on each side of the turret.
Armour: Second generation, Chobham type.
Dimensions: Length 37ft 8in (11.5m); width 11ft 6in (3.52m); height (to turret roof) 8ft 2in (2.5mm).
Weight: Combat 137,500lb (62,500kg).
Ground pressure: 12.8lb/in^2 (0.9kg/cm^2).
Engine: Perkins CV-12 TA Condor V-12 12-cylinder diesel, 1,200bhp at 2,300rpm.
Performance: Road speed 35mph (56km/h); range 280 miles (450km); vertical obstacle 2ft 10in (0.9m); trench 7ft 8in (2.34m); gradient 60 per cent.
History: Prototypes 1990; entered service with the British Army in 1998; in service with British Army (386) and Omani Army (38).

The private company, Vickers Defence, started design work on a successor to Challenger 1 in the mid-1980s and in 1988 was awarded a contract to proceed to a demonstration phase, which required that nine prototypes be built, all of which were completed by late 1990. In June 1991 a production contract for 140 Challenger 2s was placed: 127 main battle tanks and 13 driver training tanks. Formal type acceptance was given in mid-1994, completing a process in which the Challenger 2 was the first tank for the British Army to be designed and developed entirely by an independent industrial company (rather than in government R&D centres) since World War II. The initial intention of the British Army had been to replace only half its Challenger 1 fleet with Challenger 2s, but in July 1994 this decision was rescinded and an additional 268 (259 MBTs, 9 driver training tanks) were ordered so that the entire Royal Armoured Corps would be equipped with Challenger 2s. Despite entering many competitions, the only overseas order from Challenger 2 is from the Oman, which ordered 18 in 1993 and a further 20 in 1997.

The Challenger 2's hull is similar top that of the Challenger 1. The driver sits

Below: A Challenger 2E ploughs through some virtually liquid mud at a test-track, its gun kept stationary by the action of the very advanced and sophisticated stabilisation system.

Above: Desert Challenger (since renamed Challenger 2E) was developed for possible orders from the Middle East. It has air conditioning and cooling and systems to suit the hot, dry climate.

centrally, with an unusual trough in the glacis plate to enable him to see. The other three crewmen are in the turret, which is a totally new design, fabricated from new, second-generation Chobham armour, with the commander and gunner on the right of the gun, and the loader on the left. The hull and turret are constructed of welded steel and Chobham armour, and are of exceptionally good ballistic shape. The gun control and stabilization systems are all-electric.

Main armament is the new Royal Ordnance L30 rifled gun, which is fitted, as is normal practice, with a thermal sleeve, fume extractor and muzzle reference system. It is the first British tank gun to be chrome-plated and is 55 calibres long. This new gun is part of the CHARM (CHallenger ARMament) package, which included the gun, a new charge system, and a new and more effective anti-tank round with a depleted uranium (DU) penetrator. Sixty-four projectiles are carried, together with 42 charges, the latter being stowed in armoured boxes below the turret ring for maximum safety. The L30 gun is also being retrofitted to the Challenger 1 tanks, replacing their L11A5 guns.

The Challenger 2 was the only new MBT in the 1990s to mount a rifled (as opposed to smoothbore) 120mm main gun. This is due to the British Army's

Below: Challenger 2 is fitted with the British 120mm L30 rifled gun. The box above the muzzle houses the Muzzle Reference System which measures even the tiniest variation in the barrel.

continuing belief in the value of the HESH round. When such a round hits a tank the high-explosive forms, for the briefest moment of time, a circular cake which is then exploded by a charge in the base of the projectile. The shock from this explosion dislodges a large scab from the inside wall of the tank, and this then ricochets at high velocity around the crew compartment. The British Army firmly believes that this type of round is needed to complement the high-velocity, kinetic energy round (APDS and APFSDS) and has therefore insisted on retaining a rifled barrel, since such a round depends on spin stabilization for in-flight stability and cannot be fired from a smoothbore barrel.

A McDonnell Douglas 7.62mm Chain Gun is mounted co-axially with the main gun and a second 7.62mm anti-aircraft machine-gun is mounted on the turret roof.

The power unit is a Perkins diesel with a rated output of 1,200hp. The TN37 transmission of the Challenger 1 has been described as being insufficiently flexible and is replaced in the Challenger 2 by the TN54 model, which has six forward and two reverse gears. This power train was, in fact, installed initially in the Challenger Armoured Repair and Recovery Vehicle (ARRV) and 12 of these were deployed to Saudi Arabia for Operation Desert Storm where they posted 100 per cent availability, a truly remarkable achievement.

The Omani version has some modifications to cope with the high temperatures of the Gulf region. These include improved airflow in the engine compartment and air-conditioning. A newer version, now being offered for export, is the Challenger 2E, which has an MTU power pack, increased fuel tankage, steering wheel (as opposed to tillers) and a 12.7mm machine-gun on the turret roof replacing the 7.62mm MG.

The British and Omani armies have also purchased Challenger 2 driver training tanks, which weigh the same as the MBT, but have a fixed turret which accommodates the instructor (who has full dual controls) and four students.

Above right: Initially intended to replace only half the Challenger 1 fleet, Challenger 2 is now re-equipping all armoured regiments in the British Army; current total order is for 389 MBTs.

Centre right: Challenger 2 is powered by the very successful Perkins 12-cylinder diesel (1,200hp at 2,300rpm) driving a David brown TN-54 epicyclic transmission with six forward and two reverse gears.

Below right: Challenger 2E at speed in the environment for which it was designed, the deserts of the Middle East. Its predecessor, Challenger 1, proved an outstanding success in Operation Desert Storm.

Below: Challenger 2 fires its 120mm at night, showing the very flat trajectory of this weapon. Only the British and Indian armies use a rifled 120mm gun, all others having adopted a smoothbore.

Note the number of sensors on and around the turret; they include a stabilised sight; wind, humidity and temperature gauges; laser detectors; and other classified devices.

Vickers Main Battle Tank

Country of origin: United Kingdom.
Crew: 4.
Armament: One Royal Ordnance L7A1 105mm rifled gun; one 12.7mm co-axial ranging machine-gun; one co-axial L37A2 7.62mm general-purpose machine-gun; one L37A2 anti-aircraft machine-gun; two six-barrel smoke grenade dischargers.
Armour: Maximum 80mm (3.15in).
Dimensions: Length (including main armament) 32ft 1in (9.79m); length (hull) 24ft 10in (7.56m); width overall 10ft 5in (3.17m); height 10ft 1in (3.1m).
Weight: Combat 88,107lb (40,000kg).
Ground pressure: 12.66lb/in² (0.89kg/cm²).
Engine: Detroit Diesel 12V-71T turbocharged 12-cylinder engine developing 720bhp at 2,500rpm. Perkins 4,10 4-stroke diesel auxiliary power unit.
Performance: Road speed 31mph (50km/h), range 330 miles (530km); vertical obstacle 2ft 9in (0.83m); trench 9ft 10in (3m); gradient 60 per cent.
History: Entered service with the Indian Army in 1965. Now in service: Mark 1 – India (2,200), Kuwait (70); Mark 3 – Kenya (76), Nigeria (72).

In the 1950s it was decided to set up a tank plant in India and teams were sent abroad to select a design which would meet the requirements of the Indian Army. The Vickers design was successful and in August 1961 a licensing contract was signed. Two prototypes were completed in 1963, one being retained by Vickers and the other being sent to India in 1964. Meanwhile plans were being drawn up for a factory to be built near Madras. Vickers delivered some complete tanks to India before the first Indian tank was completed early in 1969. These first tanks had many components from England, but over the years the Indian content of the tank steadily increased until the Indians built over 90 per cent of the tank themselves. Production eventually passed the two thousand mark, and the tank gave a good account of itself in the last Indian-Pakistani conflict.

The Indians call the tank *Vijayanta* (Victorious). In designing the tank, Vickers sought to strike the best balance between armour, mobility and firepower within the limits of a tank weighing 850,045lb (38,610kg). The layout of the tank is conventional. The driver is seated at the front of the hull on the right with ammunition stowage to his left, and the other three crew members are located in the turret: the commander and gunner to the right and the loader to the left. The engine and transmission are at the rear of the hull.

The engine and transmission are the same as those used in the Chieftain MBT. The suspension is of the torsion-bar type and consists of six road wheels with the drive sprocket at the rear and the idler at the front, there being three track-return rollers.

The Vickers MBT is armed with the standard L7 series 105mm rifled tank gun, this having an elevation of +20° and a depression of –7°, traverse being 360°. A .3in machine-gun is mounted co-axially with the main armament and a similar weapon is mounted on the commander's cupola. Six smoke dischargers are mounted each side of the turret. Some 44 rounds of 105mm and 3,000 rounds of .3in machine gun ammunition are carried. The main armament is aimed with the aid of the ranging machine-gun method, which was used so successfully in the

Right: The Vickers MBT was built by India at Madras as part of a licence deal with the British designers. Over 2,000 examples of what the Indian Army knows as the *Vijayanta* (Victorious) eventually rolled off the production line. Main armament is a tried and tested L7A1 105mm rifled gun which was also manufactured in India under licence.

Above: Sporting an all-cast turret and a laser range-finder, the Vickers MBT has also found sales success in Kenya (76) and Nigeria (108). An enhanced version of the Mark 3, the Mark 3 (Improved), has yet to win an order.

Above: A Vickers Mark 1 MBT on the firing ranges. The 105mm gun in this model is aimed by a 12.7mm ranging machine-gun mounted co-axial with the main armament, firing in three-round bursts.

Above: A Vickers Mark 1 MBT powered by a General Motors 720bhp turbo-charged diesel engine, and sporting a thermal sleeve for its L7A1 105mm gun.

Centurion tank with the 105mm gun. The gunner lines up the gun with the target and fires a burst from the .5in ranging machine-gun, and can follow the burst as the rounds are all tracer. If they hit the target he knows the gun is correctly aimed and he can then fire the main armament. Some 600 rounds of ranging machine-gun ammunition are carried. Two types of main-calibre ammunition are used: High Explosive Squash Head and Armour-Piercing Discarding Sabot. A GEC-Marconi stabilisation system is fitted, and this enables the gun to be aimed and fired whilst the vehicle is moving.

Indian production ended at 2,200. Kuwait also bought 70 Mark 1s, which were built by Vickers in the UK. A developed version, the Mark 3, was also built by Vickers, with 76 going to Kenya and 108 to Nigeria.

In the mid-1980s Vickers carried out a redesign of the Mark 3, with an improved hull, better suspension, new powertrain, wider tracks and the latest electronic and optical devices. The result, the Vickers MBT Mark 3 (Improved), is a very modern-looking and capable tank, but has yet to win any production orders.

Vickers also produced prototypes of the Advanced MBT Mark 7 in conjunction with Krauss-Maffei of Germany, which is basically a Leopard 2 chassis with the turret developed for another Vickers private venture MBT, the Valiant. Trials were successful, but no orders were received.

Also in the mid-1980s, Vickers co-operated with FMC, a US company, to produce an export version of FMC's Close combat Vehicle (Light) CCV(L), relatively light and fast, the FMC 5 was armed with a 105mm gun and was protected by a mixture of aluminium and steel armour.

Vickers Mk 3(M) Main Battle Tank

Country of origin: United Kingdom.
Crew: 4.
Armament: One Royal Ordnance L7A1 105mm rifled gun; one L37A2 7.62mm machine-gun and one 12.7mm ranging machine-gun co-axial with main armament; one L37A2 anti-aircraft machine-gun on turret roof; eight single-barrelled smoke grenade dischargers on each side of the turret.
Armour: All-welded rolled steel with added ERA.
Dimensions: Length (including main armament) 32ft 0in (9.78m); length (hull) 24ft 10in (7.56m); width overall 10ft 8in (3.25m); height 10ft 1in (3.1m).
Weight: Combat 87,963lb (39,900kg).
Ground pressure: 12.66lb/in^2 (0.89kg/cm^2).
Engine: Detroit diesel 12V-71TA turbo-charged 12-cylinder diesel, 720bhp at 2,500rpm; Perkins 4.10 4-stroke diesel auxiliary power unit.
Performance: Road speed 31mph (50km/h); range 370+ miles (600+km); vertical obstacle 2ft 9in (0.83m); trench 9ft 10in (3m); gradient 60 per cent.
History: Developed specifically for the Malaysian Army. Prototype running in 1997. Orders awaited.

The Malaysian Army has had an operational requirement for 10 years for a main battle tank and various companies have offered products for

Below: One of 76 Vickers Mk 3 MBTs in service with the Kenyan Army. The Nigerian Army is currently taking delivery of 108 Mk3 MBTs, together with 15 ARVs and 18 AVLBs.

Above: Vickers Mk 3 on a training exercise with British troops. Full backing and testing by the producer's national forces are essential for export orders for private venture military equipment.

consideration by the Malaysian General Staff. The British company, Vickers Defence Systems, produced a special version of their successful private venture Mark 3 MBT, which was modified to meet the Malaysian requirements, two important elements of which were the ability to cope with the heat and humidity of tropical conditions and a lighter weight than the usual 50+ tons of contemporary main battle tanks. A standard Vickers Mark 3 was taken to Malaysia for trials in 1995, where it travelled some 1,300 miles (2,100km) without a break-down. It also fired 80 rounds of 105mm ammunition, with great success. However, since the Malaysian Army does not currently have a tank firing range with the necessary large safety zones, APFSDS and APDS could not be fired and the demonstrations were limited to HESH (high-explosive squash-head, also known as high-explosive, plastic [HEP]), and SH/P (squash head practice). These trials having been successfully completed, design work on the Mark 3(M) (M = Malaysia) was completed and a standard Mark 3 modified to the new standard was completed in 1996 and ran trials in the UK in 1997.

The Mark 3(M) has a standard Mark 3 hull and running gear, but the hull and turret are fitted with specially designed explosive reactive armour (ERA) package which is closely tailored to the contours of the tank. There is also a further package for fitting to the skirts. Together, these provide a high degree of protection against HEAT (high explosive anti-tank) warheads, particularly from short range missile launchers, such as the widely-used Russian RPG-7.

The Mark 3(M) has a combat weight of 39.2 UK tons (39,900kg) and a four-man crew, and is armed with the standard Royal Ordnance L7A1 rifled 105mm gun, for which a wide range of ammunition is available. One unusual feature is that for ranging it retains the ranging machine-gun system pioneered by the British Army in the late 1950s, in which a co-axially mounted 12.7mm machine-gun fires rounds ballistically matched to the main armament. This proved both simple and highly effective in service and was particularly popular with tank crews.

The Far Eastern economic problems in the late 1990s forced the Malaysian Army to put its plans for a tank force in temporary abeyance.

The Mk 3(M), latest in a long line of successful private venture tanks produced by Vickers for the export market. Note the carefully conformal ERA panels and the 105mm gun.

Mark VIII (Liberty) International Heavy Tank

Heavy (Infantry) tank ("Liberty Tank"), also known as the "International".
Country of origin: UK/USA.
Crew: 10-12.
Armament: Two 6pounder QF guns of naval origin in sponson mounts, one per side; up to seven Browning .3in machine-guns in armoured mounts.
Armour: 6mm to 16mm (0.24 to 0.63in).
Dimensions: Length 34ft 2in (10.4m); width 12ft 6in (3.81m); height 10ft 3in (3.12m).
Weight: Combat 37-44 tons (37,594-44,707kg).
Ground pressure: approximately 5.2lb/in^2 (0.37kg/cm^2).
Engine: Liberty V-12 water-cooled inline aircraft engine developing 338bhp at 1,400rpm.
Performance: Road speed 6.5mph (10.4km/h), road range 50 miles (80km); vertical obstacle 4ft 3in (1.3m); trench 14ft (4.3m); gradient climbing ability stated to be "good".
History: Entered service with US Army in 1920. Never used in action, but surplus US Army vehicles used by Canada for training in 1940.

In 1916 General John J. Pershing detailed an officer to plan a Tank Corps for the US Army. This officer, Major James Drain, was sent to London where he discussed his task with Lieutenant-Colonel Albert Stern, who had been appointed Secretary to the Royal Naval Air Service Landships Committee. (It is interesting to note the tri-service flavour of this pioneer committee!) A provisional order for 600 Mk VI tanks was placed, but in September 1917 Major Drain recommended that the British Mk VIII, then in the design stage, be substituted. In those early days the attractions of Allied standardisations were apparent and a proposal was made to use British expertise combined with American production capability. A draft tripartite agreement was submitted to Winston Churchill, then Minister of Munitions, on 11 November 1917. The agreement provided, *inter alia*, for a programme to design and build a new tank incorporating British experience and American resources, and to assemble the tank in a new factory in France. Churchill approved the proposal in December and early in 1918 the Anglo-American Tank Treaty was signed in London by Arthur Balfour, the British Foreign Secretary and Walter Page, the United States Ambassador.

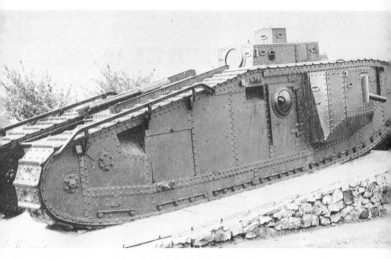

Design of the tank was undertaken by the Mechanical Warfare Supply Department of the Ministry of Munitions, Lieutenant G. J. Rackham being responsible for the design drawings. The British contribution was to be the armour plate, structural members, track shoes and rollers, and armament. The United States was to provide the automotive components, whilst France would provide the facilities for the new assembly plant, which would be built with construction equipment from the United Kingdom. The first design conference held by the Allied Tank Commission took place in France on 4 December 1917 and it was anticipated that initial production would be about 300 tanks per month, later increasing to 1,200 per month.

The high ideals expressed by the Anglo-American Tank Treaty were unfortunately overtaken by events. The German offensive of March 1918 extracted a heavy toll of British *matériel*, and the failure of the American aircraft programme prevented the diversion of Liberty engines to tank production. Thus by the time of the Armistice in November 1918 only 100 sets of components had been produced in Great Britain, whilst the United States had completed enough parts for half of the initial production of 2,950.

Below: Side view of a Mk VIII, showing one of the sponson-mounted 6-pounder guns, for which 208 rounds of shot were carried.

The French withdrew from the project after the Armistice and British involvement had to all intents and purposes lapsed after the losses in March 1918, so it was left to the United States to assemble 100 tanks at Rock Island Arsenal in 1919 from parts purchased from Britain. These tanks served the US Army until 1932, when they were withdrawn and stored. In 1940 about 90 were provided at scrap value to Canada, where they formed the basis of General Worthington's Tank Corps.

The Mark VIII had the familiar lozenge shape of the tanks of World War I and was intended from the outset to be capable of crossing a 14ft (4.3m) trench. The hull was of rivet face-hardened armour, .875in (22.2225mm) thick on the front and sides but somewhat less elsewhere on the vehicle. Incorporated for the first time was a bulkhead to seal off the engine room at the rear from the fighting compartment. This latter was provided with a positive overpressure to expel fumes, and reduced heat and noise as well as the risk of fire, and was the first real attempt to apply "Human Factors Engineering" to a tank. Unfortunately it was still necessary for an engineer-mechanic to travel in the engine compartment and his discomfort was doubtless heightened by this innovation.

The Mark VIII used a steering system devised by Major W. G. Wilson in probably the first practical application of the geared steering system, in which power is divided between tracks, rather than merely disconnected, when steering. Engine cooling was a problem in the Mark VIII, and this deficiency meant that the tank could not sustain its maximum speed for long periods, much to the relief of the mechanic in the engine room. As late as 1929 attempts were being made to improve the engine cooling.

Although it never saw action, the Mark VIII is significant as the first collaborative venture. But for the Armistice, production of the Mark VIII in 1919 would have outstripped all other Allied tank production to date.

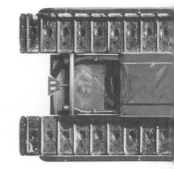

Above and right: Side and top views of the Mk VIII tank, which had a crew of 10-12 men and was armed with two 6-pounder QF naval guns and up to seven Browning .30in machine-guns. Each US-manufactured tank cost $85,000 to build in 1918-1919.

Right: Front view of a Mk VIII, showing the side sponsons designed to swing inward to reduce the width of the tank for transportation. In 1918, the Allies planned to establish a factory in France to build 300 tanks per month, with components supplied by Britain and the United States. In fact, only 100 were built in the US and 7 in Britain.

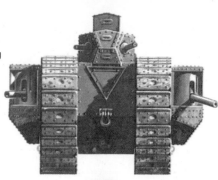

Right: Rear view of the Mk VIII, designed as the spearhead of the Allied advance planned for 1919. The Armistice meant the tank never saw action. The US Mk VIII was powered by a Liberty 12-cylinder water-cooled aero-engine. The first British Mk VIII had a Rolls-Royce power unit, but the rest had two Ricardo 150hp engines.

Right: Badge of the US 67th Armored Regt, which used the Mk VIII until 1932. About 90 were sold to Canada for training early in WWII.

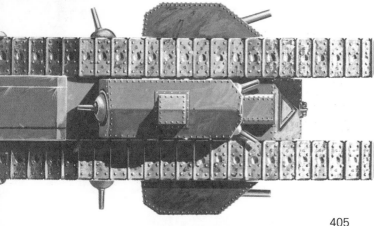

T3 Christie Medium Tank

M1919, M1921, M1928, TS M1931, Combat Car T1, T3E1 and BT-1.
Country of origin: USA.
Crew: 3.
Armament: One 37mm gun; one .3in machine-gun mounted co-axial with main armament; one .3in machine-gun in each side of turret; one .3in machine-gun in hull.
Armour: 16mm (0.625) maximum; 12.7mm (.5in) minimum.
Dimensions: Length 19ft 1in (5.82m); width 8ft 1in (2.46m); height 7ft 7in (2.31m).
Weight: Combat 24,200lb (10,977kg).
Ground pressure: 9.96lb/in^2 (0.7kg/cm^2).
Engine: Ordnance Liberty 12-cylinder water-cooled petrol engine developing 338bhp at 1,400rpm.
Performance: Road speed (wheels) 46mph (74km/h), road speed (tracks) 27mph (43km/h); vertical obstacle 3ft (0.9m); trench 8ft 3in (2.5m); gradient 42 per cent.
History: Small number used by US Army in 1930s. Christie's emphasis on speed differed from US Army's preference for reliability and official interest waned accordingly. Precursor of British Cruiser and Soviet T-34 series.

Although J. Walter Christie gave his name to a form of suspension which greatly influenced tank development in the 1930s and 1940s, his first designs gave little indication of such promise. An enterprising engineer, he had first set up a company to motorise horse-drawn fire engines and proceeded from there to motorise gun carriages for the US Army. He was attracted by the possibility of the newly-publicised tank, and produced a design of his own which was tested by the US Army as the M1919. While his self-propelled gun carriages had been successful, the tank was hastily conceived and constructed and did not perform well as it was seriously underpowered. In its favour it must be pointed out that the M1919 showed considerable ingenuity and originality, drawing little from the first designs produced in Europe. Although it did not feature all-round traverse of its armament, the gun was mounted in a barbette which allowed good visibility, and the trackwork incorporated a form of springing.

Christie's next design, the M1921, remedied some of the shortcomings of the M1919 and resembled even more the conventional modern turreted tank despite the fact that it still did not have a traversing turret. Nonetheless, Christie's bread and butter came from his self-propelled artillery designs, of which there were several in the early 1920s. He also investigated amphibious tanks with a certain degree of success but was unable to interest the US authorities in his designs.

The breakthrough came in 1928 when the first "Christie Tank" appeared. The classic Christie suspension consisted of four big road wheels mounted on large coil springs and tracks consisting of large plates. The tracks could be removed, allowing the vehicle to run on its road wheels. Extremely high speeds were achieved on roads, a figure of 70mph (113km/h) being quoted, and even on rough terrain a speed of 30mph (48km/h) was claimed.

Above: Front view of the Christie T3.

Below: The three T3s that went into service with the US 67th Regiment: the "Tornado", the "Hurricane" and the "Cyclone".

Below: Side view of the "Tornado" with its tracks in the stowed position, showing the chain drive from the sprocket to the rear road wheel. Several countries, notably the USSR, experimented with the wheeled/tracked vehicles in the inter-war years.

A demonstration of the M1928 to the US Army resulted in an order for five examples to be known as the T3 Medium Tank, and Christie set up the US Wheel and Tracklayer Corporation to produce these. The T3, or M1931, was constructed of face-hardened armour of .5in (12.7mm) thickness and had four large, rubber-tired road wheels of 27in (68.6cm) diameter on each side. These were mounted on swinging arms and supported by long coil springs in compression, which allowed a wheel travel of 16in (40.65cm). Thus each wheel could be raised until the tyre was level with the hull floor, and this feature allowed the suspension to conform with very uneven terrain. The tracks were steel plates approximately $10in^2$ ($645cm^2$), and a disadvantage of Christie's system was the large angular movement required of such large track plates, resulting in heavy wear. Another disadvantage was the reduction in available space in the hull because the suspension springs were enclosed by the side plates. Two men could remove the tracks in 30 minutes to prepare the vehicle for road running – in this mode the two front wheels could be steered and the two middle pairs were raised.

The engine was essentially the Liberty engine of the Mark VIII tank. Even in this standard state, the T3 was overpowered. With the Liberty engine "tweaked" by Christie to develop 387hp, the power was excessive and resulted in an intolerably high oil consumption, with the coil springs for the front wheels anchored at a common mounting inside the pointed nose of the hull – another Christie characteristic. The turret mounted a short-barrelled 37mm gun with 360° traverse and was advanced for its time, presenting few shot traps.

The US Wheel and Tracklayer Corporation built nine examples of the M1931 design, of which five were the T3 (in fact three of these were for the cavalry and were designated Combat Car T1 to conform with the 1920 National Defense Act), two were for the Polish Army and were taken into US Army service as the T3E1, and two were sold to the Soviet Union, where they became BT-1s and led to the development of the T-34.

Christie was a volatile character and was apt to offend his customers by continually improving his design, thus delaying delivery. This tendency to

Above: T3 "Hurricane". The T3s were used largely in a tactical training role while in service in the 1930s.

apply his own interpretation to contracts, and to refine his product at the client's expense and delay meant that when in 1932 the US Army required a further five T3 tanks the contract was let to the American La France and Foamite Company, and Christie built no further vehicles for the US Army. Christie's inventive and impetuous approach is well illustrated by the fact that in 1930, in the middle of developing his M1931, he was proposing to the US Army a plan to modernise its Renault M1918 light tanks by converting them to steam propulsion. His idea, using Christie suspension and rubber tracks, envisaged a road speed of some 85mph (137km/h). Nothing further was heard of this project.

In 1936 one example of the M1931 was bought and tested by the British Army. While the vehicle performed satisfactorily it did not conform with current British thinking. It was instead used as the basis of the A13E2 cruiser tank. Poland, despite having defaulted on her contract for two M1931s, copied Christie's design in the 10TP and 14TP tanks.

Christie's preoccupation with speed led to both his success and his failure. One the one hand his suspension allowed improved mobility and was exploited by both Britain and the Soviet Union; on the other hand the poor reliability did not impress the US Army, and the renowned reliability of the M3 and M4 series tanks was probably of more value in World War II than high speed and minimal protection.

Left and below: Front, side, top and rear views of the Christie T3 "Tornado" of the US 67th Infantry (Tanks) Regiment.

M2 Medium Tank

Country of origin: USA.
Crew: 6.
Armament: One 37mm M6 gun with a co-axial .3in M1919A4 machine-gun in turret; four .3in machine-guns, one at each corner of barbette superstructure; two .3in machine-guns in hull, firing forward in fixed mount.
Armour: 9.5mm to 32mm (0.37–1.26in).
Dimensions: Length 17ft 8in (5.38m); width 8ft 7in (2.62m); height 9ft 4½in (2.86m).
Weight: Combat 47,040lb (21,337kg).
Ground pressure: 11.67lb/in² (0.82kg/cm²).
Engine: Wright nine-cylinder air-cooled radial petrol engine, supercharged, developing 400hp at 2,400rpm.
Performance: Road speed 26mph (43km/h), cross country speed 17mph (27km/h); road range 130 miles (209km); vertical obstacle 2ft (0.6m); trench 7ft 6in (3.54m); gradient 25 per cent.
History: Obsolete before entering production and superseded by M3 medium tank. Never used in action.

Between the wars, US tanks were generally still hand-built by government arsenals, although the turret and some of the hull of the M2 were welded, which was an innovation. In spite of the fact that the M2 never saw action, it was the first tank to which production-line thinking was applied. In the rapidly changing situation in the summer of 1940, industry prepared itself for the

production of 1,000 M2 medium tanks at Detroit Arsenal, which had still to be built. Events in Europe showed that the M2 would be obsolete before it could enter production, but the M3 medium tank armed with a 75mm gun was ordered into production in place of the M2.

The M2 was of straightforward construction. The turret and parts of the hull were welded face-hardened armour, while the remainder was riveted. The suspension was derived from the M2 light tank and was of the familiar vertical volute spring type with rubber-tyred bogie wheels. The tracks were rubber-padded for quietness and smooth running, although combined with the rubber brushings of the track pins this entailed a build-up of static electricity which made use of the radio difficult when the tank was on the move.

As well as being the forerunner of the M3, the M2 formed the basis of several experimental variations, one of which, the T9 medium tractor, was standardised as the M4, served as a prime mover throughout World War II and remained in service with the Spanish Army until the 1980s. Complaints about a lack of power led to the M2A1, in which the Wright aircraft engine was supercharged to deliver another 50hp. The tracks were also widened and some armour increased. The Rock Island Arsenal produced some 94 M241 tanks, most of which were used for training until sufficient numbers of the M3 became available. The M2 was the only medium tank standardised whilst the 1920 National Defense Act remained in force and reflected the short-sighted and out-dated nature of this legislation. But it did have a significant contribution to the development of the M3.

Left: The M2 medium tank was never used in combat but had a valuable training role.

M3 Light Tank

M3, M3A1, M3A2 and M3A3.
Country of origin: USA.
Crew: 4.
Armament: One 37mm M5 gun; one .3in M1919A4 machine-gun co-axial with main armament; two .3in machine-guns in hull sponsons; one M3in machine-gun on turret roof.
Armour: 44.5mm (1.75in) maximum; 10mm (0.375in) minimum.
Dimensions: Length 14ft 10½in (4.53m); width 7ft 4in (2.23m); height 8ft 3in (2.51m).
Weight: Combat 27,400lb (12,428kg).
Ground pressure: 10.5lb/in² (0.74kg/cm²).
Engine: Continental W-670 seven-cylinder air-cooled radial petrol engine developing 250hp at 2,400rpm.
Performance: Road speed 36mph (58km/h), cross-country speed 20mph (32km/h); road range 70 miles (112km); vertical obstacle 2ft (0.6m); trench 6ft (1.8m); gradient 60 per cent.
History: Entered service with US Army in 1941. Also widely used by British and other Allied armies during World War II.

Below: Stuart Mark I light tank of the 8th (King's Royal Irish) Hussars, at the Battle of Sidi Rezegh in November 1941. The M3 was the first American-built tank to be used in action by the British Army during the war. The 8th Army in North Africa received its first shipment of 84 Lend-Lease M3s in July 1941 and by November the same year 163 were ready for Operation Crusader. The M3 was officially called the General Stuart in British Army service but was commonly known as the "Stuart" or "Honey". Some later had their turrets removed for use in command role.

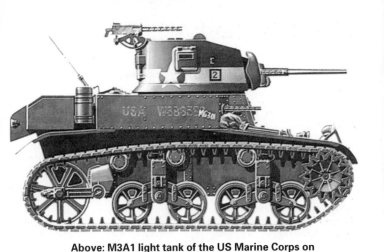

Above: M3A1 light tank of the US Marine Corps on Guadalcanal Island in the Solomons, September 1942. Clearly shown in this drawing is the .3in M1919A4 machine gun on the turret roof and one of the two sponson-mounted M1919A4 machine guns. The latter were often removed to allow for more internal stowage space, always at a premium in any AFV. Production of the M3 was finally completed in October 1943 after 13,859 tanks had been built.

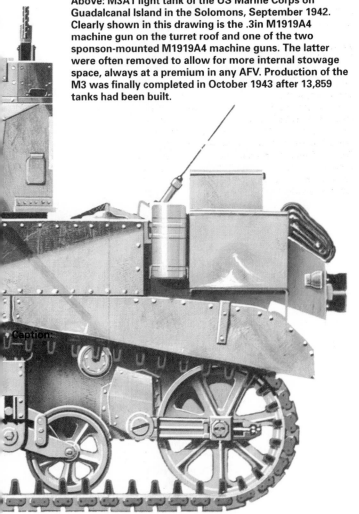

Caption:

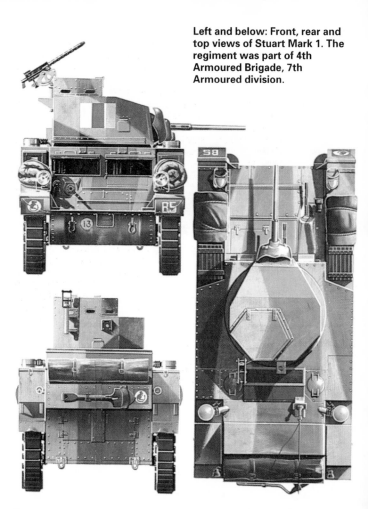

Left and below: Front, rear and top views of Stuart Mark 1. The regiment was part of 4th Armoured Brigade, 7th Armoured division.

The standard US light tank in June 1940 was the M2A4, standardised in 1939 and the culmination of a development which began with the M2A1 in 1935. The M2A4 weighed some 12 tons (12,193kg), had a 37mm turret-mounted gun and was constructed from riveted armour plate. Increasing the thickness of the armour of the M2A4 called for the use of a trailing idler in the suspension system. This, with improved protection from aircraft attack, led to the standardisation of the type as the M3 light tank in July 1940. The Continental seven-cylinder radial engine of 250hp had been inherited from the M2A4, but in 1941 shortages of this engine meant that the Guiberson T-1020 diesel engine was authorised for 500 M3 light tanks. Additional fuel capacity in the form of two external fuel tanks, which could be jettisoned, was provided as a result of battle experience in British hands in North Africa.

The M3 was produced in quantity by the American Car and Foundry Company, 5,811 having been built by August 1942. The M3A1 light tank incorporated an improved turret of welded homogeneous plate (as opposed to the earlier brittle, face-hardened armour) with power traverse, a gyro-stabiliser to permit more accurate firing of the 37mm gun on the move, and a turret basket. The M3A1 was standardised in August 1941 and used the hull of the M3, which was still constructed from riveted plate. A pilot with both hull and turret formed of welded armour, the M3A1E1, led eventually to the M5 light tank. The next model, the M3A2, was also to be of welded

414

construction but similar to the M3A1 in all other respects. The M3A2 was not built, but American Car and Foundry produced 4,621 of the M3A1, of which 211 were diesel-engined. The M3A3 was a much more comprehensive redesign and included changes in the turret, hull and sponsons, and it was considered worthwhile to continue producing the M3A3 even after the production line for its successor, the M5, was established. Some 3,427 M3A3s were built. There were several experimental models of the M3 series, mostly involving different automotive installations.

In British service the M3 provided a much-needed addition to the tank strength in the Western Desert in 1941 and 1942. It subsequently appeared in all theatres of World War II, but is chiefly remembered for its service in the desert, with the empire forces in Burma, in the capture of Antwerp, and with the American forces in the Pacific. It was under-gunned and poorly armoured but mobile and reliable, and was affectionately known as the "Honey" by British cavalry regiments. Indeed, many units preferred it to the Daimler armoured car in the reconnaissance role. The M3 was the most widely used light tank of World War II and was built in larger numbers than its two successors, the M5 and M24. A total of 13,859 had been produced by October 1943, even though the type had been declared obsolete in July of that year. Although it was fast and had good ground-crossing ability for the "cavalry" scouting role for which it was intended, the M3 had little scope for development or adaptation. The hull was too narrow, effectively limiting the size of the main armament to below the required 75mm, and it was too high and angular, offering a high silhouette and many shot traps. It did lead directly to the M5 light tank, however, and its history continued under that heading.

Below: The M3 light tank was developed from the earlier M2 shown here with its higher rear idler wheel. The M2 was designed and built at Rock Island Arsenal with the first model, the M2A1, being standardised in late 1935. In addition to the prototype, just 19 production M2A1s were built.

M3 Grant/Lee Medium Tank

M3, M3A1, M3A2, M3A3, M3A4, M3A5, and variants.
Country of origin: USA.
Crew: 6.
Armament: One 75mm M2 or M3 gun in hull sponson; one 37mm M5 or M6 gun in turret; one .3in M1919A4 machine-gun co-axial with turret gun; one .3in machine-gun in cupola on turret; two .3in machine-gun in bow.
Armour: 12mm to 37mm (0.47–1.46in).
Dimensions: Length 18ft 6in (5.64m); width 8ft 11in (2.72m); height 10ft 3in (3.12m).
Weight: Combat 60,000lb (27,216kg).
Ground pressure: 13.4lb/in^2 (0.94kg/cm^2).
Engine: Continental R-975-EC2 nine-cylinder air-cooled radial petrol engine developing 340hp at 2,400rpm.
Performance: Road speed 26mph (42km/h), cross-country speed 16mph (26km/h); road range 120 miles (193km); vertical obstacle 2ft (0.6m); trench 6ft 3in (1.9m); gradient 60 per cent.
History: Entered service with US Army and British Army in 1941. Also widely used by Canadian and Russian armies.

Battlefield experience reported from Europe in 1939 showed that the 37mm gun of the American M2 medium tank was not powerful enough for modern warfare, and accordingly the 75mm pack howitzer was experimentally mounted in the right-hand sponson of the Medium Tank T5 Phase III, a vehicle closely related to the M2. Such a vehicle would previously have been classed as a howitzer motor carriage. Meanwhile, in the United States rearmament programme William S. Knudsen, president of the General Motors Corporation, had been co-opted to the National Defense Advisory Committee to co-ordinate the capabilities of industry to the needs of defence.

The existing contract for 329 M2A4 light tanks was clearly insufficient and industry did not seem able to cope with the order for 1,500 M2 medium tanks which was then envisaged. In 1940 it was suggested that the M2 be

Left: While the 75mm gun of the Grant was a great improvement over that installed in other tanks used by the British Army it was sponson-mounted on the right side and therefore only had a total traverse of 30°. The tank had tractor-type ("scissors") suspension, in common with most US tanks until late in the war. A total of 6,258 M3s were built for the Allied armies.

Above: M3 Grant medium tank negotiating rough terrain. In October 1940 the British Tank Commission placed orders with Baldwin and Pullman in the United States for 200 M3 Grant tanks. These were all shipped to the 8th Army in North Africa, with the first tanks arriving in early 1942. During the battle of Gazala in May 1942, 167 Grants formed the main equipment of the 4th Armoured Brigade and at last gave the British Army a tank that could outrange those used by the German *Afrika Korps*, but the tank had several weak features. The M3 was also used by Canada and the Soviet Union.

Left: Grant tank fitted with a dummy lorry body as a disguise in North Africa. In addition to being used as a tank, many M3s were modified for special roles including tank recovery vehicle, full-track prime mover for 155mm gun, mine exploder (trials), .3 inch gun motor carriage (trials), 40mm gun motor carriage (trials), heavy tractor (trials) and also as the basis for the 105mm M7 "Priest".

Right: Top view of M3 Grant medium tank clearly showing the multiplicity of weapons with which the vehicle was armed, arranged in three tiers. The tank commander could operate the .30 Browning machine-gun in the independently rotating cast cupola, while the turret gunner could engage armour with the 37mm anti-tank gun or infantry with the co-axial Browning machine-gun, and the 75mm M2 or M3 hull-mounted gun could fire either AP or HE ammunition. This M3 is of all-riveted construction but others (eg, the M3A1) had a cast hull. There were very many experimental non-tank variants of the M3.

improved by increasing its armour and adapting the 75mm M1897 gun (as the T7) to a sponson mounting in the hull. This new tank was designated the M3 medium tank by the Ordnance Committee on 11 July 1940, and on 28 August 1940 the contract for 1,000 M2A1 medium tanks, signed only 15 days previously, was changed in favour of the M3.

Up to this point, America's tank needs had been met largely by the heavy engineering industry. Knudsen, now a lieutenant-general, took the view that apart from the manufacturing and casting of armour, there was little difference between manufacturing a car and a tank. He therefore arranged with K. T. Keller, president of the Chrysler Corporation, for Chrysler to lease a 113-acre (45,73-hectare) site for a new tank factory. The site at Warren, Michigan, was to become the government-owned, Chrysler-operated arsenal responsible for the production of some 25,000 armoured vehicles during World War II. The M3 was ordered into production from the drawing board and Chrysler, the American Locomotive Company (Alco) and the Baldwin Locomotive works all produced pilot models by April 1941. Production began in August 1941 and continued until December 1942, by which time 6,258 vehicles of the M3 series had been built. Of this total Chrysler built 3,352. Alco 685, Baldwin 1,220, Pressed Steel 501 and Pullman 500. These figures are quoted to illustrate what was basically the first application of motorcar mass-production techniques to tank production.

During production it became necessary to make various modifications to overcome shortages and to improve the tank. The M3A1 used a cast hull produced by Alco, this hull having no side doors for reasons of strength. A welded hull, stronger than the riveted hull of the M3, was used to save weight in the M3A2, of which Baldwin built 12. Baldwin also built 322 of the M3A3 which used two General Motors 6-71 diesel bus engines coupled together as an alternative to the Wright radial engine. Otherwise the M3A3 was identical to the M3A2. The M3, M3A1 and M3A2 could also be fitted with a Guiberson diesel engine, in which case the designation became, for example, M3A1 (Diesel). To overcome a critical shortage of the Wright engine in 1941, Chrysler combined five standard car engines to provide a tank powerpack. This "Eggbeater" engine required modifications to the hull and suspension, resulting in the M3A4. The hull was riveted as in the M3, and 109 were built. The M3A5 resulted from the installation of the twin GM diesels of the M3A3 in the riveted hull of the M3, and Baldwin built 591.

In British service the M3 was known as the Grant (after General Ulysses S. Grant) and the Lee (after General Robert E. Lee). A British Tank Commission had arrived in June 1940 with the intention of ordering British-designed tanks from American firms. But as at that time the defeat of the British appeared imminent, the National Defense Advisory Committee refused to allow tanks to be produced to British designs. As a result of this refusal the M3 was chosen as being the next best choice. Those purchased by the British Tank Commission from Pullman and Pressed Steel had a British-designed turret and were known as Grant 1. The name Lee was given to the standard M3 (Lee 1), M3A1 (Lee II), M3A3 (Lee IV), M3A3 (Diesel) (Lee V), and M2A4 (Lee VI), while the M3A5 was known as the Grant II, these tanks being supplied under the terms of the 1941 Lend-Lease Act.

The Grant I had its first impact at the battle of Gazala on 27 May 1942, the first time the 8th Army had managed to achieve any degree of parity with the 75mm gun of the *PzKpfw* IV, although it was some time before problems

associated with fuses for the HE shell could be resolved. By October 1942 a further 350 M3s had been supplied and these tanks made a significant contribution to the success at El Alamein in November of that year. Some M3s were shipped to the UK for training units, but the majority were used in North Africa and the Middle East.

By April 1943 the M4 was in full production, and the M3 was finally declared obsolete on 16 March 1944. Despite this the M3 lived on in the form of variants such as the M7 "Priest" and the M31 Tank Recovery Vehicle. The chassis was also used for many experimental variations, including: Mine Exploder T1, Tank Recovery Vehicle T2 (M31), 155mm Gun Motor Carriage T6 (M12), Shop Tractor T10 (Canal Defense Light, or searchlight tank), Cargo Carrier T14, Heavy Tractor T16, 3in Gun Motor Carriage T4, 105mm Howitzer Motor Carriage T25, 75mm Gun Motor Carriage T26, 105mm Howitzer Motor Carriage T32 (M7 'Priest'), 40mm Gun Motor Carriage T36, 3in Gun Motor Carriage T40 (M9), 25pounder Gun Motor Carriage T51, Flamethrower Vehicles (several were made, using the E3 and M5R2 flame guns). Vehicles of the M3 series supplied to the British Army were also modified for various purposes, for example as recovery vehicles, command vehicles, mineclearing vehicles, and as a canal defence light.

M4 Sherman Medium Tank

Country of origin: USA.
Crew: 5.
Armament: One 75mm M3 gun; one .3in M1919A4 machine-gun co-axial with main armament; one .3in M1919A4 machine-gun ball mount in bow; one .5in M2 machine-gun on turret roof; one 2in M3 smoke mortar in turret roof.
Armour: 15mm (0.6in) minimum; 100m (3.94in) maximum.
Dimensions: Length 20ft 7in (6.27m); width 8ft 11in (2.67m); height 11ft 1in (3.37m).
Weight: Combat 69,565lb (31,554kg).
Ground pressure: 14.3lb/in^2 (1kg/cm^2).
Engine: Ford GAA V-8 water-cooled inline petrol engine developing 500hp at 2,600rpm.
Performance: Road speed 26mph (42km/h), road range 100 miles (160km); vertical obstacle 2ft (0.61m); trench 7ft 6in (2.29m); fording depth 3ft (0.91m); gradient 60 per cent.
History: Entered service in 1942, and saw extensive service with US Army and most Allied armies during and after World War II. The most prolific medium tank of World War II, and widely adapted to other uses. Also used in action in Korea and Middle East and still in service with some armies.
(*Note: Data relate to a typical M4A3.*)

On 29 August 1940, the day following the decision to produce the M3 medium tank in place of the M2A1, work began on a new medium tank which would mount the 75mm gun in a turret with a full 360° traverse. The new tank was designated the T6 medium tank, and its design was based on the use of components of the M3 as far as possible. Elimination of the sponson mount would reduce the hull space enclosed by armour, and thus reduce weight or permit greater thickness of armour. The T6 was standardised in September 1941 as the M4 medium tank, but in all its many models it was more widely and popularly known as the "Sherman".

Below: side view of M4A3E8, known as to the Americans as the "Easy Eight" because of its HVSS suspension which gave a good ride across country. The vehicle is shown as it appeared on ceremonial parade with the United States Occupational Forces in Munich, South Germany, in June 1945.

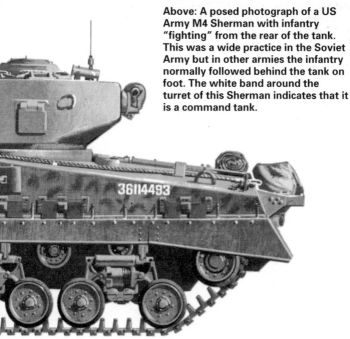

Above: A posed photograph of a US Army M4 Sherman with infantry "fighting" from the rear of the tank. This was a wide practice in the Soviet Army but in other armies the infantry normally followed behind the tank on foot. The white band around the turret of this Sherman indicates that it is a command tank.

36114493

As adopted, the Sherman weighed about 30 tons (30,482kg) and was armed with the 75mm M3 gun. The turret was a one-piece rounded casting, 3in (76.2mm) thick at the front, and power operated. A gyrostabiliser controlled the gun in elevation. The lower hull was welded, while the construction of the upper hull provided a certain degree of identification of the various models. The M4 had a welded upper hull, while the M4A1 had a cast, rounded upper hull. Both were approximately 2in (50.8mm) thick. Variations between the major models in the M4 series were mainly due to different engine installations, apart from the difference in hull construction in the case of the M4 and M4A1.

Production of the Sherman was authorised to replace the M3 as soon as possible. Facilities involved included the Chrysler-operated Detroit Arsenal, the Fisher Body Division of GMC, the Ford Motor Company, Pacific Car and Foundry, Federal Machine and Welder Company, Lima Locomotive Works and the Montreal Locomotive Works, and 49,230 Shermans of all variants were produced. Product improvement was a continuous process throughout, and indeed after production had ceased. The most significant improvements centred on armament stowage of ammunition and suspension.

The gun conceived for the T6 medium tank prototype was the unsatisfactory 75mm T6 gun. The next model, the T7, was better and became the 75mm M2 gun in May 1941, but was still relatively short-barrelled and had a muzzle velocity of only 1,850fps (564m/s). Early models on the Sherman had the M2 gun, but even in September 1940 the Armoured Force had requested a higher muzzle velocity, and this request was met in the 75mm T8 gun, adopted in June 1941 as the M3. This gun fired armour-piercing shot at a muzzle velocity of 2,030fps (619m/s) and was also more suited to tank use. The longer barrel was better balanced for installation in a gyrostabiliser mount and rotation of the breech to allow the block to open horizontally permitted greater depression of the gun in a turret mount.

Although the 75mm gun was accepted as the standard weapon, the Ordnance Department felt that more penetrating power would be required. The .3in gun of the M6 heavy tank was not ideal, but adapting the 75mm breech to the .3in barrel produced a most satisfactory weapon. At first known

as the .3in T13 gun but later as the 76mm T1 gun, this weapon was mounted on the Sherman in a project which began in August 1942. The project, although promising, found no support and was dropped in November of the same year. Later the T23 medium tank turret, with the 76mm gun, was mounted on the Sherman. The improvement was so marked that the Armoured Board admitted to a requirement for 76mm guns to supplant 75mm guns when the extra firepower was needed. This was a face-saving gesture to allow production to begin after the earlier refusal. The fact that by July 1944 over 2,000 76mm gun tanks had been produced illustrates just how much the extra firepower was needed – and this after vehicles armed with the 76mm gun had been declared obsolete in May 1943!

Another innovation in armament concerned the 105mm howitzer. In April 1941 the Aberdeen Proving Ground had suggested that the Sherman would conveniently mount the 105mm howitzer, but it was not until late 1942 that two M4A4s were modified for this purpose. Further tests were carried out on a similarly modified vehicle, the M4E5, and the howitzer in the M52 mount was adopted as a standard item. These vehicles were used in headquarter companies to provide fire support and some 4,680 were built

Right and below:
Front and rear
views of M4A3E8
with insignia: from
left to right,
denoting 7th Army,
191st Tank Batt., A
Company, Tank No.
12. Top view shows
gun travelling lock
on glacis plate.
Lower view shows
.5in M2 MG stowed
to turret rear.

Left: The M4A3E8
Sherman mounting
a 105mm howitzer
with which it gave
close support to the
medium tank
formations of the
US Army, replacing
the older M8 75mm
SP howitzer. This
Sherman has a
welded hull, cast
turret with
commander's
cupola and HVSS
suspension. Over
4,600 105mm armed
M4 Shermans were
built from 1943. The
105mm M4
howitzer had an
elevation of +35°
and a depression of
−10°, 66 rounds of
105mm ammunition
being carried.

Above: Rear view of Red Army Shermans before Kharkov in 1943. Note the appliqué armour on the hull side below turret and the fuel drums at the rear to increase operating range.

on the M4 and M4A3 hulls.

Early models of the Sherman had a somewhat unfortunate reputation for "brewing-up" when hit by anti-tank fire. To overcome this fault attempts were made to protect the ammunition showed in the tank. Stowage racks were provided in the lower hull and those for 75mm and 76mm ammunition were surrounded by water jackets, while the semi-fixed howitzer ammunition was protected by armour plate. The suffix "wet" was added to nomenclature in May 1945 to distinguish those tanks with water jacket stowage.

To improve the ride and stability, and at the same time reduce the specific ground pressure of the Sherman, experiments were made with different suspensions and tracks. The original and highly characteristic vertical volute spring suspension of the Sherman series originated with the M2 medium tank, as did the 16in (0.41m) track, but both were more suited to a 20 ton (20,321kg) vehicle than the 30-plus tons of the M4. Eventually a new horizontal volute spring suspension and 23in (0.58m) track were perfected and incorporated in production. The suffix "HVSS" was often added to designations to indicate the newer suspension.

The type lent itself to the production of many variants and most authorities list over 50 significant American experimental models. Tanks and other vehicles of the M4 series were supplied to many countries during and after World War II, and more Shermans were manufactured than any other single tank. Critics pointed out its deficiencies compared with the Panther, for example, but it made up for these shortcomings in reliability, endurance and sheer weight of numbers. Scores of years after its introduction the Sherman lived on in many armies and appeared in almost every armoured conflict between 1945 and the late 1970s.

Above: The Sherman DD (Duplex Drive) was fitted with a flotation screen and propelled in the water by two propellers at the rear of the hull, these being driven by a PTO from the engine.

Below: The Sherman Firefly VC was a M4A4 re-armed in Britain with the 17pounder gun, bussle fitted to turret and hull MG and gunner left out for increased ammunition stowage.

M22 Locust Light Tank (Airborne)

Country of origin: USA.
Crew: 3.
Armament: One 37mm M6 gun; one 37mm M1919A4 co-axial machine-gun.
Armour: 9mm to 25mm (0.35–0.98in).
Dimensions: Length 12ft 11in (3.32m); width 7ft 4in (2.23m); height 5ft 8in (1.74m).
Weight: Combat 17,024lb (7,722kg).
Ground pressure: 7.2lb/in² (0.51kg/cm²).
Engine: Lycoming 0-435T six-cylinder horizontally-opposed petrol engine developing 162hp at 3,000rpm.
Performance: Road speed 40mph (64km/h), cross-country speed 27mph (43km/h); road range 135 miles (216km); vertical obstacle 1ft 4in (0.4m); trench 5ft 5in (1.65m); gradient 52 per cent; fording depth 3ft 6in (1.1m).
History: Entered service with US Army in 1944. Also used by British and Egyptian armies.

Having taken note of the development by both Germany and the Soviet Union of airborne capability, the US Army decided in February 1941 that it too should have such forces. In order that these forces might have armoured support an airportable tank, weighing no more than 7½ tons (7,620kg), was proposed, and the General Motors Corporation, J. W. Christie and Marmon-Herrington were all invited to submit designs. The Marmon-Herrington proposal was selected, and in May 1941 one pilot model was ordered under the designation Light Tank T9 (Airborne). At the same time development of an aircraft capable of carrying the T9 was begun.

The first T9 weighed 7.9 tons (8.027kg), but this increase was accepted by the Army Air Corps and also by the British Army who had by now become interested in the project. The vehicle had a welded hull and cast turret, and the familiar vertical volute spring suspension of contemporary American light

tanks. In January 1942 two pilot models of the improved T9E1 were ordered. The shape of the turret was altered, power traverse and a gyrostabiliser were added, the front plate was modified and the two bow machine-guns were removed. Brackets were added to enable the tank to be slung beneath the C-54 cargo aircraft, and the T9E1 was tested in this form by the 28th Airborne Tank Battalion. For transporting this way it was necessary to remove the turret, a feature which severely limited the surprise effect of delivering the tank by air. The Army Service Forces ordered 500 T9R1 tanks in April 1942 before service tests had begun. Problems in manufacture and continual amendments to the design meant that of the anticipated total order of 1,900, only 830 were delivered by February 1944, when production came to an end.

The T9E1 received the designation M22 in August 1944, but was always better known by its popular name of "Locust". The Locust was supplied to the British Army in small numbers and it was in British service that is saw its only operational use. Some Locusts were used by the Airlanding Brigade of the 6th Airborne Division in the crossing of the Rhine in March 1945. For this operation the tanks were carried in the Hamilcar glider, which could also carry the British Tetrarch airborne tank.

In general, tanks are considered to combine firepower, protection and mobility to produce a fighting machine, and in practice a shortcoming in one particular factor may be offset by a superiority in another. The unfortunate Locust possessed none of these vital attributes. Because the United States had not managed to develop an aircraft or glider capable of carrying the Locust without the need to disassemble the tank, no advantage could be taken of the light weight. The Locust had very thin armour, which could be defeated by the .5in AP round, and by the standards of 1945 it was underpowered and undergunned. An attempt was made in the T9E2 to provide more HE firepower in the form of a breechloading 81mm mortar, but this project, although successful, was dropped at the cessation of hostilities in 1945.

Left: The M22 Locust airborne tank was developed specifically for use by US airborne forces. Although 830 were built by Marmon-Herrington by February 1944, the tank was not used in large numbers. The British 6th Airborne Division used some Locusts during the crossing of the Rhine in March 1945. After the war, some were supplied to the Egyptian Army.

M24 Chaffee Light Tank

T17, M8, M8A1, T24, M24, M37, M19, M41, T77, T9, T13, T22, T23, T33, T42, T9, T6E1 and T31.
Country of origin: USA.
Crew: 5, sometimes reduced to 4.
Armament: One 75mm M6 gun; one .3in M1919A4 machine-gun co-axial with main armament; one .3in M1919A4 machine-gun; one .5in M2 machine-gun; one 2in M3 smoke mortar.
Armour: 109mm (0.375in) minimum; 38mm (1.5in) maximum.
Dimensions: Length 18ft (5.49m); width 9ft 8in (2.95m); height 8ft 2in (2.77m).
Weight: Combat 40,500lb (18,370kg).
Ground pressure: 11.3lb/in^2 (0.79kg/cm^2).
Engine: Two Cadillac 44T24 V-8 water-cooled petrol engines each developing 110hp at 3,400rpm.

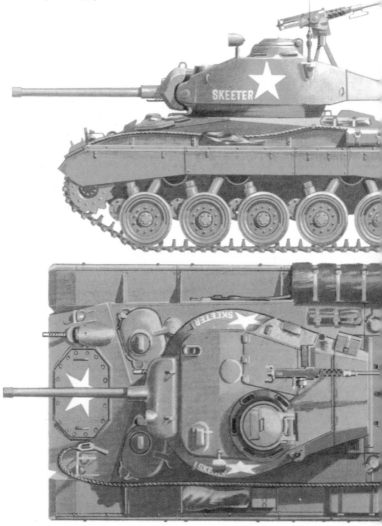

Performance: Road speed 34mph (54km/h), road range 100 miles (160km); vertical obstacle 3ft (0.91m); trench 8ft (2.44m); fording depth 3ft 4in (1.02m) unprepared and 6ft 6in (1.98m) prepared; gradient 60 per cent.

History: Entered service in 1944. Supplied to many other countries including (in small numbers) UK, and still in wide use in 1981. Basis of original "Lightweight Combat Team".

Below: Four views of the M24 Chaffee light tank used by the US Army in Europe from late 1944. Development of a new light tank to replace the M3 and M5 commenced in March 1943 and the M24 was in fact standardised in mid-1944 after it had already been in production for several months. By 1945 4,070 had been built. The French used the Chaffee in Vietnam in the 1950s.

Compared with the M5 light tank which it replaced, the M24 was a quantum advance. In two of the three attributes of armour – firepower and protection – the M24 surpassed all other light tanks of World War II, while its mobility was comparable with the exceptionally agile M5. Its 75mm gun was almost the equal of that of the Sherman and more powerful than the armament of most medium tanks in 1939. The vastly improved hull and turret shape increased protection by the elimination of shot traps, reduction of the silhouette and better sloping of the armour. Today, it is normal to consider ease of maintenance as another attribute of the tank and the M24 was designed with accessibility of major assemblies in mind.

Military characteristics defined for the new light tank were that the power train of the M5A1 should be retained; the suspension should be improved; the gross weight should not exceed 16 long tons (16,257kg); and that the armour should reach a maximum of 1in (25.4mm) thickness and be acutely angled to the horizontal. The M5A1 light tank was limited in the space available within the turret, a fact which precluded the installation of the 75mm gun. A T21 light tank was considered, but at 21.5 tons (21,845kg) this would have been too heavy. The T7 light tank was examined exhaustively by the Armoured Force. It had been designed around the 57mm gun at the request of the British Army and when the Armoured Force asked for a 75mm gun, the resultant weight increase moved the T7 into the medium tank category. In fact standardisation as the M7 medium tank, with the 75mm gun, was approved but later cancelled to avoid the logistic disadvantage of having two standard medium tank types.

The Cadillac Motor Division of the General Motors Corporation delivered pilot models of a vehicle to meet the stated requirements in October 1943. The T24, as it was designated, was found satisfactory and 1,000 were ordered before service tests had begun. In addition, pilots of the T24E1 with the power train of the M18 tank destroyer were also ordered, but this development was later cancelled. The T24 mounted the T13E1 75mm gun in a Concentric Recoil Mechanism T33 with a .3in machine-gun in the Combination Gun Mount T90. The gun was a lightweight weapon developed from the M5 aircraft gun, and although the standardised nomenclature M6 was assigned, this merely indicated tank use as opposed to airborne use. The twin Cadillac engines of the T24 were mounted on rails for ease of maintenance – a feature of the T7 light tank – and

Above: M24 Chaffee with wider tracks for use in muddy terrain at firing practice. The M24 was replaced in the US Army in the 1950s by a M41 Walker Bulldog.

Left: Although the M24 Chaffee light tank entered service as long ago as 1944, as late as the 1980s it was still in service in many armies around the world, especially in the Far East and South America.

were identical with those of the M5A1. Indeed, it was because the T24 shared the same power plant as the M5A1 that Cadillac was chosen to produce the T24 in quantity, although later American Car & Foundry and Massey-Harris were to be included in production.

The torsion-bar suspension of the M18 tank destroyer was used in the T24. Although the invention of this suspension is often ascribed to German tank designers, the American patent on torsion bar suspension was granted in December 1935 to G. M. Barnes and W. E. Preston. Five pairs of stamped disc wheels, 25in (63.5cm) in diameter and rubber-tyred, were mounted on each side and a sprocket at the front drove the 16in (40.6cm) tracks. The hull of the T24 was of all welded construction, reaching a maximum thickness on frontal surfaces of 2.5in (63.5mm) although in less critical places the armour was thinner to conform to the concept of the light tank. A large cover in the glacis plate could be removed for access to the controlled differential steering, and dual controls were provided for the driver and assistant driver. In July 1944 the T24 was standardised as the M24 Light Tank, popularly known as the "Chaffee", and by June 1945 a total of 4,070 had been produced.

In keeping with the idea of a Lightweight Combat Team, other vehicles using the M24 chassis were designed for specialist applications. A variety of gun and mortar carriages was developed, of which the T77 Multiple Gun Motor Carriage is one of the more interesting. A new turret mounting six .5in machine-guns was mounted on a basically standard M24 chassis and in a way this vehicle foreshadowed the modern six-barrelled Vulcan Air Defense System. Two armoured utility vehicles, the T9 and T13, were designed and three cargo carriers also developed. The T22E1 and T23E1 were adaptations of the T22 and T23 which were based on the M5 light tank. The T33 Cargo Carrier was a later development which, with the substitution of the medium tank engine and torque converter transmission of the Hellcat, became the T42 Cargo Tractor. The T43 Cargo Tractor was a lighter version of the T42. A bulldozer kit, the T9, was developed and adopted as the M4 but was not widely used. Various aids to flotation were tried, as in the case of the Hellcat, but none was adopted for widespread use. Each of the Combat Team families was provided with a recovery vehicle, and the T6E1 Tank Recovery Vehicle was the model compatible with the M24 series. Although pilots were built, development was not pursued.

M26 Pershing Heavy Tank

T25, T26, T26E1, T26E2, T26E3, M26, M45, M46 and many variants.
Country of origin: USA.
Crew: 5, sometimes reduced to 4.
Armament: One 90mm M3 gun; one .3in M1919A4 machine-gun co-axial with main armament; one .3in M1919A4 machine-gun in hull front; one .5in M2 machine-gun on turret roof.
Armour: 13mm (0.51in) minimum; 102mm (4in) maximum.
Dimensions: Length 28ft 5in (8.65m); width 11ft 6in (3.51m); height 9ft 1in (2.78m).
Weight: Combat 92,355lb (41,891kg).
Ground pressure: 13.1lb/in² (0.92kg/cm²).
Engine: Ford GAF V-8 water-cooled petrol engine developing 500hp at 2,600rpm.
Performance: Road speed 30mph (48km/h), road range 100 miles (160km); vertical obstacle 3ft 10in (1.17m); trench 8ft (2.44m); fording depth 4ft (1.22m); gradient 60 per cent.
History: Although doubts existed as to the need for such a tank, the Pershing entered US service in 1945. Saw service in Korea and in the 1950s with many foreign armies. Development of the M60 main battle tank can be traced to the M26.

When the M26 heavy tank was introduced into service with the US Army in 1945, it marked the end of the line of development which began in 1938 with the M2 medium tank. By the same token it marked the birth of a line culminating in the M60 series, the main battle tank of the 1960s.

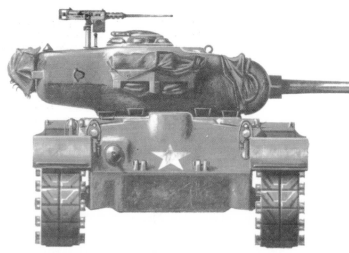

Above and right: Front and side views of M26 tank showing the cast hull and turret and the long barrelled 90mm M3 gun with its double baffle muzzle brake. Pershings were produced by the Chrysler operated Detroit tank plant which built 246 between March and May 1945, while the Fisher Body Division of General Motors Corporation's Grand Blanc tank arsenal built 1,190 between November 1944 and June 1945. Postwar, the M26, and its improved version, the M46, saw combat with UN forces in South Korea.

The story of the M26 begins in 1942 when the Ordnance Department received the approval of the Services of Supply for its proposed development of the T20 medium tank. This tank was intended to be an improvement on the M4 series, but Ordnance hoped to be able to use the vehicle for comparative tests of armaments, transmissions and suspensions. Thirteen different models of the T20, T22 and T23 medium tanks were developed and these variously tried different weapons – for example the 76mm gun; different transmissions – for example the "gas-electric" transmission, also used in the M6 heavy tank; and different suspensions – for example the early form of horizontal volute spring suspension of the Sherman. Development of two heavy tanks followed and these were designated T25 and T26. Both mounted the new T7 90mm gun and used the Ford GAF engine with electric transmissions.

Above: M26 Pershing heavy tank from the rear. Twenty T26E3 prototypes were sent to Europe as the Zebra Mission early in 1945 and were used by the 3rd and 9th Armored Divisions. The T26E3 was standardised as the M26 Pershing heavy tank in 1945 and production continued postwar. In May 1946 the M26 was reclassified as the M46 medium tank.

The T26 was given a higher priority, and in the T26E1 the Ford GAF engine drove the vehicle through a hydraulic torque converter in series with planetary reduction gearing. This transmission gave three forward ratios and one reverse and was known as the "torquematic" transmission. Torsion-bar suspension with a 24in (61cm) track was fitted. The turret was cast, while the hull was fabricated from a combination of castings and rolled plate.

At this point the feelings of the various interested parties began to emerge, and opinions differed widely. Early in 1943 the Armored Command had expressed the view that the war would be won or lost with the M4 medium tank, and as a result of this Ordnance embarked on several improvements to crew safety, mechanical reliability and combat efficiency in the Sherman. The Armored Command also objected to heavy tanks in general on the grounds of weight and size. Army Ground Forces, however, wanted 1,000 of the T26 and 7,000 of the lighter T25, the T26 to be armed with the 76mm gun and the T25 with the 75mm gun. On the other hand the Armored Command wanted neither the T25 nor the T26 but did require the 90mm gun. The T26E2 mounted the 105mm howitzer in a mount which was interchangeable with the 90mm mount, and in the T26E3 Ordnance believed that the best compromise had been reached.

Army Ground Forces preferred to delay any standardisation action until the Armored Board had indicated its satisfaction and approved the vehicle's battleworthiness, so the Secretary of War provided the necessary impetus by sending 20 tanks into the European Theatre of Operations. This "Zebra Mission" proved the battleworthiness of the T26E3 in the hands of the 3rd and

Below: During the 1945 advance into Germany, the Pershing destroyed a Tiger and two *PzKpfw* Mk IV tanks in a single action. The US M60 series was a direct descendent of the M26 via the M46, M47 and M48 tanks.

9th Armored Divisions and standardisations and production then proceeded. It is interesting to note that in June 1944, the European Theatre had reported to Washington that there was no requirement for either the 75mm or 76mm guns but that a mix of 90mm guns and 105mm howitzers in the ratio of 1:3 was preferable. This was consistent with the perceived role of the tank in 1944 but conflicts with today's concept of the tank primarily as an anti-tank weapon. The T26E3 was adopted as standard in January 1945 under the designation M26 Heavy Tank, and the name "Pershing" was given, after General John J. Pershing. At the same time the T26E2 with the 105mm howitzer was adopted as the M45 for the close-support role.

The Pershing, although introduced as a heavy tank, was soon reclassified as a medium tank and production continued well past the end of World War II. Although too late to make any real contribution to that war, the M26 was widely used in the Korean War and later supplied to many armies in the Free World.

As was usually the case, the Pershing led to a family of specialist vehicles. The "Heavyweight Combat Team" was intended to consist of the T84 8in Howitzer Motor Carriage, the T92 240mm Howitzer Motor Carriage, the T93 8in Gun Motor Carriage, the T31 Cargo Carrier and the T12 Recovery Vehicle. A flamethrower tank, cargo tractor and combat engineer vehicle were also produced and consideration was also given to a mine resistant vehicle, based on the M26 chassis, to breach anti-tank minefields. Improvements to the engine and gun resulted in the M46 Medium Tank, the first "Patton", although the poor turret and cupola shape were retained. From the T26 series, further heavy tanks resulted under the designations T29, T30, T32 and T34. The T30 was equipped with a 155mm gun which fired semi-fixed ammunition, but development was dropped when it became apparent that such a vehicle would not be sufficiently effective relative to its weight. The same fate befell the T29, T32 and T34 for similar reasons.

M41 Walker Bulldog Light Tank

Country of origin: USA.
Crew: 4.
Armament: One 76mm gun; one 7.62mm machine-gun co-axial with main armament; one 12.7mm anti-aircraft machine-gun.
Armour: 9.25mm-38mm (0.36in-1.49in).
Dimensions: Length (gun forward) 26ft 11in (8.21m); length (hull) 19ft 1in (5.82mm); width 10ft 6in (3.12m); height (including 12.7mm machine-gun) 10ft 1in (3.07m).
Weight: Combat 51,800lb (23,495kg).
Ground pressure: 10.24lb/in^2 (0.72kg/cm^2).
Engine: Continental or Lycoming AOS-895-3 6-cylinder petrol engine developing 500bhp at 2,800rpm.
Performance: Road speed 45mph (72km/h), range 100 miles (160km); vertical obstacle 2ft 4in (0.71m); trench 6ft (1.83m); gradient 60 per cent.
History: Entered service with the US Army in 1951. Still in service with Brazil (287), Chile (60), Denmark (DK-1, 53), Dominica (M41A1, 12), Guatemala (10), Republic of China (5004), Thailand (250, most in reserve), Uruguay (22, upgraded).

The standard light tank in use with the United States Army at the end of World War II was the M24 Chaffee, which weighed 40,500lb (18,370kg) and was armed with a 75mm gun. Shortly after the end of the war work

Right and below: The M41 light tank was one of three tanks developed by the United States in the early 1950s, the others being the M47 medium tank and the M103 heavy tank. The M41 shares many common components with the M42 twin 40mm self-propelled anti-aircraft gun and the M44 (155mm) and M52 (105mm) self-propelled howitzers. It was replaced in the United States Army by the M551 Sheridan but large numbers of M41s remain in service with other countries in all parts of the world. Main armament consists of a 76mm gun.

started on a new light tank called the T37. The first prototype of this was completed in 1949 and was known as the T37 Phase I. This was followed by the T37 Phase II, which had a redesigned turret and different fire-control system. This model was then redesignated as the T42 and a slightly modified version of this, the T41E1, was standardised as the M41. The M41 was authorised for production in 1949 and was named the Little Bulldog, although the name was subsequently changed to the Walker Bulldog after General W. W. Walker, killed in an accident in Korea in 1951. Production of the M41 was undertaken by the Cadillac Car Division of the General Motors Corporation at the Cleveland Tank Plant, and first production models were completed in 1951. Further models of the M41 were the M41A1, M41A2 and the M41A3. These have a slightly different

gun control system, whilst the M41A2 and M41A3 have a fuel-injection system for the engine.

The M41, as one of the three main tanks developed for the US Army in the early 1950s, the others being the M47 medium and the M103 heavy tanks, was the first member of a whole family of vehicles sharing many common components. The family included the M42 self-propelled anti-aircraft gun, the M44 and M52 self-propelled howitzers and the M75 armoured personnel carrier. In addition there were many trials variations in the 1950s. Some M42s were also used a targets by the United States Navy as the QM41. Fitted with remote-control equipment, they are used as mobile targets for new air-to-ground missiles.

The hull of the M41 is of all-welded steel construction, whilst the turret is of welded and cast construction. The driver is seated at the front of the hull on the left, with the other three crew members in the turret, the commander and gunner on the right and the loader on the left. The engine and transmission are at the rear of the hull, and are separated from the fighting compartment by a fireproof bulkhead. Like most American AFVs of that period, the M41 is provided with a hull escape hatch, thus enabling the crew to leave the vehicle with a better chance of survival than if they baled out via the turret or driver's hatch. The suspension is of the torsion bar type and consists of five road wheels, with the drive sprocket at the rear and the idler at the front. There are three track return rollers.

The main armament of the M41 consists of a 76mm gun with an elevation of +19° and a depression of –9°, traverse being 360°. A 7.62mm machine-gun is mounted to the left of the main armament and there is a 12.7mm Browning machine-gun on the commander's cupola. Some 65 rounds of 76mm, 2,175 rounds of 12.7mm and 5,000 rounds of 7.62 ammunition are carried. The barrel of the 76mm gun is provided with a bore evacuator and a "T" type blast-deflector, the latter's function being to reduce the effects of blast and obstruction caused by the flow of propellant

gases into the atmosphere. These gases otherwise raise a dust cloud and make aiming of the weapon more difficult.

The M41 was replaced by the M551 Sheridan in US Army service and has also been discarded by a number of other armies. Many remain in service, however, and several armies, including those of Brazil, Taiwan and Denmark upgraded their fleets to extend their service. Various upgrade packages were offered to other users, most of which involved replacing the 76mm gun with a 90mm (or even 105mm) weapon and replacing the original six-cylinder petrol engine with a more fuel-efficient diesel powerplant.

Below: An M41 Walker Bulldog light tank of the Danish Army. Introduced in 1951, the M41 has been replaced in US services by the M551 Sheridan, but it is still used by many countries and has proved to be a very reliable tank.

M47 Medium Tank

Country of origin: USA.
Crew: 5.
Armament: One M63 90mm gun; one M1919A4E .3in machine-gun in bow; one M1919A4E1 machine-gun co-axial with main armament; one M2 .5in machine-gun on commander's cupola.
Armour: 12.7mm-112mm (0.50in-4.60in).
Dimensions: Length (gun forward) 28ft 1in (8.1m); length (hull) 20ft 8in (6.1mm); width 10ft 6in (3.51m); height (including anti-aircraft machine-gun) 11ft (3.35m).
Weight: Combat 101,775lb (46,170kg).
Ground pressure: 13.3lb/in^2 (0.93kg/cm^2).
Engine: Continental AV-1790-5B 12-cylinder air-cooled petrol engine developing 810hp at 2,800rpm.
Performance: Road speed 30mph (48km/h), range 80 miles (130km); vertical obstacle 3ft (0.914m); trench 8ft 6in (2.59m); gradient 60 per cent.
History: Entered service with the US Army in 1952. Exported in large numbers; none remains in front-line service but a few may still be in reserve in some armies.

When the Korean War broke out the M62 and M46 were the standard US Army tanks, but a new medium tank was needed urgently. This was produced by mounting the turret of a new experimental tank, the T42, on the hull of the existing M26 Pershing. The new tank, which was considered an interim design by the US Army, became the M47 Patton and 8,676 were built between 1950 and 1953 – not a bad number for a "stop-gap"!

The hull and turret are of all-cast construction. The driver is seated at the front of the hull on the left. The other four members of the crew are the bow machine-gunner to the right of the driver, and the usual turret crew of commander, gunner and loader. The main armament is the M36 90mm gun, which has a T-shaped blast deflector and which fires a variety of rounds,

Below: The M47 was developed during the Korean War and is essentially a modified M26 Pershing chassis fitted with the turret developed for the T42 tank. Over 8,500 M47s were completed in the 1950s.

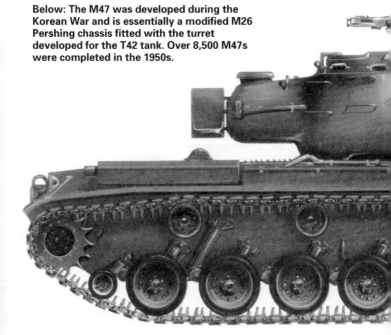

including HEAT and HEAT (Fin-Stabilized). MECAR in Belgium and IMI in Israel developed 90mm APFSDS rounds for this weapon. 71 rounds of 90mm ammunition are carried. There is a co-axial .7.62mm machine-gun, a 12.7mm anti-aircraft machine-gun, and a 7.62mm bow machine-gun.

The USA Army relegated the M47 to reserve status after only a few years, but many were supplied to NATO countries, and, although few of these remain in front-line service, there are many in storage. A new tank factory was built in Iran between 1970 and 1972 and the first tank selected for production there was a developed version of M47 designated M47M. This retained the 90mm main gun, but had a number of components from the M48A3 and M60A1 series, including engine, transmission, electrics and optical equipment. This resulted in a much superior vehicle, with greatly extended range. Some 400 were produced, but none remains in service.

Above: An M47 moves up to the battlefield with infantry support. The M47 was soon replaced in the US Army by the much-improved M48. Large numbers were exported but none remains in service today.

M103 Heavy Tank

M103, M103A1, M103A2.
Country of origin: USA.
Crew: 5.
Armament: One M58 120mm gun; one .3in M57 or M1919A4E1 machine-gun co-axial with main armament; one .5in M2 anti-aircraft machine-gun.
Armour: 12mm-178mm (0.47in-7.12in).
Dimensions: Length (gun forward) 37ft 1½in (11.315m); length (hull) 22ft 11in (6.984mm); width 12ft 4in (3.758m); height 9ft 5½in (2.88m).
Weight: Combat 125.000lb (56,700kg).
Ground pressure: 12.85lb/in² (0.9kg/cm²).
Engine: Continental AV-1790-5B or 7C 12-cylinder air-cooled diesel engine developing 810hp at 2,800rpm.
Performance: Road speed 21mph (34km/h), range 80 miles (129km); vertical obstacle 3ft (0.914m); trench 7ft 6in (2.286m); gradient 60 per cent.
History: Entered service with the US Army in 1957/58. Last used by Marine Corps and phased out of service in 1972-73.

Towards the end of World War II the Americans had a number of heavy tanks under various stages of development, including the T28 (this was really an assault gun and weighed 90 tons (91,445kg), and was later redesignated the T95 Gun Motor Carriage), T29, T30, T32 and T34. None of these progressed beyond the prototype stage, however. After the war trials with these tanks continued, but it was eventually decided to start work on a new tank, the T43. Two prototypes of this were completed in 1948 and these were followed by four modified versions designated T43E1. The latter model was placed in production and 200 were built between 1952 and 1954 by Chrysler. The T43E1 was not standardised as the M103 until 1953. Many faults became apparent in service and the US Army promptly declared the type unfit for front-line use. It was not until 1957-58 that the tank was considered fit for service as over 150 different modifications were required for each tank. The cost of an M103 in 1954 was just over $300,000, compared with the cost of a M60A1, 20 years later, of $297,000.

The M103 was designed to fulfil a role similar to that of the British Conqueror heavy tank: engaging the Russian IS-3, and later the T-10, at long range. It was not surprising that the M103 had the same limitations as the Conqueror: on the battlefield it was underpowered and therefore lacked mobility. It had the same engine and transmission as the M47 tank, which weighed 10 tons (10,161kg) less. The M103 often broke down, and had a very short operational range. It was intended to fit auxiliary fuel tanks to the rear of the hull, but although tested these were not adopted. The M103 did not remain in front-line service with the United States Army for very long, and once the M60 was in production the older vehicle soon passed away. The M103A1 (development designation T43E2) was a rebuilt M103 with an improved fire-control system and a basket on the rear of the turret. The M103A2 (development designation M103A1E1) was basically an M103A1 with many improvements, including a new AVDS-1790-2Ad diesel engine. Three prototypes were built in 1963 and these were followed by 153 conversions, all of which were for the Marine Corps, the last users of the M103 heavy tank.

With the introduction of the M103 in service, a recovery vehicle also had to be developed as existing vehicles could not handle the heavy tank. This was designated M51 (development designations being the T6 and later T6E1) and 200 of these were built by Chrysler, remaining in service until 1972-73.

The hull of the M103 was a homogeneous steel casting with the floor welded into position. The turret was also cast, but the floor of the bustle (that is the part underneath the turret rear) was welded into position. The hull was divided into three compartments, the driver's at the front, the fighting compartment in the centre and the engine and transmission at the rear. The suspension system was of the torsion-bar type and consisted of seven road wheels, with the drive sprocket at the rear and the idler at the front, there being six

Above: An M103 heavy tank of the US Army. The tank proved a most troublesome weapon – to its users! It often broke down, had a short operational range, was once declared unfit for front-line use and had to have over 150 modifications before it could enter service. Each M103 cost more than an M60A1, which entered service some 20 years later.

track-return rollers.

The main armament consisted of a 120mm gun with an elevation of +15° and a depression of –8°. A .3in machine-gun was mounted co-axially with the main armament and there was a Browning .5in machine-gun on the commander's cupola for use in the anti-aircraft role. Some 38 rounds of separate loading 120mm, 5,250 rounds of .3in and 1,000 rounds of .5in ammunition were carried. The main armament was not stabilised. The ammunition was of the separate loading type and the following types were available – Armour Piercing with Tracer, High Explosive, High Explosive with Tracer, Target Practice with Tracer, White Phosphorus and White Phosphorus with Tracer. The crew of five consisted of commander, gunner, two loaders and the driver. The M103 was fitted with infra-red driving lights and most Marine tanks had an infra-red/white light searchlight over the main armament. The M103 can ford streams to a maximum depth of 4ft (1.219m).

Below: Top view of the M103, with turret reversed. The hull was divided into three compartments: driver's at the front, fighting compartment in the centre and engine and transmission at the rear. Main armament was a 120mm gun; other weapons were a .3in machine gun and a .5in A/A gun.

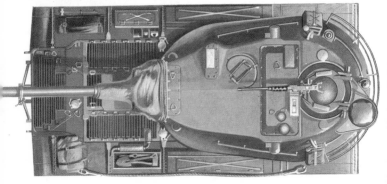

M48 Medium Tank

M48, M48C, M48A1, M48A2, M48A2C, M48A3, M48A4, M67, M67A1, M67A2, M48A VLB.
Country of origin: USA.
Crew: 4.
Armament: One 90mm gun M41; one .3in M1919A-4E machine-gun co-axial with the main armament (some have a 7.62mm M73 MG); one .5in machine-gun in commander's cupola.
Armour: 12.7mm-120mm (0.50in-4.80in).
Dimensions: Length (including main armament) 24ft 5in (7.442m); length (hull) 22ft 7in (6.882mm); width 11ft 11in (3.631m); height (including cupola) 10ft 3in (3.124m).
Weight: Combat 104.000lb (47,173kg).
Ground pressure: 11.80lb/in^2 (0.83kg/cm^2).
Engine: Continental AVDS-1790-2A 12-cylinder air-cooled diesel engine developing 750hp at 2,400rpm.
Performance: Road speed 30mph (48km/h), range 288 miles (463km); vertical obstacle 3ft (0.915m); trench 8ft 6in (2.59m); gradient 60 per cent.
History: Entered service with the United States Army in 1953. M48A1 and M48A3 remain in service with Greece (18), South Korea (c100), Taiwan (100), Tunisia (14) and Turkey (c700).

Once the M47 was authorised for production, development started on a new medium tank as the M47 was only a stop-gap measure. So in October 1950 Detroit Arsenal started design work on a new medium tank armed with a 90mm gun. This design study was completed two months later and in December 1950 Chrysler was given a contract to complete the design work and build six prototypes under the designation T48. The first of these prototypes had to be completed by December 1951. In March 1951, before

Right: Taiwanese M48 armed with 90mm gun and blast deflector. The commander's cupola has a 0.50in Browning machinegun.

Above: An M67 flame-thrower tank of the United States Marine Corps attacks VietCong positions in South Vietnam.

the prototypes were even completed, both the Ford company and the Fisher Body Division of the General Motors Corporation were given production orders for the T48, or M48 as it was to become known. Production started in 1952 and first deliveries were made to the US Army the following year. M48s were also built by Alco Products of Schenectady, New York, and production was finally completed by Chrysler at its Delaware plant in 1960.

The M48 was followed in production by the M60, essentially an M48A3 with a 105mm gun and other detailed changes, production of this model being undertaken at the Detroit Tank Plant.

The hull of the M48 is of cast armour construction, as is the turret. The driver is seated at the front of the hull with the other three crew members located in the turret, with the commander and gunner on the right and the loader on the left. The engine and transmission are at the rear of the hull, and

are separated from the fighting compartment by a fireproof bulkhead.

The suspension is of the torsion-bar type and consists of six road wheels, with the drive sprocket at the rear and the idler at the front. Depending on the model there are between three and five track-return rollers, and some models have a small track tensioning wheel between the sixth road wheel and the drive sprocket.

The main armament consists of a 90mm gun with an elevation of +20° and a depression of –9°, traverse being 360°. A .3in M1919A4E1 machine-gun is mounted co-axially with the main armament, although most M48s in US Army service have a 7.62mm machine-gun. There is also a 0.5in MZ machine-gun in the commander's cupola (except on the M48A1 which has a simple mount). This cupola can be traversed through 360°, and the machine-gun can be elevated –10° to +60°. The amount of ammunition carried depends on the model, the M48A3 carrying 62 rounds of 90mm, 6,000 rounds of .3in and 630 round of .5in machine-gun ammunition.

The M48 can be fitted with a dozer blade, if required, at the front of the hull. All M48s have infra-red driving lights and some an infra-red/white

Below: M48 of the Israeli Army fitted with 105mm gun. This is also fitted to Israeli Centurion, M60, M60A1 and more recent Merkava MBTs.

searchlight mounted over the main armament. The type can ford to a depth of 4ft (1.219m) without preparation or 8ft (2.438m) with the aid of a kit. Components of the M48 are also used in the M88 armoured recovery vehicle and the M53/M55 self-propelled weapons (the M55 is no longer in service).

The first model to enter service was the M48, and this has a simple cupola for the commander, with the machine-gun mounted externally. The second model was the M48C, which was for training use only as it has a mild steel hull. The M48A1 was followed by the M48A2, which has many improvements including a fuel-injection system for the engine and larger capacity fuel tanks. The M48A2C was a slightly modified M48A2. The M48A3 was a significant improvement as this has a diesel engine, which increases the vehicle's operational range considerably, and a number of other modifications including a different fire-control system. The M48A4 was to have had the turrets taken from M60 tanks when they were refitted with a new turret with the 152mm Shillelagh. There is also a .5in M2 machine-gun in the commander's cupola missile system, but this plan was dropped so the M48A4 never entered service.

Approximately 1,000 early model M48s remain in service, although many have been upgraded to M48A5 or equivalent standards. The unmodified versions can be expected to waste out in the next few years.

M48A5 Main Battle Tank

Country of origin: USA.
Crew: 4.
Armament: One M68 105mm rifled gun; one M60D 7.62mm co-axial machine-gun; two M60D 7.62mm anti-aircraft machine-guns.
Armour: Maximum 12.7mm-120mm (.5in-4.8in).
Dimensions: Length (including main armament) 30ft 6in (9.31m); length (hull) 21ft 1in (6.42mm); width 11ft 11in (3.63m); height 10ft 2in (3.09m).
Weight: Combat 107.900lb (48,987kg).
Ground pressure: 12.51lb/in^2 (0.88kg/cm^2).
Engine: Continental AVDS-1790-2D 12-cylinder, air-cooled, diesel engine developing 750hp at 2,400rpm.
Performance: Road speed 30mph (48km/h), range 310 miles (500km); vertical obstacle 3ft 0in (0.92m); trench 8ft 6in (2.6m); gradient 60 per cent.
History: Entered service with the US Army in 1953. Now in service with: Greece (714), Iran (60), Israel (500), Jordan (c.200), South Korea (850), Lebanon (104), Morocco (224), Pakistan (345), Portugal (86), Spain (164), Taiwan (286), Thailand (75), Tunisia (28), Turkey (2,961), Vietnam (number not known).
(Specification data apply to M48A5.)

A product of the rush to rearm consequent on the outbreak of the Korean War in 1950, the M48 design was completed in two months, prototypes were running a year later and the first production models were delivered in 1953 – a timetable that would be literally impossible today. The M48 was armed with a 90mm gun, had a crew of four and had a much-improved suspension compared to that of the M47. The original version was quickly followed by the M48A1 and M48A2, each of which had relatively minor improvements, and the first major advance was with the M48A3, with virtually all -A1s and -A2s in US Army service being upgraded to this standard. The M48A3 has a diesel engine replacing the petrol engine and improved fire control systems.

It was eventually realised that the day of the 90mm gun had passed, and it was decided to upgrade the M48 yet again by installing an M68 105mm main gun. This involved many other changes and produced an almost new tank, which was little different from the M60 (which itself had originally been simply an M48A3 with a 105mm gun).

Right: The M48A5 is an earlier M48 with many improvements, the most notable of which is the use of an M68 rifled gun in place of the 90mm weapon. Over 6,500 M48s remain in use.

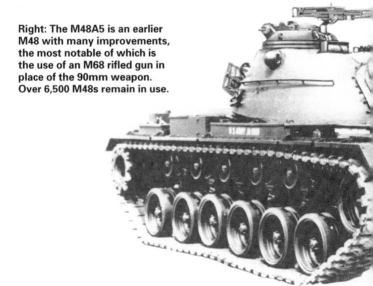

Above: M48A5s of the US Army. This version of the M48 was armed with the M68 105mm gun (licence-produced British L7), but also included many other minor improvements.

The M48 was exported in very large numbers and remain in service with 15 armies. A small number of these are M48A2 or -A3s which retain their 90mm guns, but the vast majority have been upgraded to take the 105mm. Apart from the US Army's M48A5 conversions, one of the biggest of these programmes was that of Wegmann in Germany, which has converted 650 tanks to a new M48A2GA2 standard, with a L7A3 105mm rifled 105mm gun, and improved optical and fire control equipment. Other similar programmes were undertaken in Turkey, Iran and Israel.

MBT-70/KPz-70 Main Battle Tank

MBT-70 and XM803.
Country of origin: USA/ Federal Republic of Germany.
Crew: 3.
Armament: One 152mm smoothbore gun/missile launcher; one 20mm cannon on turret roof; eight single barrelled smoke grenade launchers on each side of turret.
Armour: Cast steel.
Dimensions: Length not known; width 11ft 6in (3.51m); height 7ft 6in/6ft 6in (2.29m/1.98m) (see text).
Weight: Combat 105,273lb (47,750kg).
Ground pressure: Not known.
Engine: US version, Continental multi-fuel, air-cooled engine, 1,475hp; German version, Daimler-Benz multi-fuel, water-cooled engine, 1,500hp.
Performance: Not known.
History: Prototypes ran in 1967; after increasing delays and cost rises, cancelled in 1972.

Although the MBT70 (Main Battle Tank 1970) never got beyond the prototype stage it remains a salutary example of what can go wrong in a military development project. For the US Army, the MBT70 story began in the mid-1950s, a time when the M48A1 (*qv*) was just entering service, and centred on an experimental programme involving a totally new tank design, the T95. This started with a 105mm main gun, a four-man crew and a 700hp diesel engine, but the design was recast on several occasions, first, to take the M48's 90mm turret and, secondly, in 1959, to take the M60's 105mm turret. Then in the early 1960s the T95 was given a squatting hydropneumatic suspension and an experimental gas-turbine engine, only to be reworked yet again to incorporate an experimental 152mm gun/missile launcher. Needless to say, by this time not only did the T95 bear little resemblance to the original design, but it was also considerably over-weight and it was cancelled in 1960.

Meanwhile, the early 1960s were a time of political ferment – President John F. Kennedy took office in January 1961 – and both technological revolution and risk-taking were in the air, while within NATO the fashion was for collaboration, standardization and, albeit at a lower level, there was the ill-fated multi-fuel policy. All of these came together in the MBT70 project – with disastrous results. An earlier attempt at a

Below: One of the US MBT-70 prototypes, showing the huge turret which housed all three crew members: commander, gunner and driver. The latter had his own, independent cupola.

Above: MBT-70/PZ-70 main weapon was the 152mm gun/missile launcher capable of firing guided missiles at long-range targets and conventional HEAT rounds in shorter-range engagements.

collaborative tank project between France, Germany and Italy had already proved abortive: the Italians left the project early, while the French and Germans eventually went their separate ways, to produce the national AMX-30 and Leopard I (*qqv*), respectively. In 1963, the West Germans and the USA realised that they were both looking for successors to their current tanks and they agreed to pool their resources in order to develop a tank, which was designated MBT70 by the USA and *Kampfpanzer 1970* (KPz70) by the Germans, the figure "70" indicating the desired in-service date. Development began in 1965, with the designers being given carte blanche to develop the most advanced tank in the world, which would, it was hoped, remain in service at

Below : A German PZ-70 prototype, demonstrating how the hydropneumatic suspension could be adjusted to enable the tank to adopt a hull-down firing position.

least until the end of the century. The resulting MBT 70 was the most complex armoured fighting vehicle of its day, and, by a wide margin, the most expensive.

Everything about the MBT 70 was innovative, none more so than the weapons system, which was a 152mm gun/missile launcher. The relatively short barrel fired the 152mm M409 round, which had a HEAT (high-explosive, anti-tank) warhead, although even this round was unconventional, because it used a totally combustible cartridge case, to overcome the usual problem of extracting and disposing of a brass cartridge case. The other round was the missile, which was accelerated down the tube at high subsonic speed, but then accelerated by a single-stage rocket motor to a speed of 2,630mph (4,233km/h) out to a maximum effective range of 5,700yd (5,200m). All the gunner had to do was to place the optical cross-hairs on the target and the missile guidance system then steered the missile onto the IR beam; minimum gathering range was 1,240yd (1,143m). The warhead was a 15lb HEAT. The tactical concept behind this combination was that the missile would be used at longer ranges where its accuracy would be essential while the gun would be used for shorter ranges, where its accuracy and higher rate of fire made it better than the missile. Development of the Shillelagh missile system was lengthy and troublesome, and although it achieved IOC in 1967 it was not fully operational until 1973. The Germans, however, were sceptical about this gun/missile system from the start and designed a second turret, incorporating a Rheinmetall 120mm gun, which would have been installed in their tanks had the project come to fruition.

The MBT70 design included an autoloader in order to reduce the crew size to three – a novel idea at the time – but all three were concentrated in the turret, in order to reduce the height of the hull. The driver sat in a counter-rotating cupola, which was supposed to face forward whatever movements the turret made. This again proved to be a major problem and all drivers complained of disorientation and motion sickness.

Another innovation was the variable-height hydropneumatic suspension, which was intended to enable the tank to squat to reduce its silhouette in a static fire position, but then to rise for high cross-country mobility. The control was very sophisticated and could be used to adjust the tank position either front/rear, left/right, or any combination.

The engine was required not only to provide a high power output, but also to comply with the NATO policy of being multi-fuel in order to ease logistic problems in war. The outcome was a variable compression ratio 1,500hp engine that could use a wide variety of fuels; but, again, the Germans did not like this and powered their version with a Daimler-Benz diesel.

Other elements of the design included full turret stabilization, a laser range finder, a ballistic computer, a remotely controlled 20mm cannon, and an environmental control/life support system. Finally, the design was supposed to incorporate quality

A dramatic picture of XM-803, the "austere" version of the MBT-70. The entire project was an example of the dangers of incorporating too many innovations into one programme.

Above: Another view of one of the PZ-70 prototypes, with the suspension in the fully lowered ("squatting") position, intended to enable it to make maximum use of cover in while firing.

assurance and reliability in service to a standard never before realised.

The first prototypes were unveiled simultaneously in Germany and the USA in July 1967 but technical difficulties abounded, with major delays on most individual systems, coupled with difficulties in integrating the whole. Costs spiralled remorselessly, a contemporary assessment being that a production MBT70 would cost $US1 million while an M60A1 would cost $US220,000. In an effort to save the project the design team came up with an austere version, designated XM803, of which a prototype was running in 1970, but even that would have cost $US600,000 in production. Congress became increasingly critical and in 1969 the House of Representatives Appropriations Committee demanded that the project with Germany be ended and that the US Army should design a tank with far less sophistication at about one-third of the then projected cost of the MBT70. The entire project ground to a halt in 1972 when Congress simply denied any further funds and insisted on a fresh start. The whole saga proved to be an object lesson in how not to run and control a development project and, in particular, the dangers of trying to make too many advances all at once.

M60A2 Main Battle Tank

Country of origin: USA.
Crew: 4.
Armament: One M162 152mm gun/launcher; one 7.62mm M73 machine-gun co-axial with main armament; one 12.7mm M85 anti-aircraft machine-gun in commander s cupola.
Armour: Not known.
Dimensions: Length (gun forward) 24ft 0in (7.33m); length (hull) 22ft 11in (7.0m); width 11ft 11in (3.63m); height 10ft 10in (3.31m).
Weight: Combat 128,120lb (58,115kg).
Ground pressure: 12.2lb/in^2 (0.76 kg/cm^2).
Engine: One Continental AV1-1790-2A, V-12, four-stroke diesel, 750bhp at 2,400rpm.
Performance: Road speed 31mph (50km/h); range 370 miles (595km); vertical obstacle 3ft 0in (0.91m); trench 8ft 8in (2.66m); gradient 60 per cent.
History: First prototype 1965; entered service in 1971; withdrawn in 1979; 526 built, all for the US Army.

In the early 1960s the US Army found itself with the (apparently) very promising Shillelagh tank missile system nearing the end of its development

but, with delays to the MBT70 programme there was no vehicle to field it in, particularly in the region of major threat, Western Europe. As a result, it was decided to develop what appeared to be a low risk interim solution, by taking the existing hull, suspension and power-train of the M60A1 (*qv*) and mating them with an entirely new turret mounting the revolutionary gun/missile system. This new project was designated M60A1E2 and was authorized in 1964 with the first pilot vehicle being completed in September 1965.

The M60A1E2 had a turret of cast steel, but of a completely novel shape, being very long and narrow, which was intended, at least in part, to present the minimum cross-section to the enemy. The commander's position was at the rear of the turret with the 152mm gun/launcher at the front. The tank carried 13 Shillelagh missiles and 33 conventional rounds, both of which had HEAT warheads.

The fire-control system was particularly complicated for its day, with the commander sitting in a fully rotating, independently stabilized cupola, in

Below: The M60A2 was intended to make use of the 152mm gun/launcher system which had been developed at such cost for MBT-70. In the event, M60A2 also proved to be a costly failure.

order to provide an accurate, fire-on-the-move capability. There was a full-solution, ballistic computer coupled to a laser rangefinder, and both commander and gunner had passive night vision devices. Only the gunner was able to launch and guide the missile, but the commander was able to aim and fire the main weapon in a gun engagement, by day or night, with the same accuracy as the gunner. In addition, the commander, having acquired a target using his cupola, could then press a button to align the turret with the target in order to designate the target to the gunner.

The hull was that of the M60A1, but despite the original intentions some modifications were necessary, including the installation of air compressors and compressed-air storage bottles. These were required to provide a closed-breech scavenging system to clear the gun tube after firing, so that noxious fumes from the propellants were not allowed back into the turret.

The programme was beset by difficulties from the start; these involved the missile system, the combustible cartridge for the conventional round, turret stabilization, and the integration of the new turret into the M60A1 hull. Because of all these problems, overall system reliability was very poor. There were tactical problems as well, since the weight had crept up from a planned

Above: M60A2 combined a standard M60 chassis with a new turret mounting the gun/launcher and associated systems, but this proved to be much more difficult than expected.

52 tons to 57 tons, and the overall height of 11ft 11in (3.63m) was very considerable, particularly for European-type warfare.

The controversy came to a head in 1966 with a dispute between those who wanted to put the new tank into production as soon as possible and others who wanted to find answers to the great number of unresolved problems before the system was put into the hands of troops. Unfortunately, the former won and an order for 300 was placed in 1967 and some tanks were actually deployed to the 7th (US) Army in Europe. So severe were the problems, however, that production was suspended in 1969 and it was not until late 1971 that the tank was accepted into service as the M60A2. A total of 526 M60A2s were eventually built, which were deployed to US units in Western Europe and the Continental USA. The M60A2s in Europe were quietly withdrawn to the USA in 1979 and then all were withdrawn from service in the early 1980s.

M60A3 Main Battle Tank

Country of origin: USA.
Crew: 4.
Armament: One M68 105mm rifled gun; one M73 7.62mm co-axial machine-gun; one M85 12.7mm anti-aircraft machine-gun.
Armour: Classified.
Dimensions: Length (including main armament) 30ft 11in (9.4m); length (hull) 22ft 9in (6.95m); width 11ft 11in (3.63m); height 10ft 9in (3.27m).
Weight: Combat 107,900lb (48,987kg).
Ground pressure: 12.37lb/in² (0.87kg/cm²).
Engine: Continental AVDS-1790-2c, 12-cylinder, air-cooled, diesel engine developing 750hp at 2,400rpm.
Performance: Road speed 30mph (48km/h); range 300 miles (480km); vertical obstacle 3ft 0in (0.92m); trench 8ft 6in (2.6m); gradient 60 per cent.
History: Entered service with the US Army in 1960. Now in service with: Austria (168); Bahrain (180); Bosnia (45); Brazil 91); Egypt (1,459); Greece (669); Iran (150 approx); Israel (1,350); Jordan (268); Morocco (300); Oman (79); Portugal (100); Saudi Arabia (460); Singapore (number not known); Spain (310); Sudan (20); Taiwan (300); Thailand (178); Tunisia (84); Turkey (932); USA (200); and Yemen (64).

Above: A US Marine Corps M60A1 MBT moves inland after being landed during an amphibious exercise in Turkey.

Below: The commander and gunner of an M60 confer over a map while on a US Army exercise in northern Europe.

In the 1950s the standard tank of the US Army was the M48. In 1957 and M48 series tank was fitted with a new engine for trials purposes and this was followed by a further three prototypes in 1958. Late in 1958 it was decided to arm the new tank with the British 105mm L7 series gun, to be built in the United States under the designation M68. In 1959 the first production order for the new tank, now called the M60, was placed with Chrysler, and the type entered production at the Detroit Tank Arsenal in late 1959, with the first production tanks being completed the following year.

From late 1962, the M60 was replaced in production by the M60A1, which has a number of improvements, the most important being the redesigned turret. The M60A1 has a turret and hull of all-cast construction. The driver is seated at the front of the hull with the other three crew members in the turret, commander and gunner on the right and the loader on the left. The engine and transmission are at the rear, the latter having one reverse and two forward ranges. The M60 has torsion-bar suspension and six road wheels, with the idler at the front and the drive sprocket at the rear; there are four track-return rollers.

The 105mm gun has an elevation of +20deg and a depression of -10deg, and traverse is 360deg. Both elevation and traverse are powered. An M73 7.62mm machine-gun is mounted co-axially with the main armament and there is a 12.7mm M85 machine-gun in the commander's cupola. The latter can be aimed and fired from within the turret, and has an elevation of +60deg and a depression of -15deg. Some 60 rounds of 105mm, 900 rounds of 12.7mm and 5,950 rounds of 7.62mm ammunition are carried. Infra-red driving lights are fitted as standard and and infra-red/white light is mounted over the main armament. All M60s have an NBC system.

Below: M60A3s on exercise with the US Marine Corps.

The tank can also be fitted with a dozer blade on the front of the hull. The tank can ford to a depth of 4ft (1.22m) without preparation or 8ft (2.44m) with the aid of a kit. For deep fording operations a schnorkel can be fitted, allowing the M60 to ford to a depth of 13ft 6in (4.11m). A radical departure was made with the M60A2, developed in the mid-1960s, in which a standard M60 hull was mated to a new turret mounting the (then) new 152mm gun/launcher (see M60A2 entry).

Meanwhile, plans were being made to improve the 105mm gun-armed version. A new fire control system, a laser rangefinder and a computer substantially enhanced the probability of a first-round hit, later helped even more by the addition of a Tank Thermal Sight. Many of these M60A3s came from new production, but others were upgraded M60A1s. The M60 series was phased out of US service in 1997, although a few remain in the inventory.

Second largest user of the M60 series was the Israeli Army, which has some 1,350 M60s, M60A1s and M60A3s, which are being constantly upgraded. All have been given more powerful versions of the Teledyne Continental diesel engine, while the locally produced M68 105mm rifled gun has been fitted with an Israeli-developed thermal sleeve. Israeli M60s have also been fitted with Blazer explosive reactive armour, which consists of specially tailored blocks bolted to the outside of the hull and turret, to give protection against chemical energy (CE) warheads. A newer add-on armour, called MAGACH-7, is now being fitted; this is more bulky and substantially changes the appearance of the tank, particularly of the turret. It gives increased protection against both CE and kinetic energy projectiles. A new fire control system called MATADOR is also being installed.

With many thousands still in service, the M60 series will be found in front-line service well into the 21st Century.

A line-up of US Army M60A3s just prior to *Desert Storm*.
Note the additional ERA armour around the turrets.

M551 Sheridan Light Tank

Country of origin: USA.
Crew: 4.
Armament: One 152mm gun/missile launcher; one 7.62mm machine-gun co-axial with the main armament; one 12.7mm anti-aircraft machine-gun; four smoke dischargers on each side of turret.
Armour: Classified.
Dimensions: Length 20ft 8in (6.30m); width 9ft 3in (2.82m); height (overall) 9ft 8in (2.95m).
Weight: Combat 34.898lb (25,830kg).
Ground pressure: 6.97lb/in² (0.49kg/cm²).
Engine: Detroit 6V53T six-cylinder diesel developing 300bhp at 2,800rpm.
Performance: Road speed 45mph (70km/h), water speed 36mpg (59km/h); range 373 miles (600km); vertical obstacle 2ft 9in (0.83m); trench 8ft 4in (2.54m); gradient 60 per cent.
History: Entered service with the United States Army in 1966 and remained in service with 82nd Airborne Division until 1997.

In August 1959 the United States Army established a requirement for a "new armoured vehicle with increased capabilities over any other weapon in its own inventory and that of any adversary". The following year the Allison Division of General Motors was awarded a contract to design a vehicle called the Armored Reconnaissance Airborne Assault Vehicle (ARAAV) to meet the requirement. The first prototype, designated XM551, was completed in 1962, and this was followed by a further 11 prototypes. Late in 1965, a production contract was awarded to Allison, and the first production vehicles were completed in 1966, these being known as the M551, or Sheridan. Production was completed in 1970 after 1,700 vehicles had been built.

The hull of the Sheridan was of all-aluminium construction whilst the turret was of welded steel. The driver is seated at the front of the hull and the other three crew

members were in the turret, with the loader on the left and the gunner and commander on the right. The engine and transmission were at the rear of the hull. The suspension was of the torsion-bar type and consisted of five road wheels, with the drive sprocket at the rear and the idler at the front. There were no track-return rollers.

The most interesting feature of the Sheridan was its armament system. This consisted of a 152mm gun/launcher with an elevation of +19° and a depression of –8°, traverse being 360°. A 7.62mm machine-gun was mounted co-axially with the main armament and a 12.7mm Browning machine-gun on the commander's cupola. The latter could not be aimed and fired from within the turret, and as a result of combat experience in Vietnam many vehicles were fitted with a shield for this weapon. The 152mm gun/launcher, a version of which was fitted to the M60A2 and MBT-70, fired a Shillelagh missile or a variety of conventional ammunition including HEAT-MP, WP and canister, all of them having a combustible cartridge case. The Shillelagh missile was developed by the United States Army Missile Command and the Philco-Ford Corporation, and had a maximum range of about 3,281 yards (3,000m). The missile is controlled by the gunner, who simply kept the cross-hairs of his sight on the target to ensure a hit. This missile itself weighed 50lb (26.7kg) and had a single-stage solid-propellant motor with a burn time of 1.18 seconds. Once the missile left the gun/missile-launcher, four fins at the rear of the missile unfolded and it was guided to the target by a two-way infra-red command link which eliminates the need for the gunner to estimate the lead and range of the target. A Sheridan normally carried eight missiles and 20 rounds of ammunition, but this mix could be adjusted as required.

It was announced in 1978 that the M551 would be withdrawn from service, but a number remained operational until 1997 with the 82nd Airborne Division and took part in the liberation of Kuwait (Operation *Desert Storm*). Others remained in service in training roles at the National Training Center at Fort Irwin, California, some of which were altered to resemble Soviet AFVs, and at Fort Knox, located in Kentucky.

Courtesy of the 1.8 second burn time of its single-stage solid-propellant motor, a Shillelagh missile, its rear-mounted guidance fins beginning to deploy, streaks away from the 152mm gun/launcher atop an M551 Sheridan. A normal on-board complement was eight missiles per Sheridan.

Commando Stingray Light Tank

Country of origin: USA.
Crew: 4.
Armament: One Royal Ordnance LRF 105mm rifled gun; one 7.62mm M240 co-axial machine-gun; one M2 12.7mm anti-aircraft machine-gun.
Armour: Classified.
Dimensions: Length (including main armament) 30ft 6in (9.30m); length (hull) 21ft 2in (6.45m); width 8ft 11in (2.71m); height 8ft 3in (2.55m).
Weight: Combat 46.707lb (21,205kg).
Ground pressure: 10.24lb/in² (0.72kg/cm²).
Engine: Detroit-Diesel 8V-92 TA diesel developing 535hp at 2,300rpm.
Performance: Road speed 41mph (67km/h), range 300 miles (480km); vertical obstacle 2ft 6in (0.76m); trench 7ft 0in (2.13m); gradient 60 per cent.
History: First production Stingray completed in 1988; 108 now in service with Royal Thai Army.

For many years the world's major armies have concentrated on developing MBTs whose intended battlefield has been either the rolling plains of central Europe or the open deserts of the Middle East. As a result these MBTs have become ever larger, more sophisticated, more expensive and heavier, and armed with a gun of ever-increasing calibre. Some sales have been achieved outside these major theatres, but many Third World countries, who happily bought the relatively uncomplicated M47s or Centurions in the past, find these new MBTs increasingly unsuitable. The reasons can vary from sheer expense to something as simple as the fact that these heavyweight monsters are just too heavy for the local bridges.

There are, of course, a number of light tanks on the market, such as the British Scorpion family and the (albeit ageing) French AMX-13. However, many armies are looking for something in between, weighing about 30 tons and armed with a 105mm gun. Various tanks have been developed to meet this market. The British firm of Vickers developed a series of tanks, which have sold in some numbers to India, Kenya, Kuwait and Nigeria (*see Vickers MBT*), while Thyssen Henschel of Germany developed the TAM for the Argentine Army.

In the United States, Cadillac Gage also decided to target this market. After conducting some market research they set their priorities as: firepower (preferably a 105mm gun firing NATO-standard ammunition), high mobility, good operational range, minimum size, light weight, and transportability in a Lockheed C-130 Hercules aircraft. Conceptual work started in January 1983, design work in September 1983, with a prototype running in August 1984

Below: A modern, light tank of relatively straightforward design and construction, the Stingray totes an LRF 105mm rifled gun.

Above: The sleek lines of the Stingray's turret are indicative of the manufacturer's aim to produce a tank with a low profile.

Below: To date, the sole customer for the Stingray has been the Royal Thai Army, with an order for 108 placed in October 1987.

and on demonstration two months later. Cynics would say that such a very rapid development programme was only possible due to the total absence of government involvement, reinforced by the completely commercial pressures in the project up to this point! The prototype went to Thailand for trials in 1986 and the Royal Thai Army placed an order for 108 Stingray tanks in October 1987, which were delivered between 1988 and 1990.

With firepower and mobility given such high priority, protection is inevitably somewhat reduced. The hull is constructed of steel armour, which is capable of resisting penetration by a Soviet 7.62mm round over the entire vehicle, with increased protection at the front to resist a Soviet 14.5mm round. Since producing tanks to this specification for Thailand, Cadillac Gage has been investigating improvements to the armour protection to attract orders from other customers.

The gun is designed and produced by the British firm of Royal Ordnance and is developed from their very successful L7A3 weapon. The 105mm tube is fitted with a muzzle brake and a redesigned fume extractor, together with a thermal sleeve and muzzle reference system. The major change lies in the totally new recoil system, which reduces maximum trunnion force by a surprising 60 per cent to 30,000lb (13,608kg). 44 rounds of standard 105mm ammunition are carried, eight in the turret and the remainder below the turret ring in the hull. There is a coaxial 7.62mm machine-gun and either a 12.7mm or another 7.62mm machine-gun can be mounted on the turret roof above the commander's hatch. The Stingrays delivered to the Royal Thai Army are fitted with a British Marconi Digital Fire Control system, but a gun stabiliser is not fitted as standard, although this is an optional extra.

The Stingray is powered by the well-proven Detroit Diesel 8V-92 TA and the torsion bar suspension is based closely on that used for many years on the M109 155mm self-propelled howitzer.

Cadillac Gage Stingray Mk II Light Tank

Country of origin: USA.
Crew: 4.
Armament: One Royal Ordnance 105mm Low Recoil Force (LRF) gun; one M240 7.62mm machine-gun mounted co-axially with the main gun; one M2HB 0.50in heavy machine-gun on turret roof; one four-barrelled smoke grenade launcher on each side of the turret.
Armour: All-welded.
Dimensions: Length (including main armament) 30ft 8in (9.35m); length (hull) 21ft 1in (6.44m); width 8ft 11in (2.71m); height 8ft 5in (2.55m).
Weight: Combat 49,720lb (22,600kg).
Ground pressure: 11.4lb/in^2 (0.80 kg/cm^2).
Engine: Detroit Diesel 8V-92TA, 550bhp at 2,300rpm.
Performance: Road speed 44mph (71km/h); range 280 miles (450km); vertical obstacle 2ft 8in (0.84m); trench 7ft 0in (2.13m); gradient 60 per cent.
History: Prototype completed in 1996; ready for production, but no order had been announced as of January 2000.

The Cadillac Gage Stingray II is an evolutionary development of the Stingray I light tank. It was developed specifically for export to countries requiring an armoured fighting vehicle capable of bringing mobile firepower to the battle-field but in a vehicle that is considerably lighter than contemporary MBTs. Thus, its combat weight of 22.5 tons (22,600kg) compares very favourably with even the lightest of main battle tanks, such as the Vickers Mk3 (38.9 tons/39,500kg) or the French AMX-30 (36.4tons/37,000kg).

Below: Main armament is the Royal Ordnance rifled 105mm LRF (low recoil force) gun with a new recoil system, reducing trunnion pull from 75,000lb (34,020kg) to 30,000lb (13,608kg).

Above: Stingray II was developed for export to countries needing an AFV bringing mobile firepower to the battlefield in a vehicle considerably lighter than contemporary MBTs.

The main armament is the Royal Ordnance rifled 105mm LRF (low recoil force) gun, which is fitted with a thermal sleeve, fume extractor and muzzle brake. It is mounted on a new, longer recoil system, which enables the maximum trunnion pull to be reduced to 30,000lb (13,608kg), compared to 75,000lb (34,020kg) in the normal British L7A1/US M68 gun.

The armour has been designed to enable the user to choose between several protection options. The basic all-welded hull and turret are made from a specially hardened steel, which provides protection against small and medium calibre weapons, up to 23mm.

M1A1 Abrams
Main Battle Tank

Country of origin: United States of America.
Crew: 4.
Armament: One M256 Rheinmetall 120mm smoothbore gun; one M240 7.62mm co-axial machine-gun; one M2 12.7mm and one M240 7.62mm anti-aircraft machine-gun.
Armour: Classified.
Dimensions: Length (including main armament) 32ft 3in (9.83m); length (hull) 25ft 11in (7.92m); width 11ft 11in (3.66m); height 9ft 6in (2.89m).
Weight: Combat 125,890lb (57,154kg).
Ground pressure: 13.65b/in² (0.96kg/cm²).
Engine: Textron Lycoming AGT-1500 gas-turbine developing 1,500hp at 30,000rpm.
Performance: Road speed 41mph (67km/h), range 300 miles (480km); vertical obstacle 3ft 6in (1.07m); trench 9ft 0in (2.74m); gradient 60 per cent.
History: First production M1 completed in 1980 and first production M1A1 in 1985. Users in 2000: Egypt (555), Kuwait (218), Saudi Arabia (315), US Army 8,444), US Marine Corps (403).

In June 1973 contracts were awarded to both Chrysler Corporation (which built the M60 series) and the Detroit Diesel Allison Division of the General Motors Corporation (which built the MBT-70) to build prototypes of a new tank designated M1, and later named the Abrams tank. These tanks were handed over to the US Army for trials in February 1976. In November 1976 it was announced after a four-month delay that the Chrysler tank would be placed in production. Production commenced at the Lima Army Modification Center at Lima in 1979 with the first batch of full production M1s being completed early in 1980.

The M1 has a hull and turret of British Chobham armour, which is claimed to make the tank immune to attack from both missiles and tank guns. Its crew consists of four, the driver at the front, the commander and gunner on the right of the turret, and the loader on the left. The main armament consists of a standard 105mm gun developed in Britain and produced under licence in the United States and a 7.62mm machine-gun is mounted co-axially with the main armament. A 12.7mm machine-gun is mounted at the commander's station and a 7.62mm machine-gun at the loader's station. A total of 55 rounds of 105mm, 1,000 rounds of 12.7mm and 11,400 rounds of 7.62mm machine-

Right: The most recent – and by far the most important – addition to the US Army's MBT force during the 1980s, the baseline M1 Abrams has given rise to four distinct versions. In addition to its US Army service, the M1/M1A2 Abrams has won orders from the USMC and the Egyptian, Kuwait and Saudi Arabian armies.

Above: The angular front and sides of the M1's turret are among this MBT's most distinctive features. Atop the turret and to the left can be seen the M2 12.7mm AA machine gun.

One of the prototype XM1 Abrams is put through its paces at the Aberdeen Proving Grounds in Maryland, USA. The first of 2,374 full production M1 Abrams MBTs were delivered to the US Army during 1980.

gun ammunition are carried. The main armament can be aimed and fired on the moved. The gunner first selects the target, then uses the laser rangefinder to get its range and depresses the firing switch. The computer makes the calculations and adjustments required to ensure a hit.

The M1 is powered by a multi-fuel Textron Lycoming gas-turbine. This has proved to be reliable in service and gives the M1 the high power-to-weight ratio of 27hp/tonne and the very rapid acceleration of 0-20mph (0.32km/h) in six seconds! It is also mechanically simple and particularly easy to service. Conversely, it is noisy and emits a very hot exhaust (and thus has a strong infra-red (IR) "signature"), but perhaps the most serious fault is that it is very thirsty on fuel. There is a fully-automatic transmission, equipped with four forward and two reverse gears.

After producing 2,374 basic M1s production switched in February 1985 to the M1 (Improved), which has better armour, but is otherwise identical to the basic M1. The major change came with the M1A1, which started to leave the production lines in 1987. This is armed with the Rheinmetall M256 120mm smoothbore gun, which had been originally developed in Germany to arm the Leopard 2. 40 120mm rounds are carried, compared to 55 rounds in the 105mm-armed m1. An integrated NBC protection system is also installed and the suspension system improved.

In the M1A1 with the Heavy Armour Package certain areas of the hull, particularly the front, are constructed of a new type of armour, consisting of depleted uranium (DU) encased in steel, which gives a density 250 per cent greater than that of normal steel. This is designed to counter the latest kinetic energy penetrators and is used for those M1A1s intended for deployment in Europe. The DU has a very low radiation emission rate, but raises the tank's overall weight.

A series of developments known as "Block II Improvements", if accepted,

Above: A tight squeeze for a US Army Europe M1 Abrams, as it trundles through a German town while on exercise.

Below: An impressive line-up of M1 Abrams in the deserts of Kuwait, awaiting the word to advance on Iraqi ground forces.

will result in the M1A2. The improvements involved are mostly associated with the command-and-control, electronic, optical and electrical systems.

In all, 403 M1A1s were built for the US Marine Corps to replace its ageing M60A1s. This model is almost identical to the Army's M1A1, except that all Marine Corps tanks will be fitted with the Deep Water Fording Kit for use in amphibious landings.

The M1A1 is also produced in Egypt, under an agreement signed in 1988. The first tanks were sent from the USA fully-assembled, tfollowed partly-assembled versions and then by kits. Egypt manufactured certain components, but hulls, gun, ammunition and electronics are supplied by the USA.

By early 2000, the delivery/order picture was:

US Army	**M1**	2,674	All to be converted to M1A2.
	M1 Improved	894	Production complete.
	M1A1	4,796	Production complete.
	M1A2	77	New build; production complete.
USMC	**M1A1**	403	Production complete.
Egypt	**M1A1**	555	Production under way.

Kuwait	**M1A2**	218	Production complete.
Saudi Arabia	**M1A2**	315	Production complete.
TOTAL		9,932	

Various improvement programmes are under way. AIM XXI (Abrams Integrated Management System for 21st Century) is intended to refurbish M1A1 to "as new" condition. To overcome concern about high fuel consumption a diesel-engined version has been developed for the export market. Other improvements are more detailed and include new tracks, suspensions and electronics. What is certain is that the M1 series is going to be around in large numbers for many years to come.

Below: The sand billowing from its tracks and in its wake denotes an M1A1 Abrams travelling at high speed through the desert. This elevated view clearly shows the distinctive angling of the turret's front and side plates, as well as the Rheinmetall M356 120mm smoothbore gun.

United Defense LP M8 Armored Gun System

M8 Levels I, II, and III.
Country of origin: USA.
Crew: 3.
Armament: One Watervliet Arsenal M35 rifled 105mm main gun; one M240 7.62mm machine-gun co-axially mounted with main gun; one 0.50in M2HB machine-gun, or one 7.62mm machine-gun, or one 40mm grenade launcher; two eight-barrel smoke grenade dischargers.
Armour: All-welded aluminium (optional ERA).
Dimensions: Length (including main armament) 29ft 1in (8.85m); width 8.ft 7in (2.62m); height 7ft 10in (2.38m).
Weight: Combat 58,600lb (26,586kg)(see text).
Ground pressure: 9.4b/in² (0.66kg/cm²).
Engine: Detroit Diesel 6V-92TA 6-cylinder multi-fuel diesel, 550hp at 2,400rpm.
Performance: Road speed 45mph (72km/h); range 300 miles (483km); vertical obstacle 2ft 7in (0.8m); trench 7ft 0in (2.13m); gradient 60 per cent.
History: Several prototypes and type-classified by US Army; no orders to date.

The story of the light tank for the US Army is a lengthy and twisted tale, which has already been partly told in the M551 Sheridan entry, but it continued with the LP M8. In the late 1980s a need arose for a replacement for the remaining M551 Sheridans, which were still serving with one armoured battalion in 82nd Airborne Division and as "hostile" vehicles at the National Training Center. United Defense won this competition for an Armored Gun System (AGS) with a development of their Close Combat Vehicle – Light (CCV-L), which had been developed as a private venture in the 1980s, but failed to attract any orders. The main innovation with the AGS was that it was armed with the new Watervliet Arsenal rifled 105mm gun and autoloader, although there were also other, more minor changes. The vehicle was type-classified by the US Army as the M8 AGS in late 1995, but only a few months later all work was first suspended and then

Below: The M8 AGS has an all-welded aluminium alloy hull and turret; armour packages are added to match the vehicle's role and the threat and the degree of protection required.

Above: M8 AGS is armed with an M35 rifled 105mm, fully stabilised gun, which fires all standard US 105mm ammunition. Some 31 rounds are carried, of which 21 are in the autoloader.

cancelled, since which time United Defense has been seeking orders from overseas customers, particularly Turkey, but so far without success.

The design concept of the M8 AGS involves a basic all-welded aluminium alloy hull and turret, to which can be added armour packages, depending upon the vehicle's role and the degree of protection required. The Level I package is designed for the rapid deployment role and provides protection against small arms fire and shell splinters; all-up weight is 39,800lb (18,052kg). The Level II package is for light forces in a more serious threat environment; all-up weight is 44,270lb (20,082kg). The Level III package is for contingency operations and consists of a large number of bolt-on armoured tiles which give protection against hand-held anti-tank weapons, such as the RPG-7; all-up weight is 52,000lb (23,586kg).

In order to reduce production costs, maximum use is made of off-the-shelf items. Thus, the Detroit Diesel 6V-92TA engine has 65 per cent commonality with the power unit in the US Army's 8x8 HEMTT (Heavy Expanded Mobility Tactical Truck), while both the hydromechanical transmission system and the cooling fans are identical to those used in the M2 Bradley. The engine, transmission and cooling systems are mounted on rails for ease of removal for maintenance or replacement.

The layout of the M8 AGS is conventional with the driver at the centre front under the glacis plate, while inside the turret the automatic loader is mounted on the left, with the gunner forward and the commander to the rear on the right. The commander sits inside a rotating cupola with seven x1 periscopes. Either gunner or commander can fire the gun, and their gun and turret controls are based on those used in the M1-series MBTs.

The 105mm gun is fully stabilized and can be traversed through a full 360 degrees although full depression (-10 degrees) is not possible over the rear arc due to the high decking. The M38 105mm gun fires all standard US 105mm ammunition and 31 rounds are carried, of which 21 are immediately available in the autoloader. The fire control system is provided by Computing Devices of Canada and is identical to that used in the British Challenger 2 MBT.

All versions of the M8 are air transportable, with the C-5 taking five and the C-17 three. The load possible in a C-130 depends upon the armour package: Level I can be carried and air-dropped; Level II can be carried, but must be air-landed; Level III cannot be carried.